Criminal Investigation

Basic Perspectives

ELEVENTH EDITION

Charles A. Lushbaugh

Retired Lieutenant, Sacramento County Sheriff's Department
Sacramento, California

Lecturer of Criminal Justice
California State University
Sacramento, California

FBI NA, 185th Session

Paul B. Weston

(Deceased)

PEARSON

Prentice
Hall

Upper Saddle River, New Jersey
Columbus, Ohio

Library of Congress Cataloging-in-Publication Data

Weston, Paul B.
    Criminal investigation: basic perspectives/Paul B. Weston, Charles A. Lushbaugh. — 11th ed.
        p. cm.
    ISBN-13: 978-0-13-244748-5
    ISBN-10: 0-13-244748-7
    1. Criminal investigation—United States.   I. Lushbaugh, Charles.   II. Title.
    HV8073.W44 2008
    363.250973—dc22   2008002465

Editor in Chief: Vernon R. Anthony
Senior Editor: Tim Peyton
Developmental Editor: Elisa Rogers
Editorial Assistant: Alicia Kelly
Project Manager: Stephen C. Robb
AV Project Manager: Jackie Portisch
Production Coordination: Vishal Harshvardhan, Aptara, Inc.
Design Coordinator: Diane Ernsberger
Cover Designer: Kristina D. Holmes
Cover Photo: SuperStock
Operations Supervisor: Patricia A. Tonneman
Director of Marketing: David Gesell
Marketing Manage: Adam Kloza
Marketing Coordinator: Alicia Dysert

This book was set in Palatino by Aptara, Inc. It was printed and bound by Edward Brothers, Inc. The cover was printed by Phoenix Color Corp.

Photo Credits: Orlando/Getty Images Inc., Hulton Archive Photos, p.36; Forensic Technology WAI Inc., p.36; Mikael Karrison/Arresting Images, p.53; Spencer Grant/PhotoEdit Inc., p.55; Efield/Getty Images Inc., Hulton Archive Photos, p.93; Mikael Karrison/Arresting Images, p.95; Dwayne Newton/PhotoEdit Inc., p.159; Robert E. Daemmrich/Getty Images Inc., Stone Allstock, p.162; AP Wide World Photos, p.175; Spencer Grant/PhotoEdit Inc., p.179; Mike Stewart/Corbis-Sygma, p.225; AP Wide World Photos, p.226 AP Wide World Photos, p.245; AP Wide World Photos, p 354; J. Markowitz/Corbis-Sygma, p. 355; Jim McDonald CORBIS-NY, p. 375; Bob Daemmrich/Corbis-Sygma, p.376; AFP PHOTO/FILES/Agence France-Presse/Getty Images p.378.

Pearson Education Ltd.
Pearson Education Canada, Ltd.
Pearson Education Australia Pty. Limited
Pearson Educación de Mexico, S.A. de C.V.
Pearson Education Singapore Pte. Ltd.
Pearson Education—Japan
Pearson Education North Asia Ltd.
Pearson Education Malaysia Pte. Ltd.

10 9 8 7 6 5 4 3 2 1
ISBN-13: 978-0-13-244748-5
ISBN-10:   0-13-244748-7

*This edition
is dedicated
to the memory of
Sue Lushbaugh,
a loving wife,
mother,
and friend.*

Contents

Preface

The eleventh edition of *Criminal Investigation: Basic Perspectives* was written to keep abreast of changes in the field of criminal investigation. A new chapter on the rules of evidence is included, and the segment on terrorism has been extensively rewritten into a new chapter. These changes reflect new insights in these areas. In addition, new segments were added to three chapters:

Development of forensic science (Chapter 1, The Initial Investigation)
Lineups (Chapter 7, Major Investigative Techniques)
Child sexual abuse: pedophilia (Chapter 12, Sexual Assaults)

Two new case studies, designed to enhance the learning process, have been added to this edition. The case study method of instruction facilitates learning by linking case content to textbook topics and by encouraging the exchange of opinions and viewpoints among students during discussion sessions. The case studies in this book are designed to contribute to this type of learning process. Each case provides factual information that is likely to promote analysis and discussion and thus aid in developing the student's ability to analyze, evaluate, and reason. The topic of discussion is focused on the facts of each case study, but only the range of student opinions and ideas limits the scope of the discussion.

Some cases are presented in straight narrative style, while others are written in dialogue form as the best means of joining the personalities and the situations of a case study. Each case presents a real-life situation or episode experienced sometime in the past. No "doctoring" has been done to develop points, theories, or problems. However, names, dates, and locations have been altered in some instances to avoid embarrassing any persons or their families.

Also new to this edition are the multiple-choice or fill-in review questions at the end of each chapter. All 190 of these questions are designed to enhance the learning process.

I thank the reviewers for this edition, whose insights and suggestions have made this a better book. They include: Dexter Cummins, Antelope Valley College; Jeffrey R. Hislop, San Joaquin Delta College; Rebecca Nathanson, Lake-Sumter Community College; Thomas R. O'Connor, Austin Peay State University; and Harry D. Ulferts, Sauk Valley Community College. I extend special thanks to Robert Pennal, Special Agent Supervisor, California

Department of Justice, Bureau of Narcotic Enforcement; and to David Lushbaugh and Christopher Baker for their assistance.

Supplements

Several online supplements available to instructors using this text include:

- Online Instructor's Manual with Test Bank (0-13-159825-2)
- Online PowerPoints (0-13-159812-0)
- Online TestGen (0-13-135216-4)

Instructor
Resource
Center

Register today at www.prenhall.com
to access instructor resources digitally.

To access supplementary materials online, instructors need to request an instructor access code. Go to **www.pearsonhighered.com/irc,** where you can register for an instructor access code. Within 48 hours after registering you will receive a confirming e-mail including an instructor access code. Once you have received your code, go the site and log on for full instructions on downloading the materials you wish to use.

part **one**

The Initial Investigation

chapter **one**

The Initial Investigation

CHAPTER OUTLINE

After reading this chapter you will be able to:

- Discuss the historical development of the major events that have led to the field of forensic science and the persons responsible for these breakthroughs.
- Identify the steps investigators take in processing a major crime scene.
- List the various methodologies available to search for evidence at a crime scene.
- Recognize the potential hazards involved in the handling of violent crime scenes where the victim may have a lethally infectious disease.
- Describe the symbiotic relationship between the media and law enforcement at major crime scenes.

Criminal investigation is a lawful search for people and things useful in reconstructing an illegal act or **omission** and analysis of the mental state accompanying it. It is a probing from the known to the unknown, backward in time. The objective of criminal investigation is to determine truth as far as it can be discovered in any inquiry. Successful investigations are based on fidelity, accuracy, and sincerity in lawfully searching for the facts, and on an equal faithfulness, exactness, and probity in reporting the results.[1]

The joining of science with traditional criminal investigation techniques offers new horizons of efficiency in criminal investigation. New perspectives in investigation bypass a total or major reliance on informers and custodial interrogation and, instead, increasingly utilize a skilled scanning of the crime scene for physical evidence and a search for as many witnesses as possible. Mute evidence tells its own story in court, either by its own demonstrativeness or through the testimony of an expert witness involved in its scientific testing. Such evidence may serve in lieu of—or as a corroboration of—informers, custodial interrogation, and testimonial evidence of witnesses found and interviewed by police in an extension of their responsibility to seek out the truth of all circumstances of a crime. An increasing certainty in solving crimes is possible and will contribute to the major deterrent of crime: the certainty that a criminal will be discovered, arrested, prosecuted, and convicted.

DEVELOPMENT OF FORENSIC SCIENCE

Forensics, the use of science to answer legal questions, has developed over time. Scientists schooled in a variety of disciplines have made meaningful contributions to the field of **criminalistics**, the application of scientific techniques in collecting and analyzing physical evidence. The following are a few of the earliest contributors to this endeavor.

Mathieu Orfila (1787–1853) is thought by many to be the father of forensic **toxicology**—that is, the study of the effects of poisons. His work on the detection of poisons and their effects on animals established the science of forensic toxicology.

Hans Gross (1848–1915) was the earliest advocate of criminal investigation as a science. Gross was a native of Austria, born in Graz. Educated in law, he became interested in investigation while serving as an examining magistrate. He became a professor of criminology at the University of Vienna. Perhaps it was the legal training, or the education in rational theory joined with the study of law, that made Magistrate Gross unhappy with the lack of science in police investigation. In any event, he deserves credit for developing a system of investigation. His *System der Kriminalistik (Criminal Investigation)*, translated into English and published in 1906, is a classic text in this field. Gross strongly supported scrupulous accuracy and high ethics in criminal investigation. His greatest contribution to the introduction of science in criminal investigation was the advocacy of a parallel system of inquiry based on the crime scene.

Alphonse Bertillon (1853–1914) developed the first means of human identification, known as **anthropometry**. This system involved the taking of eleven measurements of various parts of the body—such as height, reach, head width, and length of left foot—along with a photograph of the subject. Bertillon based his system on the assumption that it would be virtually impossible for two people to look alike and to have the same physical measurements. His system worked well for over two decades until unraveled by the Will West case in 1903. When West was being processed into the Fort Leavenworth prison, it was discovered that another prisoner, already in custody, had the same measurements and appearance, as if they were identical twins. Bertillon's system was eventually replaced by the identification of individuals through fingerprints, but he is still considered to be the father of criminal identification.

Francis Galton (1822–1911) provided the first definitive study of fingerprints in his book *Finger Prints*. His pioneering efforts in this area led to the creation of a classification system that was capable of filing these prints in a logical searchable sequence.

Albert S. Osborn (1858–1946) authored in 1910 the first significant text in the field of questioned documents. The book remains a primary resource for document examiners and was responsible for the acceptance of documents as scientific evidence by the courts.

Edmond Locard (1877–1966) in 1910 persuaded the police department in Lyons, France, to finance a small police laboratory. Locard's research and accomplishments became known throughout the world. He eventually became the founder and director of the Institute of Criminalistics at the University of Lyons. The institute developed into an international center for the study of and research in forensic science. Locard is perhaps best known today for his **exchange principle**. He believed that when a criminal came in contact with another object or person, a cross-transfer of evidence occurred, primarily of hairs and fibers.

Leone Lattes (1887–1954) expanded upon the discovery that blood can be grouped into four different categories: A, B, AB, and O. Lattes, a professor of medicine in Turin, Italy, devised a procedure for determining the blood group from dried bloodstains and applied this technique to criminal investigations.

Calvin Goddard (1891–1955) was aware that the determination of whether a fired bullet originating from the suspect's weapon required a comparison with a bullet that had been fired and retrieved from the suspect's gun. Goddard refined the techniques for making these determinations by using a comparison microscope.[2]

THE LEGAL SIGNIFICANCE OF EVIDENCE

Evidence is the only means of satisfying the triers of fact of the truth or untruth of allegations and accusations made by the parties in their pleadings. Inasmuch as investigators must collect all the evidence, and prosecutors and the court must weigh the significance of any evidence in relation to its possible presentation in court, the first item of importance is whether the evidence will be admissible in court. Admissibility usually depends on the evidence being relevant, material, and competent.

The legal significance of evidence rests in its influence on the judge or juror. Once evidence has passed the test of admissibility and is part of the court record, it has a potential for influencing the outcome of the trial. Any piece of evidence, either alone or in combination with other evidence, must be persuasive to the triers of fact—this is the **impact energy** of an item of evidence.

Investigators must learn the difference between evidence and facts to avoid confusion in evaluating evidence in its role as proof. Evidence is not synonymous with fact. Evidence may be ambiguous—that is, subject to different interpretations. It may be false, exaggerated, planted, or perjured. It may be modified by forgetfulness, inattention, or silence. On the other hand, a fact is the truth—insofar as the truth can be determined by the triers of fact in a criminal trial. A fact in this sense of the term is the effect of evidence, and it is dependent upon evidence. A fact is established from a very personal evaluation of the evidence presented in a particular case by the trier of fact. Evidence may tend to prove a fact, may be sufficiently strong to compel a conclusion of fact, or may be just strong enough to create a reasonable doubt.

The U.S. system of justice presumes the defendant to be innocent and requires the prosecution to prove the case against the defendant beyond a reasonable doubt—to a moral certainty. These legal principles of the adversary system of justice have a simple reality: accusations of crime must be supported in court by legally significant evidence.

Knowledge of evidence and its legal significance is essential to success as an investigator. The investigator must know what evidence is required to support the issue of guilt or innocence; whether such evidence indicates guilt or innocence; and, when guilt is apparent, whether such evidence—in total—is likely to prove guilt beyond a reasonable doubt. In the final analysis, the success of an investigation depends on the evidence collected and its legal significance.

COORDINATION OF THE CRIME SCENE

The crime scene is the focus of the preliminary investigation. En route to the scene, the assigned investigator plans his or her action and upon arrival reviews the problems usually connected with any crime scene. The type of crime determines the type of approach. For example, where injured victims need immediate response, lights and sirens would be appropriate. However, lights and sirens would not be appropriate for a robbery in progress, as the sirens would notify the suspect of the response and thus aid escape or encourage a hostage situation.

The initial response should include a notation of any persons or vehicles leaving the scene. The area should be scanned to determine if the crime is ongoing and if the suspect is still on the scene. It is the first responder's responsibility to neutralize the crime scene, making it safe for other personnel to enter the area. Neutralization of the crime scene includes the arrest of any suspects and the elimination of any hazards that might present a threat.

The next responsibility is to ensure that medical attention is provided if required with as little impact on the crime scene as possible. The best way to minimize this impact is to work with the medical personnel so they know the importance of limiting the number of persons who enter the area and respect the need to minimize the possible destruction of evidence. The investigator, however, must be mindful that the possibility of saving a life takes precedence over the possible destruction of evidence.

The first step in processing a crime scene for clues and evidence is to make an accurate survey of the surroundings and carefully evaluate the situation—to take "a long, hard look." Deliberate action at this time guards against false moves and mistakes. The impact of the overall appearance of the scene on an experienced investigator will provide guidelines for modifying a base plan of action. The assigned investigator must ascertain as soon as possible where the crime happened. Usually the crime scene is readily discernible.

A search for evidence starts with effective protection of the crime scene. The searcher must be certain that nothing has been removed from or added to the scene since the arrival of responding police—in short, that the scene is intact. Posting freeze signs ("Keep Out—Crime Scene Search in Progress") and placing barrier tape aid in delineating the crime scene area. Officers posted at the perimeter will also prevent the entry of unauthorized persons. Crime scene boundaries should be established beyond the initial scope of the crime scene with the understanding that the boundaries can be reduced in size if necessary but cannot be easily expanded.[3]

The officers guarding the perimeter of the crime scene are responsible for preparing a **chronological log** of events as they occur at the scene. This is typically a time-based log that documents when an officer enters and leaves the scene. This notation includes the time and the officer's full name, agency, rank, and reason for entering the scene. This logging process also serves to keep unnecessary officers from entering the scene just to look around.

The main purpose of a search—to look for clues and for evidence of what happened during the crime—must always be kept foremost in the mind of the investigator. It is not a random grouping but rather a selective looking for objects and materials. The expertise of the investigator, acquired by training and experience, indicates what is to be found at the scenes of different types of crimes. For a search to be successful, its main purpose must be aligned with knowing precisely what to seek and scrutinize. Otherwise, the search lacks the necessary professional direction.

The work of the preliminary investigator concentrates on three of the basic elements of investigation: searching the crime scene, collecting and preserving evidence found at the scene, and locating and interviewing available witnesses at or near the crime scene. When crimes are not witnessed or when a reliable witness cannot be located at this stage of the investigation, the investigative leads likely to produce a solution to the crime will originate with the physical evidence found at the crime scene.

The command at a crime scene is often hectic. Most law enforcement agencies specify that the first officer to arrive at the scene is in charge until a patrol sergeant arrives. This sergeant (or officer of higher rank) is in command until he or she is relieved by a detective or an officer of even higher rank. In minor crimes, the sergeant may relinquish command by calling the dispatcher and reporting that he or she is leaving the scene and reporting the name of the officer now in charge. At the scene of a more serious crime, the sergeant waits at the scene for the detective's arrival, briefs him or her about what the police at the scene have learned about the circumstances of the crime, and turns over command of the investigation to the detective. However, the sergeant will remain at the scene in command of the uniformed personnel guarding the limits of the scene, monitoring new arrivals, and performing similar duties.

At the scene of more serious crimes, particularly homicides, larger police units field a mobile crime laboratory to process the crime scene either with detectives trained in forensic science or with crime laboratory forensic scientists. At this point, it becomes even more difficult to determine who is in charge. Despite this identification problem, most police units have men and women who are self-starters and work together to get organized and ready for the search of a crime scene.[4]

SYSTEMATIC SEARCH PROCEDURES

The methodology of searching depends on the case and the scene. Staffing problems in police units, as well as problems associated with the proffering of evidence in court, have brought about the development of the **single-officer search**. Associates of this single officer often assist in locating evidence, but they do not disturb it or collect it. The goal is to limit the number of officers in possession of crime scene evidence to the officer searching the scene. The use of double coverage in searching crime scenes is valuable as a double-check for evidence, but it frequently results in conflicting testimony by searching officers.

When the search must cover a wide area, the available investigators should be assigned in teams. One member of each team serves as the single officer collecting evidence, and each team is assigned responsibility for the search of a specified segment of the crime scene. A designated investigator or a superior officer commands the entire searching operation.

A crime scene is the place of the crime, including any adjoining entry or exit area. Therefore, prior to a search, the assigned investigator surveys the scene, noting its dimensions and the presence or absence of an adjoining entry (approach) and exit (flight) area. This evaluation is the basis for setting limits on the area of the search, for determining how to organize the search procedure, and for ascertaining what assistance is needed.

Traditionally, systematic searching has utilized the following methods (Figure 1–1):

1. A **point-to-point movement**, following a chain of objects that are obviously evidence
2. An **ever-widening circle** technique, in which the searching officer starts at the focal point of the scene or the center of the security area and works outward by circling in a clockwise or counterclockwise direction until the fringes of the protected area are reached
3. An **ever-narrowing circle**, the reverse of an ever-widening circle, in which the searching officer starts at the outskirts of the crime scene and works toward its focal point
4. A **zone or sector search** in which the scene is subdivided into segments and each sector is searched as an individual unit
5. A **strip or grid search** for outdoor areas in which the area to be searched is plotted like a football field. Searching starts at a

FIGURE 1–1 Search methods: (a) indoors, (b) outdoors, (c) immediate area, (d) extended area, (e) strip search of large area, (f) grid search of large area.

sideline and moves across the field to the other sideline, with searchers working back and forth across the field until the entire area is searched. The **grid search** begins after the strip search is completed. It covers the same area in a similar manner but at right angles to the previous search pattern. Metal or wood stakes and heavy cord are used to direct and control outdoor searches.

Some experienced investigators dislike describing any searching method by name because it emphasizes technique rather than purpose and has often led to criticism during cross-examination. When queried on the witness stand about searching the crime scene, investigators should state that they began the search by looking around, moved generally in a clockwise movement (if that was the technique), and made field notes as items of evidence were discovered. Their field notes then support the search as a systematic examination of the scene.

When a criminal act is suspected as being involved in a death, a search of the deceased person is often assigned to field representatives of the coroner's or medical examiner's office. In some jurisdictions, the coroner or medical examiner will permit body searches by the police upon request. In any event, the search must be methodical and thorough. Many police units require the investigator to delay such a search until it can be made in the presence of a disinterested witness and also require the investigator to record the name of such a witness in his or her field notes. A complete list of all property found on the deceased victim, as well as where it was found (e.g., right-side pocket of trousers, hidden in bra), are made part of the officer's notes.

The ability to discover and recognize evidence is a prerequisite to successful searching. As the investigator surveys the crime scene preparatory to searching, he or she develops some concept of the type and nature of evidence that should be the objective of the crime scene search. Physical evidence can be anything from massive objects to microscopic traces. The nature of the crime offers the first clue: weapons are used in assaults; an entry occurs in burglaries; a fire is set in arson cases. The victim, the **modus operandi** or method of operation of the offender, and other circumstances that can be observed during this survey may suggest possible clues.

Where to search for physical evidence is based on the type of evidence the investigator is seeking. In assaults and homicides, the injuries sustained by the victim suggest a weapon and orient the search toward it. In burglaries, the means used to gain access to the premises and the place of entrance indicate the possible location of tool marks. Tabletops, glassware, and other smooth surfaces guide the search for imprints. Soft earth, mud, and dust are known sites for foot and tire impressions.

When searching a crime scene, the investigator should be mindful of Locard's exchange principle, which states that suspects will bring items of evidence into the crime scene and will take items with them when they leave. This exchange of trace evidence involves such items of evidence as hairs, fibers, dirt, dust, blood, body fluids, skin cells, and other microscopic materials.[5]

Initially, it is a case of identifying the type of evidence one wants to find and its likely area of discovery, then of making a systematic search, and finally of recognizing it when it is found. The experienced investigator is always alert for evidence that may seem unimportant but is, in fact, material and relevant.

COLLECTING EVIDENCE

Investigators should not rush to pick up evidence since its significance may be destroyed in doing so. The investigator's field notes should record the discovery. In addition, photographs and accurate measurements are necessary to show the original position and nature of all evidence. In searching for evidence at crime scenes, never alter the position of, pick up, or touch any object before it has been described in minute detail in an official note and photographed.

The integrity of evidence is maintained by keeping it in its original state. No alterations are made to any item that is or may be evidence. Blood, rust, grease, and dirt are not removed from objects, nor does the investigator add his or her fingerprints to the evidence or smear or wipe off any such clues. An item of physical evidence inherently important in its own substance may have another item of evidence added to it. This can range from a fingerprint on a fragment of glass to blood and fibers on weapons.

Evidence likely to be found at crime scenes and amenable to scientific analysis is divided into seven major groups: (1) weapons, (2) blood, (3) imprints or impressions (traces of a person or a vehicle), (4) marks of tools used to gain access to locked premises or containers, (5) dust and dirt traces, (6) questioned documents, and (7) miscellaneous trace or transfer evidence.

MARKING EVIDENCE

Marking evidence serves to identify it. Marking must not impair the value of evidence or restrict the number and kind of examinations to which it might be subjected by criminalists and other experts. Consideration should also be given to the monetary value of the item of evidence and whether the item will be returned to the rightful owner when no longer needed. Will the marking of the evidence destroy or diminish the value of the item? If so, another means of marking the items should be considered. Tamperproof evidence tags and bags might suffice, as might the use of correction fluid that can be applied to the item of evidence, written on, and later removed without causing permanent damage.

Crime scene being processed with items of evidence identified with numbered tags.

Traditional marking of objects includes the investigator's initials, date, and report number if ample space is available. Counterfeit money should have a dual marking. The name of the person last in possession should be signed across a corner of the bill, or such person should be asked to scratch his or her initials on a coin. In addition, the investigator should place his or her own mark of identification on the money. When currency is mutilated by marking with a tracing powder or dye, it should not be cleaned but should be placed immediately in a sealed envelope and handled with care. Later, when no longer required as evidence, this mutilated currency should not be returned to general circulation but should be redeemed at a local bank with a statement that it contains stained material added to develop it as evidence.

The item of overriding importance in identifying evidence exhibits in court is how the investigator knew that this exhibit was, in fact, the object he or she found. On direct examination, questions usually have the following format:

Q.   Officer, I show you this revolver, now marked as people's exhibit number 7. Do you recognize it? (Officer takes the revolver, looks for his mark, finds it, and answers.)
A.   Yes, I do.

Q.   How do you recognize it?
A.   By my mark here on the butt (pointing to rear and bottom of revolver).

Q.   Where and under what circumstances did you first see this revolver?

The witness proceeds with the testimony; the identification serves as a foundation for the remainder of the testimony.

ESTABLISHING THE CHAIN OF POSSESSION

Continuity of possession—the **chain of possession**—must be established when evidence is proffered in court as an exhibit. Whenever possible, if the officer locating the evidence is not the investigator assigned responsibility for the case, the evidence should not be disturbed until its location and nature can be brought to the attention of the responsible investigator, nor should it be moved until its location and description have been noted, photographs taken at the scene, and measurements made to place it.

Adherence to standard and required procedures in every case is the best guarantee that the collection and possession of physical evidence will stand a court test of what happened—or could have happened—to it from the time of its finding to its presentation in court. Any deviation from standard procedures in processing physical evidence can affect credibility and contribute to a reasonable suspicion in the minds of the triers of fact about the entire police investigation.

In narcotics cases in many areas, investigators seal the evidence in manila envelopes, initial the sealing, and drop all the envelopes through a slot into a locked box at local headquarters. The chemist who will make the examination has the only key to this box. He or she removes the evidence by cutting open the sealed envelope, examines it, and replaces it in the original manila envelope, reseals the envelope, initials the sealing, and places the envelope in a locked box. An idea of the ritual used to prove the continuity of the possession of evidence is illustrated by the questions and responses recorded during a grand jury hearing in a case of possession and sale of narcotics. The testimony, on direct examination, of the finding investigator relative to this evidence was as follows:

Q.   I believe you found a large quantity of what you believe to be drugs in the house?

A.   Yes, sir.

Q.   Do you recognize this plastic bag as containing the quantity you discovered?
A.   Yes, sir.

Q.   Where were the drugs taken?
A.   They were brought to the station.

Q.   Where were they put?
A.   In the interrogation room and locked up.

Q.   The next day did you take the drugs from the interrogation room to the Bureau of Narcotics Enforcement?
A.   Yes, sir, I did.

Q.   In the Bureau of Narcotics Enforcement, were they put in a locker?
A.   Yes.

Q.   Was this locker locked?
A.   Yes.

Q.   Did you have a key to open it again?
A.   No, sir.

Q.   Where is this locker located?
A.   The chemist's office.

The chemist was then sworn and questioned.

Q.   Do you recall having seen that plastic bag (indicating bag identified by previous witness) and the contents of it?
A.   Yes, I have.

Q.   Did you bring it with you today?
A.   Yes, I did.

Q.   When did you first come into contact with that particular bag?
A.   On December 28 of last year.

Q.   Where did you find it?
A.   This was removed by me from a locked locker at the Narcotics Bureau. It is an evidence locker in my office that is used to submit evidence for analysis when I am not present to take it personally and to which I have the only key.

Q.   Now, did you subsequently make an examination of those drugs in this bag?
A.   Yes, I did.

Since the basic legal integrity of the evidence had been shown, the witness continued his testimony about his examination of the contents of this plastic bag.

PACKAGING PHYSICAL EVIDENCE

Evidence must be packaged to avoid breakage, loss, or contamination in transit. Tweezers, forceps, and similar tools are used to collect and place traces and small items in their containers. Latex gloves are suggested for handling some physical evidence.

An evidence box or board can be used for transporting evidence over short distances. An evidence box with pegboard sides allows for tying or wiring small- and medium-size objects in place. A series of drilled holes and appropriately sized dowels can serve the same purpose. Items of evidence that will undergo comparison analysis for possible relationships should be packaged in separate containers to obviate any allegation of cross-contamination. No wet or soiled materials or boxes or bottles should be used. Thoroughly clean and dry containers, wrapping paper, corrugated paper, boxes, and sealing tape are the basic safeguards for physical evidence in transport.

Documentary evidence is first placed in transparent envelopes without folding or bending; then between two pieces of firm, corrugated cardboard; and then in a manila envelope or other wrapper.

Plastic pill bottles or film containers with pressure lids are unbreakable, can be easily sealed with tape, and are excellent containers for hairs, fibers, and other small articles. They also are ideal for spent bullets, empty cartridge cases, and cartridges because they can be packed with cotton gauze to minimize movement of such evidence.

Plastic envelopes and bags are available in various shapes and sizes and also are easily sealed. However, when they are used to transport soil, debris, or clothing that may contain bloodstains, bacterial action contaminating the blood sample becomes a strong possibility. Use plastic containers with caution. To an unusual degree, they can act as greenhouses for the cultivation of mold that can destroy the integrity and identity of some types of evidence.

Use only the tubes or vials with stoppers found in blood collection kits for blood samples and swatches used to collect bloodstains, and follow directions on these kits for refrigeration and other care.

If the stain is on a solid object that can be moved, such as a firearm or other weapon, transport the object, protecting the area of the stain or completely enclosing the object in a package if it is small in size. If the stain is on clothing, wrap the garments separately in paper, mark them appropriately, and package them. This is a better procedure than any technique for removing a sample of a stain for analysis.

Articles of clothing, tablecloths, and other fabric evidence should be folded as little as possible and without applying pressure. If the areas of the fabric to be examined are known, they should be protected from friction with wrapping paper or another appropriate form of containment.

Take a soil-stained or mud-soaked object to the laboratory rather than attempting to remove and transport the soil or mud as separate items. When such traces are picked up as individual items of evidence, it is vital that every precaution be taken to keep the evidence in separate sealed containers to avoid any accidental loss or mixing in transit.

Charred wood, carpet, and drapery material from the scene of a suspicious fire may be wrapped in metal foil and sealed in an airtight container. Smaller objects, such as paper and rags, or solid samples should be sealed in the container in which they were found or placed in airtight bottles or cans. This prevents the fire accelerant and its residues from evaporating.

Pills and other noncaustic substances should be left in their original containers for transport to the laboratory. Such containers often provide useful information. The investigator should count the number of pills or capsules or accurately determine the bulk quantity of fluids or powders and should place this data in the field notes.

Caustic poison should not be transported until the investigator has made certain that the container in which it was found (or placed after its recovery from sink, bathtub, or other place) is safe for a period of time equal to at least twice the likely transport time.

Food, body substances, and fluids should be placed in as many separate moisture-proof bottles or containers as necessary to avoid any contamination of evidence. Food or other substances suspected of containing or known to contain poison should be plainly labeled as suspected or known samples of poison.

If a weapon is suspected of containing hair, blood, or fragments of flesh, it should be packaged in a sealed container of appropriate size.

Microscopic traces, hairs, and fibers should be sealed in folded paper or placed in a clean, sealed envelope or box of appropriate size.

MATCHING PHYSICAL EVIDENCE WITH KNOWN STANDARDS

Criminalistics includes the identification of physical evidence and the finding of its origin. This individualization of evidence often requires that physical evidence collected at a crime scene be matched with a **known standard of evidence** or a control. Known standards may be collected at the crime scene, from the victim, from a suspect, or from other sources and must be collected in exactly the same manner as any other evidence because they have equal evidential value. As for other evidence, known standards must be recognized and followed so that possession is obtained legally, evidence is marked appropriately, samples are properly preserved, and the acquisition process is reported accurately.

Locating a known standard of fingerprints may require no more than a search of records for a suspect's fingerprints. Shoe prints may require the collection of a known standard of soil from the area close to a footprint or heel print for comparison with soil traces on the shoes of a suspect. Collection of a sample of hair is often required, as is the search for and the recovery of a coat or sweater or other garment that may be a known standard for fibers recovered at the crime scene.

Known samples of blood start with the victim. Samples can be secured only by a medical practitioner upon the request of the investigator. Since the

Schmerber case, it is lawful to take a sample from an arrested person charged with a crime in which blood collected as evidence requires a known sample for comparative analysis.[6]

The self-incrimination clause of the Fifth Amendment to the U.S. Constitution protects against compelling a person or suspect to communicate or testify to matters that may incriminate him or her. However, the Fifth Amendment does not protect a person or suspect from being compelled to be the source of "real or physical evidence." The recovery of blood, clothing, and hair without consent is not prohibited by the Fifth Amendment because these are all considered "real or physical evidence" and thus are subject to the controls of the right to privacy and search and seizure clauses of the Fourth Amendment, rather than to the self-incrimination clause of the Fifth.

Handwriting analysis requires exemplars, or samples, as well as proof of authorship. These known standards are classed as either "requested" (by the investigator) or "regular course of business." In death cases in which a suicide note is found, the only exemplar possible is some "regular course of business" handwriting found on the victim or at the scene, or secured from relatives and associates and identified by a responsible person as being the victim's handwriting. In other cases, such exemplars may be available at the crime scene, at the place of employment, or in the public record. Exemplars that have been requested are often less reliable because of intentional disguising of normal writing style or distortions due to nervousness.[7]

Investigators obtaining handwriting samples from a suspect should supply him or her with paper and a pen or pencil similar to what was used for the questioned writing, dictate the material to be written or printed, and allow the suspect to spell words as he or she would usually spell them. Misspelled words can contribute to the physical **match** between sample and questioned writing.[8] In addition, the suspect should be asked to write out and sign a statement as to the validity and source of the sample or samples.

Requiring a suspect to give handwritten exemplars is not considered to be a request for communications that fall within the protection of the Fifth Amendment. The Fifth Amendment only prohibits the compulsion of communicative or testimonial evidence from a defendant. In writing to produce the exemplar for identification, the defendant is no more than the source of identification. Handwriting exemplars have been specifically held to be such an identifying physical characteristic.[9]

As with handwriting exemplars, compelling the accused to utter words spoken by an alleged thief is not within the scope of the Fifth Amendment privilege against self-incrimination. However, voice identification is subject to the Sixth Amendment's right to representation by an attorney clause and is regarded as belonging to a critical stage of the proceedings against a suspect.[10]

The justices of the U.S. Supreme Court have expressed a minority viewpoint that handwriting exemplars and voice identification are within the scope of constitutional protection. Therefore, compelling these two types of evidence against the will of a person is at least questionable if either is the key evidence in the case. It would be a better policy to obtain handwriting exemplars and speech for identification by consent and not by force. If the investigation is beyond the general inquiry stage and has focused on a suspect, the

Miranda admonishment should be given to inform the person of his or her constitutional protection against self-incrimination.[11]

Many manufacturers of paint and glass provide scientific laboratories with known standards of their products, and criminalistics laboratories maintain many reference files of known standards. However, one should not assume that such standards are on file. It is the responsibility of the investigator to seek known standards until such time as he or she is informed that they are not required.

Because the legal significance of physical evidence often is based on comparison to a known standard, it is of vital importance that physical evidence and its collection be viewed as a dual process of collecting and preserving the basic physical evidence and of collecting and preserving the known standards of such evidence.

TRANSPORTING EVIDENCE

Transporting physical evidence to a laboratory, to a place of storage, or to the prosecutor's office or the courtroom is the responsibility of the investigator who found the evidence. It is usually delivered personally, but when distance is a problem it may be shipped by registered mail, insured parcel post, or express mail. When food or physiological fluids or substances are collected, temperature control is a primary precaution. Refrigeration without freezing will prevent deterioration, and insulating containers are now available for the transport of such material. Evidence should be shipped by the fastest available route. Local delivery should be made in person by the finding investigator or by authorized personnel of his or her employing agency.

When physical evidence is sent to a laboratory for scientific examination, it must be accompanied by an informative report. The report must, in effect, bring the crime scene into the laboratory. This report must be on the official letterhead of the law enforcement agency with jurisdiction in the case and should contain the following:

1. Name and address of the agency submitting the evidence
2. Crime classification of case by type and grade of offense
3. Case number of agency submitting evidence
4. Copy of the offense report, the report of the preliminary investigation, or a brief history of the case
5. List of evidence consecutively numbered by item with a brief description of each item and a notation as to (a) when and where found, (b) whether the item is a known standard for comparison, and (c) whether any change has taken place in the evidence either through accidental mishandling or because a sample is being submitted, rather than the full amount of evidence collected
6. List of suggested scientific examinations
7. Brief statement of the problems in the case
8. The name and address of the investigator to whom the exhibits should be returned upon completion of the examination

Packages in which physical evidence is to be shipped to a laboratory should be marked "Evidence for Examination" and the written request for an examination should be pasted securely to the outside of the package, with the notation "Letter" or "Invoice" indicating its location. The criminalist receiving the package can read the request letter and have some idea of the nature of the evidence before opening the package itself.

Packages containing blood or other body fluids suspected of being contaminated by a person with acquired immune deficiency syndrome (AIDS), hepatitis B, or tuberculosis should be marked "CAUTION", followed by the name of the disease suspected. The technician in charge at the crime laboratory should be consulted before submitting this type of evidence.

Laboratory technicians carefully mark, tag, and otherwise identify all items of evidence while such evidence is in their custody. It is this careful handling of physical evidence by crime laboratory technicians that preserves the integrity of such evidence. Upon return of the evidence, the report of the expert examiner who conducted the laboratory examination is integrated with other information collected in the investigation to date. At no time should an investigator return any part of the evidence to its rightful claimant without the authority of the prosecutor. If the prosecutor believes that the evidence is not required in the trial of the offender, he or she has the authority to return it to the rightful owner or to store it until such time as it is disposed of according to law. When the case is completed, the prosecutor has the authority to release the evidence.

HANDLING INFECTED EVIDENCE

AIDS, hepatitis B, and tuberculosis are potentially lethal infectious diseases more likely to be encountered at crime scenes today than in the past. The scenes of crimes of violence involving victims with one of these diseases are likely to contain blood and possibly other infectious body fluids. Therefore, it is imperative that all possible precautions be taken.

Investigators arriving at the crime scene should question other officers as to the possibility of the victim having a lethal infectious disease. The high-risk groups include injection drug users and possibly prostitutes (male and female). A quick survey of the crime scene may indicate some warning signals—for example, condition of the victim and the presence of prescription or nonprescription drugs.

The first line of defense against infectious diseases is to wear disposable gloves. A surgical mask and protective eyewear may also be suggested with any likelihood that liquid or dried blood may come into contact with the face of the investigator or the crime scene technician. The second line of defense is to avoid cutting or puncturing a finger or other portion of the body while conducting the crime scene search and collecting evidence. A collateral line of defense is to seek medical assistance immediately if you do receive an accidental cut or other wound or believe that particles of possibly infected blood may have come in contact with your mouth or eyes.[12]

To protect others, any evidence suspected of contamination should be placed in clearly marked plastic bags and sealed. However, these bags should not be forwarded to the crime laboratory until it is certain that the laboratory will accept this type of evidence.

Because of the epidemic spread of AIDS, investigators are urged to meet with local health officials to discuss how to best protect all concerned. Health personnel should be able to outline possible signs at crime scenes that might indicate that a victim should be suspected of having an infectious disease; to explain the proper procedure for disposing of latex gloves after their use at a "suspect" crime scene; and to denote the best procedure to follow from the time an investigator or technician believes that he or she has been in contact with blood or other body fluids likely to be infected to the time when medical assistance will be available.

IDENTIFYING PHYSICAL CHANGES AT THE SCENE

Investigators search for and collect evidence of any observable damage to objects at the scene—furniture turned over, broken, or moved from its normal location at the scene and other items that are bent, broken, dented, or scratched. Disarrangement, damage, and theft may be useful in determining what happened and who did it. A fight or struggle of some kind is indicated by overturned and broken furniture. Damage may indicate the direction of force. Photographs of the scene preserve the "as is" quality of the change or disarrangement.

Not only may articles taken from the scene lead to a major suspect, but they also may supply incriminating evidence when recovered from the possession or control of a suspect at the time of arrest. The responsible investigator includes a description of the stolen property in the alarm broadcast. Even articles of little value, such as snapshots or ashtrays, have potential value as evidence when recovered.

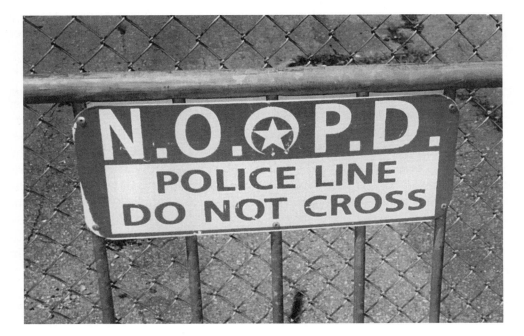

A crime scene can be well defined by using barrier tape or barricades.

A crime scene can be anywhere, even in the middle of nowhere.

CONDUCTING A FINAL SURVEY OF THE SCENE

The officer in charge should take a final survey of the scene before relinquishing control of the crime scene area. This final survey ensures that all of the evidence has been identified and collected and that the scene has been properly processed prior to release. This review of the crime scene also ensures that equipment and materials generated by the investigation are not left behind inadvertently. Investigators should keep in mind that to return to the scene to do follow-up crime scene work because items were inadvertently overlooked may require a search warrant, because once the area is released it no longer carries the legal status of a crime scene.[13]

MEDIA RELATIONS

The vast majority of crime scenes will not attract the attention of the media. However, the media's need for law enforcement is obvious: crime and the police make news. Recent studies, for example, have shown that crime reporting has made up one-third of all the coverage in local television newscasts. Newspaper, radio, and television reporters have a real hunger for news about crime and the police.

Law enforcement also needs the media. The media is essential for publicizing information on wanted suspects or alerting residents to crime trends. In addition, the news media can be a valuable tool for advertising various activities that build public support for the agency's mission.[14]

This symbiotic relationship between the media and law enforcement should be used to develop a long-term professional working relationship. The best way to accomplish this goal is to work with the media honestly and to provide information that can be released in a timely manner.

Usually the following information can be released to the media:

1. The type of crime committed, including a brief description of what happened, where, and when
2. Identity of the victim, which is usually not released unless the victim is deceased, in which case this information would be withheld pending notification of the next of kin. (In cases of sexual assault, per applicable rape shield laws, the victim's identity is also withheld.)
3. Facts concerning the arrest of the suspect or suspects can include the name, age, and circumstances of the arrest and the time, place, resistance, and weapons involved

Information that should not be released to the media includes the following:

1. Prior criminal charges and convictions or comments regarding the reputation, character, guilt, or innocence of suspects
2. Identification of any juvenile suspects
3. Comment on any admission or confession or the fact that an admission or confession has or has not been made
4. Identity of any possible witnesses
5. Precise description of the amount of money or other items taken[15]

CASE STUDY

Incredible Evidence

Late Sunday afternoon on June 12, 1994, Nicole Brown Simpson, the former wife of football great O. J. Simpson, attended her daughter's dance recital in West Los Angeles. Also in attendance was her former husband, who is the father of her two children. When the recital ended, Nicole, her children, and her other family members dined at the Mezzaluna restaurant near her home in Brentwood. She arrived home at approximately 8:30 p.m. and called the restaurant to inquire about her prescription sunglasses that she had left behind. A waiter friend, Ron Goldman, found the glasses and offered to bring them to her on his way home from work. Goldman left the restaurant at about 9:45 p.m.

At approximately 10:45 p.m., a limousine driver arrived at O. J. Simpson's estate to pick him up and take him to the airport. The driver noted that his passenger was "agitated and sweaty." At 11:45 p.m., Simpson's plane left for Chicago. At this time, an acquaintance noted that Simpson appeared composed and talkative about playing golf the next day in Chicago.

On Monday morning, June 13, at about 12:10 a.m., a neighbor found Nicole's dog wandering around the neighborhood. He returned the dog to Nicole's townhouse and discovered the bodies of Nicole Brown Simpson and Ron Goldman outside the front entrance to Nicole's home. Both victims had been stabbed and had their throats slashed.

The police were notified and quickly responded to the scene. The first officer on the scene located the victims and searched the interior of the townhouse, finding Nicole's two children unharmed, asleep in their beds. The area was cordoned off and the crime scene technicians and homicide detectives were requested to respond. During the initial search for evidence at the crime scene, a bloody leather glove was found at the feet of victim Ron Goldman.

By 5:00 a.m., the detectives assigned to the case had determined the identities of the victims and decided to go to the Simpson estate a few miles away to notify him of the death of his ex-wife. Upon arrival at the estate, the detectives noticed what appeared to be blood on the driver-side door handle of Simpson's Ford Bronco, which was parked on the street outside the estate. A string of what could have been blood droplets led from the Bronco to the front entrance of the residence. The detectives received no response at the gate intercom or to follow-up phone calls to the residence. Believing the safety of O. J. Simpson and other family members was at risk, one of the detectives scaled over a five-foot wall surrounding the estate and opened the gate, allowing the other detectives to enter.

The detectives entered the residence, but O. J. Simpson was not there. The detectives found two navy blue socks on the floor of the master bedroom. A search of the grounds led to the discovery of a bloody leather glove, similar to the one found at the crime scene, on the rear walkway on the south side of the estate. The detectives seized these items and the Ford Bronco as possible items of evidence. These items of evidence were eventually forwarded to the crime laboratory for processing.

O. J. Simpson's whereabouts in Chicago were then determined. He was contacted by telephone in the early morning hours and informed of his ex-wife's death. Simpson arranged to catch the next flight back to Los Angeles. Upon arrival in California, Simpson was taken to police headquarters, questioned by the homicide detectives, and later released.

On June 17, Simpson was charged with two counts of murder and a warrant was issued for his arrest. On June 20, Simpson entered a plea of not guilty and his trial was scheduled to begin on January 24, 1995. During his eight-month-long trial, Simpson did not take the witness stand in his defense, and the prosecution did not use any portion of his statement given to the police on June 13. No eyewitnesses to the crime came forth, so the prosecution relied primarily on the physical evidence to make its case against the defendant, which included the following:

Simpson's Ford Bronco. A crime scene technician collected blood samples from the vehicle's interior two days after the murders. The test results on the samples indicated that these bloodstains matched the blood of both victims, as well as that of the defendant. On cross-examination, the crime scene technician who collected the samples admitted that she had used the same cotton swab on different bloodstains. This was contrary to her training, and this unapproved method of collection could have led to possible contamination of the samples.

Blood at the Crime Scene. In addition to finding the victims' blood, investigators found bloodstains at the crime scene that matched the blood of the defendant. Some three weeks after the crime was committed, a drop of Simpson's blood also was found on the rear gate at the scene of the crime. The prosecution maintained that Simpson cut himself while attacking his two victims. The defense countered that the three-week delay in finding this evidence would have given the police ample time to plant the evidence.

Navy Blue Socks. Tests revealed that the socks found in Simpson's master bedroom contained bloodstains that matched the blood of both victim Nicole Brown Simpson and the defendant.

Leather Gloves. Tests indicated that the bloodstains on the glove found at the crime scene and the glove found at the Simpson estate matched the blood of both victims and the defendant. The defense countered by suggesting that one of the gloves had been transported by the police from the crime scene and then was planted on the estate's rear walkway.

Simpson's Blood Sample. The defendant had supplied a blood sample at police headquarters shortly after being questioned by the homicide detectives. Detective Vannatter then took the sample from police headquarters to the Simpson estate. Detective Vannatter gave the sample to the crime scene technicians who were still collecting evidence. The defense argued that this was contrary to established standard procedure. The detective should have booked the blood sample at police headquarters. In addition, the defense maintained that a small quantity of this sample, 1.5 milliliters, was unaccounted for by the crime laboratory. The defense suggested that the missing blood was used by the police to plant the defendant's blood samples at the crime scene and on various pieces of evidence.

EDTA.   In its analysis of blood evidence, the defense found minute quantities of a preservative known as EDTA. The defense contended that such a finding could suggest that the blood attributed to the defendant had come from Simpson's sample. The prosecution refuted this contention by arguing that had the evidence been sprinkled with blood from Simpson's reference vial, the level of EDTA would have been much, much higher.

After eight months of trial testimony, most experts expected the jury to deliberate for days, if not weeks, before reaching a verdict. However, within only a few hours, the jury completed deliberations and reached a unanimous verdict of not guilty. Juror Brenda Morgan, interviewed after the verdict was announced, told the press that the jury found Detective Vannatter's decision to carry Simpson's blood sample around with him for several hours "suspicious because it gave him the opportunity to plant evidence." Another juror put it this way: "not a conspiracy with all the police officers, but maybe with some."

Source: Adapted from Vincent Bugliosi, *Outrage: The Five Reasons Why O. J. Simpson Got Away with Murder* (New York: Norton, 1996), 309–320, 344.

CHAPTER REVIEW

KEY TERMS

anthropometry *4*
chain of possession *12*
chronological log *7*
criminalistics *4*
ever-narrowing circle *8*
ever-widening circle *8*
exchange principle *5*

forensics *4*
impact energy *6*
known standard of
  evidence *15*
match *16*
modus operandi *10*
omission *4*

point-to-point
  movement *8*
single-officer search *8*
strip or grid search *8*
toxicology *4*
zone or sector search *8*

REVIEW QUESTIONS

1. The person who first developed a system of human identification, known as anthropometry was:
   a. Alphonse Bertillon
   b. Calvin Goddard
   c. Edmond Locard
   d. Francis Galton

2. The scientist who theorized that when a criminal came into contact with another object or person a cross-transference of evidence could occur was:
   a. Alphonse Bertillon
   b. Calvin Goddard
   c. Edmond Locard
   d. Francis Galton

3. The scientist who refined the technique necessary for the determination of whether or not a bullet was fired from a suspect weapon was:
   a. Alphonse Bertillon
   b. Calvin Goddard
   c. Edmond Locard
   d. Francis Galton

4. The first officers responding to a crime scene are responsible for making sure that the scene is safe for other personnel to enter the area. This step in the coordination of a crime scene is known as:
   a. Initializing the scene
   b. Neutralizing the scene

c. Crime scene security

d. Crime scene basis

5. The crime scene search pattern that starts at one end of the scene and in which searchers work back and forth until the entire area is searched is known as what type of search?
   a. Ever-widening
   b. Ever-narrowing
   c. Zone or sector
   d. Strip

6. Being able to account for an item of evidence from the time of its finding to its presentation in court is known as:
   a. Contingency processing
   b. Chain of possession
   c. Possession accountability
   d. Chain of accountability

7. Which of the following should *not* be released to the media by investigators?
   a. Identity of possible witnesses
   b. Type of crime committed
   c. Details of the offense
   d. When and where the crime occurred

8. The study of the effects poisons have on the human body is known as:
   a. Forensics
   b. Typing
   c. Anthropometry
   d. Toxicology

9. Officers guarding the perimeter of a crime scene are responsible for maintaining a chronological log. This log is based on what?
   a. Resources expended at the crime scene
   b. Movement of persons into and out of the crime scene
   c. Time of occurrence of events at the crime scene
   d. Importance of the events that occur at the crime scene

10. The use of science to answer legal questions is known as:
    a. Toxicology
    b. Criminology
    c. Forensics
    d. Modus operandi

See Appendix D for the correct answers.

DISCUSSION QUESTIONS

1. Trace the growth in the use of physical evidence in criminal proceedings.
2. Will physical evidence really establish a case for or against a suspect? Does it have real legal significance?
3. Describe standard procedures in collecting and preserving evidence.
4. Can any one rule of evidence gathering be identified as of primary importance?
5. Explain when and why known standards of evidence should be collected.
6. Why are blood samples exempt from the scope of the Fifth Amendment's privilege against self-incrimination?
7. What other types of identification samples, in which a defendant is the source, are exempt from the protection of the Fifth Amendment?
8. Regarding the case study, discuss how a deviation from standard operating procedures in the handling of physical evidence can affect the outcome of a criminal trial.
9. Regarding the case study, is the perception of wrongdoing as persuasive to a jury as actual wrongdoing?

RELATED WEB SITES

To find out more about crime scene investigation, contact the National Criminal Justice Reference Service, the research agency of the U.S. Department of Justice, at *www.ncjrs.org*.

To learn more about the role of public information officers (PIOs) and media relations, contact the National Information Officers Association at *www.nioa.org*.

New technologies are constantly being developed to help investigators to find evidence and solve crimes. Learn more about these emerging technologies at *www.officer.com*.

Interested in being a crime scene investigator? If so you might be interested in some information from the International Crime Scene Investigators Association at *www.icsia.org*.

chapter **two**

Direct and Circumstantial Evidence

CHAPTER OUTLINE

After reading this chapter you will be able to:

- Explain the distinction between willing and unwilling witnesses and their motivations.
- Discuss the various methods investigators use to identify and locate potential witnesses to a crime.
- Articulate the distinction between circumstantial and direct evidence.
- Identify the various types of fingerprints found at crime scenes and the methods used to recover these items of evidence.
- List the various types of information that can be obtained through ballistic examinations of firearms.

Two kinds of proof are used during a criminal trial to answer the question of guilt or innocence: direct evidence and circumstantial evidence. **Direct evidence** involves eyewitnesses who have, through one or more of their five senses, experienced something relative to the crime in question or its circumstances. A **willing witness** is often found at the scene of the crime. However, unwilling witnesses must often be located through the techniques of revisiting the crime scene, neighborhood canvasses, and pleas for public cooperation. In contrast, **circumstantial evidence** is defined as evidence from which an inference can be drawn and which includes items such as physical evidence. The major types of circumstantial evidence include weapons, blood, imprints or impressions, tool marks, dust and dirt traces, questioned documents, and miscellaneous trace or transfer evidence.

LOCATING WITNESSES AT THE CRIME SCENE

Witnesses at the crime scene include those discovered in the view area and neighborhood. It is the duty of the first officer at the scene of a suspected crime to "contain" it. Standard regulations require responding officers to detain witnesses and other persons at the scene. These officers secure adequate information about the identity of all persons found at a crime scene; their names, addresses, and telephone numbers; and their employers' names and business addresses. Of course, the perpetrator is arrested if he or she is at the scene and so identified, but at this time the major concern with regard to witnesses is to locate them, secure a description of the perpetrator and the facts of the crime, and record their identities and where they can be located.

The degree of difficulty involved in locating a particular witness is directly related to the willingness of that person to be a witness and the knowledge that person has that he or she is, in fact, a witness to a crime. A willing witness may wait at the crime scene until the police arrive or contact the police to supply information. Many willing witnesses are motivated by a sense of civic responsibility. Others may be motivated to assist the police to eliminate business competitors. It is not uncommon, for instance, for one drug dealer to inform on another drug dealer whose territory he covets. Relatives, spouses, and lovers will also provide the authorities with information regarding the whereabouts of wanted loved ones in the hope that the offender will get the necessary treatment or learn the lesson that crime does not pay. Perhaps one of the most powerful motivations is revenge: people who have been wronged by the suspect in one way or another will cooperate with the investigation to get even.

The **unwilling witness** does not want to cooperate with the investigation and will usually disappear from a crime scene when the police arrive. The motivation of such witnesses varies. It may be a simple dislike for authority or that the witness has outstanding warrants or is a suspect in a criminal act. Many unwilling witnesses will say simply that they do not want to get involved. The basis here may be selfishness or a genuine concern for loss of income or another inconvenience that might result from having to testify at a lengthy criminal trial.

Some potential witnesses may be unaware that they witnessed a crime or its circumstances. For example, the witness may have observed the arrival or departure of the suspect from the crime scene but not the crime itself. Although the nature of the crime may be unknown, this potentially important witness can place the suspect at the scene of the crime.

REVISITING THE CRIME SCENE

Revisiting the crime scene has been effective in locating witnesses. Motorists and pedestrians who do not live or work in the area but who travel the area at about the same time daily or weekly are often witnesses, but they leave the scene prior to the arrival of responding officers, sometimes not even knowing that the event they witnessed has become a police case.

The technique of revisiting a crime scene to search for witnesses has been adapted from the investigation of hit-and-run crimes. Solving such cases, in which motorists are involved in an accident and flee the scene, usually requires locating the vehicle involved. Investigators can use only the identification potential of the physical evidence found at the scene and, when the suspect vehicle is located, the damage to the suspect car. For this reason, witnesses who can give some clue to the identity of the vehicle and its operator must be discovered. When the initial inquiry at the scene does not produce witnesses, investigators revisit the scene for a week or two for an hour or more each day, spanning the time of the accident, then revisit on the same day of the week for three or four weeks. Traffic accident investigation units have used this technique for years to find witnesses and collect information about the identity of a hit-and-run vehicle. Key witnesses have been located as much as a month after an accident. The procedure is now formalized as follows:

1. Revisit the accident scene daily for no less than a week and weekly on the day of the week of the accident for no less than a month at the same time of day that the accident occurred.
2. Question motorists and pedestrians, with particular attention to school children and service personnel, such as operators of delivery vehicles.[1]

VIEW AREA CANVASS

An inquiry in the **view area** of the crime scene is also standard practice (Figure 2–1). When a crime is committed within a building, as in an office or apartment, the universe of possible witnesses may be small. When the crime is committed in a store or on the street, a large group of persons might have witnessed it. This requires a search for persons who may have been witnesses but who have not been so identified. Officers visit places of business, apartments, and residences near the scene. Customers and employees of markets, taverns, and service stations, and residents at home and their visitors, are all questioned. This is a solicitation for information about the crime and about anyone who might have seen the event, witnessed suspicious persons in the area before the crime, viewed the perpetrator's flight from the

30

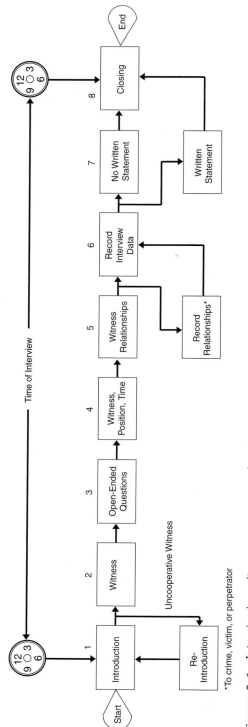

FIGURE 2–1 Interviewing witnesses—nonsuggestive structure.

scene, heard anything unusual, or knows of someone who has or might have information.

THE NEIGHBORHOOD CANVASS

Superior officers supervising the criminal investigation often assign additional personnel to an extensive **neighborhood canvass** in order to find a witness. The plan used in such a canvass may be based on the approach and flight route of the perpetrator, the travels of witnesses, or the path of a bullet in sniper cases. A canvass for witnesses in the neighborhood of the crime follows a pattern. It starts with revisits to persons residing or employed in the view area of the crime scene and extends to establishing contacts with employees of delivery service firms and public utilities. This canvass expands to nearby areas and bus stops and public transit stations beyond the crime scene but within a convenient distance of it. Such a canvass involves the traditional task of ringing doorbells. Often it appears to be a hopeless assignment, yet time and again an investigator canvassing an area finds a witness or, equally important, a person who knows the identity of a witness.

This knocking on doors and asking questions is a very productive source of evidence in homicide cases. The seriousness of the crime impresses most people, and they respond meaningfully when questioned. In these cases, investigators are seeking information about the victim, as well as the killer or killers.[2]

The attempt to locate witnesses in a canvass of a neighborhood includes the following steps:

1. Friends and immediate relatives of the victim living in the neighborhood are located and interviewed.
2. A house-to-house, apartment-to-apartment, door-to-door canvass is made of
   a. residents and shopkeepers and their employees
   b. delivery, utility, and other service personnel
   c. bus and taxi drivers

Supermarkets, which are isolated within the moats of their immense parking lots, have created problems in locating witnesses. The problem is not that the viewing area is curtailed, since people are still in and about this area. The problem is that the people in the view area are transients. They do not reside in it, nor is it a place of employment. They walk or drive to a view area, then leave it and return to their homes or places of business. The tremendous population of people and vehicles in and about shopping centers complicates the problem of locating witnesses to crimes and has led to the concept of the shopping-area canvass for witnesses (Figure 2–2). Unlike the neighborhood canvass developed by detectives in large urban central cities, this shopping area canvass can be very extensive geographically. The canvass in urban centers encompasses the area in which the perpetrator may have traveled to and from the crime scene; the shopping area canvass encompasses the area in which witnesses travel to and from the crime scene.

FIGURE 2–2   Shopping area canvass for witnesses.

It may seem that the distinction is highly technical or abstract, but many individuals who are otherwise very cooperative with the police reject any semblance of the informer role. These persons often feel that revealing the name or whereabouts of a witness is not in the same category as revealing the identity of a person who might have committed the crime.

Investigators successful in locating witnesses in this way are skilled in establishing liaisons with persons likely to have information and in maintaining contacts with such individuals until their cooperation is needed. This is not normally a procedure that can be developed for a specific investigation. The contacts must be established first. Then when a crime occurs, and this type of cooperation is needed, the investigator has sources of information available.

ISSUING PLEAS FOR PUBLIC COOPERATION

In serious felony cases receiving unusual publicity, the police receive a great many investigative leads from members of the community. These offers of help proliferate when the crime is child molesting, a series of murders or rapes, and robberies or thefts of very large sums of money or immensely valuable jewelry. Unfortunately, the great majority of these calls are from persons justly classified as cranks. Most of the leads are useless, and the time spent making inquiries is lost entirely. An investigator cannot afford to verify every offer of information from such sources. Selectivity is necessary, and techniques for auditing these unsought messages should be developed. In the audit, all messages containing the name and address or other data identifying a potential witness are separated from letters and calls presenting theories of the crime or suspicious persons. A prompt follow-up inquiry is made on the witness leads, and the remainder are set aside for later analysis.

Police officials, in attempting to locate witnesses to crimes of importance, use all the communications media: newspapers, radio, local television outlets, and the Internet. In New York, Chicago, San Francisco, Miami, and other large cities, the standard plea to the public is to contribute any information about the case to police, and it is now made easier for them to do so by publication of a special telephone number. In some cases, the posting of a reward hastens the response to these pleas for public cooperation. However, this mercenary inducement for help should be avoided unless it is deemed absolutely necessary. For gain, some persons may supply false or meaningless information solely in the hope of making a future claim. A **silent witness program** seeks the same help but offers rewards and confidentiality.

A technique has been developed by local television stations: a telecast of clues about an unsolved and recent crime. This "clue-in" offers the viewers a minimum of facts about the case, and the core of the program is a request for listeners to call the local station if they believe they may have witnessed any of the travels of the suspected offender or offenders. Several radio stations across the country have cooperated with police in a similar fashion. Listeners in either instance are conditioned to respond by calling the station because of the growth of contests and opinion polls requiring a prompt telephone response.

In both types of clue-ins, the emphasis is not on finding people with theories of the crime or ideas of techniques the police should use in searching for the offender but rather on locating witnesses. Listeners and viewers are asked to call a specific, easily remembered telephone number under any of the following conditions:

- If you witnessed any segment of this crime, any act concerned with its preparation, any of the postcrime travels or other activities of the criminal or his or her associates
- If you know the identity of the criminal or his or her associates from other sources of information
- If you know the identity of any other person who might have been a witness or who might know the identity of the offender and his or her associates

Police in the United States have been having problems securing the cooperation of the public in solving crimes. However, when the crime is widely recognized as vicious and hurtful, the potential for community support is excellent. Persons who would not normally cooperate will do so when the atrocity of a crime inspires their sympathy for the victim and the public appeal for information orients them to the police. It is a technique in searching for witnesses that has optimum potential because everyone in the community is exposed to multimedia. Notices in the media do communicate to people and can be used successfully in discovering witnesses.

SEPARATING WITNESSES

The scene of the crime is the one place where a number of witnesses will be together at the same time. The first officer on the scene should identify potential witnesses and separate them as soon as possible.[3] Witnesses should not be allowed to discuss the crime among themselves as the investigator wants only that information that the witness independently observed or experienced. When witnesses discuss the crime or overhear others talking about the crime, they tend to adopt some of this information as their own or alter their recollections to fit with those of other witnesses. This process is normal and is known as **retroactive interference**.[4]

GETTING A COMMITMENT

In the process of identifying potential witnesses, the officers at the scene of a crime will encounter people who are uncooperative or state that they have no knowledge of the crime. This is not unusual. However, as soon as it is determined that these persons were in a position to be a witness to the crime, they should be identified and their refusal to give information or their statement of ignorance should be properly recorded in the police report. This process makes a record of the fact that these potential witnesses were given the opportunity to assist the investigation at the time the crime occurred. Any statement made by a potential witness refusing to cooperate or denying knowledge of the crime can be used to impeach the witness when at trial he or she becomes the star defense witness.

CIRCUMSTANTIAL EVIDENCE

Evidence likely to be found at crime scenes and amenable to scientific analysis is divided into seven major groups: (1) weapons, (2) blood, (3) imprints and impressions (traces of a person or a vehicle), (4) tool marks, (5) dust, dirt, and other traces, (6) questioned documents, and (7) miscellaneous trace or transfer evidence.

WEAPONS

Firearms should be handled to preserve ballistic identity. **Ballistics** is the identification of firearms, bullets, cartridges, and shotgun shells. **Interior ballistics** refers to the functioning of firearms through the firing cycle, and **exterior ballistics** is the study of projectiles in flight. As primary sources for identification, ballistics uses the inside of the barrel (the bore, with its lands and grooves), the firing pin, the breech face in which the firing pin hole is located, the chamber, and the ejector and extractor.[5]

Investigators reject such techniques for picking up firearms as the insertion of a pencil in the barrel of a handgun and follow procedures that will not change the portions of the weapon commonly used for ballistic comparison and identification. Firearms should be picked up by their rough or checkered wooden portions, if possible, or any external metal portion except the trigger guard and trigger area, and promptly placed in a container or tied to a board or strong piece of cardboard. Firearms should not be handled unnecessarily, nor should the mechanism be actuated time and time again.

A collection of weapons commonly encountered by investigators.

Safety is of paramount importance. The minimum procedure for emptying a gun should be followed to unload a firearm. No attempt should be made to fire a gun, dismantle it, or interfere with the mechanism in any way.

A description of a firearm should start with the name of the manufacturer and the serial number. These data are necessary for tracing the weapon. Record all names and numbers stamped on the firearm, along with their locations on the gun. Some numbers are part numbers, and one- or two-digit numbers are usually model numbers. Some marks may indicate the maker, others proof testing. (Emblems and symbols are **proof marks** that indicate tests performed to prove the strength of the chamber of a firearm by actual firing with maximum loads.) All these marks help identify the gun. Sometimes a number has been obliterated by grinding, filing, or center punching. The investigator should describe the damage and its location and request laboratory services to restore the number. (It is difficult to restore when center punched, but it may be possible, and even a fragment may be helpful.)

The **caliber** of the weapon or its gauge (if a shotgun) is also an identifying characteristic. It is often marked on the firearm in a stamping associated with the name of the manufacturer or model number. If the caliber is not marked, the investigator should qualify any estimate of the caliber by putting "unknown" in his or her field notes and noting a measurement across the bore of the weapon in fractions of an inch. This is in line with the requirement of accuracy in collecting evidence. A defense attorney can raise doubt about testimony in relation to firearms (and possibly doubt about the entire police case) by questioning failure by police to make accurate notations regarding the caliber of a weapon. Professional conduct requires an investigator to qualify any lack of knowledge, and it is more desirable to write "unknown" than to specify an approximate caliber and later to find it is grossly wrong.

Fired (empty) and unfired cartridge cases, shotgun shells, and spent bullets should also be handled with particular attention to the portions

When a firearm is discharged, residues are deposited on the shooter's hands.

used in ballistic identification—that is, the base and the rim just above the base of the case, and the side of the cartridge or the shell immediately above the base (extractor marks). When empty cartridge cases or shotgun shells are picked up, the location should be pinpointed with measurements for future reference. Because some firearms throw out, or eject, the cartridge cases with some distinctiveness as to direction and force, the exact location of the cases can indicate the position of the person firing the gun, sometimes for each shot fired.

Spent bullets are excellent clues to the firearm used in the crime. They must be carefully removed from their point of impact, and the location at

A test bullet on the right-hand side of this vertical line matches the bore marks on a bullet found at the scene of a crime.

Fingerprinting a Gun

A gun can be identified through several distinctive markings it leaves on bullets and casings. Just like human fingerprints, each gun leaves its own unique markings as identification. The Bureau of Alcohol, Tobacco and Firearms wants to take fingerprints of new guns to create a national database prior to their sale. These images along with ones of gun fingerprints from crime scenes can then be searched for matches. If a match is found in the database, the gun that created the match can be traced to other crimes and back to where and to whom it was sold.

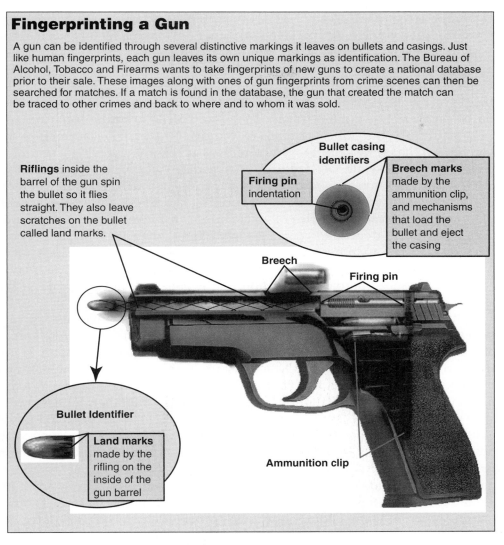

Bullet casing identifiers

Firing pin indentation

Breech marks made by the ammunition clip, and mechanisms that load the bullet and eject the casing

Riflings inside the barrel of the gun spin the bullet so it flies straight. They also leave scratches on the bullet called land marks.

Breech

Firing pin

Bullet Identifier

Land marks made by the rifling on the inside of the gun barrel

Ammunition clip

FIGURE 2–3   Interior ballistics identification.

which they are found must be recorded accurately in the investigator's field notes. Investigators must search at crime scenes for bullets embedded in walls and furniture. A spent bullet can be ruined by digging it out with a pocketknife. Care must be taken so that the drill or cutting instrument used in this operation does not ruin identifying characteristics on a bullet by coming into contact with the softer metal (Figure 2–3). Bullets also should be handled as little as possible and packaged to prevent movement and to protect the side portions used in ballistic comparison and identification. When the victim is dead and an autopsy is performed, one of the **postmortem forensic science** procedures is the removal of spent bullets without damage to their original condition. In the United States, physicians and surgeons are very conscious of the evidential value of spent bullets.

Because it is sometimes necessary to establish the position of a person in crimes involving a shooting, the investigator at the crime scene should look closely for places the bullet has struck in its flight.[6] These marks or holes are items of evidence and are correlated with other positioning factors, such as the location of ejected cartridge cases found at the scene and the path of a bullet in the body of a victim.

A question that must be answered concerns whether or not a victim of a suicide or the suspect of a homicide recently fired a weapon. This question can be answered through a **gunshot residue (GSR) examination**. This test starts with applying adhesive tapes to the person's hands. These tapes are then sent to the **crime laboratory** where they are examined using a scanning electron microscope interfaced with an energy-dispersive X-ray.[7] This examination is used to search for the presence of the major components in a center-fire cartridge: antimony sulfide, barium nitrate, and lead styphnate, as well as supporting metallic particles of zinc, copper, or nickel. These compounds and elements are deposited on a person's hands when they fire a weapon, and they undergo an intense **exothermic reaction** due to the rapid increase in temperature followed by a sharp decrease. This supercooling phenomenon leads to a unique spheroidal formation that is generally not observed in the natural environment.[8]

Other weapons commonly encountered by police investigators are knives and various blunt instruments. Accuracy in describing such evidence may depend on a general description. The presence of serial numbers is not common, and clubs and similar weapons are not stamped with the name of the maker. The lengths of a knife blade and a knife handle are easily determined without excessive handling, as are the lengths and other dimensions of clubs and bludgeons. Distinctive features of the object should be noted in the investigator's field notes. The greatest possibility of error in connection with these weapons results from the tendency, when searching, to ignore common items of furniture or equipment at the scene of the crime as suspect weapons. In one case, the bludgeon used in a killing was a piece of 2-inch by 4-inch lumber about $3\frac{1}{2}$ feet long. The scene of the crime was a lumberyard. In another case, an apparently innocuous empty soft drink bottle was collected; later, the autopsy report cited a depressed fracture of the skull of the victim as the cause of death, and laboratory tests discovered blood traces on the bottle.

BLOOD

Blood is a trace that can divulge a great deal of information about the criminal, the victim, and what happened during a crime. The police who are first to arrive at the scene of assaults are often smeared with blood in their efforts to help a victim. In some cases, it is almost impossible to walk about the scene without stepping into some trace of blood and then transporting it around the scene. Still, investigators often fail to recognize bloodstains on clothing and other objects and, therefore, fail to collect valuable evidence. To complicate the problem of blood and its stains and residues as evidence, quite frequently a mixture of this residue is found at crime scenes when both the victim and the offender have been wounded. In addition, the evidence may come from an animal source, as well as a human one, or a common liquid may dilute the blood.

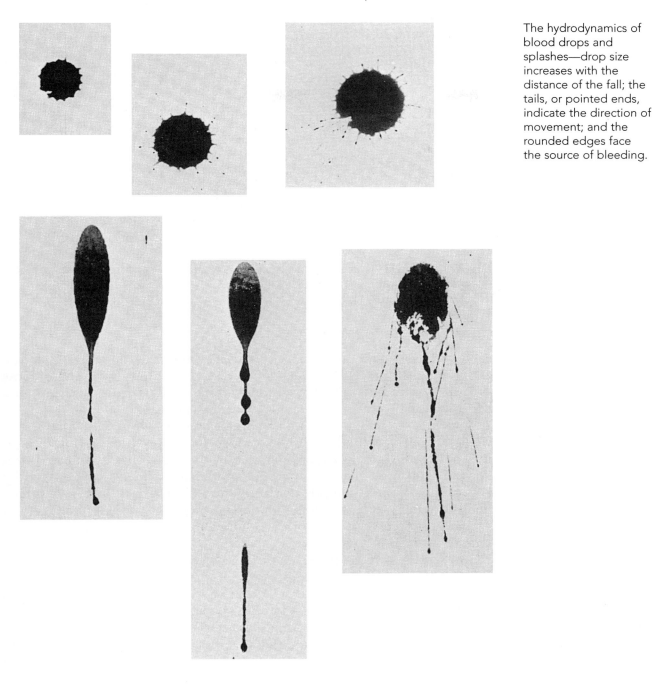

The hydrodynamics of blood drops and splashes—drop size increases with the distance of the fall; the tails, or pointed ends, indicate the direction of movement; and the rounded edges face the source of bleeding.

Despite some of the problems associated with this type of human trace, blood drops and splashes help to narrow the size of the suspect group, support identity when a suspect is located, and plot the movements of the victim and the assailant (Figure 2–4). Information that can be discovered through careful bloodstain pattern analysis includes the angle of the impact; the nature of the force involved in the bloodshed and the direction from which that force was applied; the nature of any object used in applying the force; the approximate number of blows struck during the incident; and the

FIGURE 2–4   Blood trajectory—wall stains.

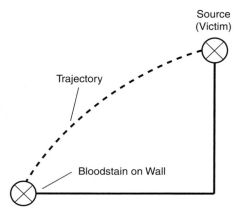

relative position in the scene of the suspect, victim, or other related objects during the incident.[9]

IMPRINTS AND IMPRESSIONS

Personal imprints and impressions found at crime scenes identify or tend to identify a person or vehicle as having been at the crime scene. These traces hold promise as areas of inquiry, although they usually require a suspect or a suspect vehicle before their evidential value can be realized.

Imprints are markings left on a surface by protruding parts of a person or vehicle. Imprints found at a crime scene include bloody handprints or footprints, or tire tread marks left behind after the tire has been contaminated with oil or mud. Such evidence is first photographed and then may be lifted by dusting with a contrasting powder, applying a clean, sticky, transparent tape to the dusted area to pick up the markings, and then pressing the tape to a clean card to preserve it. The object with the imprint sometimes can be transported to the laboratory.

Impressions are made by a person or object in a material softer than the item of evidence making the impression. Impressions include tire tracks or footprints left in snow or soft dirt. A trail of shoe prints or footprints offers some clues about the size or weight of the person making them, the speed of movement, and any gait abnormalities. Impressions are collected as evidence by first photographing and then casting the impression with plaster of Paris or dental plaster. Tire marks of vehicles are highly individual. When suspects are identified and located, vehicles used by such persons can be processed for comparison with the tire marks found at the scene. Furthermore, tire marks can be clues that aid in solving a crime inasmuch as the type of vehicle used may indicate fruitful lines of investigation. It can help to know, for example, that the vehicle was a large, late-model, high-priced car or a ten-year-old automobile. Shoe or heel prints and footprints in soft earth or other material that will take and hold a likeness are excellent to use for matching after a suspect is located.

Fingerprints can be found at crime scenes as either imprints or impressions. Bloody fingerprints left on weapons or at the scene of a crime are called

Heel of suspect's shoe (left) and heel impression taken at a crime scene (right). Lines show points of comparison—a "match."

contaminated prints. Such prints are observable with the naked eye and are collected by first photographing and then dusting and lifting with transparent tape. Fingerprints are impressions that a burglar might leave behind when his or her fingers come into contact with soft glazier's putty around the edges of a window. These are called **plastic prints** and are collected by first photographing and then casting with dental plaster. These prints can also be observed with the naked eye.

Latent prints usually cannot be seen with the naked eye and need to be developed to be seen. These fingerprints are caused by the transfer of body perspiration or oils present in finger ridges that are deposited on the surface of an object. Latent prints found on smooth nonporous surfaces such as glass can be developed by dusting with a powder, the color of which should contrast with the surface on which the print is found. Latent fingerprints on porous surfaces such as paper are developed in the laboratory through an **iodine fuming or ninhydrin process**. The iodine fumes react with the amino acids in the print and appear purple in color when developed. Prints left on smooth, slippery surfaces such as plastic bags, which are resistant to the dusting process, can be developed using the **cyanoacrylate fuming process**. Cyanoacrylate, a common glue product, is heated in a covered tank and the resulting fumes settle on the fingerprint, which is now observable and photographable.[10]

Traditionally, fingerprints have been taken from persons by inking the tips of the fingers and then rolling the contaminated print onto a card. These cards were then sent to the FBI or to a state agency to be read and classified. This process took weeks or months to complete. Unclassifiable cards were

Dusting powder, brush, and tape used to develop and lift latent fingerprints.

Computers are now being used to finger-print and electronically transmit fingerprints to a database.

returned, and often the person who supplied the prints was no longer available to supply another set of prints, resulting in loss of the opportunity to have this person's prints on file.

Computer technology now allows for a person's fingerprints to be captured electronically. The person's hand is placed on a platen and a scanner reads and records the fingerprints digitally. The machine reads the prints and indicates, while the person is still at the machine, whether or not a classifiable set of prints has been obtained. With the touch of a button, the set of prints is electronically sent to the FBI's database, which contains 41 million sets of prints. This automated system has reduced the FBI's criminal ten-print processing time from forty-five days with the inked card system to less than two hours.[11]

TOOL MARKS

Just as weapons are likely to be found at the scene of assaults and homicides, the marks of tools are likely to be found at the scene of burglaries or other crimes in which the offender forced entry into the premises or forced open locked containers at the crime scene. The criminal must gain access by force. Windows, doors, and skylights are the traditional means of ingress for such criminals. Roofs and walls have been cut and pounded in to provide entry. In some cases the criminals exit from another area of the building. The modus operandi of many burglars is multiple entry through rows of offices or commercial establishments, with the burglars burrowing through interior walls in a molelike progress from store to store. The places of entry or exit and all the locked desks and cabinets that were forced open along the way will bear some mark of the tools used. Safes, unless found open or opened with a combination or key, also bear traces of prying, ripping, or battering. Scientific laboratory procedures can individualize these marks and impressions. When suspect tools are discovered, laboratory technicians can make comparison analyses.

The initial procedure for collecting the marks of tools used to gain access is to locate accurately the impression at the scene and to record the general description and measurements. Accuracy, again, is the key. The impressions must be measured with an accurate rule, and the dimensions must be recorded in the investigator's field notes. Photographs of the impressions should be made. When feasible, the substance bearing the mark should be transported to the crime lab. It is sometimes possible to make a cast impression of the mark, and this will make an effective trial exhibit. Inasmuch as the mark is small, a material more costly than plaster of Paris can be used to form the impression. Various dental waxes and molding materials can be pressed into the imprint and allowed to harden. The overriding factor in reporting and collecting tool impressions at the scene of a crime is the preservation of the impression, or its reproduction, for future comparison with a suspect tool.

Quite often an investigator finds a tool that might have made an impression at the scene of the crime and attempts to match the tool visually with the impression by fitting it to the mark. This second contact of the tool to the impression ruins the evidence. Prevailing practices suggest that the best procedure is to treat any likely tool as suspect and to collect it for laboratory comparison by an expert.

Tools found on a suspect or under his or her control at the time of arrest (or traced to the suspect) become incriminating evidence when laboratory examinations show that the particularities of the suspect tool relate to the tool impressions found at the crime scene.

DUST, DIRT, AND OTHER TRACES

Traces have value as associated evidence when laboratory examination can establish identity and origin and can connect a suspect with a crime. The evidence potential of soil and mud, the debris from the underside of a vehicle, and dust in various forms, particularly on persons and their clothing, is excellent. Minute samples of glass and paint recognized as evidence may be processed to demonstrate similarities or differences in identity and origin. Larger samples of glass may be matched physically, and chips of paint at crime scenes now can be matched layer by layer with a suspect sample. Laboratory analysis now includes an amazing range of methods of identification for comparing these substances and for tracing origins to the crime scene, the victim, or the perpetrator.

In arson cases, potential evidence exists when the nature of the trace can be identified as a flammable fluid or its residue. Traces of volatile fluids of suspicious origin are lost if not searched for promptly and retrieved without delay. Precautions should be taken primarily to avoid loss by evaporation.

The residue of explosives should be handled in similar fashion. The primary requirement is to find and collect as much of the bomb as possible. Fragments of the container and timing mechanism of the bomb, if any, are loaded with residues, as are the objects close to the center of the explosion.

A direction-of-force potential is inherent in arson cases and crimes involving explosives. The survey of the fire scene may indicate fire trails resulting from the natural downward flow of liquid fire accelerants; laboratory tests that study the depth of charring in burnt wood collected at the scene may indicate the origin and spread of the fire. The expansion of gases in an explosion is discernible in a visual examination at the scene and can indicate the type of explosive and its placement. Distinctive damage at explosion sites can indicate the amount and type of explosive used in the blast.

The direction of force can be determined and some data on the force used can be gained by studying glass and its fragments found at crime scenes. Glass breaks first on the side opposite the force applied to it. When bullets penetrate a glass window, the projectile blasts out a cone-shaped hole on the side of the glass away from the shooter. The shape of this exit crater gives some indication of the direction or angle at which the bullet struck the glass.

QUESTIONED DOCUMENTS

In cases involving checks, the check itself is a **questioned document** and an important item of evidence. In apparent suicides, the victim may leave a note. This is an evidence item, and when found it is often processed as a questioned document.

Documents that have been destroyed or partially destroyed by fire can sometimes be restored by laboratory technicians. Charred paper must be

"Cratering" of a bullet hole in a glass window indicates the direction of travel. The bullet enters from the bottom, or small side of the crater and exits from the top, or large side.

sprayed with a preservative and requires special packaging and transport to the place of examination. This is a critical and time-consuming process, but the potential of charred paper as evidence is worth the work involved in its recovery.

The general style of a typewritten document, margins, separation of words at the end of the typed lines, spelling errors, paragraphing, and other indentation may all contribute to identification of the person who typed it.[12] It is quite possible to match a suspect typewriter, printer, or copying machine by comparing exemplars obtained from the machine and the document under suspicion.

Indented or embossed writing is sometimes found on telephone pads, blotters, and other impressionable surfaces despite the fact that the original paper on which the writing was made has been removed.

MISCELLANEOUS TRACE OR TRANSFER EVIDENCE

Hairs and fibers have excellent potential for identification. The primary problem with this type of evidence is finding it. When laboratory examination indicates that hairs or fibers found on the victim or on the victim's clothing are not the victim's, the possibility exists for future identification when a suspect is located. In addition, examination of the suspect for such traces may uncover hairs or fibers belonging to the victim.

The stains of seminal fluid are a trace found in sex crimes. Such stains are often meaningful to the investigation. They are useful and, at times, vital to show the commission of a crime when the victim is too young to testify or to remember having been molested or when the sexual attack is part of a homicide.

In narcotics and dangerous drug cases (possession and sale of drugs), the evidence must be identified as possession of a drug in violation of the law. The examination need only identify the drug as an illegal one.

Drugs and poisons may be the means of attack in homicide and assaults and the fatal substance in suicides. As such, they must be searched for and collected. When the victim becomes ill in a suspected poisoning case or is given an emetic to bring up a poisonous fluid or substance, the investigator must collect all material vomited. If the victim is still alive, urine specimens also should be collected. In poison cases, precautions must be taken primarily to prevent loss, contamination, or deterioration of the substance in transit. The collected physical evidence, as well as the stories of any witnesses about the circumstances of death, should be recorded in the officer's field notes. Such data help the medicolegal experts prepare a clinical history of the death.

Cigars and cigarettes, butts, and ashes have evidence potential. Unique brands, lipstick smears, and chewed ends with teeth marks may be of particular value. Wooden matchsticks and a distinguishable method of breaking them have been rewarding to searchers in some cases. Paper matches, torn from a book of matches, are evidence at the scene likely to reward a searcher if the book from which the matches were torn can be located and traced to a known suspect.

CASE STUDY

Revenge

His plan was simple, yet effective. He would get up around noon, and on those days he needed money he would leave the apartment around 3:00 in the afternoon. He would go to one of the supermarkets in the area and throw a few items into a cart. He would walk around the store in search of a victim. What he was looking for was a woman who put her purse in the grocery cart, usually in the child seat. When he found his potential victim, he would follow at a discrete distance, and when she turned away from the cart to select a cut of meat or to handle produce, he would approach her cart. If she was still occupied, he would grab the purse, conceal it under his jacket, and calmly walk out of the market.

On his return to the apartment he would get comfortable at the kitchen table, where he would spread the contents of the purse on the table. Any money he found was pure profit, but what he really wanted was the ATM cards. Once he located them, his real search began. He didn't find too many personal identification numbers (PINs) in these purses, but what he did make note of was any four-digit numbers. He would write down the person's address, telephone number, birth dates, and the last four numbers of the person's Social Security number. Armed with these numbers, he would venture out again around 11:00 p.m. to the proper ATM. He preferred local banks, for he thought the security was not as tight as at the bigger banks. He would be dressed in a hooded sweatshirt and dark sunglasses. He would insert the stolen card and begin using the list of possible PIN numbers he compiled from the victim's personal information. He would try a couple of numbers before midnight and a few after. Once into the victim's account he would take out as much of the money as he could before the machine cut him off.

I first heard of this case during a call I received from one of the local bank managers. The banks were assisting us in getting our neighborhood community-oriented policing office online, and they had the number to my direct line. I sent one of my detectives to the bank to make contact, and I called our robbery detail to get the initial police reports. My detective returned with a series of photos of the suspect. He had hit four times, and the ATM's cameras had great photos of a male suspect wearing a hooded sweatshirt and dark glasses. We didn't have much to work with, so the detectives did a neighborhood canvass, a modus operandi check, and surveillance, all with negative results. We worked the case for the next six weeks and got very little for our efforts, although the suspect kept hitting the bank on a regular basis.

I sensed that my detectives were getting frustrated by the lack of results, so I invited them out to lunch. One of the detectives was not hungry, so he declined and stayed behind to watch the office. While we were gone a woman came in to have a domestic violence report taken and to see about a restraining order. The detective invited her to sit at his desk so he could take the report. As she sat down, she noticed the photos of our hooded thief staring up at her and said, "I see you already know my boyfriend." She then gave a complete statement regarding her knowledge of the suspect's activities and later took the detectives to her apartment where the hooded sweatshirt and several of the victims' purses were recovered. She even gave us the address of his new girlfriend's apartment, where he was arrested without incident shortly before 5:00 p.m. that day.

CHAPTER REVIEW

KEY TERMS

ballistics *34*	circumstantial	contaminated
caliber *35*	evidence *28*	prints *42*

REVIEW QUESTIONS

1. The type of evidence that involves eye-witnesses who through one or more of their five senses have experienced something relative to the crime in question is known as:
   a. Direct evidence
   b. Circumstantial evidence
   c. Physical evidence
   d. Substantial evidence

2. When a witness discusses the crime or overhears others talking about the crime, he or she may unconsciously incorporate some of this information as his or her own. This process is known as:
   a. Interference
   b. Retroactive interference
   c. Reactive interference
   d. Proactive interference

3. Bloody fingerprints, such as those left on weapons or at the crime scene, are known as what type of prints?
   a. Contaminated
   b. Deteriorated
   c. Plastic
   d. Latent

4. Fingerprints found in soft material, such as tacky tar or glazier's putty, are known as what type of prints?
   a. Contaminated
   b. Deteriorated
   c. Plastic
   d. Latent

5. Fingerprints that cannot be seen with the naked eye and must be developed to be seen are known as what type of prints?
   a. Contaminated
   b. Deteriorated
   c. Plastic
   d. Latent

6. Approximately how many sets of fingerprints are contained within the Federal Bureau of Investigation's national fingerprint database?
   a. 40 million
   b. 80 million
   c. 160 million
   d. 320 million

7. The question of whether or not a victim or a suspect has recently fired a firearm can be answered by the examination of which of the following?
   a. Exothermic reaction
   b. Postmortem forensics
   c. Gunshot residue
   d. Heliopathic reaction

8. The first officers on the scene of a crime should identify potential witnesses and _____ them as soon as possible.
   a. Interview
   b. Separate

c. Interrogate

d. Dismiss

9. Fingerprints left on smooth, slippery surfaces such as plastic bags can be developed by using which process?

a. Dusting powder

b. Iodine fuming

c. Ninhydrin process

d. Cyanoacrylate fuming

10. Fingerprints left on smooth, nonporous surfaces such as glass can be developed by using which process?

a. Dusting powder

b. Iodine fuming

c. Ninhydrin process

d. Cyanoacrylate fuming

See Appendix D for the correct answers.

DISCUSSION QUESTIONS

1. Describe the various methods investigators use to locate potential witnesses.
2. Discuss the need to separate witnesses at a crime scene and the group dynamics involved.
3. Discuss the motivation of the woman involved in the case study. Can you think of other cases that have been solved in this or a similar manner?
4. Explain the difference between internal and external ballistics as it relates to examination of firearms.
5. Describe the three types of fingerprints likely to be found at a crime scene. How are these various types of prints processed?
6. Explain the advantages of capturing a person's fingerprints electronically compared to the traditional ink and paper system.

RELATED WEB SITES

To learn more about firearms, visit the University of Utah College of Medicine firearms tutorial at *www-medlib.med.utah.edu/WebPath/TUTORIAL/GUNS/GUNINTRO.html.* This site has information regarding the anatomy of firearms, ballistics, laboratory methods, and gunshot residue testing.

Tour a virtual comparison microscope used in firearms identification at *www.firearmsid.com.*

For more information regarding the history of fingerprints, fingerprint examinations, and the legal challenges to fingerprints, visit *www.onin.com/fp.*

chapter **three**

Rules of Evidence

CHAPTER OUTLINE

After reading this chapter you will be able to:

- Define the process for obtaining a search warrant and the information required in the warrant application.
- Recognize the various exceptions to the search warrant requirement.
- Explain the situations that would place an investigator in a lawful position to view and seize evidence according to the plain view exception.
- Discuss the justification for the motor vehicle exception to the search warrant requirement.
- Describe the action taken by the courts in dealing with evidence that does not meet the standards established by the Fourth Amendment.

N o evidence is admissible in a court of law unless it is relevant. **Relevance** is the connection between a fact offered in evidence and the issue to be proved. Evidence must also be material. An item of evidence is considered material if it is important or substantial, that is, capable of properly influencing the outcome of the trial. Evidence becomes immaterial when it is so unimportant compared to other easily available evidence that the court should not waste time admitting it. The third and most contentious criterion is that evidence must also be obtained lawfully. A search for evidence must be reasonable, and any search conducted as a result of a lawful warrant is, on its face, reasonable. However, a number of exceptions apply to the search warrant requirement. The court's remedy for the handling of evidence seized illegally is to exclude the evidence from trial.

SEARCH WARRANTS

The Fourth Amendment to the U.S. Constitution provides protections against unreasonable searches and seizures by all government officials and reads as follows:

> The right of the people to be secure in their persons, houses, papers, and effects, against unreasonable searches and seizures, shall not be violated, and no Warrants shall issue, but upon probable cause, supported by **Oath or affirmation**, and particularly describing the place to be searched, and the persons or things to be seized.

This amendment is intended to provide a means of balancing society's need to deal with criminals and criminal activity with the need to protect individual rights. The issuance of a warrant makes a search reasonable by placing an unbiased third party—a magistrate or judge—in the process. The role of the magistrate is to review the application for a search warrant and determine if the request is reasonable and meets the guidelines established by the Fourth Amendment. The magistrate will determine reasonableness by considering all the circumstances in each case.

To obtain a search warrant, an investigator must prepare a written application that outlines the probable cause for the search and describes the place to be searched and the person or things to be seized. The investigator must swear, or affirm, to the **magistrate** that the information contained in the warrant application is true.

Probable cause, as used in the warrant requirement, exists when enough facts lead a reasonable and prudent person to believe that criminal activity is fairly probable. This standard of proof is well below what is required at a criminal trial: guilt beyond a reasonable doubt. For example, an undercover police officer making a buy of illegal drugs at a residence would be sufficient probable cause to lead a reasonable and prudent person to believe that controlled substances were being sold at that location.

For the description of the place to be searched, the investigator must provide sufficient detail in the warrant application to identify the location of the requested search. In urban areas, a street address—with an apartment number, if applicable—would be required. In rural areas the court may be more flexible

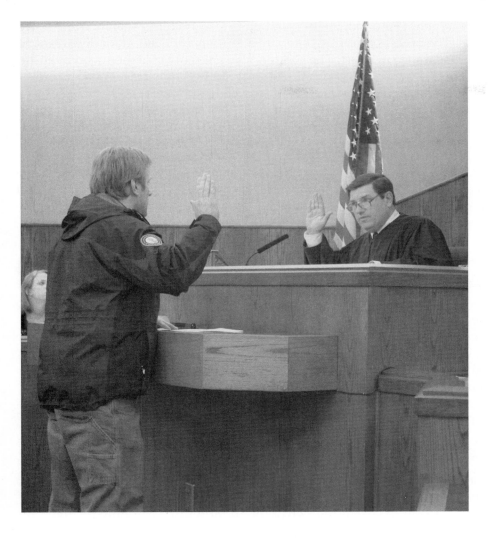

A plain-clothes detective swearing to the judge that the information contained in a warrant application is true.

and allow a general description, such as "a yellow house with a detached barn located on Mill Pond Road one half mile north of Highway 212."

For the description of the persons or things to be seized, the investigator must outline exactly what is being sought, as an approved warrant is not a license to rummage through a person's home or personal effects. Usually the type of crime being investigated will dictate where the investigator can search. The investigation of stolen 42-inch plasma TV sets, for example, would allow a search of any area where a TV set could be hidden or stored; the search of smaller areas, such as a dresser, would not be allowed as a TV set could not be hidden there and such a search would, therefore, be unreasonable.

The application for a search warrant must be supported by oath or affirmation as required by the Fourth Amendment. This means that the investigator must raise his or her right hand before the magistrate and swear—or affirm, if he or she does not believe in God—that the information is true and correct to the best of his or her knowledge under the penalty of perjury. This means that an investigator could be charged with a crime if he or she knowingly presents false information in a search warrant application.

In emergency situations, an investigator can obtain a search warrant by telephone. The investigator must prepare a written application for a warrant as if for an appearance in court. The written warrant request is then read over the telephone to the magistrate, who then transcribes what is read in order to prepare the warrant. The magistrate has the investigator swear to the truthfulness of the application. The authorization for the search warrant, if granted, is authorized over the phone and made available in the magistrate's court the following business day, at which time the investigator must pick up the warrant.

Search warrants must be executed within a prescribed time period, normally within ten days. The magistrate or the legislature, by law, can limit the time of execution to daylight hours only, as well as to no weekend or holiday service. The restrictions of the Fourth Amendment do not apply to private persons as long as they are not acting as agents of the government.[1]

WARRANTLESS SEARCHES

While conducting a search with a lawful warrant is a reasonable process, it is, however, not always practical. Emergency situations, the possible destruction of evidence, and other considerations make obtaining a warrant impractical at times. The U.S. Supreme Court has defined as reasonable some specific searches that may be conducted without a warrant. These exceptions to the warrant requirement include consent searches, stop and frisks, plain view exceptions, searches incident to a lawful arrest, motor vehicle stops, open fields, and emergency circumstances.

CONSENT SEARCH

A person can voluntarily consent to the police to search their person, home, and property. Any evidence found as a result of a **consent search** is admissible in court. The consent to search the person of an individual can only be given by that individual. The waiver of the Fourth Amendment is a personal right and can only be waived by the affected individual. Consent to search property can only be given by the actual owner or by a person in charge of that property.

A person has an absolute right to refuse to consent to a search when asked by the police and may revoke consent at any time. When a person agrees to a consent search, the investigator should obtain the consent in writing to substantiate the voluntariness of the consent and subsequent search.

The courts have held that a consent search was unreasonable if the consent was obtained by deceit, trickery, or misrepresentation by investigators. The courts typically justify consent searches by the voluntariness test: the consent was obtained without coercion or promises and was, therefore, reasonable.[2]

STOP AND FRISK

The U.S. Supreme Court has held that a police officer may temporarily detain a person for questioning if the officer has a reasonable suspicion that criminal activity may be involved. The person may also be patted down for weapons if the officer has the additional **reasonable suspicion** that the pat down was necessary for officer safety. Such a temporary **stop and frisk**

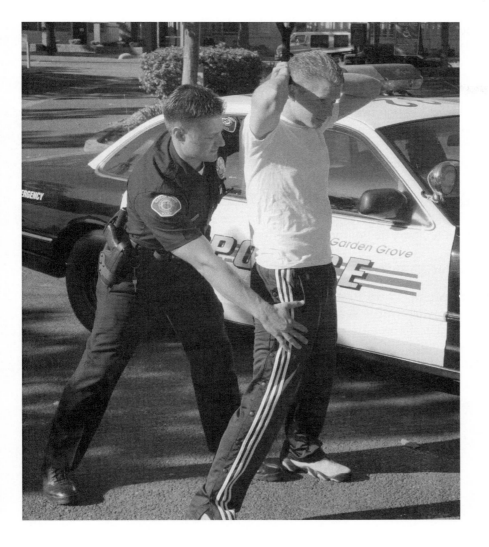

A police officer frisking a subject.

detention is not considered to be an arrest. A temporary detention is based upon reasonable suspicion, which is less than the necessary probable cause needed for an arrest.

Reasonable suspicion for a detention must be based on facts that can be articulated in court. The investigator must have a reasonable suspicion that criminal activity is occurring, is about to occur, or has recently occurred and that the person or vehicle to be detained is related to that criminal activity. The detention must be fairly short in duration and only long enough to clarify the reasons for the detention. Any evidence discovered during this detention would be admissible in court.[3]

PLAIN VIEW EXCEPTION

The **plain view exception** permits investigators to observe and seize evidence without a warrant if the officer is lawfully in a position to view an object and if the incriminating character of the object is immediately apparent. In a number of situations, law enforcement officers may make a seizure of evidence based on the plain view exception.

Effecting an arrest.   An officer may lawfully seize an object that comes into view during a lawfully executed arrest or search incident to arrest.

Executing a search warrant.   An officer executing a valid search warrant can legally seize items of evidence lying in plain view even though they were not specifically described in the warrant.

Pursuing a fleeing suspect.   Officers who are lawfully on the premises in hot pursuit of a dangerous person may seize items of evidence in plain view.

Responding to an emergency.   Officers responding to emergency situations, such as crimes in progress or crimes of violence, shooting, stabbings, etc., may seize items of evidence in plain view.[4]

SEARCH INCIDENT TO A LAWFUL ARREST

The U.S. Supreme Court has recognized that police officers have the authority to conduct a warrantless **search incident to a lawful arrest**. The scope of this search includes the person of the arrestee, including a wallet or purse immediately associated with the arrestee. Also included in the scope of this search is the area into which the arrestee could reach at the time of the arrest to

An officer conducting a search incident to an arrest.

An officer conducting a search of the trunk of a vehicle.

retrieve a weapon or to destroy evidence. The officers may also search adjoining areas for persons posing a threat to the officers or the arrest scene. This search must be made contemporaneously with the arrest, and any items of evidence in plain view may be seized.[5]

MOTOR VEHICLE STOP

The U.S. Supreme Court has created an exception to the warrant requirement for motor vehicles due to their mobility, their use as transportation to and from crime scenes, and their use in transporting weapons, stolen goods, and contraband. A lawful search under the **motor vehicle exception** requires the existence of probable cause to believe that the vehicle contains evidence of a crime, or contraband, and that the searching officers have lawful access to the vehicle. Other mobile conveyances, such as motor homes, houseboats, and airplanes, are included in this exception.

Locked containers, such as vehicle trunks and suitcases, may also be searched without a warrant, provided probable cause exists relating to these locked containers. In other words, the scope of the warrantless search is no broader or narrower than if a search warrant had been obtained.[6]

In the interest of public safety, vehicles are frequently taken into police custody when the driver is arrested or intoxicated or if the vehicle is used in a crime or has been reported stolen. The impound procedure involves the police taking possession of the vehicle and moving it to a secure area for safekeeping. Once in police custody, the police are potentially liable for the vehicle and its contents.

Therefore, the courts allow the inventorying of the vehicle's contents. The inventory procedure is not a search but rather a routine administrative custodial procedure. However, if contraband or items of evidence are observed during the inventory, they may lawfully be seized and are admissible as evidence.[7]

OPEN FIELDS

The U.S. Supreme Court has held that **open fields** are not protected by the Fourth Amendment and that investigators may enter and search unoccupied or undeveloped areas. The rationale here is that only "homes, person, effects and paper" are protected by the Fourth Amendment and that there is a lesser expectation of privacy in open fields. The term *open fields* includes open lands and forests. Even if ownership of the area is posted, the area may be searched without a warrant. The exception would be the area immediately surrounding a dwelling, known as the **curtilage**.[8]

EMERGENCY CIRCUMSTANCES

Investigators who have established probable cause that evidence is likely to be at a certain place may make a warrantless entry into the premises if exigent or **emergency circumstances** exist. Such circumstances include the following:

1. A reasonable belief that the evidence may be immediately destroyed
2. Hot pursuit of a suspect whom the investigators reasonably believe is in the area to be searched
3. An immediate need to protect or preserve life
4. A threat to the safety of the officers conducting a protective sweep of the premises, for other suspects[9]

EXCLUSIONARY RULE

The **exclusionary rule** is applied when investigators violate a person's constitutional rights by conducting an unlawful search and seizure. This rule prevents illegally obtained evidence from being admitted into evidence. This is the method the courts use to uphold the Fourth Amendment and to control investigator's actions and prevent illegally obtained evidence from being used at trial. An extension of the exclusionary rule is the "fruit of the poisonous tree doctrine," which holds that evidence derived from an illegal search or seizure is inadmissible because of its original taint.

CASE STUDY

Weeks v. United States

232 U.S. 383 (1914)

The defendant, Weeks, was arrested by a police officer, so far as the record shows, without warrant, at Union Station in Kansas City, Missouri, where he was employed by an express freight company. Other police officers had gone to the house of the defendant. When told by a neighbor where the key was kept, officers found it and entered the house. They searched the defendant's premises and took possession of various papers and articles found there, which were turned over afterward to the United States marshal. Later that day, police officers returned with the marshal, who thought he might find additional evidence. On being admitted by someone in the house—probably a boarder, in response to a knock—the marshal searched the defendant's room and carried away certain letters and envelopes found in the drawer of a chiffonier. Neither the marshal nor the police officers had a search warrant. The defendant filed a petition requesting the return of his private papers, books, and other property pertaining to the alleged illegal sale of lottery tickets. In his petition, the defendant contended that these items were seized in violation of the rights secured to him by the Fourth Amendment to the Constitution of the United States, which provides the following:

> The right of the people to be secure in their person, houses, papers, and effects, against unreasonable searches and seizures, shall not be violated, and no Warrants shall issue, but upon probable cause, supported by Oath or affirmation, and particularly describing the place to be searched, and the person or things to be seized.

The trial court denied the defendant's request, citing the underlying principle that the court will not take notice of the manner in which a witness has possessed himself of papers or other chattel, subjects of evidence, which are material and properly offered in evidence. Accordingly, the defendant was found guilty. He appealed to the U.S. Supreme Court.

The Court held that the letters and property in question were taken from the house of the accused by an officer of the United States, acting under color of his office, in direct violation of the constitutional rights of the defendant; that having made a reasonable application for their return, which was heard and passed upon by the Court, there was involved in the order refusing the application a denial of the constitutional rights of the accused, and a statement that the court should have restored these letters to the accused. The Court determined that, in holding the letters and permitting their use during the trial, prejudicial error was committed.

The judgment of the trial court was reversed, and the case was remanded for further proceedings in accordance with the opinion.

CHAPTER REVIEW

KEY TERMS

consent search *54*
curtilage *58*
emergency
    circumstances *58*
exclusionary rule *58*
magistrate *52*

motor vehicle
    exception *57*
Oath or affirmation *52*
open fields *58*
plain view exception *55*
probable cause *52*

reasonable suspicion *54*
relevance *52*
search incident to a
    lawful arrest *56*
stop and frisk *54*

REVIEW QUESTIONS

1. _____ exists when enough facts lead a reasonable and prudent person to believe that a fair probability of criminal activity exists.
   a. Reasonable suspicion
   b. Probable cause
   c. Exigent circumstances
   d. Contingent cause

2. Which constitutional amendment provides the citizens of the United States protections against unreasonable searches and seizures?
   a. First Amendment
   b. Second Amendment
   c. Third Amendment
   d. Fourth Amendment

3. A person can waive constitutionally provided protections against unreasonable searches and seizures and allow an investigator to search home, person, and property. Such a search is known as:
   a. Consent search
   b. Plain view search
   c. Stop and frisk
   d. Search incident to an arrest

4. The U.S. Supreme Court has held that a police officer may temporarily detain a person for questioning if the officer has reasonable suspicion that criminal activity may be involved. The person may also be patted down for weapons. This police action is known as:
   a. Consent search
   b. Plain view search
   c. Stop and frisk
   d. Search incident to an arrest

5. This doctrine permits investigators to observe and seize evidence without a warrant if the officer is lawfully in a position from which an object and the incriminating character of the object are immediately apparent. This exception to the search warrant requirement is known as:
   a. Consent search
   b. Plain view search
   c. Stop and frisk
   d. Search incident to an arrest

6. Investigators who have established probable cause that evidence is likely to be at a certain place may make a warrantless entry into the premises if what type of conditions exist?
   a. Exclusionary
   b. Inclusionary
   c. Emergency
   d. Conclusively

7. The method the courts use to uphold the constitutional protections against unreasonable searches and seizures, as well as to control the investigator's actions and prevent illegally obtained evidence from being used at trial, is known as the:
   a. Exclusionary rule
   b. Inclusionary rule
   c. Emergency rule
   d. Conclusively rule

8. In the interest of public safety, vehicles are frequently taken into police custody, such as when reported stolen or when used in the commission of a crime. These vehicles may be examined, inside and out, and any evidence of a crime may be lawfully seized under which theory of law?
   a. Search incident to arrest
   b. Motor vehicle exception
   c. Procedural search
   d. Inventory procedure

9. The areas that are not protected by the Constitution and may be searched without a warrant are known as _____ .

10. An application for a search warrant must be supported by _____ or _____ .

    See Appendix D for the correct answers.

DISCUSSION QUESTIONS

1. Explain the Court's reasoning behind the motor vehicle exception to the search warrant requirement.
2. Discuss the difference between probable cause and reasonable suspicion, and explain how these concepts apply in criminal cases.
3. Describe the process for obtaining a search warrant.
4. Explain in detail the various emergency situations that would justify a search without a warrant.
5. Using the case study as an example, explain how the exclusionary rule applies in criminal cases.

RELATED WEB SITES

To review U.S. Supreme Court decisions go to the Court's Web site at *www.supremecourtus.gov.*

For information regarding the United States code sections relating to crimes and criminal procedure, go to *www.access.gpo.gov/uscode/title18/title18.html.*

chapter **four**

Recording the Crime Scene

CHAPTER OUTLINE

After reading this chapter you will be able to:

- Cite the type of information that is included in the preliminary investigation report.
- Understand the process of how crime scene photography moves the subject matter from the general to the specific.
- Explain how the crime scene sketch provides an in-depth understanding of the circumstances of the crime beyond the level of comprehension attained solely by reviewing the written report or photographs.
- Discuss the strengths and weaknesses of using videotaping as a method of recording the crime scene.
- Define the need for progress reports during a continuing criminal investigation.

Field **ield notes** made during the search of a crime scene are the basic record of the search and the evidence discovered. The investigator's report is prepared from his or her field notes. The notes and report both become permanent records in the case and have the inherent integrity of records prepared in the performance of official duties.

Photographing and sketching offer opportunities to graphically portray the scene and the evidence located during the search and must be done with care to represent the subjects accurately. **Crime scene sketches and photographs** usually are offered in evidence as exhibits that are more realistic than words or that can assist jurors in understanding the case, or both. They must withstand the basic tests of relevancy and materiality. No legal presumption states that graphic representations are correct. Sketches and photos are verified as accurate by the person who made them or by any witness having sufficient knowledge of the subject who can say that the sketch or photograph is a faithful representation of what is shown.

Maps and diagrams were used to illustrate testimony long before photographs were first offered in evidence. As early as 1857, the nonphotographic drawings of a doctor illustrating the appearance of blood as seen microscopically were admitted into evidence as exhibits to clarify the verbal description of a medical witness in a Maine case. When a drawing is admitted into evidence, its ability to clarify testimony and to orient evidence to the crime scene enhances such testimony and evidence.

Videotaping is the newest use of graphics at the crime scene. Its pictorial storytelling provides substantial benefits for investigators. Likewise, the videotape may be equally useful to defense attorneys in court.

FIELD NOTES

Field notes are memoranda made by the investigator during an investigation. They begin with assignment to the case and arrival at the scene; they are added to until the case is closed. That portion of field notes concerned with recording the search for evidence at a crime scene usually includes the time the search started, the names of assisting personnel, the weather and light conditions, a description of the area searched as the investigator proceeds, a note of any special equipment used, and an accurate note of the discovery of every significant item of evidence: when and where it was found, who found it, and what it looks like. Any measurements that place the evidence are recorded, as is the disposition of the evidence. Sketches and diagrams drawn at the crime scene are field notes that, by their graphic portrayal of the crime scene, supplement the measurements and other data recorded.

In addition, the searching officer must record in his or her field notes any damage to objects at the scene or any disturbance of furniture and other objects. Anything unusual or foreign to the scene also is noted. Moreover, the failure to locate an item of evidence commonly found at the scene of similar crimes is noted and recorded. These factual reports may be important as clues or as negative evidence to overcome defense claims regarding the theory of the crime and its reconstruction.

PRELIMINARY INVESTIGATIVE REPORT

The place and time to obtain data for a **preliminary investigative report** are at the crime scene during the initial investigation. Anything omitted or overlooked is either lost or must be ascertained later, which is usually a difficult and time-consuming task. Information about each item of importance must be collected if an investigation is to be comprehensive; the reports required of the officer processing the crime scene are incomplete without such information. The data in this report should include the following:

1. Victim's name, sex, age, occupation, residence and business addresses, and telephone numbers
2. Where the event took place
3. The time of occurrence
4. Who reported the event, if other than the victim, and personal data about this person
5. Date and time reported, and sometimes how reported—in person, by mail, or by telephone
6. Time that the reporting officer arrived at the crime scene
7. Witnesses—full information along with personal data
8. Arrestee, if any, and available personal data
9. Suspects, named or described, with available personal data
10. Name of reporting officer

While at the crime scene, the reporting officer must determine the method of operation of the perpetrator and collect data about this phase of the crime. These are the modus operandi data and have a stylized form because data storage and retrieval are based on major segments of a criminal's technique. Attention to all these segments by the officer processing the crime scene ensures a thorough reporting of the technique used in the crime. The modus operandi segments include the following (Figure 4–1):

- Type of crime
- Person attacked
- How attacked
- Means of attack
- Trademark of perpetrator (peculiarities)
- Words spoken (or the written note used)
- Vehicle used
- Property stolen
- Name or physical description of suspect

Investigators must collect pertinent data under each segment. For this reason a checklist should be prepared as a reminder of the data to be collected in various crimes. Crimes can be grouped for this purpose as crimes against property, crimes against persons, and other crimes. Investigators also must

| DIST. | SECT | SUB. | □ CUSTODY □ PEND.
 □ CITATION □ CLEARED ADULT
 □ FURTHER INVEST. □ CLEARED JUV. | **CRIME REPORT** | **REPORT NUMBER** |

| INDICATION OF OCCURRENCE | REPORT DATE | DAY | TIME | EVENT NO. |

| OCC. DATE FROM | DAY | TIME | OCC. DATE TO | DAY | TIME | CONNECTED REPORT(S) — NUMBER AND TYPE |

CODE SECTION	F	M	CRIME TITLE
		A	
		B	
		C	
		D	

SPECIAL CRIME CATEGORIES EXIST?   □ NO   □ YES — CATEGORY FROM REVERSE _____

| **V** | NAME (LAST, FIRST, MIDDLE) | RES. PHONE | BUS. PHONE |

| RESIDENCE ADDRESS | CITY | STATE | ZIP | BUSINESS ADDRESS (SCHOOL IF JUVENILE) | CITY | STATE | ZIP |

DOB	AGE	SEX	RACE	VICTIM'S VEHICLE (YR., MAKE, MODEL, LIC. NO.)	A	B	C	D	E
					F	G	H	I	J

| **V/R** | NAME (LAST, FIRST, MIDDLE) | RES. PHONE | BUS. PHONE |

| RESIDENCE ADDRESS | CITY | STATE | ZIP | BUSINESS ADDRESS (SCHOOL IF JUVENILE) | CITY | STATE | ZIP |

DOB	AGE	SEX	RACE	VICTIM'S VEHICLE (YR., MAKE, MODEL, LIC. NO.)	A	B	C	D	E
					F	G	H	I	J

A. PLACE of CRIME
1 □ STRUCTURE   4 □ STREET/ALLEY   7 □ OTHER
2 □ VEHICLE   5 □ LOT/PARK
3 □ RES/YARD   6 □ BUS/STORAGE

B. DESCRIPTION OF SURROUNDINGS
1 □ RESIDENTIAL   4 □ RECREATIONAL   7 □ OPEN SPACE
2 □ BUSINESS   5 □ INSTITUTIONAL   8 □ OTHER
3 □ INDUSTRIAL   6 □ CONST. SITE

TYPE OF STRUCTURE □ N/A	G POINT OF ENTRY	J METHOD OF ENTRY	INVESTIGATIVE NOTATIONS

C NON-RESIDENTIAL
□ 1 CONVENIENCE
□ 2 FAST FOOD
□ 3 RESTAURANT/BAR
□ 4 DRUG/MEDICAL
□ 5 GAS STATION
□ 6 RETAIL
□ 7 SCHOOL
□ 8 FINANCIAL INST.
□ 9 ENTERTAIN/REC.
□ 10 PUBLIC BLDG.
□ 11 OTHER _____

D TARGET(S)
□ 1 SHOP
□ 2 CASH REG/DRAWER
□ 3 OFFICE
□ 4 SAFE/BOX
□ 5 VENDING MACHINE
□ 6 DISPLAY ITEMS
□ 7 CLASSROOM
□ 8 OTHER _____

E RESIDENTIAL
□ 1 SINGLE FAMILY
□ 2 APT/CONDO
□ 3 DUPLEX/TOWN
□ 4 MOTEL/HOTEL
□ 5 MOBILE HOME
□ 6 OTHER _____

F TARGET(S)
□ 1 STORAGE BLDG.
□ 2 CLOSET
□ 3 BATHROOM
□ 4 DEN
□ 5 FAMILY ROOM
□ 6 GARAGE/CARPORT
□ 7 KITCHEN
□ 8 LIVING ROOM
□ 9 STORAGE ROOM
□ 10 BEDROOM
□ 11 DINING
□ 12 OTHER _____

1 □ N/A   4 □ SIDE
2 □ FRONT   5 □ GR LEV.
3 □ REAR   6 □ UP LEV.

H
□ 1 UNKNOWN
□ 2 DOOR
□ 3 WINDOW
□ 4 SLIDE GLASS
□ 5 DUCT/VENT
□ 6 ADJ. BLDG.
□ 7 ROOF/FLOOR
□ 8 WALL
□ 9 BASEMENT
□ 10 OTHER _____

I ALARM SYSTEMS
□ 1 YES   □ 2 NO
SET OFF
□ 3 YES   □ 4 NO

□ N/A
□ 1 ATTEMPT ONLY
□ 2 NO FORCE
□ 3 KEY/SLIP
□ 4 BODY/FORCE
□ 5 SAW/DRILL
□ 6 HID IN BLDG.
□ 7 CHANNEL LOCK
□ 8 PRY TOOL
□ 9 LIFT OUT
□ 10 BRICK/ROCK
□ 11 BOLT CUTTERS/PLIERS
□ 12 WINDOW SMASH
□ 13 TAPE/WIRE
□ 14 DOOR PUNCH
□ 15 DOOR KICK
□ 16 OTHER _____

SUSPECT INFO PAGE
(NUMBER SUSP _____)   ____YES____NO

PHYSICAL EVIDENCE
GATHERED BY R/O   ____YES____NO

CSI REQUESTED   ____YES____NO

IDENTIFIABLE PROPERTY   ____YES____NO

ADDITIONAL VICTIMS/
WITNESSES   ____YES____NO

NEIGHBORHOOD CANV   ____YES____NO

PROPERTY LOSS   ____YES____NO

PROPERTY LIST ATTACHED   ____YES____NO

INVESTIGATIVE DIV. PERS. NOTIFIED

K SUSPECT'S ACTION □ N/A	L PROPERTY TAKEN □ N/A

K SUSPECT'S ACTION
□ 1 ENTERED OCCUPIED BLDG.
□ 2 ENTERED UNOCCUPIED BLDG.
□ 3 VACANT RES./BLDG.
□ 4 VANDALIZED/RANSACKED
□ 5 USED MATCHES/SMOKED AT SCENE
□ 6 DISABLED ALARM
□ 7 ATE/DRANK ON PREMISES
□ 8 VEHICLES NEEDED FOR LOOT
□ 9 USED VICTIM'S TOOLS
□ 10 KNEW LOCATION OF HIDDEN CASH
□ 11 SELECTIVE IN LOOT
□ 12 USED LOOKOUT DRIVER
□ 13 BOUND/GAGGED VICTIM
□ 14 RIPPED/CUT CLOTHING
□ 15 MOLESTED VICTIM
□ 16 FORCED VICTIM TO MOVE
□ 17 DISABLED PHONE/ELECTRIC
□ 18 INJURED VICTIM
□ 19 THREATENED VICTIM
□ 20 MASTURBATED
□ 21 DISROBED FULLY/PARTIALLY
□ 22 FIRED WEAPON
□ 23 SUSPECT ARMED
□ 24 OTHER _____

L PROPERTY TAKEN
□ 1 LARGE LOSS VALUE
□ 2 TOOK CHECKS/CREDIT CARDS
□ 3 CONSUMABLE GOOD
□ 4 OFFICE EQUIPMENT
□ 5 CAMERA
□ 6 POWER TOOLS/LAWN EQUIP.
□ 7 FIREARMS
□ 8 SILVERWARE
□ 9 FINE JEWELRY
□ 10 MONEY
□ 11 LARGE APPLIANCES
□ 12 SMALL APPLIANCES
□ 13 CLOTHING/FURS
□ 14 DRUGS
□ 15 CONSTRUCTION MATERIALS
□ 16 AUTO PARTS/ACCESSORIES
□ 17 TOOLS/CARP./MECH./ELECT.
□ 18 GOLD/SILVER COINS
□ 19 TV/STEREO/VIDEO
□ 20 NO LOSS _____
□ 21 OTHER_____

SYNOPSIS OF CRIME

| INVESTIGATING OFFICER | BADGE | DIVISION | SUPERVISOR |

PAGE ____ OF ____

FIGURE 4–1   Crime report—information called for on this printed form is the primary record of the circumstances of a crime.

ORIGINAL REPORT USE ONLY

THIS PORTION OF THE REPORT IS REQUIRED BY LAW. REFER TO UNIFORM CRIME REPORTING STANDARDS FOUND IN THE REPORT WRITING MANUAL. IT IS **NOT** TO BE FILLED OUT ACCORDING TO CALIFORNIA PENAL CODE STANDARDS. IF YOUR CRIME CLASSIFICATION INVOLVES A BURGLARY, ROBBERY, THEFT, HOMICIDE, ASSAULT, OR RAPE, BE CERTAIN TO CIRCLE WHATEVER CATEGORY BELOW IS APPROPRIATE. CODE ONLY THE TYPE AND VALUE OF PROPERTY STOLEN AS INDICATED BELOW. RECOVERED PROPERTY IS TO BE CODED DIRECTLY ON THE RECOVERED PROPERTY REPORT, UNLESS RECOVERED SIMULTANEOUSLY AT THE TIME OF THE CRIME REPORT.

PROPERTY	Stolen Value	Recovered Value	BURGLARY	ROBBERY	THEFT
			VEHICLE AND SHOPLIFT BURGLARIES ARE TO BE CODED UNDER THEFT	TYPE	TYPE
A CURRENCY, NOTES, ETC.	$	$		031 FIREARM	0610 PICKPOCKET
B JEWELRY, PRECIOUS METALS	$	$	ENTRY	032 KNIFE	0620 PURSE SNATCH
			051 FORCIBLE	033 OTHER WEAPON	0630 SHOPLIFT
C CLOTHING, FURS	$	$	052 UNLAWFUL	034 STRONGARM	0640 FROM VEHICLE
E OFFICE EQUIPMENT	$	$	053 ATTEMPT FORCIBLE	LOCATION	0650 AUTO PARTS & ACCESSORIES
F TV, CAMERA, STEREOS	$	$	STRUCTURE	1 HIGHWAY	
G FIREARMS	$	$	1 RESIDENCE	2 COMMERCIAL HOUSE	0670 FROM BUILDING
H HOUSEHOLD GOODS	$	$	2 NON-RESIDENCE (CLOSED)	3 SERVICE STATION	0680 COIN-OPERATED MACHINE
I CONSUMABLE GOODS	$	$		4 CONVENIENCE STORE	0690 ALL OTHER
J LIVESTOCK	$	$		5 RESIDENCE	
K MISCELLANEOUS	$	$		6 BANK	ATTEMPT VEHICLE THEFT
				7 OTHER	
TOTAL	$	$			0710 AUTO
					0720 TRUCK/BUS
					0730 OTHER VEHICLE A

REPORTED DATE _____ DATE OCC. _____ FROM ___ TO ___
REPORTED TIME _____ TIME OCC. _____

SPECIAL CRIME CATEGORY				NUMBER OF VICTIMS ASSAULTS	
A CRIMES AGAINST CHILDREN	0110	MURDER NON-NEG MANSLAUGHTER	0410	GUN	0440 HANDS/FEET (SERIOUS INJURY)
01 NEGLECT/ABUSE			0420	KNIFE	
02 SEXUAL	0120	MANSLAUGHTER BY NEGLIGENCE	0430	OTHER DANGEROUS WEAPON	0450 HANDS/FEET (MINOR OR NO INJURY)
B CRIMES AGAINST ELDERLY					
C DOMESTIC VIOLENCE					
D GANG AFFILIATION					
E CRIMES MOTIVATED BY:		NUMBER OF VICTIMS		RAPE	
01 RACE					
02 RELIGION		0210 FORCIBLE		0220 ATTEMPT FORCIBLE	
03 SEXUAL PREFERENCE					

ARSON				
PROPERTY CLASSIFICATION		INHABITED	UNINHABITED	TOTAL ARSON $ DAMAGE
091 SINGLE OCCUPANCY RESIDENTIAL	(House, Townhouse, Duplexes, etc.)	1	2	$
092 OTHER RESIDENTIAL	(Apartments, Tenements, Flats, Hotels, Motels, Inns, Dormitories, Boarding Houses, etc.)	1	2	$
093 STORAGE	(Barns, Garages, Warehouses, etc.)	1	2	$
094 INDUSTRIAL MANUFACTURING		1	2	$
095 OTHER COMMERCIAL	(Stores, Restaurants, Offices, etc.)	1	2	$
096 COMMUNITY/PUBLIC	(Churches, Jails, Schools, Colleges, Hospitals, etc.)	1	2	$
097 ALL OTHER STRUCTURE	(Outbuildings, Monuments, Buildings under Construction, etc.)	1	2	$

0981 MOTOR VEHICLES	(Automobiles, Trucks, Buses, Motorcycles, etc.)			
0982 OTHER MOBILE PROPERTY	(Trailers, Recreational Vehicles, Airplanes, Boats, etc.)			
0990 OTHER	(Crops, Timber, Fences, Signs, etc.)			

FIGURE 4–1 (*continued*)

report the details of the crime. This segment of the crime or offense report should be structured to tell the story of the circumstances of the crime to supplement the facts contained in the primary information or the modus operandi segments of the crime report. Many police departments suggest the following organization for this segment of the preliminary investigation:

1. Suspect(s).   Additional information should be recorded to describe the suspect or suspects, from aliases (the designation *a.k.a.*, "also known as," is used to indicate aliases) and nicknames, to physical oddities and dress, including any data on employment or school attended.

2. Property Taken.   In thefts, additional descriptive data on property stolen should be recorded, including the value as set by the victim, the approximate date of original purchase or acquisition by other means ("age" of article), and the original purchase price or estimated value at the time.

3. Physical Evidence.   All items of evidence—including traces, tool marks, and other imprints or impressions—should be described in detail, along with full information as to when and where such evidence was found and who found it, handled it, and disposed of it.

4. Victim's Statement.   The victim or victims who make statements are identified by name, address, age, and employment (or school attended), and the essential facts of the victim's story are stated.

5. Statement of Witness(es).   Each witness making a statement is identified (as in item 1), and the essential facts of the story told by the witness are stated. In addition, this segment of the report should include: (a) data as to the location of the witness at the time of observation, (b) the light conditions, and (c) any relationship of the witness to the victim or suspect(s).

6. Observations by Reporting Officer.   Facts are recorded that are not evidence, such as weather, conditions at the scene, and sobriety of persons contacted. Opinions based on observations are permissible in this segment, with both the opinion and its objective base being reported (opinions not based on some objective fact do not belong in a crime report).

Offense or **crime reports** originate at the operational level. Their basic purpose is to record and transmit information. Such reports inform interested persons of the action taken at a crime scene by the reporting officer. They place the data reported in the possession of others who can take appropriate action, and they ensure the continuity of an investigation with little or no need to backtrack or duplicate the work of the preliminary investigator.

Primary data, modus operandi information, and the details or narrative of the crime and its circumstances must be written legibly and in clear and simple language; they must be complete in that all available and related facts are included, but they also must be brief; and they must be accurate, with all facts reported as they are known to the reporting officer, and opinions clearly noted and differentiated from the factual content of the narrative report.

PHOTOGRAPHING THE CRIME SCENE

So that the scene can be shown in its original condition, an investigator should not disturb the scene or any objects at the scene before photographing. Crime scene photography provides a permanent record of the facts at the crime scene. Photography is one means of recording facts for future use so that they can be used in reconstructing the crime scene and, sometimes, the crime. Photography is not a substitute for field notes, accurate measurements, and sketches of the scene. Pictures supplement the other forms for recording the facts of a crime scene, and they are often the best way of recording and illustrating the details of a crime scene and its evidence. Sometimes, indeed, they are the only feasible means of recording and illustrating certain features of a crime and the scene.

Photographing a crime scene serves two purposes: it provides a pictorial representation of the appearance and position of objects at the scene, and it serves as evidence to support the testimony of the investigator as to what he or she found at the scene, its location, nature, and condition.[1]

Investigators who do not take their own photographs should be on the crime scene ready to supervise the work of the photographer. As a general rule, police photographers working crime scenes are responsive to instructions from an assigned investigator because they realize that the investigator is the person responsible for the adequacy of the photographs taken.

The camera positions and the range at which photographs are taken should take advantage of the natural composition at the scene. The story of the scene is to be told graphically, and coherence requires an orderly progression in picture taking. In this type of camera work, objects cannot be moved to gain better composition, but the camera is mobile and its mobility should be used to best advantage.

In general, the subject matter of crime scene photography should move from the general to the specific. Long-range views should tell a story of what happened at the crime scene and serve as a backdrop to locate the subjects of close-up photographs of items of physical evidence. The **long-range photos** may show the locale, the approach route, the means of ingress to the scene or its premises, a hallway, two connected rooms, or a view of the scene from the normal entrance. **Mid-range photos** (ten to twenty feet) pinpoint a specific object of evidence or a significant segment of the crime scene. **Close-up photos** are used for recording evidence in position and detail—location, nature, and condition.

Aerial photos are excellent for studying crimes in series to ascertain whether the locations of past crimes suggest a pattern of criminal behavior on which the location of the next crime in the series can be projected. They are also excellent for locating outdoor crime scenes or controlling search patterns when large areas must be searched for evidence.

To prove the **corpus delicti**, the essential elements of the crime, a close-up crime scene photograph is needed. This graphic exposition of the full story of the crime, insofar as it can be revealed from any mute viewing of the place of occurrence and its evidence, may be extremely important in preparing the case for presentation in court. Composition varies with the crime: for example, a full-length picture of the homicide victim to show the position of the body or the location of a wound or wounds, the place of forced entry in burglaries,

One of the many uses of helicopters is to take aerial photographs of crime scenes.

and the point of origin of the fire in suspicious blazes. Examples of close-ups include views of the weapon and wounds in homicides, tool marks at the site of forced entrance, and a fire-setting contrivance or distinctive charring along the fire trails of the accelerant often used in arson.

Photographs also can be used to trace the modus operandi of the criminal and the continuity of crimes occurring in a series. Photographs of tool impressions record the characteristics of any tools used. Enlargements can be made, and prints can be cut in half for comparison. Quite often a jimmy or pry bar can be traced from crime to crime. Linking the impressions sometimes results in a basic lead for an investigator and often provides multiple evidence when a matching tool is found in the possession of a crime suspect.

Evidence photography of crime scenes can be used to reveal blood and hair on weapons, the trajectory of flying objects from marks on floors and walls, the location and characteristics of imprints and impressions, and the full extent of injuries and wounds. Important details can be developed from close-up photography. When a close-up view does not indicate the entire item of evidence, the photographer should show a progression from one end or side of the object to the other side, in a series of sectional views. Sectional photography reassures the triers of fact that the entire surface of the item of evidence was examined. Thus the number of photographs taken of any single item of evidence depends on the dimensions of the evidence and the need for photographic detail.

Measurements and measurement markers always have been a problem in crime scene photography because they intrude upon the photographer's reproduction of the scene as he or she found it. One acceptable procedure is to take a photograph without any change (as is) and then to take another picture with the measurement marker (a flat ruler, or the beginning section of a steel tape stretched out flat) placed in position. The use of a measurement marker is necessary to put the size of the item in the photograph in perspective.

Identification cards or markers are used in some photographs to record the date, time, location, photographer, and agency involved. However, they are not placed on the evidence, nor do they conceal any part of the major subject of the photograph.

All photographs of a crime scene in a series are dated and numbered consecutively (starting with 1) or identified by a series of film file numbers. Information that will supply data that can be written on each photographic print should be linked with these numbers in the field notes of the photographer. Pertinent data consist of the case number and subject of the picture, the crime classification, the date and time taken, the name of the photographer, the camera's location, the direction in which the camera was aimed, and the distance (in feet) to the subject of the picture.

SKETCHING THE CRIME SCENE

The basic reason for sketching a crime scene is to provide an in-depth understanding of the circumstances of the crime beyond the level of comprehension that can be attained solely reading a written report or studying photographs. A sketch is more than a written report and less than a photograph in depicting a crime scene. Because of its unique virtues, it can supplement both reports and photographs. The advantage of a sketch is that unnecessary detail can be eliminated, whereas it cannot be eliminated from a photograph. Sketching a plan or diagramming the scene in the regular course of police business records the facts available to the viewer (sketcher) so that at any time in the future the assigned investigator and the triers of fact both have a graphic representation of the crime scene (Figure 4–2).

FIGURE 4–2   Floor-plan sketch showing walls of room and location of (1) body, (2) blood, (3) gun, and (4) empty cartridge cases.

A necessary timeliness is involved in sketching a crime scene. The rough sketch must be made by the investigator as part of his or her field notes during the search of the scene. A field sketch is marked for identification by inserting the following:

1. The investigator's full name
2. The time, date, case number, and crime classification
3. The full name of any person assisting in taking measurements
4. Orientation—address; position in building; location adjacent to building; landmarks and compass direction, if outdoors

A common error in sketching the crime scene is to attempt to make an architectural reproduction or to include too many details. The crime scene sketch is not unlike the diagram of a traffic accident: items that do not aid in reproducing the accident should not be shown.[2] Standard symbols are used to indicate characteristics of the sketch, such as roads, walks, fences, common items of furniture, and evidence frequently encountered at crime scenes (Figure 4–3). A sketch shows and locates important objects at the scene; unimportant ones are omitted for simplicity. No one except the sketcher should mark or correct a field sketch in any way. This is the first permanent graphic record of the investigation. It is kept for years, beyond any possible need in court, and a photocopy is attached to the investigator's report of the case.

When a graphic illustration is meant to clarify a written report, accurate measurements are needed. Steel tapes are the approved means of measuring distances in criminal investigations. The so-called measuring wheel is an accurate device, but the investigator must show that he or she knows how to use it and did use it in a manner that produced an accurate measurement. The investigator should test it against a known distance measured with a steel tape to verify its accuracy before use. The greatest disservice an investigator can render is to record an erroneous measurement on a drawing or in his or her field notes, for in that case, no matter how many persons subsequently certify the correct measurement, a question will always remain about the initial recording and why it was erroneous.

In general, measurements are made of the area searched. They are made first with the eye. The investigator surveys the crime scene and decides what to measure and where to start. The distance lines between two objects are drawn on the sketch plan; then the actual measurements are made and recorded on the plan. Measurements should extend along and from fixed and identifiable points. Avoid any distance measurement with a floating base: that is, a reference point that may be moved or cannot be located with accuracy. Angular measurements can serve as coordinates to locate a point on the sketch only if the angle is broad and has two reference measurements (constituting a set of measurements) from identifiable fixed points or objects. Two sets of measurements are used for large items, such as a body, to fix the rotational position of that object (see Figure 4–2).

If at all possible, nothing should be moved in the process of measuring. Remember, the movement of objects changes the scene. The sketcher can claim that the object was returned to exactly the same spot, but this is an unnecessary taint of the officer's testimony.

Distance (Measurement) Line		Television	
Items of Evidence	1, 2, 3, etc.	Bed	
Light Pole		Dresser	
Traffic Signal		Bath (Tub)	
Gun		Shower (Stall)	
Knife		Toilet Bowl	
Road or Driveway		Stove (Range) (Circles Indicate Number of Burners)	
Fence		Refrigerator	◀— Door
Railroad		Sink	One Bowl Two Bowls
Tree		Built-Ins (Place Open Side Against Wall)	
Hedge, Low Shrubbery		Counter (Island in Kitchen, Merchandise in Store or Showroom)	
Footpath, Walkway		Cash Register	CR
Vehicle	▷ Front	Safe	S
Bicycle or Motorcycle	▷ Front	Door	(Indicates Direction of Opening)
Camera (Position)		Double Doors	
Blood		Sliding Door	
Body (Victim)		Folding Door	(Hinge or Fastened Side)
Chair		Wall (Building, Interior or Exterior)	
Sofa, Couch, Daybed		Casement Window (Drawn in Extension of Wall)	
Table (Coffee or Large)		Stairs (Arrow Indicates Up)	
Table (Small)			
Table (Round)			
Lamp			

FIGURE 4–3   Crime scene sketch graphic symbols.

A crime scene area diagram can supplement a crime scene diagram. The former is warranted when one or more of the basic facts in the case is beyond the crime scene itself. Such sketches pinpoint the location of shoe prints, tire tracks, weapons, and similar evidence linked to the crime scene (Figure 4–4).

Erasures may be made on such drawings. In fact, the drawings usually are completed in pencil, then inked in with a permanent ink, and the pencil marks are erased after the ink has dried completely. The drawings are identified in the same way as the crime scene sketch, and similar symbols may be used and annotated as necessary. Colors may be used for special effects, and overlays of semitransparent paper may be used to diagram the movements of participants in the crime. Schematic diagrams are often used to show the travels (paths) of the victim, offender(s), bullets, and other moving objects.

FIGURE 4–4 Crime scene area diagram. Each numbered location represents an item of physical evidence.

Case:
Crime:
Drawn By:
Date:

Many graphic illustrations are drawn to scale, using the investigator's rough sketch and measurements. Recommended scales range from one-eighth of an inch equals 1 foot (1:96) for indoor scenes to 1 inch equals 20 feet (1:240) for larger outdoor areas. These scales usually permit the work to be presented on an $8\frac{1}{2}$ by 11-inch sheet of paper. Ideally, the investigator should select a scale that permits reproduction of the scene without completely filling the $8\frac{1}{2}$ by 11-inch paper and allows space for a key or legend and necessary identification.

The professional assistance of individuals with special training is often used to prepare an investigator's sketches and diagrams for use in court. These may be enlarged (blown up) but will be kept to the scale noted on the drawing. Such reproductions are usually endorsed or certified by the investigator as being a reproduction of his or her original crime scene sketch. Software is now available that will allow investigators to prepare their own sketches. These two-dimensional applications are user friendly and investigators can learn to create their own diagrams in just a few lessons.[3]

Traditionally, the crime scene sketch has been used as a single-purpose tool merely to indicate the position of physical evidence at the crime scene. Its major purpose has been to place various items of physical evidence at the crime scene rather than to serve as a complete graphic report. Basically, the objective of crime scene sketching should be to graphically present the crime scene in a manner that will permit reconstruction of the crime from the details of the sketch. Thus, an ability to draw must be placed high among the necessary skills of an investigator.

For years, sketching has been particularly effective in vehicular traffic accidents. However, it is a standard investigative technique for pictorial recording in all types of investigations.

VIDEOTAPING THE CRIME SCENE

Videotaping is pictorial storytelling, and it offers compelling reasons for investigators to use it. The videotaper is not limited by the borders of a photograph or the lens of a camera, but he or she should be more careful when using the video camera to record the graphics of a crime scene record, knowing that the defense counsel could use the videotape to discredit the police case during the trial.

Discovery is the term used for a request by the defense counsel to the prosecutor before trial for disclosure of the police case against his or her client (see "Discovery"). Its objective is to aid in making certain the defendant receives a fair trial. Detectives have become accustomed to disclosing the fruits of their investigations, knowing that when a discovery request is made by the defense counsel in local courts, prosecutors must provide all crime reports, photos, sketches, and other pertinent materials.

Videotaping has been used to advantage by prosecutors at trial to show jurors meaningful views of the crime scene, but it has also been used by defense attorneys to destroy the credibility of investigators by using select segments of the video to contradict court testimony. The segment may show only a minor oversight on the part of the officer, but it may be enough to destroy a police case by linking suspicion to police conduct at the crime scene. Today, investigators participate in making decisions about the use of videotapes, along with prosecutors, local judiciary, and defense attorneys.[4]

Videotape has several advantages over photography: (1) it provides immediate results without the need for developing film; (2) tapes can be reused by recording over the images on the previously used tape; (3) visual movement allows the viewer to perceive the scene as it is shown; and (4) sound may be used.[5]

The low cost of camcorders, as well as their portability, user-friendly sophistication, high-quality images, and the ease with which the tape can be moved for viewing from the camcorder to a tabletop or large-screen monitor are all sound reasons for police departments to adopt this graphic system and adapt it to their needs.

In crime investigation, videotape has been used successfully in clandestine observation of suspicious places and persons, as well as transactions in "sting" operations. It is now being used more extensively to record interviews with witnesses and the built-in statement feature, which documents what was actually said, has been helpful to investigators when a witness attempts to change or deny his or her initial version of the crime's circumstances. Videotaping at crime scenes has become more commonplace.

PROGRESS REPORTS: THE CONTINUING INVESTIGATION

Progress reports are made either to inform the commanding officer of a new development in an investigation or at specified intervals: for example, daily when there is a lot of progress or every five days while the case is still active. The purpose and scope of progress reports prepared during a continuing investigation depend on the assignment of the investigator. If the assignment is limited—to check out one of the basic leads in a case or to interview a witness— the scope of the report is limited to this assignment, with the purpose being to collect data on a possible lead or the story of a witness. However, if the investigator is assigned to complete a continuing investigation, he or she will prepare as many reports as necessary to record the work done, the data collected, and the status of the investigation.

Reports made during a continuing investigation have four primary objectives:

1. To inform persons reading the report of the findings resulting from an assigned investigation, including both (a) information and (b) the precise source of the information
2. To facilitate understanding of the entire investigation to date
3. To foreshadow the uncompleted portion of the investigation, if any
4. To fulfill the duties of the assignment (basic lead, witness interview, etc.)

A frequent and successful arrangement is to structure these reports according to the classic queries of news reports: when, where, who, what, how, and why. These queries and the segments of the report responsive to them need not be in this order, but such queries serve as reminders to report writers to tell the entire story within the scope of their assignment.

Because a major segment of the work done in the continuing investigation is interviewing, investigators should develop a standard method of reporting interviews. This should not extend to the content of the interviews but should list such standard items of information as the time and date of the interview, the name and other identification data on the interviewee, any relationship to others involved, and the place of the interview.

This standard method can be extended to another major segment of the continuing investigation: physical evidence. First, the item of physical evidence is identified, and then whatever facts are to be reported in connection with it are supplied.

DISCOVERY

Discovery is the term used for a request by the defense counsel for the prosecutor to disclose the police case against the defendant before the trail. The objective of discovery is to aid in ensuring that the defendant receives a fair trial. Detectives have become accustomed to disclosing the fruits of their investigation, knowing that when the defense counsel makes a discovery request in local courts, prosecutors must provide all crime reports, photographs, sketches, and other pertinent materials. Consequently, the importance of accurately recording the crime scene—regardless of the methods used—should always be foremost in the investigator's mind.

CASE STUDY

The Lucky Market Case

Police reports summarize the armed robbery of a supermarket, the subsequent investigation, and its results:

Details of Crime

On July 23, officers received a call at 1854 hours regarding a 211 P.C. (robbery) at the Lucky Market, 56th and Broadway. Upon arrival, officers were met by the holdup victim, Edith Sheridan, who stated she was checking out at a cash register for customers. The next person in line was Suspect No. 1, and he left the groceries in the cart and didn't unload them, so victim started to take them out and Suspect No. 1 said, "Leave them alone." Suspect No. 1 took a gun from his belt with his right hand and said, "Empty the till and hurry up!" Victim took the money from the till and Suspect No. 1 said, "What's underneath?" Victim said, "Nothing but checks." Suspect came around and looked for himself, taking out the drawer. Suspect then said to the victim, "Go to the next till and pull out the cash." Victim asked if he wanted the coins and Suspect No. 1 said, "No, I don't want them." Victim went to the next till and Suspect No.1 said, "Hurry up, you're not going fast enough." Suspect said he wanted all the coins in this till. Victim told Suspect No. 1, "There's no money in the last two tills," and Suspect No. 1 said, "Open them anyway," which the victim did. Suspect told victim to "stay put," and then the two suspects went out the front door separately, the short man in front.

 John Cox, off-duty Sacramento Police Officer, Badge #178, at this time was standing at the checkout counter waiting in line and knew the holdup was in progress. When the suspects left the front door, Cox pulled his gun on the way to the front door and caught up with Suspect No. 2 and told Suspect No. 1, who was seated in the car, "Hold it right there."

 Suspect No. 2 at this time was standing beside Cox. Suspect No. 2 wheeled behind Cox and pinned his arms and pushed him down. Cox then went down and Suspect No. 2 pulled his gun from his belt and shot Cox in the neck. The next thing the victim saw was Cox lying on the pavement. Victim stated she heard no shot.

 Victim stated Suspect No. 2 was possibly standing behind her in the store. She did not get a good look at him.

 Victim also stated she felt that if she didn't obey Suspect No. 1's commands, she would be shot.

 Victim also stated that the bag boy walked back to unload suspect's basket of groceries as they were at the counter and Suspect No. 1 said, "Hey, stay right there." This incident happened at No. 1 check stand.

 The amount of cash taken is not known at this time. Victim will advise.

Officers: Joseph Bals, #196/George Maloney, #189

27'

C

E

B

D

LEGEND:
A - Front door
B - Light pole
C - Victim
D - Revolver (victim)
E - Glasses (victim)

38'6"

N

68'

56'

Sidewalk
Roof

Flower Bed

A

Building (Lucky Store)

FIGURE 4–5   Crime scene diagram—Lucky Market case study.

Casualty Report

On July 23, police officer John Cox, age 38, white male, off-duty, was shot by one of two holdup men, during robbery at Lucky Market, 56th Street and Broadway. Victim taken by Superior Ambulance to Sutter Hospital, Unit 50 following ambulance, and reporting officer was present in Sutter Hospital Emergency Room when Dr. Meehan pronounced victim DOA (dead on arrival) at 1912 hours. Victim had been shot in the neck.

Officer: Edward Leonard (Unit #50)

Supplementary (Progress) Investigation Reports

On July 23–24, 2015 to 0115 hours, I took the following photographs at the Lucky Market, 56th Street and Broadway (Figure 4–5):

1. The front of the store: blood stains in the parking lot in front of the NW corner of the store (color)
2. The check stand area from four (4) different angles (black and white)
3. A wire basket with grocery items in it located in front of the store office, NW corner of the store (black and white)

I checked the following items found in the wire basket for fingerprints:

1. A potato bag
2. A paper bag of ice
3. A carton (six-pack) of Busch Bavarian beer
4. A box of Lucky detergent (giant size; 1 lb., 15 oz.) (On the face of the box of detergent I found two partial tips of fingers; latents protected with an Ace tab lift. No other latents of value found.)

I took color photographs of the deceased police officer, John Cox, at the coroner's morgue. These show the powder-burned area and a bullet hole in the officer's left neck, a small black-and-blue spot on the officer's right neck, a photograph of the officer's face, and a photograph of the officer showing his gun holster strapped to his belt on the left side of his body. (All photographs in color and taken at f/8 and 1/50 second.)

I checked a red Cadillac convertible with a black top bearing California license MYY-625 for fingerprints in the police yard. Numerous partial latent fingerprints were found.

Officer: Joseph Green

On July 23, at 1854 hours. Mr. LeRoy Kennedy, a clerk in the market, stated he was standing alongside Aisle 31 in the Lucky store when an unidentified man tapped him on the shoulder and said, "There's a holdup going on." Kennedy walked to the cash register at the front of the store and observed two male subjects with a female clerk, Edith Sheridan (615 Crown Road, 675-6404), as she removed money from various cash registers at the direction of a suspect wearing an orange-colored nylon shell-type jacket, who will be designated as Suspect No. 1.

His accomplice, Suspect No. 2, wearing a blue jacket of somewhat the same type, was standing by. Kennedy further stated that he could see that Suspect No. 1 had some bulky object in the waistband at the front of his trousers, and he (Kennedy) concluded that it was a gun.

When the clerk (Edith Sheridan) had emptied several registers, Suspect No. 1 took the bag and left the store. Suspect No. 1 went to a vehicle parked to the west of the front doors in the parking area and got behind the wheel as Suspect No. 2 left the store, walking toward the vehicle.

Mr. Kennedy stated that he then observed a customer (later identified as off-duty Officer John Cox) pursuing the suspects from inside the store and approaching them at their vehicle. Cox had a gun in his hand and turned slightly away from Suspect No. 2 as he pointed the gun at Suspect No. 1 seated in the vehicle.

At this point, Suspect No. 2 wheeled around behind Cox and appeared to pin Cox's left arm behind him and then pushed down on Cox's shoulder or head with his left hand, while pulling a gun from his waistband, shoving it tight against Cox's neck, and firing once. Cox fell to the asphalt, his gun fell from his hand.

Suspect No. 2 then entered the vehicle and both suspects left, driving east on Broadway and then south on 59th Street, and out of sight.

Physical Descriptions of Suspects

Suspect No. 1—WMA, taller than Suspect No. 2, possibly 68, 165 lbs., dark skin, medium build, wearing orange-colored nylon windbreaker-type zipper jacket, same age group as Suspect No. 2

Suspect No. 2—WMA, 5889, 165 lbs., mid 20s to early 30s, wearing faded blue nylon windbreaker and hunting-type cap with bill, dark in color

Officer: George Maloney, #189

On July 23, at 1910 hours. This officer received a call via radio that a police officer had been shot and that the subjects were last seen in a late-model Cad headed possibly E/B on U.S. 50 beyond the Elvis Freeway. This unit responded and rolled to the intersection of Watt Ave. and U.S. 50, and upon arrival at the Watt Ave. on ramp E/B observed the late model Cad E/B in the No. 1 lane with one man at the wheel. The vehicle was a late-model Cad, black top over red bottom, convertible, license number MYY-625 California. The subject was ordered to the curb with the red light, and the vehicle stopped. The driver alighted and stood by the rear of his vehicle. This officer was out with gun in hand and ordered the driver to lie on the ground spread-eagled, and then the rear of the Cad was approached and the car was seen to move as if someone was still in it. This officer then poked his gun into the Cad's interior and the subject hiding in the rear came out from under several coats and trousers and surrendered. Subject driving was Harry W. Burrell, and the passenger hiding in the rear seat area was James Brainard.

The subjects were taken out of the car and laid on the ground on their stomachs, head to head, with their hands cuffed together. The subjects offered no resistance and were handcuffed without incident. The driver, Harry Burrell, stated as he watched this officer poke his gun into the car, "Come on out, Brainard. Looks like they have got us."

The subjects were transported from the scene to the county jail.

Note: Two Colt .38 police positive revolvers, No. 1 loaded with four rounds and No. 2 loaded with five rounds, were found together in the front seat of the car when it was stopped.

Officer: John Gayne, #111

On July 23, at 1920 hours. Upon my arrival at the scene (outbound U.S. 50, near Watt Ave.), Officer John Gayne had two suspects on the ground on the shoulder of the freeway, handcuffed. I observed two handguns in a red 1970 Cad convertible. The guns were on the right front seat of above Cad. Subjects transported to county jail in my unit, number 245.

While en route to county jail, Subject Brainard stated that he had shot the policeman. He stated he did not know that the man was a police officer until he (the police officer) pulled his gun on the two subjects. Subject Brainard stated he told the police officer to drop the gun, and when the officer moved, the subject's gun went off and the officer fell.

Officer: Walter Morris, #622

On July 23, at 2330 hours. Following the arrest of the two subjects, Brainard and Burrell, the two weapons were brought into the Detective Bureau and examined by Harkness of the State CII (Criminal Investigation and Identification Division) and myself:

1. One .38 caliber revolver, serial No. 325597, was found to contain five live rounds of .38 caliber ammunition. This gun was marked and turned over to Harkness, CII.
2. One .38 caliber revolver, serial No. 333563, was found to contain four live rounds of .38 caliber ammunition and one spent .38 caliber casing. This gun was marked and turned over to Harkness of CII.
3. Both guns received by Harkness of CII at 2310 this date.

On July 23, at 2355 hours. Referring to attached diagram, following articles removed from Cad 2-dr convertible bearing California license MYY-625 in county jail yard:

1. Paper bag containing a tag from Grants dated July 23, one light socket, and one jar of hand cream
2. Paper bag, brown, containing $1,370.51 in currency and coin
3. Paper bag, empty
4. Cigarette package, opened, Marlboros
5. Dark glasses, bubble type
6. Dark glasses, flat
7. Hat, green with white webbing in front, bearing new price tag
8. Bag, empty, between seat and door on floor
9. Hat, green with white webbing in front, bearing new price tag. Identical to item 7
10. Glove, brown cotton
11. Man's Naugahyde jacket, pile lining
12. Dark glasses, flat
13. Shirt, khaki tan, cotton
14. Shirt, orange-colored with several buttons missing
15. Jacket, rain repellant, dark color with white lining
16. One glove, dark color identical to glove item 10 and found wrapped in item 13
17. Bag, small size, found wrapped in shirt, item 13
18. Watch, Timex
19. One green metal tool box containing:
    a. empty brown paper bag
    b. cloth glove similar to items 10 and 16
    c. jar, Cover Girl makeup
    d. tube lipstick, lavender color
    e. one box .38 caliber ammunition containing 33 Peters cartridges

20. One man's green hat, soft
21. One white coverall, J. C. Penney, Big Mac brand with light-colored paint over all
22. Boots, brown, medium high with light-colored paint on same
23. Two buttons, 4-hole, pearl color

Regarding articles from the Cad (MYY-625):

1. Items 1 and 3 to 23 inclusive were turned over to Allen Harkness, State CII.
2. Item 2 was booked with Jail Sergeant.
3. Brown paper bag, item 2, containing $1,370.51 in currency and coin consisted of the following:

CURRENCY

25 held together by paper clip	$ 1.00 bills	$ 25.00
Loose	$ 1.00 bills	208.00
Loose	$ 5.00 bills	535.00
Loose	$ 10.00 bills	350.00
Loose	$ 20.00 bills	220.00
	Currency, total:	$1,338.00

COINS

1 roll 25-cent pieces	$10.00
3 rolls 10-cent pieces	15.00
3 rolls 5-cent pieces	6.00
3 rolls 1-cent pieces	1.50
1 loose penny	.01
Coins, total:	$32.51

Officer: John Gayne, #111

On July 24, at 0830 hours: The officer listed below was sent to the county morgue to pick up the cartridge belt and the clothing of Officer Cox.

Officer was present when Dr. Prisinzano removed the bullet or slug from the mouth of Officer Cox. I witnessed the doctor mark same, and he then handed the slug to me and I then marked same and placed in envelope. This envelope was later turned over to Allen Harkness of the CII at approximately 2230 hours.

The slug entered the neck of Officer Cox on the left side, approx. 5" below and 1" to the rear of the ear. It then passed through the neck and then lodged itself in the lower jaw on the right side.

This slug appears to be that of a .38 cal., and it is badly damaged, having smashed against the jawbone.

Deputy Shiner of the Coroner's Office advised that he will dry the shirt and other items of clothing and will then turn same over to Allen Harkness, CII, in the morning.

Joseph Green of our B of I took colored photos of the deceased, showing close-ups of the wounds, including the powder burns. Dr. Prisinzano removed a large section of flesh from around the wound, showing the powder burns, and this will be preserved and turned over to the CII by the Coroner's Office.

Officer: Harry Wells, #233

CHAPTER REVIEW

KEY TERMS

aerial photo   *69*
close-up photo   *69*
corpus delicti   *69*
crime report   *68*
crime scene sketches
    and photographs   *64*

discovery   *75*
field notes   *64*
long-range photo   *69*
mid-range photo   *69*

preliminary
    investigative
    report   *65*
progress report   *76*

REVIEW QUESTIONS

1. Which of the following is *not* one of the nine elements of modus operandi?
   a. Who committed the crime
   b. Type of crime
   c. Means of attack
   d. Words used

2. The essential elements of the crime are known as the:
   a. Modus operandi
   b. Corpus delicti
   c. Corpus operandi
   d. Modus delicti

3. Close-up photographs should include a/an _____ for scale.

4. The advantage of a crime scene sketch that cannot be accomplished with any type of photography is the:
   a. Ability to improve lighting conditions
   b. Elimination of unnecessary detail
   c. Unique ability of the artist comes through
   d. Addition of missing necessary detail

5. The type of police report used to document the results of ongoing investigative efforts and often prepared on specified intervals are known as:
   a. Field notes
   b. Preliminary reports
   c. Progress reports
   d. Periodic reports

6. When the basic objective of this type of police report is the reconstruction of the crime scene, the report is known as:
   a. Field notes
   b. Preliminary report
   c. Progress report
   d. Crime scene sketch

7. The process of providing all crime reports, photos, sketches, and other pertinent materials to the defense in a timely manner is known as:
   a. Discretionary
   b. Disclosure
   c. Discovery
   d. The fairness doctrine

8. In general, the subject matter of crime scene photographs should move from the _____ to the _____.

9. _____ photographs are excellent for studying crimes in a series to ascertain whether the locations of past crimes suggest a pattern of criminal behavior from which the location of the next crime in the series can be projected.

10. Opinions based on observations are permissible in a police report. However, opinions not based on objective facts _____ belong in a crime report.

See Appendix D for the correct answers.

DISCUSSION QUESTIONS

1. What is the meaning of the inherent integrity of records prepared in the performance of official duties? Can this designation be applied to field notes of a crime scene search? To photographs of a crime scene? To sketches?
2. Explain the requirement that photographs and sketches must be a faithful representation of the thing shown.
3. Relate the purposes of photographing a crime scene to the need for planned picture taking.
4. What are the advantages of a floor-plan sketch?
5. Who is responsible for the adequacy of crime scene photography? Why? Discuss.
6. What are the primary objectives of reports made during a continuing investigation?
7. What is the most appropriate form or structure of investigative reports?
8. What is meant by chronological order in the preparation of reports of a continuing investigation?
9. What are the six classic queries of reporters useful in guarding against the omission of details in an investigative report?

RELATED WEB SITES

To learn more about crime scene photographing and sketching visit the following sites.

www.crime-scene-investigator.net

www.feinc.net/cs-proc.htm

chapter **five**

Laboratory and Technical Services

CHAPTER OUTLINE

After reading this chapter you will be able to:

- Explain the fundamental scientific concepts involved in DNA typing as it relates to criminal investigation.
- Recognize the types of information a crime laboratory can supply regarding the processing of physical evidence.
- Discuss the major pieces of crime laboratory equipment and their capabilities.
- Understand the scientific principles involved in voiceprint identification.
- Distinguish between the various ciphers used by criminals and the types of criminal activity likely to be involved.

T he trustworthiness of an expert is important to the net worth of the entire investigation. Any suspicion of subjectivity or dishonesty destroys the legal significance of evidence because the average trier of fact may easily view such conduct as affecting the credibility of the entire investigation. An unusual unanimous vote for reversal of an Illinois murder conviction by the judges of the United States Supreme Court in the case of *Miller v. Pate* illustrates this reaction.

> Lloyd Eldon Miller, Jr., was convicted of murder in an Illinois state court in a prosecution for the death of a girl resulting from a sexual attack. A piece of compelling evidence against Miller was a pair of reddish-brown stained men's shorts found in an abandoned building a mile away from the scene of the crime and known as Van Buren's Flats.
>
> The prosecution theorized that the stains on the shorts were human blood and that the petitioner had been wearing these shorts when he committed the crime. The judgment of conviction was affirmed on appeal by the Supreme Court of Illinois (13 Ill. 2d 84, 148 NE2d 455). On application for a writ of habeas corpus to the U.S. District Court for the Northern District of Illinois, the court granted the writ (225 F Supp 541), but the Court of Appeals for the Seventh Circuit reversed it (342 F2d 646). In the federal habeas corpus proceeding it was established that the reddish-brown stains on the shorts in question were not blood, but paint, and that counsel for the prosecution had known at the time of the trial that the shorts were stained with paint.[1]

In words of unusual bluntness the unanimous Supreme Court opinion stated:

> More than 30 years ago this Court held that the Fourteenth Amendment cannot tolerate a state criminal conviction obtained by the knowing use of false evidence. There has been no deviation from that established principle. There can be no retreat from that principle here. The judgment of the Court of Appeals is reversed, and the case is remanded for further proceedings consistent with this opinion.[2]

CRIMINALISTICS: FORENSIC SCIENCE

The crime laboratory in which physical evidence obtained by police in the course of an investigation is examined may now be known as a **forensic science laboratory**, and laboratory technicians are often identified as **forensic scientists**. The professional group in this field, however, still identifies with the term **criminalistics**.

Criminalistics is the profession and scientific discipline directed to the recognition, identification, individualization, and evaluation of physical evidence by application of the natural sciences in matters of law and science.[3]

Identification in criminalistics is aligned with the logic of **set theory**. All objects can be divided and subdivided into various sets on the basis of their properties. Identification in relation to physical evidence and its analysis is defined as the determination of some set to which an object or substance belongs or the determination as to whether an object or substance belongs to a given set. Fingerprints, tool marks, blood, hair, glass, paint, and other types of evidence can be so classified. In addition, criminalistics is concerned with identity or origin. Given a bloodstain found and collected at a crime scene, the criminalist is asked to determine from whom it originated; given a spent bullet recovered from a human body, the criminalist is asked to decide if a particular firearm fired the bullet. In reaching a decision about identification, the criminalist also is asked to individualize the identification by specifying how individual or unique the item of evidence examined is within the set of its origin.

The crime laboratory is staffed by technicians educated and trained in criminalistics. It is a subsystem in the administration of justice that studies the effect of a criminal upon a crime scene (and other sites of criminal activity) and vice versa. The informational output of a crime laboratory depends on its input: the physical evidence collected at crime scenes and forwarded to the laboratory for examination. The forensic science staff is responsible for deciding whether or not to develop information from physical evidence within a laboratory operation. Depending on the circumstances of the case, the general strategy is to order analyses so that the maximum amount of information is secured.[4]

When scientific findings are interpreted, the deductions of the criminalist reconstructing the event and the person or persons associated with it cannot be made with certainty and usually are made with prudence. Criminalists offer the most probable reconstruction on the basis of reasonable criteria and do not assign mathematical probabilities to the occurrence of two materials from different sources (two items of evidence, or one item of evidence and one known standard) having a common origin. Even the most sophisticated and specific analysis techniques do not, as a general rule, offer an opportunity for a criminalist to evaluate identification in terms of mathematical probability.

The effect on an accused person and his legal counsel of such identification and its individualization is considerable. Associative evidence placing a suspect at the crime scene ruins a not guilty pleading based on a general denial of presence at the crime scene or of contact with the victim at any time, and it seriously damages a defense based on an alibi. Tracing an item of evidence found at the crime scene to the accused person or an item found on the suspect back to the scene has serious implications for any successful defense unless a reasonable explanation is forthcoming. This effect is not necessarily an inducement to confess, but it does function in this fashion by its influence on the defendant and his or her legal adviser.

DNA FINGERPRINTING

DNA testing has become an established part of criminal justice procedure. Despite early controversies and challenges by defense attorneys, the admissibility of DNA test results in the courtroom has become routine. Understanding the importance of DNA typing to criminal investigations requires knowledge of some fundamental biological facts.

Each molecule of DNA, the primary carrier of genetic information in living organisms, consists of a long, spiral structure that has been likened to a "twisted ladder." The handrails of the ladder string together the ladder "rungs." Each rung consists of a **base pair**, two of four varieties of nucleic acid, and are combined in pairs called **nucleotides**. The sequence of these base pairs constitutes the genetic coding of DNA.

DNA in humans is found in all cells that contain a nucleus—except red blood cells. Each nucleated cell (with the exception of sperm and eggs cells)

1. A blood sample is taken.

2. DNA is extracted from blood cells.

3. The DNA is cut into fragments by a restriction enzyme.

4. The DNA fragments are separated into bands during electrophoresis in an agarose gel.

5. The DNA band pattern in the gel is transferred to a nylon membrane by a technique known as *Southern blot.*

6. The radioactive DNA probe is prepared.

7. The DNA probe binds to specific DNA sequences on the membrane.

8. Excess DNA on the probe is washed off.

9. At this stage 25, the radioactive probe is bound to the DNA pattern on the membrane.

10. X-ray film is placed next to the membrane to detect the radioactive pattern.

11. The X-ray film is developed to make the pattern of bands that is known as a DNA fingerprint visible.

FIGURE 5–1 DNA identification process.

usually contains the full complement of an individual's DNA, called the **genome**, that is unvarying from cell to cell. The genome consists of approximately 3 billion base pairs, of which about 3 million actually differ from person to person. However, the base pairs that vary represent a virtually incalculable number of possible combinations. Person-to-person differences within a particular segment of DNA sequence are referred to as **alleles**.

DNA typing focuses on identifying and isolating discrete fragments of these alleles in a sample and comparing one sample with another. For example, a forensic scientist might compare a semen sample retrieved from a rape victim to a DNA sample taken from a suspect. If identical fragments appear in both samples, a match is declared. To determine the likelihood of a match being mere coincidence, a particular combination of alleles is compared to the frequency with which the combination appears in the statistical population.

Many of the frequently encountered specimens found at crime scenes are either contaminated, degraded, or small in quantity. These problems are surmounted by **polymerase chain reaction (PCR) analysis**. This technique involves extracting DNA from a small evidence sample and then replicating it through a complex operation of repeated heating and cooling cycles and exposure to an enzyme. Because each cycle doubles the quantity of DNA, the original extraction can be replicated several million times within a short time. By examining several locations (loci) where variation occurs, a typing profile can be produced. The FBI has selected thirteen **short tandem repeats (STR)** loci to serve as a standard battery of core loci, each of which contains a short region where a sequence of three, four, or five nucleotides is repeated a different number of times in different people. Samples identified by a radioactively labeled, allele-specific probe are blotted onto a membrane, according to standard PCR protocol. Each dark spot that appears can be read as "yes" or "no" to the question of whether a particular individual possesses a given allele. When comparing DNA samples from known individuals with evidence samples, a difference of a single allele can exclude someone as the donor of that evidence sample. The more locations that show the same allele pattern, the stronger the evidence that the two samples came from the same individual.[5]

DNA is found in all body tissues and fluids. Saliva, skin cells, bone, teeth, tissue, urine, feces, and a host of other biological specimens, all of which may be found at crime scenes, are also sources of DNA. Saliva may be found in chewing gum and on cigarette butts, envelopes, and possibly drinking cups. Fingernail scrapings from an assault victim or a broken fingernail left at the scene by the perpetrator may also be useful DNA evidentiary specimens. Even hatbands and other articles of clothing may yield DNA. Because the DNA molecule is long lived, it is likely to be detectable for many years in bones or body fluid stains from older criminal cases in which questions of identity remain unresolved.

Today almost all states have legislation related to DNA data banking, most of which focuses on collecting and testing DNA from individuals convicted of sexual assaults or homicides. The FBI is supporting this effort by linking these state databases together to form a national database known as **CODIS (Combined DNA Index System)**. This system networks to link the typing results from unsolved criminal cases in multiple jurisdictions and by alerting investigators to similarities among unsolved crimes.[6]

LABORATORY DETERMINATIONS

After scientific examination of physical evidence, laboratory personnel report their findings. These determinations in past cases have led to a stylized set of expectations from field investigators. It is not always possible for a finding in a specific case to achieve the optimum expectations. As a result, the field investigator may be disappointed and, perhaps, reluctant to request such technical or laboratory assistance in the future. On the other hand, an optimistic view of the determinations that are possible through scientific aid should lead field investigators to a more extensive use of technical and laboratory services.

Great expectations may be rewarded. For this reason, an optimistic but realistic view of possible technical and laboratory determinations is necessary. The findings that possibly may result from a scientific examination of physical evidence have been organized in the following list for ready reference according to the types of evidence common to police cases:

1. Weapons—Firearms
   a. identification of bullets, shells, or cartridge cases with a specific gun
   b. operating condition of firearms, functioning of safety and trigger pull
   c. distance at which gun was fired
   d. position of the shooter at time of firing
   e. ownership traced
   f. obliterated serial number restored
   g. imprints (latent fingerprints), impressions, or transfer evidence developed
   h. used in other crimes

2. Weapons—Knives and Bludgeons
   a. description of cutting, stabbing, or striking surfaces
   b. comparison with wounds
   c. tracing ownership
   d. imprints, impressions, or transfer evidence developed
   e. used in other crimes
   f. direction of force
   g. position of assailant
   h. identity of assailant; sex, strength, and which hand held weapon
3. Drugs and Poisons
   a. analysis by type (name)
   b. determination of quantity of fatal dose
   c. origin (purchase, manufacturer, growth)
   d. comparison with effect—wounds, body functions
   e. used in other crimes
4. Imprints and Impressions
   a. nature of object making imprint or impression
   b. identity by manufacturer or group
   c. individual identity—comparison (imprint or impression made by or not made by submitted suspect object)
   d. individual identity—fingerprints (Figure 5–2)
   e. individual identity—footprints[7]
   f. direction of movement
   g. transfer evidence developed
5. Tool Marks
   a. nature of tool
   b. identity by manufacturer or group
   c. identity—for search

FIGURE 5–2 Latent fingerprint found at a crime scene (left), compared with the rolled fingerprint of the suspect (right). Twelve points of identity indicate a match.

    d. origin (purchase)

    e. individual identity (mark made or not made by submitted suspect tool)

    f. transfer evidence developed

    g. used in other crimes

6. Traces of Identity—Blood

    a. identification as blood

    b. determination (human or animal, grouping, direction, and velocity of drops and splashes)[8]

    c. direction of force

    d. position of assailant

    e. individual identity (blood of victim or defendant)

    f. found at other crime scenes

    g. transfer evidence developed[9]

7. Blood (Test)

    a. alcohol in blood (percentage)

    b. interpretation of percentage as to degree of intoxication

8. Hairs and Fibers

    a. origin (human, head, body, pubic; animal; clothing)

    b. identity (sex, race—a broad grouping)

    c. individual identity—comparison of known standards of hair of victim with hair of defendant; comparison of fibers from clothing of victim (or found at scene) with material found on suspect

    d. Dog hair (victim's pet to clothing of suspect; suspect's pet to crime scene or victim)

9. Dust, Dirt, Debris

    a. origin (locale, occupation)

    b. identity (group)

    c. individual identity or transfer evidence developed

10. Flammable Fluids—Fire and Explosive Residue

    a. identity by physical properties

    b. origin (purchase, manufacturer)

    c. direction of force (flow)

    d. used in other crimes

11. Glass

    a. identity and comparisons

    b. direction of force

    c. transfer evidence developed

    d. similar damage at other crime scenes

12. Paint

    a. identity (group)

    b. origin (purchase, usage, manufacturer)

    c. individual identity—the same as or similar to submitted sample

    d. transfer evidence developed

13. Semen Stains
    a. identity of stain as semen
    b. location and extent of stain
    c. origin—individual identity in relation to blood or other body substances or fluids of a suspect in custody[10]
14. Wood
    a. identity (type, group, name)
    b. origin (purchase, production, growth)
    c. identity—same as or similar to submitted suspect sample
15. Suspected Poisoned Food
    a. isolation and identity of noxious or poisoned substance
    b. origin (source, process)
16. Documents
    a. authenticity of document or signature or both
    b. authorship (handwriting); authorship (typewriter); identity—"trademarks" of writer (form, spelling, vocabulary, etc.); fraudulent check "trademark"
    c. age (date written)
    d. nature of alteration or erasure
    e. copy traces, carbon paper, embossed writing, typewriter ribbons
    f. transfer evidence developed
    g. dating of ink and paper[11]
    h. used in other crimes
17. Feces
    a. comparison with samples taken from other crime scenes
    b. undigested food residues possible and informative
18. Vomit
    a. comparison for identity when suspect is located with vomit at crime scene and traces on clothing of suspect
    b. in suspected poison cases, analysis for content and identification of poison, if present
19. Urine
    a. analysis of submitted specimens (alcohol level in blood)
    b. analysis in suspected poisoning cases

Investigators should become acquainted with the language used by criminalists in reporting their determinations. If any doubts exist in the mind of the investigator as to the level of uniqueness achieved by the criminalist, a request for clarification should be made. A high level of exactness in identification is not always possible because of the nature of the evidence or the type of examination. Investigators should be particularly alert for the following phrases in the reports of technicians examining physical evidence:

1. consistent with
2. similar to
3. indistinguishable from

4. of the type used
5. matching
6. indicates that
7. has the appearance of

LABORATORY EQUIPMENT

The work of the criminalist concerns the physical and biological science laboratories, examination of substances involved with crimes and suspects, and the use of selected equipment normally associated with scientific techniques in such disciplines. Equipment designed especially for identification of firearms and examination of questioned documents is part of the inventory of a criminalistics laboratory.

   Major items of equipment, other than the basic assortment of test tubes, retorts, burners, and the like that may be found in a modern laboratory of considerable size, range from optical equipment through X-ray and spectrographic devices to machines and measuring devices that use the latest space-age technology. Microscopes usually span the range of magnification from low-power instruments of comparatively low cost to high-power instruments of high cost. The comparison microscope, designed for work in the identification of

A ballistic expert adjusts a comparison microscope.

firearms, and photographic equipment necessary for microphotography are common optical tools in these laboratories.

Equipment for spectrographic analysis has been part of the criminalistics scene for many years. In **spectrography**, the radiation from an incandescent gas or vapor is concentrated in certain discrete wavelengths. Such wavelengths are characteristic of the emitting elements in the gas, with each element emitting a unique and characteristic pattern of wavelengths, or **spectrum**. A spectrograph has a narrow slit to admit the radiation, a prism or grating to distribute the radiation, and a system of lenses to focus the wavelength pattern on a photographic plate. The pattern is recorded photographically as a series of short lines, each line being an image of the slit formed by the radiation of one wavelength. In analysis, the evidence sample is vaporized to incandescence by flame, arc, or spark and the radiation recorded. Evidence samples are normally composites. Therefore, spectra of all the elements comprising the evidence sample are recorded simultaneously and the criminalist analyzes the composition of the sample by sorting the recorded lines, their widths, and their positions in the spectrum. Spectra of known standards and charts of the standard wavelength of various elements are used for identification. A medium-size quartz prism instrument with a range into the ultraviolet region disperses incident light on a 10-inch photograph plate. The spectrograph is an all-purpose instrument for criminalistics, which will produce a complete elementary analysis of evidence samples containing mineral and other inorganic compounds.[12]

Chromatography is a method of separating compounds to identify the components. Modern equipment in this area is capable of identifying compounds. Gas or vapor chromatography employs a columnar device in which the evidence sample is injected into the system at the beginning of the column and carried along by a stream of carrier gas. Each constituent of the sample being tested is separated, emerges at a definite time from the time of injecting the sample (retention time), and is fed into a recorder. The recorder provides a trace in which the peaks and their position on a time axis (the retention time) identify each of the components of a sample. Gas chromatographs are valuable analytical tools because with them microsamples of such complex compositions as gasoline, fuel oil, perfumes, hair dressings, and paint thinners can be separated and identified from their constituents—a difficult problem with other scientific techniques when only minute quantities of evidence are available.[13]

X-ray crystallography is useful for the identification of any crystalline solid or compound from which a crystalline solid derivative can be made. **X-ray diffraction** is also of use in processing very small samples, in examining samples with noncrystalline impurities, and in identifying inorganic and mineral substances. X-ray spectra are used for analysis and identification. Equipment is based on standard X-ray devices adapted to testing and recording X-ray spectra and diffraction patterns.

The newest in laboratory equipment is a type of nuclear reactor used for **neutron activation analysis (NAA)**—a technique that can analyze samples one hundred times too small for ordinary spectrographic techniques. It is not equipment easily purchased by a local laboratory, but a centrally located radiochemistry laboratory can make this new technique available to any local criminalistics laboratory.

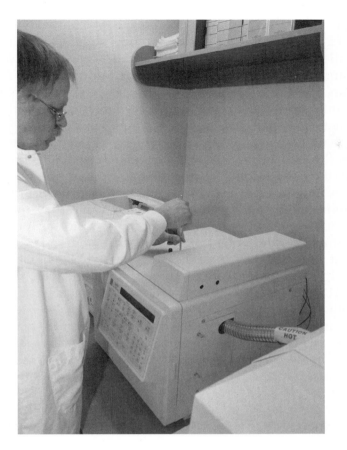

A toxicologist using a gas chromatograph to test a sample for traces of poison.

Neutron activation analysis is a very sensitive method of analyzing samples for the elements in their composition. It involves bombarding the samples with neutrons in a nuclear reactor, which causes the different elements in the sample to become radioactive, thus making it possible to identify the different radioactive elements present and to determine the quantity of each. The great sensitivity of this method allows the detection of mini-micro elements. The research reactor is much smaller and simpler than a nuclear power reactor. In operation, it produces vast numbers of neutrons by uranium fission chain reaction—but under precise control. When an evidence sample is inserted into this intense field of neutrons, the various elements in the sample undergo a nuclear reaction that causes some of these elements to become appreciably radioactive. After the irradiation, the activated sample is removed for counting. The different radioactive elements that are now present emit radiations of different energy levels and decay at different rates. Some die out within seconds, some within minutes or hours, some require days, weeks, or even longer. A very sophisticated apparatus, the **gamma-ray spectrometer**, is used to measure the distinctive radioactive gamma-ray emissions and thereby to identify the elements from which the rays originate. The data are printed on paper tape and also displayed on the face of an oscilloscope. As the number of elements found at the same concentrations in two samples increases, the matching of the two samples becomes increasingly positive.[14]

The NAA technique and its application in the study of gunshot residues has returned a potential item of evidence to investigators. Testing for gunshot traces had fallen into disuse when the paraffin test was found to react to urine and a few similar substances, as well as to gunshot residues. Now paraffin-lifting kits are used on a suspect's hands, and NAA measurements for the presence of antimony and barium, which are common gunshot residues, have indicated a new and useful discrimination and particularity. Distinctive "signatures" of handguns, tools, and other metal objects are now available to investigators through an innovative **trace metal detection technique (TMDT)**, which makes the patterns of these objects visible on the skin or clothing of suspects when treated with a test solution and examined under ultraviolet light.[15]

Ultrasonic cavitation is an etching method that may replace chemical, electrolytic, and magnetic particle methods of restoring obliterated serial numbers on firearms and other metal objects. Cavitation is similar to boiling liquids in that vapor bubbles form in a liquid agitated by a vibrator. An ultrasonic generating system is used for inducing cavitation. The high-energy bubbles produced have the effect of etching a metal surface. It is a rapid and very effective method for serial number recovery.[16]

Lasers (argon-ion or copper-vapor) are widely used in the detection of latent fingerprints. Recently, laser examination of questioned documents has been found to be useful in some alteration or obliteration cases. Laser examination can reveal information unattainable by any conventional nondestructive means.[17]

The equipment found in crime laboratories is extensive. Basic cameras, microscopes, spectrographs, and fluoroscopes are being supplemented by computers and space-age devices. As new equipment is obtained and used by laboratory technicians, the director of the laboratory informs local police managers of the additional services available. Investigators should be alert to these changes in the availability of such services and use them whenever it is in the best interest of an investigation.

VOICEPRINT IDENTIFICATION

Voiceprinting is the graphical identification of voices. Voiceprints are an innovative concept in personal identification and are fast becoming useful tools in criminal investigation. Their use is limited only by the adaptation of this new technique to the many areas of verbal communication encountered in an investigation.

Voiceprint identification is based on the physical characteristics of each individual's vocal cavities (the throat, mouth, nose, and sinuses) and the manner of manipulating the lips, teeth, tongue, soft palate, and jaw muscles. It is a technique of personal identification that may challenge fingerprints as the most positive means of personal identification. Chances are quite low that any two individuals have precisely the same size vocal cavities and have learned to use their articulators in the same manner. To date, this premise has survived some thousands of attempts to disprove it. Efforts to disguise the voice or to imitate the voice of another have been easily discerned. Whispering, muffling, nose holding—even filling the mouth with marbles—can be detected.

Suspect voices are recorded on a good-quality tape recorder. Known standards for comparison also are tape recorded. Tape recordings are fed into a specially designed spectrograph that reacts to the sound of the recorded voice and produces a voiceprint in much the same way as the polygraph produces a chart. The voice spectrograph reacts to voice frequency, to volume, and to the timing of a person's speech. Voiceprint techniques of identification are particularly applicable to the identification of voices involved in kidnappings, obscene language telephone calls, and telephoned threats.

Automatic methods of voice identification are being developed. This machine-aided speaker recognition will be used for naming, identifying, or distinguishing the speaker who has produced a given voice sample from other speakers. This is a mechanized, computerized extension of the ability of people to recognize voices. Speech samples will be processed for their unique features and categorized by these extracted features. Recognition will be automatic and will be based on digital computer technology rather than on the skill of a technician, user, or operator.[18]

CRYPTOGRAPHY

The use of simple ciphers and codes to protect the security of messages—**cryptography**—is increasing in the world of crime. It is common in unlawful gambling cases where records of wagers made by customers must be kept. It is used by organized crime personnel because written communications have been found to be less susceptible to investigative examination than telephone conversations. It is also likely to be used in communications among extremist groups planning crimes, as well as by various types of offenders who want to protect the security of personal telephone and memo books.

The most common cipher in use by criminals is a simple **substitution cipher** in which a symbol, letter, or digit stands for another symbol, letter, or digit. The simplistic thinking of many criminals confines the substitution to some simple order, such as 1 represents A, 2 represents B, 3 represents C, and so on. **Transposition ciphers** are characterized by a change in the order of the enciphered material. Investigators find it fairly common in recording telephone numbers. This may be a **reversal transposition** in which the telephone number 445-1769 becomes 967-1544, or any **split combination**, for example, 176-4459, 769-4451, 544-1769, and so on. Of help to investigators is the fact that most criminals are amateurs in cipher work, and the solution of their ciphers is a simple matter. A criminal does not have access to the few sources of information available about ciphers, and when he or she sits down to evolve a cipher, no one is there to tell the person that his or her invention is, in truth, hundreds of years old.[19]

A stolen bonds fraud case involving members of the Mafia in a typical national crime syndicate operation with international overtones was successfully solved by federal agents when a key to a code was found hidden in the wallet of one of the gang members. The code had been used in cable communications between members in New York and London to communicate secretly to name the denomination of stolen bonds available for sale and the asking price. Court action by the federal district attorney brought the records of these communications into court, and the knowledge of the code key made their content intelligible to the trial jury and showed the joint action of the conspiracy.

Investigators can learn to solve simple substitution or transposition ciphers by running down the alphabet with the first eight or ten letters of the message and then testing for substitution. This requires substituting letters one further on in the alphabet in the first run-through, then two further on in the second testing, and so on. This means to try b for a, then c for a, and so on. Julius Caesar is said to have used a cipher based on the simple substitution of a letter three letters further on in the alphabet. Simple transposition ciphers can be solved by trial and error when the enciphered work or numerical prefix in telephone numbers is known or suspected. Telephone and memo book codes usually are solved by using the local telephone exchange prefix of three numbers to break the method of transposition by trial and error. A **frequency distribution study** will solve more complex ciphers, but this requires the work of experts with tables of letter and word frequencies. However, an investigator may break a complex cipher or code if he or she has some preknowledge or can guess that a certain word is likely to appear in the message and then looks for this word.[20]

When the use of a cipher or code is suspected, the investigator should attempt to collect as much of the suspected writing as possible and to ascertain the languages and skills with which the defendant is familiar. Knowing the language fluency of the suspect and whether he or she has any particular skill, such as stenography, printing, piano playing, or the like, may be helpful in deciphering the communication because these areas of skill or experience often form the base of the cipher or code scheme. When expert assistance is required, the enciphered material should be forwarded to the police laboratory in the same manner as other questioned documents, with the relevant data noted under the details of the case, along with some of the possible words likely to be frequently used in the enciphered communications.

CASE STUDY

Child Abduction

Twelve-year-old Courtney left home around 2:00 p.m. to go to the local convenience store two blocks away. She was reportedly seen there at about 2:15 p.m. talking to a man who was seated in a dark-colored BMW. At about 7:00 p.m., when she did not return home, her parents reported her missing. More than twenty officers and volunteers began a neighborhood search, knocking on doors in the area in an effort to find her.

Searchers did not know that Courtney's body had already been found in an adjoining county some 25 miles away. At about 5:30 p.m., some fishermen approached a spot on the river by boat, which was near the highway. As they approached they noticed a subject running away from the beach, leaving behind a body. The beach where the body was found is a popular spot to fish, drink beer, fire guns, and dump dead bodies. The beach averages two to three bodies a year. A search of the crime scene disclosed some key pieces of evidence: a sun visor, boxer shorts, and sunglasses that the suspect had left behind.

Eight months after Courtney was slain, an arrest was made in the case. More than 1,200 possible suspects were considered and subsequently eliminated. Investigators traced the sun visor's lot number back to its source and were able to determine that twenty such visors had been sold in the area. Detectives then began tracking down the buyers through credit card receipts and by asking for DNA samples. One visor purchase that had been made near the time of the abduction and slaying was particularly interesting. This purchaser was already under investigation for allegedly advertising in Internet chat rooms that he had child pornography to trade. When investigators went to his residence to talk to him, they determined that he had left town and was somewhere in New Mexico.

Investigators posted a "Be on the lookout" notice for this subject on the **National Crime Information Computer (NCIC) system.** When the subject, a twenty-year-old male, was arrested a few days later for walking out of a restaurant without paying for his meal, the arresting officers ran his name through NCIC, were alerted to the notice, and contacted the case investigators.

Two detectives flew to Albuquerque to question the suspect and to obtain a DNA sample. This sample was later matched to the DNA materials found at the scene where Courtney was sexually assaulted and strangled. At the time of his arrest, the suspect was driving a dark-colored BMW. The vehicle was searched and determined to contain three newspaper stories on Courtney's death. The search also revealed an adult magazine that had faces of young girls pasted over those of the adult nude models. Investigators stated no evidence indicates that the suspect knew the victim prior to her death, and they speculated that she may have been abducted at random.

CHAPTER REVIEW

KEY TERMS

allele 88
base pair 87
chromatography 94
CODIS (Combined DNA
   Index System) 89
criminalistics 86
cryptography 97
forensic science
   laboratory 86
forensic scientist 86
frequency distribution
   study 98
gamma-ray
   spectrometer 95

genome 88
identification 86
lasers 96
National Crime
   Information Computer
   (NCIC) system 99
neutron activation
   analysis (NAA) 94
nucleotide 87
polymerase chain
   reaction (PCR)
   analysis 88
reversal transposition 97
set theory 97

short tandem
   repeats (STR) 88
spectrography 94
spectrum 94
split combination 97
substitution cipher 97
trace metal detection
   technique (TMDT) 96
transposition cipher 97
ultrasonic cavitation 96
voiceprinting 96
X-ray crystallography 94
X-ray diffraction 94

REVIEW QUESTIONS

1. Which piece of laboratory equipment would be used to determine the elements contained within mineral samples?
   a. Spectrograph
   b. Chromatograph
   c. Neutron activation analysis
   d. Ultrasonic cavitation

2. The piece of laboratory equipment that is capable of identifying the components in compounds is the:
   a. Spectrograph
   b. Chromatograph
   c. Neutron activation analysis
   d. Ultrasonic cavitation

3. Which technique is useful in determining if a suspect or victim has recently
fired a handgun?
   a. Spectrograph
   b. Chromatograph
   c. Neutron activation analysis
   d. Ultrasonic cavitation

4. Which piece of laboratory equipment
would be effective for serial number
recovery?
   a. Spectrograph
   b. Chromatograph
   c. Neutron activation analysis
   d. Ultrasonic cavitation

5. Criminals often use codes and ciphers
to protect the security of their messages
and transactions. The deciphering of
such information is known as:
   a. Cavitation
   b. Crystallography
   c. Chromatography
   d. Cryptography

6. Many DNA samples are either contaminated, degraded, or in small quantity.
These problems are overcome by the
_____ process.

7. Differences within a particular segment
of a DNA sequence are known as:
   a. Genome
   b. Alleles

   c. Polymerase chain reaction
   d. CODIS

8. DNA is found in all cells that contain a
nucleus. Each nucleated cell contains
the full complement of an individual's
DNA, which is called the:
   a. Genome
   b. Alleles
   c. Polymerase chain reaction
   d. CODIS

9. The state DNA data banks are linked
together by the FBI to form a national
DNA data bank known as:
   a. Genome
   b. Alleles
   c. Polymerase chain reaction
   d. CODIS

10. The professional name for employees in
a forensic laboratory who conduct the
scientific examinations is:
   a. Criminalist
   b. Criminalistics
   c. Laboratory technicians
   d. Forensic science laboratory

See Appendix D for the correct answers.

DISCUSSION QUESTIONS

1. Are laboratory personnel handicapped by the legal precept that the admissibility of any
scientific process in relation to evidence must be tested against acceptance of the scientific principle involved?
2. Is there any difference between the terms *forensic science* and *criminalistics*? How does
medicolegal differ from *criminalistics*?
3. Cite similarities and differences in the determinations of a criminalist and the findings
of an autopsy surgeon.
4. Project the likely growth and development of laboratory services.
5. Who decides the best strategy (or strategies) for the forensic science examination(s) of
physical evidence?

6. Describe spectrographic analysis; trace metal detection technique; ultrasonic cavitation.
7. Do criminalists make truly scientific and objective determinations?
8. Discuss the perspectives for voiceprinting in criminal investigation.
9. Explain the meaning of one word or phrase used by criminalists in describing comparison analysis determinations.
10. Define a physical match in relation to the laboratory examination of physical evidence.
11. What was the role of DNA analysis in the case study?

RELATED WEB SITES

To learn more about crime laboratory services, consult the FBI's lab home page at *www.fbi.gov/hqs/lab/labhome.htm.*

Interested in becoming a criminalist? The American Academy of Forensic Science lists employment opportunities on its Web site: *www.aafs.org.*

Answers to the most frequently asked questions regarding cryptography can be found at this Web site: *www.faqs.org/faqs/cryptography-faq.*

chapter **six**

Basic Investigative Leads and Informants

CHAPTER OUTLINE

After reading this chapter you will be able to:

- Appreciate the importance of field contact reports as an investigative lead.
- Explain how stolen property can be traced back to the person, or persons, responsible for its theft.
- Discuss how offender registration is used in the investigation of crime.

- Describe the process that is used to identify links between persons engaged in criminal activity.
- List the various types of informants and their motivation for informing others involved in criminal activity.

The problem of "Who did it?" is a simple one when the offender is caught in the act or apprehended in flight from the scene shortly after the crime. When the perpetrator is not promptly arrested, the direction of the investigation varies according to which of two categories the case falls into—known identity or unknown identity. The case is one of **known identity** when the perpetrator is known and has been named by the victim or witnesses. All other cases are of **unknown identity**. Cases involving named suspects constitute a high percentage of the cases cleared by arrest in any police agency. In these cases, the principal lead to the perpetrator's identity has been furnished by the victim or witnesses. The challenge to the skill of any investigator is the case without a named suspect. In such cases the basic investigative leads must be developed by the investigator to reveal the identity of the perpetrator.

Motive and opportunity (or presence) are broad areas of investigation basic to any crime. The people and things involved in a crime offer leads to the identity, motive, and opportunity of any perpetrator, known or unknown.

BASIC LEADS

The victim offers the initial basic lead. The background of the victim furnishes data, as do his or her activities just before the crime. A group of suspects can be developed by inquiring about who would benefit from the crime and who had the requisite knowledge about the target—the object of the crime. Field contact reports of interviews by patrol officers at and about the time and place of the crime offer data about suspects and sometimes about vehicles. When motor vehicles or weapons are involved in a crime, inquiries often link these material things with their owners or users. Latent fingerprints and other trace evidence found at crime scenes confirm that a suspect has been at the scene and indicate opportunity. Another trace of a presence at the crime scene is the manner in which the crime was committed—the modus operandi. Sometimes recovered stolen property can be traced to the thief. Police records of persons previously arrested contain photographs that can be viewed by witnesses when investigators develop suspicions about the identity of suspects. When photographs are not available, composite drawings may be used. Finally, injuries characteristic of certain crimes furnish leads that often help to link a suspect to a crime (Figure 6–1).

Experienced investigators dislike associating the development of investigation leads with any intuitive process; they believe that a hunch is out of place when dealing with people. Developing leads is a combination of know-how, the cognitive process, and an ability to work rapidly. Time is of the essence in criminal investigation and has an effect upon witnesses and investigators. It gives the criminal an opportunity to dispose of evidence, to

FIGURE 6–1   This composite sketch resulted in prompt identification of the shooter in a double homicide committed outside Central Intelligence Agency (CIA) headquarters in Virginia. From Fairfax County Police Department, Fairfax, VA, in "Report to the Chairman, Commerce, Consumer, and Monetary Affairs Subcommittee, Committee on Government Operations, House of Representatives: Bureau of Alcohol, Tobacco & Firearms Handling of Suspect Lead in Langley/CIA Headquarters Shooting Incident" (Washington, DC: U.S. Government Accounting Office, April 1994), 10.

develop defenses against the shock of being arrested, or to get farther away if he or she is in flight. No time can be lost making inquiries indicated by the basic leads of a case.

In cases of known identity, the objective is to corroborate the story of the eyewitness. The investigator follows the basic investigative leads, but particular effort is also made to corroborate the eyewitness's stories. In addition, parallel inquiries are pursued to avoid error in identity and to make the case compelling rather than subject to doubt.

In cases of unknown identity the objective is to develop suspects by following the basic investigative leads with the goal of identifying the perpetrator. The action is oriented to expanding the universe of suspects, to identifying prime suspects, and to finding the guilty person or persons among the prime suspects.

Keep in mind that determining who committed the crime should not terminate the investigation. All elements of the crime must be proved beyond a reasonable doubt. Some crimes present unique elements or possible defenses. The investigation should continue until all evidence, positive or negative, is gathered to prove the crime, to identify the perpetrator, and to disprove, when possible, defenses such as justification, excuse, lack of specific intent, lack of malice, diminished capacity, intoxication, ignorance, error, insanity, and the like.

Basic leads suggest lines of inquiry likely to provide an investigator with information (Figure 6–2). **Active information** leads to the establishment of a group of suspects. The strength of the information accumulated against each member of this group depends on the nature of the evidence, but it may indicate prime suspects. **Passive information** is associative evidence that can be of use only if a group of suspects has been developed. Passive information often confirms suspicions against a person as a prime suspect by associating him or her with the crime scene or the victim. These basic types of information lead

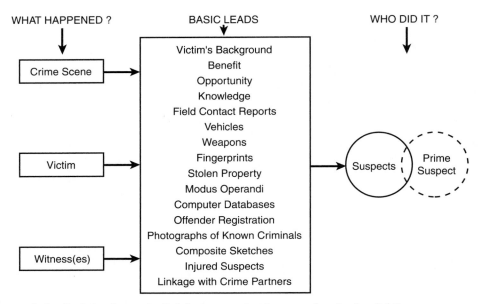

FIGURE 6–2   Basic leads are the link between what happened and who did it.

by two routes to sufficient evidence to reveal the person or persons who are guilty of the crime being investigated.[1]

VICTIM'S BACKGROUND

Police investigators have been criticized for cross-examining a victim and for probing his or her background and relationship to the crime. To the uninitiated, prying information from the unfortunate victim of a crime instead of promptly taking up the hue and cry for the perpetrator seems unjustifiable. However, a chase without a clearly defined objective is just aimless activity. Very promising leads can be developed from a review of the background of the victim, which can give the pursuit defined goals.

Many classic avenues can be probed in regard to the victim. The following are some of these classic queries:

1. Did the victim know the perpetrator? If so, what is the relationship?
2. Does the victim suspect any person? Why?
3. Has the victim a history of crime? A history of reporting crimes?
4. Did the victim have a weapon?
5. Has the victim an aggressive personality?
6. Has the victim been the subject of any field contact reports?
7. What is the license number and description of the victim's car?
8. Was the victim mistaken for someone else?

This does not mean that an investigation of crime should boomerang into an investigation of the victim. However, any fact of significance about the victim should be unearthed at this stage of an investigation inasmuch as it may contribute a vital basic lead, and it may aid in the future evaluation of the case by the prosecuting attorney.

BENEFIT

The question of who might **benefit** from a crime provides an excellent focus for making inquiry. The factor of benefit often can provide investigative leads. In homicide cases, the motive of jealousy or elimination is a standard avenue of inquiry. Whenever a wife or husband dies and the death is unexplained, the survivor is suspect. Necessary action is taken to discover the classic love triangle. If a third party is involved, the triangle is considered a promising lead. In arson cases, the benefit may be complex: a rational motivation for financial gain in fraudulent fires of insured premises or an irrational motivation in psychopathic fire setting.

These are particularized motives in that the identity of the perpetrator can be deduced from the exposure of a relationship to the victim or the crime. Generally, the relationships between the victim in homicides and persons who might benefit from the fact of death are most productive in providing significant leads. The more universal motives of profit and sexual release common to burglaries, robberies, rapes, and other sex crimes usually do not offer investigators specific leads about the identity of the person who will benefit from the crime.[2]

OPPORTUNITY

Searching for and identifying persons with the **opportunity** to commit a crime is a valid basic lead. Admitted or suspected presence at the scene of a crime at or about the time of its occurrence may be no more than an immediate investigative aid, but it is a lead.

When offenders know they are suspected of being at the crime scene and thus vulnerable to this "opportunity" line of inquiry, they often fabricate an **alibi**—a claim of being elsewhere. Investigation into an alibi will often disclose any fabrication, justifying other inquiries directed at this suspect. However, an effective alibi does not summarily exclude a suspect from further screening.

KNOWLEDGE

In theft cases, the victim is questioned about the identity of persons who might know their way about the premises and about the presence and location of articles of value. This is done in order to establish who may have had the **knowledge** necessary for committing the crime. In armed robberies, the victim is questioned about the identity of persons who knew of the routine of the victim or the business firm victimized. This tracing of knowledge provides a natural group of suspects, including the following:

1. Persons who have access to the premises at which the crime occurred or who are familiar with them

2. Persons who knew of the value and place of storage of property or the routine of the victim or the business victimized, such as:

   a. any present employee or spouse
   b. any former employee or spouse
   c. service and maintenance personnel (those employed in the area or the building, or those making frequent service deliveries)
   d. neighbors
   e. criminals with contacts among the persons with knowledge

3. Persons noticed in the area or on the premises recently who were:

   a. acting strangely (sex cases, fires, homicides)
   b. applying for work, soliciting sales, conducting surveys, etc.

Possession of the knowledge needed to commit a crime suggests possession also of the skill and capacity to have done it. What kind of criminal could accomplish the crime under investigation? Did it require a special (an identifying) skill, such as using a torch to open a safe or knowledge of the fast-cutting action of demolition-type burning bars? Did it require a special knowledge in a trade or occupation? The use of the hydraulic jimmy suggests a person who has worked in body and fender shops where this device is used to pry apart bent fenders and who knows about this tool's fast and powerful push-and-heave action. Did the crime require a person who was not afraid to kill, such as the cat burglar who enters occupied homes—even occupied bedrooms?

The multiple murders of the Clutter family in Kansas would have been solved months earlier if the basic lead of former employees had been pursued. Floyd Wells, a prisoner in Kansas State Prison, had worked on the Clutter ranch and had mentioned the extent of the ranch to a cell mate. The murders took place shortly after the release of the cell mate. Wells, weeks after the crime, identified himself as a former employee of the victims and supplied the authorities with a basic lead that identified one of the two killers. A check of this man's associates led to a rapid identification of his crime partner.[3]

FIELD CONTACT REPORTS

Field contacts are an aggressive police patrol tactic. **Field contact reports** record the stop-and-frisk interviews with persons stopped in their cars or on foot because of their suspicious appearance or actions. These reports place in police records the names and the descriptions of the persons coming to police attention and the time, date, and place they were seen and interviewed. These reports are confidential in that they are not disclosed to the public but are filed in police records systems for the use of investigators. The data on who was in the vicinity and where and when are valuable aids to investigators seeking basic leads. Field contacts represent a broad surveillance involving observations of an entire patrol sector by an alert assigned officer. Often an investigator confronted with a burglary without apparent clues to the identity of the offender will find a field contact report describing a known thief being stopped in the early morning hours not more than a few blocks from the crime scene. An apparently innocent suspect in a sex case who pleads that he hardly ever leaves his home at night may be revealed by field contacts to be a nocturnal roamer in the city's parks.

For the purpose of revealing group identification, some police units have an automated filing system for field contact cards about youngsters under seventeen or eighteen years of age. Because most juvenile crimes are committed by groups, this cross-reference offers information about the associates of an offender. When the field contact cards of a juvenile are requested, these group associations should be probed for basic leads along the lines of race, sex, age, and associates of previous arrests.

VEHICLES

There is no better clue to the identity of a criminal than the identification of a vehicle. True, time is important when a stolen vehicle is used because professional bank robbers and other criminals who plan their crimes with care abandon the getaway car before an alarm can be broadcast. However, two killers of a police officer were once observed as they changed cars, and thus a crucial basic lead that led to their arrest was gained.

Even a fragmentary description of a vehicle is often helpful. In a series of bank robberies in northern California, the robber walked away from his crimes. The first basic lead offering any promise followed the third robbery in which a witness noticed a man acting suspiciously while going from a bank to the parking lot. The witness could offer only a fragment of a license number: EPC. Federal Bureau of Investigation (FBI) agents sought help from the California Department of Motor Vehicles, which yielded no results. Then the "EPC" fragment was checked against reports of cars stopped at barricades set up after each robbery. The agents found one promising lead. A car with registration letters CPC had been stopped and passed through a roadblock. Again motor vehicle records were scanned. The vehicle was registered to William Liebscher, Jr., a used car dealer. Motor vehicle files provided an in-the-course-of-business exemplar of Liebscher's signature on a registration application. Agents compared it with another basic lead previously useless for lack of a suspect: the handwriting on a fictitious money order dropped by the robber at one of the crime scenes. The handwriting was similar. Other evidence corroborated these leads, and Liebscher was arrested and convicted.

Enterprising detectives scan stolen vehicle reports for similarities with the descriptions of cars used in crime. The anxious criminal who used his or her own car may become worried that the vehicle has been seen by witnesses and abandons it. Then, after an appropriate interval, he or she reports it stolen. The criminal hopes to throw off suspicion by such action if the car had been identified with the crime. Usually, the fragments of description are not enough to locate a vehicle, but they are sufficient for alert detectives when a criminal directs attention to an automobile by reporting it lost.

Motor vehicle records are statewide records filed under name and license (registration) number. Often a name not known to be used by the suspect under investigation is detected in searching for the owner of a vehicle used in a crime or known to be operated by the suspect. Motor vehicle records may contain a thumbprint or a photograph or both, and they usually will have some physical description of a licensed operator. Both owner and operator records usually contain a person's date of birth, previous residence, and dates of residence at such locations. Accident and violation reports, cross-indexed to these basic motor vehicle records, may reveal something of the activities of the suspect, such as dates and locations of accidents and driving record.

Of importance to investigators is the finality of identification possible using motor vehicles as a basic lead. Time and again the suspect's shock upon learning that he or she has been identified has led to full cooperation with police and a plea of guilty.

WEAPONS

Clubs and other blunt instruments are rarely engraved with an owner's name, but firearms are marked with a maker's name and a serial number, and their ownership often can be traced through sales and firearm registration records. The lead developed from such tracing may reveal that the weapon was stolen, but this fact links the crime under investigation with another crime—and that is a basic lead.

The ownership of knives often can be identified, even though knives are not marked with serial numbers. Clubs and other striking weapons often provide promising leads to identity. Poisons and drugs used in crimes sometimes can be traced, and the purchase of dynamite is often traced in bomb cases.

Bullets and fired cartridge cases, pattern wounds, and the distinctive effects of several poisons provide passive information useful for associating a suspect, when identified, with a crime.

FINGERPRINTS

Fingerprints found at crime scenes have a very high potential for identifying perpetrators of crime once the imprints of the victim and other nonsuspects are screened out. Searching for these chance imprints at crime scenes is emphasized more and more. Latent imprints, normally invisible, are developed by dusting various surfaces at the crime scene with contrasting fingerprint powders or by iodine fuming. The increase in the use of evidence technicians at crime scenes has resulted in more effective searches for these hidden fingerprints.

Computerized fingerprint searching systems permit a rapid scanning of thousands of ten-finger records against chance imprints found at crime scenes. Police expertise at other police agencies is developing slower, but equally effective, procedures for the rapid comparison of fingerprints found at crime scenes with the fingerprints of known offenders on file:

1. Crime-scene fingerprints are determined to be of value or of no value. Imprints of value have an adequate number of identifying characteristics.
2. Crime-scene fingerprints are compared with the imprints of persons who are legally at the scene: victim, witnesses, police, and other known visitors.

3. Fingerprints on file are searched to identify the suspect making the crime scene fingerprint(s):

   a. **Request search**. The investigator assigned to the case names one or more suspects and asks for a search.

   b. **Single-digit search**. Identification technicians search such files as those containing other crime-scene fingerprints or the ten-digit fingerprints of repeat or career criminals.

   c. **Cold search**. Identification technicians search through an entire ten-digit fingerprint file. Unless the police agency is small or has a computerized search capability, the scope of this cold search should be reduced to (1) known criminals operating in the same geographical area or with the same modus operandi and (2) recent arrestees.[4]

Of importance is the finality of identification in this area. Fingerprints found at crime scenes reveal the opportunity or presence factor—which provides an important lead. When fingerprints pinpoint a person with a history of like crimes or link the suspect with other latents from another crime, the lead is significant.

STOLEN PROPERTY

A search for stolen property is a search for identifiable items. Police have been using this technique skillfully for so many years that it is sometimes overlooked as a routine, albeit successful, technique. Novice investigators are not aware of its potential value until they have worked on cases in which stolen property has been recovered. In tracing its possession, they have noted the ease with which the identity of the burglar or thief has been developed.

Tracing the proceeds of a theft is facilitated by the establishment of special investigative squads whose duties are to visit pawnshops, secondhand dealers, junk shops, and other places where stolen property is likely to be offered for sale and to coordinate the local search for locally stolen property. It is also supported by laws in many states and municipalities that require the pawnbroker to report to the police the pawning or purchase of specific secondhand merchandise (guns, watches, televisions, VCRs, computers, and other articles that are commonly stolen). These laws often require places of business handling such merchandise to maintain a log or register of their business, describing each item purchased. This record is open to police inspection at any time. The level of cooperation extended to police by many such business managers—often far above the legal demands—results in the recovery of vast amounts of stolen property. In some cities, pawnshop proprietors have personally defrayed the cost of hotlines to, and silent alarms in, nearby police stations for prompt notification of offerings by suspicious persons.

The Sacramento County Sheriff's Department has established a database of information supplied by pawnshop dealers. This information includes the date of transaction, description of the item, and name and address of the person pawning it. A compilation of all transactions for that month is printed and sent to investigators. It was noted that a woman had pawned eight different wedding rings in one month. Another individual had pawned a number of televisions and VCRs at various pawnshops around the city. This information supplied investigators with important investigative leads beyond the theft and burglary investigations that might have started a search for stolen property.

A computerized stolen property record system within a police department will make possible the following:

1. Shorten the time required to search these reports for items of stolen property
2. Allow for searches leading to the identity of persons who frequently sell or pawn used property
3. Offer opportunities—long after a crime has been committed—to locate stolen office equipment by periodic examination of the records of the repair services of manufacturers (authorized agents)[5]

Serial numbers and other positive identifying data necessary for the recovery of property are not always available from the victim of a theft. It may be necessary for the victim (or the investigator) to visit the store in which the property was purchased. Most merchants keep a detailed record of sales. When jewelry and furs are stolen, merchants can provide information regarding scratch marks on items of jewelry or hidden identifications stamped on the inside lining of fur garments or on the skins themselves. These merchants, along with pawn brokers, sometimes mark this type of property when it passes through their establishments for repair or cleaning or as collateral for a cash loan. Markings often are hidden, require information about where to look for them, or must be viewed with ultraviolet light. Happily, when skilled thieves believe they have removed all labels and identifying marks from stolen property, such markings may remain for the investigator's use.

No assumptions should be made in regard to describing identifying characteristics of stolen property. Recovery depends on identification. For example, when jewelry is described, it is better to state the appearance of the metal and stones than to assume a basic classification. What is described by a victim as a yellow gold ring is best detailed in a wanted notice as a yellow metal ring, and the diamonds and rubies said to be part of the setting of such rings are best described as white and red stones of a particular size and cut. Stolen property notices sometimes contain lengthy listings of stolen property, and for this reason these notices are indexed by number to each item of property listed, starting with number one. Investigators also group property within this numbered sequence in general classifications, such as jewelry, clothing, and furs. In communicating with agencies locating the property, this numbering system aids in identification and shortens the necessary communication among agencies. Know-how based on experience and some intuition can lead an investigator to the prompt recovery of stolen property and may thereby offer a valuable investigative lead.

The process for verifying the use of stolen credit cards is similar to tracing stolen goods. It is a trail that offers many opportunities for basic leads. Large commercial organizations issuing credit cards are generally not local because a central accounting office provides nationwide coverage. However, billing procedures may provide effective assistance in tracing fugitives, which more than justifies the labor of communicating with these organizations.

Because gasoline is a prime credit card purchase, local service station dealers may be able to provide information about a suspect and the use of a credit card. Recent receipts, not yet forwarded to the central accounting office, may still be available at gas stations and may reveal the name of the purchaser, the credit card number, and the name of the gasoline company handling the account. Credit card accounts will reveal recent billings and may show the activity of a suspect on the days when purchases were charged to the credit card. Problems resulting from loss, theft, and misuse of credit cards have led to improved attention to security among the accounting personnel of these firms, and their cooperation with police is excellent.

MODUS OPERANDI

The choice of a particular crime to commit and the selection of a method of committing it is the **modus operandi** of a criminal. Not all criminals have a particular modus operandi, but enough of them have distinctive methods of operation to justify classifying crimes by their like characteristics. The modus operandi of a criminal is his or her **signature**.

For this reason, investigators compare the manner in which a crime was committed with relevant records stored in the modus operandi section of the police record systems. If any of these comparisons are successful, the detective secures data on possible suspects. The use of modus operandi by police agencies is both current and extensive. Its successful use in robbery, burglary, grand theft, fraud, sex offense, and fraudulent check cases amounts to a mandate to search the modus operandi files for basic leads in these crimes.

A modus operandi file contains information about the methods of operation of known criminals and the methods used in unsolved crimes. This file has three major capabilities:

1. Identifying a perpetrator by naming suspects whose modus operandi in past crimes fits the facts of the crime being investigated
2. Linking an unknown perpetrator with the modus operandi of past crimes committed by unknown perpetrators for the purpose of structuring the identity of a suspect from the modus operandi and leads from several connected crimes
3. Storing data on unsolved crimes according to modus operandi to allow comparison with the crime technique of an apprehended criminal and unresolved crimes with an arrestee

Of course, past offenses and the way they were committed must be sufficiently similar to be meaningful. They must possess a number of common features with a crime under investigation to warrant the inference that if the suspect committed the other acts, he or she must have committed the act being investigated. Similarities in methods of operation (in combination with other basic leads) also constitute an important tool in the realm of identity, for they decrease the likelihood of a claim of a mistake, or a real mistake, in suspecting a person of crime.

COMPUTER DATABASES

At the local level, the computer databases of police and sheriff's departments contain information regarding who has been victimized and where, as well as wanted person, criminal history, and stolen property information. At the state or regional level, motor vehicle files can be accessed for driver's license, registered vehicle, and stolen vehicle and vessel information. Other statewide or regional databases may contain wanted person, stolen property, and firearms registry files.

The National Crime Information Center (NCIC) (see Chapter 5) is the computer system dedicated to serving the needs of law enforcement throughout the United States, Mexico, and Canada. Operated by the FBI, the system processed 2 million inquiries in its first year of operation in 1967. Today the system handles 2.5 million inquiries a day, most of which are generated by local law enforcement officials. The system was upgraded in the year 2000 and now contains files or databases on wanted persons, stolen property, criminal histories, missing and unidentified persons, convicted sexual offender registrations, and convicted persons on supervised release. This system is now supported by digital images. Upon request the system can provide mugshots, fingerprints, signature samples, and as many as ten identifying photographs on wanted, missing, or unidentified persons. Photographs can also be attached to identify stolen vehicles, boats, or other property. The system has the ability to match fingerprint records and to link related records across associated NCIC files for the same crime or criminal.[6]

The **National Integrated Ballistic Information Network (NIBIN)** is a nationwide database deploying ballistic imaging equipment. This system can compare gun evidence, such as projectiles and cartridge cases that are recovered at crime scenes. The system, which is maintained by the **Bureau of Alcohol, Tobacco, Firearms, and Explosives (ATF)** automatically compares each new entry to prior entries and generates a list of potential similar entries. A firearms examiner then examines the evidence to confirm that the cases are linked.[7]

OFFENDER REGISTRATION

In 1994, Congress passed the Jacob Wettering Crimes Against Children and Sexually Violent Offender Registration Act. The act required that states create sex offender registries. Offenders who commit a criminal sexual act against a minor or commit any sexually violent offense must register for a period of ten years from the date of their release from custody or supervision. All fifty states now have sex offender registration laws. In 1996, the act was amended by establishing a national sex offender database that the FBI maintains. This national tracking system gives investigators access to sex offender registration data from all participating states.

Registry information typically includes the offender's name, address, date of birth, Social Security number, and physical description, as well as fingerprints and a photograph. Usually, offenders must register within a certain number of days following their release from custody or placement on supervision. The registration requirement is in effect for at least ten years, with some states requiring lifetime registration for all or some offenses. Most states make it a criminal offense to knowingly fail to register or report subsequent changes in information, such as the registrant's name or address.[8]

California, the first state to pass an offender registration law in 1947, requires convicted arsonists, drug offenders, and sex offenders to register. The drug offender registration terminates five years after discharge from custody or expiration of parole or probation. However, sexual offender and arson offender registration is a lifetime requirement. This registration is required of California residents even if the crime was committed in another state or federal jurisdiction.

XREF#:	**5000324**
Last:	**CARVER**
First:	**DANIEL**
DOB:	**06/06/66**
Sex:	**MALE**
Race:	**WHITE**
Height:	**6'02"**
Weight:	**210**
Hair:	**BLOND**
Eyes:	**GREEN**
Charges:	

Mug shot taken at the time of arrest.

The nationwide **Amber Alert system** is a new law enforcement tool for combating sexual predators. This system aims to assist officers in capturing kidnappers and sexual predators who have recently abducted children. The system disseminates information to the general public about the suspects and their vehicles via highway signs, television spots, and radio broadcasts. The system is named after Amber Hagerman, a nine-year-old Texas girl whose abduction and murder inspired a similar alert system in that state.[9]

PHOTOGRAPHS OF KNOWN CRIMINALS

A search through modus operandi records often provides photographs of suspects made at the time of a previous arrest. These photographs, or **mug shots**, are available, and if the crime being investigated has been witnessed, the investigator has an opportunity to ask an eyewitness to view them. The witness is not asked to identify any photo but is requested to scan no less than a half dozen photographs and to cast out those that offer no resemblance to the perpetrator. When one or more photographs appear to resemble the perpetrator, further inquiry is conducted. The investigator concentrates on the where-abouts of the persons selected as "possibles." It may be that the suspect was in prison, out of town, or living in a distant city at the time of the crime. Every reasonable circumstance that eliminates persons from a group of suspects reduces the group and allows concentration upon the remainder. The investigator or associates also cast out any suspect known to be working and living within his or her means and to have a reputation for no longer being involved with crime.

Mug books are often prepared for specific offenses. The FBI provides photos of known bank robbers to agents investigating bank robberies. These photographs were collected before the crime being investigated happened and thus permit a rapid viewing by an eyewitness of persons who have committed crimes similar to the crime under investigation.

As long as the photographs show five or ten suspects of various types and origins, this practice does not destroy the validity of future testimony of these witnesses. When a photograph of only one person is exhibited to an eyewitness, or when the other photos in the group are of a nature that a single suspect is isolated by some physical or racial characteristic, the future testimony of the witness is compromised. Such a viewing of photographs is likely to be criticized in present-day trial procedures and likened to a conditioning process. The witness may be compromised, and his or her potential credibility toward establishing identity may be ruined. When two or more eyewitnesses are available, it is possible to use one of them to view photographs for basic leads to the identity of the offender and to reserve the remaining witness or witnesses for a later identification. Little justification can be made for ruining the potential of a major witness by having him or her confirm identification at this initial stage.

COMPOSITE SKETCHES FOR IDENTIFICATION

When photographs are not available, the victim and any witnesses may be asked to collaborate with a police artist in developing a **composite sketch** of the suspect. Artists have the skills necessary to develop a portrait of a suspect from the description of a victim or witness or from the descriptions given by several witnesses. The usual procedure is for the artist to make a tentative sketch and then show it to the victim or witness and ask how closely it resembles the suspect. After some trial and error, this collaboration of the artist and the victim or witness frequently results in a drawing that is likely to be of value in identifying the suspect.

Identi-Kit is another visual means for identification through the cooperation of victims and witnesses. An **Identi-Kit system** consists of several hundred plastic slides containing photoreproductions of one small portion of a human face: hairstyle, forehead, eyes, nose, mouth, chin, ear, eyeglasses, and so on. Police personnel trained in the use of an Identi-Kit can work with a victim or witness in developing a composite sketch in accordance with the description and trial-and-error viewing.

Computer software is now available for producing composites created by a witness in response to queries in the computer program. When completed, these composites can be checked against a database of known criminal mug shots using facial recognition software. In the past, the use of composites always relied on someone recognizing that person and coming forward with that information. Facial recognition software, however, measures the spatial relationships among facial features and converts that information into a mathematical map of the face. The computer then picks the most similar set of mathematical features and displays the corresponding faces in an electronic lineup.[10]

INJURED SUSPECTS

In homicides, assaults, and arson cases, the criminal is sometimes bloodied or burned. An injured person may be a basic lead. In most states, physicians are required to report gunshot and knife wounds when patients seek treatment. In some cases, local hospitals are asked to be alert for persons seeking treatment for various injuries. In one case, the investigator believed that blood and a broken glass window suggested a wound with glass in it. The emergency room of the local hospital was requested to report any such wound, and forty-eight hours later a call came in describing "a wound with a great deal of powdered glass." In a rape case, the attacker was surprised in the act and ran off in the dark through a wooded area. Two days later the police received a call about "a patient . . . who did not seek treatment for his broken ankle for two days." An anxious suspect may wash off blood and postpone treatment for a severe injury, but chances are excellent for a basic lead if medical treatment is sought.

Searching for injured persons in developing a group of suspects is similar to an exhaustive search for witnesses. The search may or may not develop information, but this investigative work reveals a determination to follow every reasonable line of inquiry in seeking leads to the identity of the perpetrator.

Similar determination to follow every suggested line of inquiry as basic leads are developed reassures the people of a community that criminals are being sought systematically and also favors exoneration of an innocent person originally suspected of the crime. Diligent inquiry in following up basic leads gathers the active and passive information that will identify "who did it," sometimes will reveal the perpetrator's presence at the crime scene, and often will contribute to an understanding of why the crime was committed.

LINKAGE BETWEEN SUSPECT AND CRIME PARTNERS

When more than one person is responsible for a crime, the assigned investigator must develop the identity of all the individuals involved. An arrested suspect may or may not identify his or her crime partners. An identified but unapprehended suspect may be located by identifying and locating one or more crime partners.

While crime partnerships may be based on the underworld skills of an individual (ability to neutralize burglar alarms, getaway-car driving skills, torch capability for opening safes and locked boxes), they also depend on mutual trust and compatibility. When crime is a person's business, partnerships are only formed with someone who is known, liked, and trusted.

The following are six types of relationships that form strong personal **linkages** between persons engaged in criminal activity:

1. *Neighborhood friendships.*   These friendships may date from early childhood, such as from membership in a youth gang, or the social interactions among neighboring families and members of ethnic groups.

2. *Juvenile hall and prison contacts.*   Incarceration in a correctional facility brings persons who are convicted of a crime, or who are adjudicated as delinquents and made wards of a children's court, into close contact. Many of these contacts ripen into friendships that can be traced through juvenile institutions to prisons for adult offenders. Inmates band together with others they trust.

3. *Family relationships.*   Many persons have a strong sense of family trust and loyalty, which may be extended to persons without kinship linkage who have exercised some form of unofficial parental control, guidance, or support.

4. *Coethnic contacts.*   In ghetto neighborhoods, juvenile halls, and prisons, each ethnic group tends to band together, which is similar emotionally to family relationships.

5. *Buyer–seller interactions.*   This is a business relationship between the person wanting the crime committed for profit and the criminal actor. The common type of buyer–seller relationships are the business owner and the torch, the planner of a murder and the hit man, and the receiver of stolen property and the thief.

6. *Lovers.*   An identifiable and often easily traced relationship is one between husband and wife (legal or common law); a triangle relationship in which a lover of either sex is added to the husband–wife duo; and heterosexuals or homosexuals living together or otherwise identified as lovers.

When basic investigative leads do not disclose the identity of a crime partner, investigators must probe among the common kinds of relationships for "possibles."

The investigator who probes a criminal or personal relationship may gain information that is meaningful to the success of the investigation. Few relationships can survive the temptation of **"better him than me."** Ethnic gangs have their informants or potential informants; prison friendships may succumb to self-preservation; families often have hidden internal hostilities; and the instances of lovers grown cold are legion.

INFORMANTS

Informants have long been a source of information to investigators seeking basic leads to a crime under investigation (Figure 6–3). In fact, one class of informants has been termed the **basic-lead informant**. However, informants are not basic leads but rather a means through which basic leads can be developed. One criticism of criminal investigation in its early years was that police investigators were prone to rely on informants when solving crimes and paid

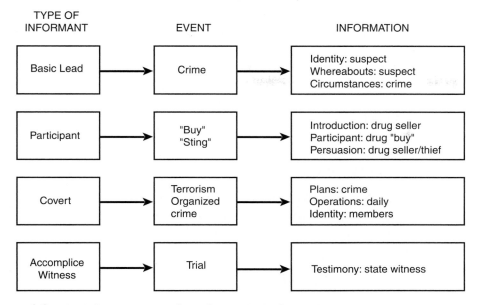

FIGURE 6–3   An informant network used in a criminal investigation.

little or no attention to processing the crime scene or to following up on available basic leads. Today, the starting point in investigating any crime is a thorough examination of the crime scene, if known, and scrutinization of the basic leads discovered in the course of this examination. The follow-up investigation picks up these data and expands and develops them. Investigators no longer depend on informants, but they do seek help from the general public in locating anyone with information about the crime under investigation.

Revealing other people's secrets is **snitching**. In the world of crime and criminals, snitching is a social felony. When a crime partner reveals his or her associates to police investigators and becomes a prosecution witness at subsequent court proceedings, he or she has committed treachery in the eyes of the underworld.

Words long used to describe individuals who inform police are denigrating. They tend to disparage the character or reputation of the informer: snitch, tipster, stool, stool pigeon, rat, canary. More recently, police investigators have employed *informant* as a generalized—and euphemistic—term. Anyone can be an informant. Most informants can testify in a criminal trial as long as they are acceptable as witnesses and their testimony meets the rules of admissibility.

Informants generally wish to remain anonymous. They particularly want to avoid the public identification inherent in becoming a witness for the prosecution. It is, therefore, especially important to conceal the identity of informers or to protect them from attack once their identity is disclosed because professional criminals are willing to maim or kill informants. It is difficult to conceal cooperation because criminals use every available source to learn the identity of informants.

Because the investigator relinquishes his or her basic role and seeks the help of criminals or persons associating with criminals, the use of informants is a questionable option in criminal investigation. Even noncriminal informants are often less objective than they claim. Some of their more common motivations for snitching are less than benevolent: hatred, revenge, jealousy, greed.

Informing is a dirty business because informants may lie to implicate innocent persons or to exculpate a favored crime partner. Inherent in some forms of snitching is that the snitch trades his or her version of what happened during a crime for immunity to prosecution, a reduced charge, or leniency at the time of sentencing.

BASIC-LEAD INFORMANTS

Despite considerations to the contrary, informants are a traditional starting point in seeking basic leads. In fact, informants sometimes offer data about an unreported or undiscovered crime or one in its planning stages.

The successful use of basic-lead informants is a complex combination of an alert and knowledgeable investigator knowing where to seek information, finding the contacts who have it, and probing and prying to gather as much meaningful information as possible.

This type of informant is motivated to divulge information to a police investigator for a multitude of reasons. He or she may have encountered it by chance or wants to do a citizen's duty by divulging it. Criminals may provide information to get rid of a competitor—a common practice in gambling, drug, and prostitution activities and not uncommon among thieves and recipients of stolen property. Jealousy and revenge sometimes motivate such informants. The "woman scorned" has done great harm to the victims of her fury by informing about their criminal activities.

Former girlfriends and wives often serve as unpaid informants. In the world of crime, the women friends of criminals often fear them with some justification. A frightened and knowledgeable ex-girlfriend or ex-wife, has often allied herself in self-defense with police efforts and delivered vital information about the criminal activities of her ex-boyfriend or ex-husband.

Other informants seek pay for information leading to arrests. Investigators with unsolved jewelry thefts, suspicious fires, and homicide cases often are contacted by such informants proposing to supply information. Recently released prison inmates may be confronted with the choice of going back into crime or earning money, and they often sell information as a stopgap livelihood until they find employment or return to crime.

In many areas of the United States, "secret witness" programs sponsored by local news media are an innovative way of paying informants for basic leads. Cooperating business firms may contribute to an informant fund. Local police may request publicity about the most serious crimes or those without substantial leads. The news media involved publish the details of the crime and specify the amount of the reward (which varies by the nature of the crime). Inherent in these programs is a means by which informants, by providing a code word or number that will substantiate their claim to the reward, can contact local police investigators without revealing their identity. Rewards are paid when police have verified the information and found it meaningful and useful in the identification of a suspect, in learning the whereabouts of a known suspect, or in discovering what happened at the time of the crime.

PARTICIPANT INFORMANTS

The role of the **participant informant** in enforcing the law against illegal drug sales is that of go-between: to identify the drug seller and to introduce the undercover investigator as a potential buyer, or to "instigate" the transaction in some fashion.[11]

Participant informants participate directly in gathering sufficient evidence to warrant an arrest. One type of participant informant is the special employee. He or she is paid a fee set in advance for this work. A special employee may be hired because of his or her knowledge of the local drug scene, friendships among local drug sellers and users, or the ability to deceive suspects as to his or her role.

Another type of participant informant on the drug scene is the arrestee who has been "turned," or "**flipped**," by the arresting officer. In this type of arrangement, the arrest is made on a minor charge of possessing or selling illegal drugs and the arresting officer persuades the arrestee to cooperate in identifying his or her source of drugs—in effect, to assist in a more important arrest—in return for some consideration by police, prosecutor, or court. At one time, this was an easily arranged and informal procedure, but current procedure usually requires discussion with and approval of the "deal" by the prosecutor. Often, a formal plea bargain is entered into between the prosecution and the defendant and his or her legal counsel.

Participant informants may be used by an investigator in solving crimes other than those involving the sale of illegal drugs. A few of these informants have been used as **shills** in police **sting** operations aimed at discovering burglars and thieves and recovering stolen property. This role requires the informant to sell property to the police playing the role of buyers in order to lure real burglars and thieves to do likewise.

The Federal Bureau of Investigation (FBI) used a participant informant to uncover political corruption in Chicago. The informant's role was to lure politicians to meetings where payoffs could be videotaped by FBI agents.[12] The sting investigation, known as ABSCAM, pioneered this videotaping of public officials accepting bribes. The name derives from the original cover story about the informant's relationship to a group of wealthy Arabs who owned "Abdul Enterprises Unlimited." In the ABSCAM prosecutions, a U.S. senator, six members of the U.S. House of Representatives, several local public officials in Pennsylvania and New Jersey, and numerous associates were found guilty. These verdicts were decided despite defense claims of unfairness and entrapment in this cash-for-political-favors "scam." The videotapes presented to the juries in these trials apparently convinced them that the government's action was not unfair, unscrupulous, or unethical.[13]

COVERT INFORMANTS

Covert informants are not classified as persons who assist in developing basic leads in a criminal investigation, nor do they serve the instigator role of participant informants. They are men and women who report information to a police investigator about a terrorist or other criminal organization from a position of trust and confidence within the group. These agents-in-place are known as **moles** in the area of international espionage, as they are often in place for years before being activated.

Covert informants may or may not be remunerated for their work. They are not used for spot intelligence. The use of such persons is akin to the practice of having spies in the enemy's camp. These agents-in-place are a spin-off from military and international intelligence.[14] They can provide information over a lengthy period as long as their identities are protected. Such individuals must be developed fully, cultivated over a long time, and used only when absolutely necessary. These sources of information are not developed solely to provide information for current investigations but can be set up to provide information at a future time.

Organized crime and hate extremist groups are sites for agents-in-place. Homicides committed by hate groups are common, and organized crime is constantly expanding its operations. Hoodlums and extremists are an ever-present threat. When information is needed, after-the-fact intelligence operations are useless with either of these groups.

A man or woman may be established within a terrorist or crime group when he or she begins cooperating with an investigator. On the other hand, the investigator may recruit a person whom he or she believes to be trustworthy and capable and suggest a means by which the new covert informant can infiltrate the target organization.

A Canadian woman, a member of the Front de Liberation du Quebec (FLQ), went to the Montreal police to avoid involvement in an armed robbery planned by members of this terrorist group. She was promptly recruited as a covert informant. She was an excellent source of information for several months as she was never suspected of being an informant by any of her terrorist associates. Her police contacts avoided disclosing her identity until the day she appeared in open court as a witness.[15]

Most terrorist groups have established high thresholds to any penetration by informants; new members are always greeted with suspicion and distrust. Therefore, in seeking a productive informant, investigators should make every effort to cultivate and recruit as an informant a person who has been an active member of the group for some time.[16]

The "family" aspect of organized crime groups, regardless of its ethnic nature, is a real handicap to infiltrating an informant as a new member. However, the need for covert informants in these groups has diminished in recent years because of the success of prosecutors in turning or flipping accomplice witnesses.

ACCOMPLICE WITNESSES

An **accomplice witness** is a person who is liable to prosecution for the identical offense charged against the defendant or defendants in a pending trial. He or she has been arrested along with one or more crime partners, and the police–prosecutor team offers leniency in return for his or her cooperation. Accomplice witnesses testify for the prosecution, identifying the defendant or defendants and testifying to acts done by them in furtherance of the crime.

Some prosecutors develop compelling evidence of guilt on the part of one person in a criminal operation, bring him or her to the prosecutor's office for a briefing on the evidence, and offer the alternatives of (1) arrest, conviction, and prison or (2) cooperation, a bargained plea to a lesser charge, and less or no incarceration.

A special state prosecutor in New York broke a complex case involving many police officers by confronting two of the police suspects with compelling evidence of guilt. Facing prison for their own crimes, these two officers flipped and agreed to inform on their coworkers in exchange for their own freedom. They continued their criminal activities (ripping off drug dealers, primarily) while being **wired** to secretly record and thereby incriminate their colleagues in crime.[17]

Recruiting a defendant in an organized crime case begins with a reiteration of the theme "Every man for himself." Once the witness seeks more information, the standard deal is finalized:

1. In return for full cooperation, the witness will be given partial or full immunity.
2. After testimony is completed, the witness will be accepted in a witness protection plan (federal/state) that will furnish the witness with a new identity, funds, and assistance in relocating the witness and his or her family and will provide security measures sufficient to conceal his or her whereabouts.

When a pending case does not involve organized crime members, the accomplice witness does not usually need the protection afforded by a witness protection plan, and the prosecutor offers the potential informant only immunity or partial immunity. In a widespread diamond fraud case involving no less than $5,500,000, the mastermind (Irwin Margolies) ordered two of his crime partners killed (his accountant and her assistant). After the contract killer in this case was sentenced to over a hundred years in prison for these two homicides plus the wanton killing of three accidental witnesses to the murder of the accountant, the prosecutor was determined to indict Margolies for murder. All the evidence secured by hard-working police investigators, however, was circumstantial. Rather than allow the mastermind to avoid trial and conviction, the prosecutor offered a coconspirator in both the fraud and the murders a deal: he would be named in future indictments in the conspiracy to murder unless he freely told all he knew and agreed to testify against Margolies in any future trial. If he did cooperate, he would be granted immunity from prosecution. He did talk. Margolies was convicted of murder, primarily on the testimony of the accomplice witness, and stated that he brought Margolies and the shooter together and was a party to the murder "contract."[18]

CASE STUDY

The Shugars and Smith Case

At 3:40 p.m. on November 5, officers on patrol were instructed to investigate a call from a Greyhound Cab Company driver who reported that the door of a pawnshop at 424 J Street was open and the owner was not there. On arrival, the officers discovered the body of the proprietor, who was apparently dead from knife wounds to the chest. Evidence of a struggle was found, and blood was observed in several areas of the crime scene. A display case, which was a container for handguns, was open; the tags (identification of guns) were there, but six guns were missing (Figure 6–4). No wallet was found on the victim. The victim was pronounced dead by the coroner

FIGURE 6–4   Crime scene diagram of the Shugars and Smith case study.

at 1624 hours (4:24 p.m.). The location of the pawnshop is in an area frequented by laborers and transients; occupancies are low-cost hotels and small stores.

The Investigation

Immediate action was instituted to develop all possible basic leads.

Eyewitnesses

1. Interviewed all employees of hotel and adjoining Greyhound taxi terminal and cabdrivers. Checked all neighborhood hotels and shops. Results negative.
2. Questioned bus driver, C. Gardner, who stopped at 4th and J Streets from 2:30 to 3:00 p.m. He noted two people in pawnshop. No definite description. States he saw a green station wagon in front of pawnshop with a woman in front seat and possibly two children in rear (not positive about children).
3. Questioned all cab drivers who worked at that time. Negative.
4. Open book in pawnshop with last entry: Richard Moriarity.
5. Contacted Richard Moriarity at his home. He had redeemed a rifle belonging to his brother at 1500 hours. Negative. Moriarity states a Mexican customer was in pawnshop. He gave a complete description of this person and said he left before he (Moriarity) left the shop. Also interviewed his wife, Celia Moriarity. Negative.
6. Interviewed George Samuel who told cabdriver Petovitch that he saw door of shop open but could see nobody inside. He was worried.
7. Petovitch interviewed, said he went to door, saw the mess, and asked dispatcher to call police. He said he had not seen any suspicious people around at the time.
8. Questioned B. Knursem, cabdriver, who picked up a man at 4th and J Streets at 4:00 p.m. Man said, "Let's get out of here. Dead man in there." States took man to 8th and E, where he had a soda with him. Six other cabdrivers interviewed. Negative.

Victim's Background

1. E. Martin, desk clerk at Olympic Hotel, had received phone call from elderly person (victim's father) earlier but was too busy at the time to call him to phone. (Victim used this phone, no phone in pawnshop.)
2. Interviewed parents of victim. They said he carried a brown wallet, no credit cards, and had a car (which was found in nearby parking lot). They said he (father) had worked with son but had no idea of inventory.
3. Outer door of the safe open, but inner door still closed. Money in safe intact, but pocket of victim turned inside out; wallet missing. Inventory made of money in safe: total was $4,693.70.
4. Questioned cabdriver Caleb Leyhe. Saw victim talking with two men and one woman at approximately 3:00 p.m. Negative.
5. Interviewed Robert Head, cabdriver. Negative.
6. Questioned Harry Isuki, jeweler, who was a friend of victim and did work at the pawnshop. He said victim had been beaten up three months ago by two men who had given no reason. No report had been made of the assault to police.

Informants

1. James Chambers came to the police station. He said he had information regarding the murder in the pawnshop. Said he had been standing on the corner of J and 2nd Streets on November 5 when a white man asked for "Jerry King." Wanted to know if he was still living on 10th Street. This man said he had heard that King was in trouble because of a "shooting" in a pawnshop someplace. Chambers stated that King runs with a man named Mason and that both are good with knives. Chambers has not seen them since the murder. King is called the "Cowboy," wears a big white cowboy hat and boots. Chambers also states that Mason bought a green station wagon, a Ford. Officer sent Chambers back to street for more information.

2. Questioned informant Chambers, who gave a complete description of one Jerry King. He is afraid to tell where he got the information that King was going to borrow a car and "knock over" a pawnshop the night of the homicide. Promises more information. Said he thinks he bought a car at Del Mar Market.

3. Questioned Joe Note at Del Mar Market. Note said that on November 3 he sold a 1990 green station wagon to Eugene Mason. He said Mason had a guy with long hair with him and that Chambers (our informant) lived with Mason.

4. Again questioned Chambers, and he admitted he had lived with Mason and King. King, Chambers states, had later lived with a Mexican woman on 10th Street. He said some man had told him that Mason and Sanchez had showed up at his house at 1815 6th St. with a 1989 or 1990 green station wagon a couple of nights ago, loaded it up, and left, and that there was a third man in the car. He also said that Mason had a reputation with a knife and had knifed someone on 6th Street some time ago. He promised more information.

5. Re: Jerry King. Information from Willie Park (1815 6th St.). Knows of suspect, refers to him as "Big Foot." Big Foot wanted Park in on a deal. Park did not want anything to do with it, so Big Foot talked about getting "Walkie Talkie" to go in on the deal with them. Park stated that Walkie Talkie is a BMA (black male adult) about 50 years, 5'8", 175 lbs., sort of heavy build; wears a cap made of corduroy material and a grayish-type suit coat and blue pants. Park stated that Walkie Talkie sometimes sleeps in the shack behind 1815 6th St. Park stated that Big Foot, in talking about the job he had lined up, said they were going to use three men on the job. One was to be on the outside, one on the roof, and one was to be let down by the fellow up on top through the skylight and into the shop. Big Foot talked about a lot of guns, watches, and cameras that were in the place. When they were done, they would take the stuff to a room they had. Big Foot is supposed to see Park tonight (1815 6th St., November 12) and bring over some pants and a bottle of wine. This was supposed to be around 1800 to 1900 hours.

6. Re: Elroy Robin (Walkie Talkie), DOB (date of birth) 7/19/49 (Texas), WMA (white male adult), gray/black (hair color), brown eyes. Elroy Robin was spoken to in the detective division regarding the above offense. Robin stated he did not know anyone by the name of Jerry King and that the nickname Big Foot meant nothing to him. Stated he only knew what he had heard on the street about the killing at the pawnshop. Robin was asked if he had ever been approached by anyone who attempted to get him to go along on a burglary of a pawnshop. He stated he had not, that he had been in prison once and didn't want to go back.

7. Re: George Brendon Williams ("Tex"), WMA, bald/gray, DOB 2/6/56 (Texas). Williams stated he was approached by a subject he knows as Jerry King on Saturday at 0900 hours at 2nd and K Streets in front of the Bank Exchange Bar the day the pawnshop man was killed. King asked him to loan him his car. Williams asked King why he wanted his car. King stated he had to go pick up some money. Williams told King that his car was not running. King was with a small man with gray hair at this time. Williams later saw the two walking east on J Street near the Olympic Hotel about 0930 hours. Williams stated he did not see King again until November 10 around 1200 hours. This was at 6th and S Streets near the park. After a short conversation of small talk, King told Williams he had a hot gun he had bought down on 2nd Street. Williams asked what kind of gun, and King replied it was a .22 caliber pistol. Williams stated he advised King that he had heard the cops were looking for him. King stated he knew they were. Williams asked King if he knew the cops were looking for him why didn't he go in and get it straightened out. King stated he was going to do that but he was going to throw the gun in the river first. The same man who was with King when they had met on 2nd Street was with him at this time. He had walked away, going to a nearby gas station. On his return, King stated he was fixing up to leave town. He was going to steal a car and make it. Williams stated that the last time he saw King, he and the other man were walking in the direction of town. Williams described the man with King as short, thin, gray hair, about 45 or 50 years old.

8. Received phone call at police department from J. Drum of 1909 P Street. Drum stated that on the previous night he was drinking at the Village Bar and a man said he had killed the pawnbroker. This man was about 37 years, 5'10". He stated the bartender seemed to know him because he changed a lot of dimes to bills for him, no questions asked.

9. Contacted bartender at Village Bar re: customer changing dimes. He stated the man works for the Purple Heart Thrift Shop, that his name is Bill Donal, and that he was drunk at the bar with Drum and probably did talk about the murder because the victim of the homicide had refused Donal a loan at an earlier date. This story was checked out with Donal. Negative.

10. Donal was in Los Angeles and en route on bus (checked out) at time of murder.

11. Willie Park (informant) called and said King would visit the 6th Street address in the evening (November 12) for sure.

Benefit and Motive

No reports.

Knowledge

No reports.

Field Interview Reports

1. Jerry King is a supposed associate of a Eugene Mason. Field interview cards checked: On July 20, Eugene Mason, PD (police dept. no.) S-7836, was stopped at 2nd and I Streets. DOB given: May 3, 1938, WMA, 5'9", 155 lbs. Add(ress) of California Apartments in Broderick. Car being used was an '85 Mercury, 4 dr. lt. blue, ANZ-009. At the time he was with an Agapito Casteneda.

2. FI (field identification) card on Agapito Casteneda shows DOB 11/20/38, 5'7", 138 lbs. Add. 100 Lucas Street, Laredo, Texas.

Weapon

1. No weapon found at crime scene.

2. Interviewed Mr. John Daven, a resident of Olympic Hotel, who said he observed a man displaying a knife with an 8-inch blade in the lobby around the time of the homicide. Daven identified Albert Richards, who surrendered the knife to officers and said he was intoxicated that day and lives in neighboring hotel. Identified himself. Negative.

Latents at Crime Scene

1. Six latent prints were lifted and photographed at crime scene.

2. Compared latent prints found at scene. Found they were of victim, of the last customer in shop (Richard Moriarity), and remainder not identified at this time.

3. The latent prints obtained were checked against all persons on the list of police and coroner's personnel present at crime scene with negative results.

Stolen Property

1. Thorough check of inventory of shop. Six tags for handguns found in showcase, but no guns. Description and serial numbers of guns on tags. This case had been broken into. Missing were one .25 caliber automatic, three .22 caliber revolvers, one Smith & Wesson .38 caliber revolver, and one .32 caliber revolver. It also appeared that some rifles were missing. Further checks with accountant.

2. With assistance of brother-in-law of victim, checked records in pawnshop and made list of all guns on hand, guns taken in pawn and not redeemed, and guns sold. Checked all guns bought by victim for past year and a half. Bookkeeper contacted. He had invoices for all new guns. Impossible to find out what weapons should be in shop—poor records.

3. After further check with accountant: 7 guns (handguns) missing.

4. Inspector Serro of the pawnshop detail called and said he had picked up a seventeen-year-old WMA by the name of Steven Russell while he was attempting to pawn some "junky" jewelry. A search of his car revealed a .38 caliber Smith & Wesson revolver, serial #190452. Inspector Serro stated that he had seen the wanted notice on the pawnbroker stabbing and noticed that some as yet unidentified guns had been stolen, and he offered this information for what it was worth.

5. Phone call received from Wayne Cooper. Has in his possession three guns obtained from a Henry Smith as security on a loan. Checked serial numbers—all three missing from pawnshop. Cooper called after he had been told by his sister that Smith was wanted. These guns were taken as evidence.

Modus Operandi Comparison

1. Checked all local pawnshop owners for any unusual occurrences. Negative.
2. Attempted holdup at Southside Junk Yard. Gun displayed but victim could not identify make. There is a good description of the robber who was scared off by a customer.

Photographs of Known Criminals

None available. Identi-Kit likeness prepared from descriptions given by informants. (The Identi-Kit is a trademarked device that uses plastic inserts of facial characteristics to reproduce a likeness of a suspect from verbal descriptions and visual supervision. It is a substitution for a police artist drawing a portrait sketch.)

Injured Suspects

1. Checked adjacent hotel. Interviewed witness who saw a man with blood on face and hands in washroom of hotel at the time of the homicide. This was traced to a resident who had a fight with another resident. Negative.
2. Went to the Olympic Hotel and took two photographs of the blood droplets in the lobby and in the bathroom in front of the toilet bowl. Obtained a sample of this blood at the same location and booked it as evidence. Receipt #30551.
3. Patrol Division Captains: Re: Homicide at 424 J St., Pacific Jewelry & Loan Co. It appears that the victim fought with the suspect and perhaps the suspect has injuries. Please be on the alert for subjects being arrested with injuries that may have been caused during a struggle and bring them to the attention of the detective division.
4. Contacted the clerk at the desk in the Travelers Hotel and obtained a list of checkouts from this morning. There were six, and R/O (reporting officer) in company with the housekeeper (Clacey Brown) checked each room; three had been made up, and the floor maids indicated that no sign of blood or other evidence was noticed. Three rooms not yet made up were checked, particularly bathrooms and towels, but no sign of blood or anything of evidential value seen. The floorman responsible for cleaning the common washrooms on each floor was also contacted, and he reported no bloodstains or anything suspicious were noticed in any of them.

The Arrest

On November 12 about 1800 hours, a team of investigators went to 6th st. in separate vehicles, positioning their cars to keep the vicinity of 1815 6th St. under observation. After a short interval a man wearing a white cowboy hat and having the general appearance of the suspect Jerry King was observed on the sidewalk walking toward the house at 1815. The suspect was stopped and questioned. Also stopped with the suspect was another man who identified himself as Henry Smith and who said they both lived at 912 S St. Smith had identification. King had none. Both men were searched; King had a .22 caliber revolver, loaded, in his belt, and Smith had a .22 caliber revolver, loaded, in his right pants pocket. Both King and Smith were handcuffed and taken to the police station.

Postarrest investigation revealed Jerry King to be Lyle E. Shugars. His companion was identified as Henry E. R. Smith, the person named as Eugene Mason during the investigation by informants. Both men were warned of their rights to silence and legal counsel (the Miranda warning) but waived these rights and made statements to police.

The Trial

Both Shugars and Smith were represented by legal counsel. However, guilty pleas were entered for both men. The proceeding was brief; both men admitted their guilt in open court. They were sentenced to state prison for life.

Critique

1. The lack of eyewitnesses, despite diligent search, indicated this case was likely to be one in which the police would not have a named suspect.
2. Investigator's reports of their day-to-day activity document a series of parallel inquiries along avenues suggested by basic investigative leads.
3. Information gathered from reliable informants was excellent.
4. Investigators followed the doctrine of warning suspects of their constitutional rights to silence and to legal counsel. Grand jury testimony indicates rights of both accused persons were fully protected while in custody during questioning. Wording of statements and content indicates voluntariness.
5. Continuing and diligent search for witnesses and evidence indicated impartial attitude of investigators, which allowed the case to focus within its own evidence structure and without any preconceived theory of who did it.

Source: Sacramento, California, Police Department and Public Defender's Office.

CHAPTER REVIEW

KEY TERMS

accomplice witness 122
active information 105
alibi 107
Amber Alert system 115
basic-lead informant 118
benefit 107
"better him than me" 118
Bureau of Alcohol, Tobacco, & Firearms (ATF) 114
cold search 111
composite sketch 116

covert informants 121
field contact report 108
flipped 121
Identi-Kit system 116
knowledge 107
known identity 104
linkages 118
modus operandi 113
mole 121
mug shot 115
National Integrated Ballistic Information Network (NIBIN) 114

opportunity 107
participant informant 121
passive information 105
request search 111
shill 121
signature 113
single-digit search 111
snitching 119
sting 121
unknown identity 104
wired 123

REVIEW QUESTIONS

1. The claim of being somewhere else at the time the crime was committed is a defense known as:
   a. Alibi
   b. Benefit
   c. Knowledge
   d. Lack of motive

2. A police report of contact with persons who are engaged in suspicious activity not amounting to a crime is known as a:
   a. Preliminary report
   b. Progress report
   c. Field contact report
   d. Pending report

3. A/an _____ file is useful in linking a perpetrator with the past crimes he or she has committed.

4. Eyewitnesses to crimes will often be asked to look at pictures of persons arrested for similar crimes. These photos are known as:
   a. Composites
   b. Portraits
   c. Mug books

5. When photos are not available, what regarding the suspect may an eyewitness be asked to collaborate with a police artist in developing?
   a. Composites
   b. Portraits
   c. Mug books

6. When more than one person is responsible for the commission of a crime and when one suspect is identified, the other suspects may be identified as well using which investigative lead?
   a. Mug shots
   b. NCIC
   c. Offender registration
   d. Personal linkage

7. Informing is a/an "_____" because informants may lie to implicate innocent persons or to exculpate a favored crime partner.

8. A person who has been arrested for a criminal offense and agrees to cooperate with investigators to supply information concerning others involved in criminal activity is known as what type of informant?
   a. Covert
   b. Participant
   c. Basic lead
   d. Accomplice witness

9. A person who supplies information to investigators about organized crime that is based on a position of trust and confidence from within the organization is known as what type of informant?
   a. Covert
   b. Participant
   c. Basic lead
   d. Accomplice witness

10. This type of informant is motivated to divulge information to the police for a variety of reasons, such as jealousy, greed, revenge, or to eliminate competition. Which type of informant is this?
    a. Covert
    b. Participant
    c. Basic lead
    d. Accomplice witness

See Appendix D for the correct answers.

DISCUSSION QUESTIONS

1. Compare the objectives of investigations in which the identity of the offender is known with those of investigations in which the identity of the offender is unknown. Compare these objectives with the basic objectives of any investigation.
2. Discuss in some depth one of the classic queries to be probed in victim–offender relationships.
3. Explain the concept of benefit in relation to motive for a crime.
4. Is the basic lead of knowledge more likely to be concerned with motive or opportunity for a crime?
5. Are field interviews justified? Why?

6. Can the imprint of a single finger found at a crime scene lead to identification of a suspect? Explain.
7. Discuss the role of tracing stolen property in the day-to-day investigation of crime and criminals.
8. Discuss the three major capabilities of a modus operandi file.
9. What is the common theme between the use of photographs for identification and the hue and cry for injured suspects?
10. What is the role of composite drawings in identifying a suspect?

RELATED WEB SITES

To learn more about the history of fingerprints and the answers to the most frequently asked questions about fingerprint examination, visit this Web site: *onin.com.*

Want to know more about computer databases? If yes, then visit the FBI's National Crime Information Center (NCIC) Web page: *www.fas.org/irp/agency/doj/fbi/is/ncic.*

chapter **seven**

Major Investigative Techniques

CHAPTER OUTLINE

After reading this chapter you will be able to:

- Explain the legal issues involved in audio surveillance.
- Distinguish between the various types of surveillance techniques and the methods employed in their application.
- Discuss the six stages involved in the police intelligence process.
- Identify the role of legal counsel during a physical lineup.
- Outline the reasons why undercover police agents make better witnesses than underworld informants.

Identifying a suspect with compelling evidence of guilt often goes beyond hours of making inquiries and miles of footwork and driving. The combination of an eyewitness, a suspect, and a police lineup may achieve this goal.

Monitoring the activities of a subject by ordinary observation can be supplemented by videotaping, court-ordered wiretaps, and fluorescent chemicals, all of which can reveal contacts and actions of great importance to an ongoing investigation—even when the suspect is aware of or fears a police interest. Patience is essential in this area: on occasion, a suspect is not as cautious as he or she should be and the investigator is able to unearth a valuable piece of information as a result.

Investigators assigned to covertly scan the activities of the known criminals of organized crime often are not the arresting officers. However, when homicides occur the information these investigators can provide their associates can lead to arrests.

Undercover police agents assume a similar role. Seeking information in this manner can be life threatening to agents; nevertheless, facts gathered in this way can become solid evidence when the agent testifies in court.

SURVEILLANCE

Surveillance is observation of people and places by investigators to develop investigative leads. Often hidden—not just unobtrusive—surveillance is a seeking for specific activity and significant information rather than merely passive observation. Its basic objective is to bring an investigation into sharp focus by supplying detailed information about the activities of a person or place and about the associates of a person or the individuals who visit a place.

VISUAL SURVEILLANCE

Visual surveillance is nothing more than keeping watch on a particular suspect, vehicle, or place. It may be aided by binoculars or a telescope or replaced by photographic surveillance. The use of binoculars permits observation from a distance of two or three city blocks. A twenty-power telescope is effective at ten to fifteen city blocks. A robot camera can replace personnel performing fixed surveillance. Infrared viewing devices permit observation in the dark.

A **fixed visual surveillance**—a **stakeout** or plant—is located within a building, if possible, with observations made through available windows or doors. Panel trucks and campers have been converted to fixed observation posts using peepholes or curtained windows for viewing. Rooftops are excellent for long-range surveillance; stores and hallways are suitable sites for short-range viewing. Sometimes long-term positions are possible; in some instances, it is necessary to move frequently to avoid notice. The static quality of a fixed surveillance requires skilled judgment in selecting a rewarding area of observation. To be effective in scrutinizing a suspect's activities, the presence of the observing investigator must not be detected. For this reason a fixed observation post in a building is preferable because the investigator is not only concealed but, through a rental arrangement, has the rights of a resident or tenant.

Some investigators, because of their height, size, race, or national origin, may have difficulty blending into certain environments as residents or tenants. In fact, several well-hidden fixed surveillances in apartments have been compromised by the appearance of the investigator entering the premises. In the de facto segregated ghetto areas of urban centers across the country, an investigator not conforming to the appearance of the residents or tenants is certain to be suspect.

A **moving visual surveillance**—a **tail (shadow)**—may be on foot, may be in a vehicle, or may use a combination of walking and riding. The suspect being followed is often alert and may take evasive action. Suspects "double door" the trailing investigator by entering a street-level shop and leaving by a rear, side, or basement entrance. They use the modern traffic system with its copious traffic and one-way streets to break contact or force the investigator too close to a point at which his or her presence can be noted by an alert suspect. It is difficult to supplement a moving surveillance optically, although camera equipment can be employed. A moving surveillance is a dynamic technique in that it does not depend on the appearance of the suspect at a certain place; rather, it keeps the subject in view from place to place.

To avoid detection, a mobile surveillance often uses a two- or three-person surveillance team, with members rotating in the position of closest contact. This leapfrogging technique for following persons under surveillance is useful on foot or in vehicles. Its particular value is that the chance of detection by the suspect is diminished because the same person is not following the suspect continuously. The close contact position is behind the suspect, and an alert and anxious suspect will identify a person who is in this position for an extended period. With the leapfrogging technique, the suspect just about makes an identification when a new member of the surveillance team or a new vehicle moves up and into close contact and the other team member drops back into a position well to the rear or across the street. All that is required of the personnel who drop back is to keep the contact position investigator in sight. When vehicles are used, such contact can be maintained by radio.

A device that electronically signals the location of automobiles, or other objects to which it is affixed, is known as a **bumper beeper**. Another device used for this purpose is the **global positioning device (GPS).** For example, wireless carriers are required by law to make all cell phone users' locations traceable when they make 911 calls. Carriers that track callers via GPS are able to locate the caller within 160 feet.[1] Sophisticated receivers in the vehicle(s) of a mobile surveillance continually trace the otherwise silent signals emanating from the bumper beeper and locate the vehicle (or other object) under surveillance. These devices are particularly helpful during investigations of ongoing, conspiratorial criminal activities involving a high degree of organization (gambling, fraud, drug selling) and in which the persons under surveillance are likely to "make" (identify) one or more of the vehicles in a mobile surveillance if they follow the target car too closely.

Monitoring beeper signals from a radio transmitter that was placed in a container of chloroform has been held not to invade any legitimate expectation of privacy and not to constitute search or seizure under the Fourth Amendment. The U.S. Supreme Court's decision in *U.S. v. Knotts*, 460 U.S. 276 (1983), noted that the scientific enhancement of the beeper raised no constitutional issues that would not be raised by visual surveillance.

Investigators develop their own methods for blending with the surroundings on mobile surveillances. A device or technique suitable to one individual may draw attention to another. Appearances can be corrected to some extent. A change of clothing may suffice for one individual; another may use clothing to suggest a trade or service. Conduct and behavior can be coordinated with appearance to communicate some cover or excuse for being in a neighborhood. Carrying something is a common practice with some investigators adept at hiding their occupation, and most persons are not suspicious of a person carrying a bag of groceries or some similar load.

Vehicles used in mobile surveillance do not blend with surrounding traffic units if they are too distinctive in design or color. The number of occupants and the seating arrangement may also identify a vehicle to a suspect under surveillance, as will the design and position of headlights at night. Apparent changes in the number of occupants and their in-vehicle positions are a defense against identification, as are driving without lights when safe or using a vehicle with the capability to change the appearance of headlights.

Fortunately for investigators, most suspects are alert but anxious; they are on the lookout for a surveillance, but they really do not want to discover it. They want to know if the police are watching them, and yet they do not want to know it. This is the only possible explanation for heavy-footed mobile surveillances going undiscovered and fixed pickup posts operating for weeks unnoticed adjacent to the meeting places of known hoodlums and crime syndicate gangsters. At Los Angeles International Airport, police intelligence unit personnel, federal agents, and state narcotics officers are frequently standing shoulder to shoulder among the throngs greeting incoming planes from Las Vegas, but the subjects of their observations never seem to notice the tail they pick up. One notorious hoodlum was so oblivious to this surveillance that he was apprehended in a minor shoplifting episode at the airport newsstand.

A combination of fixed and mobile surveillances (both on foot and by vehicle) has been found to be effective in on-the-scene apprehensions of criminals who have committed a series of crimes. The irrational arsonist who sets several fires a night and who cannot be traced by normal investigative leads can be apprehended by isolating the area of suspicious and known incendiary fires and establishing extensive surveillance. Burglars and serial rapists who enter residences and continue their operations until arrested also may be surprised in their operations by the technique of staking out an area.

The object of a surveillance is to collect information on the activities of a suspect, the persons in contact with him or her, and the places frequented. Therefore, the assigned investigator and associates must keep a running commentary, or log, of their observations. Notes are made in the field as the surveillance discloses associates of the suspect, cars used by the suspect and associates, and the ownership or reputation of places frequented. When surveillance is aligned with use of the investigator as a witness to what he or she observed, the surveillance investigator must personally verify vehicle registrations, identities of unknown persons in contact with the suspect, or data on the premises or locations frequented by the suspect or others. With such a foundation, the witness can show personal knowledge of the surveillance and the investigation that disclosed pertinent and related facts.

Visual surveillance is somewhat limited. In 1968 a federal court ruled that without a valid warrant or reasonable cause, a person should be free from the eyes of the law while within the privacy of his or her own home. Peering into the defendant's window by stealth was the complained-about action.

AUDIO SURVEILLANCE

Wiretapping and electronic eavesdropping are the primary forms of **audio surveillance** by listening. It is the observation technique that has been termed a "dirty business" by the U.S. Supreme Court and that is viewed with mixed emotions by law-abiding citizens who apparently see it as the epitome of an unjustified and nondirective invasion of privacy.

The interception of telephone communication is a difficult surveillance to detect. Telephone wires lead from the instrument cable to a house cable, to an area cable, to a main cable, and to a distant central office. At each point a junction box containing an array of wires and binding posts facilitates the work of the telephone company's service personnel in providing service to subscribers. The wires of an individual telephone appear in terminal boxes and are identified by pair and cable numbers located at various points from the telephone instrument to the distant central office. A telephone tap can be hooked up easily at any of these locations.

Testimony is sometimes required on the mechanics of the interception—for example, how the wires used were selected as the wires of the telephone that was meant to be tapped. A common practice is to use a regular portable telephone instrument equipped with wire clips. The investigator hooks up to the selected wires, makes certain no one is using the line, dials the subscriber's number, and hears the distinctive sound of a busy signal without conversation on the line. In other instances an associate may have to call and engage the subscriber in a simulated "survey" conversation while the listener clips in and verifies the line by recognizing the associate's voice. Tape recording devices permit direct recording of conversations and offer a verbatim record for review.

Places or people may be wired for sound. This has been termed **bugging**. When properly installed, the electronic equipment necessary for eavesdropping is almost as difficult to detect as wiretap connections and equipment. The pickup microphone may be wired directly to a tape recorder, or it may broadcast the conversation a short distance by radio to a receiver located on the person of an investigator or in a nearby car or building. Surreptitious or covert entry of private premises to install a microphone (bug) is in conflict with expectations of individual privacy. However, in *Dalia v. United States*, 441 U.S. 238 (1979), the U.S. Supreme Court ruled, "We find no basis for a constitutional rule proscribing all covert entries. It is well established that law officers constitutionally may break and enter to execute a search warrant where such entry is the only means by which the warrant effectively may be executed."

The facts of *Dalia* are that the U.S. District Court authorized the interception of specified oral communications at a particular location in compliance with Title III of the Omnibus Crime Control and Safe Streets Acts of 1958. Dalia was convicted of receiving stolen goods and conspiring to transport, receive, and possess stolen goods. At a hearing on petitioner Dalia's motion to suppress evidence obtained under the "bugging" order, it was shown that the order did not explicitly authorize entry of the petitioner's business office. However, the district court ruled that a covert entry to install electronic eavesdropping equipment is not unlawful merely because the court approving the surveillance did not explicitly authorize such an entry. (FBI agents assigned the task of implementing the court's order had entered the petitioner's office secretly and installed an electronic bug in the ceiling.)

The court considered two questions in *Dalia*: (1) May courts authorize electronic surveillance that requires covert entry into private premises for installation of the necessary equipment? (2) Must authorization for such surveillance include a specific statement by the court that it approves of the covert entry? The court held that (1) the Fourth Amendment does not prohibit per se a covert entry performed for the purpose of installing otherwise legal bugging equipment; (2) Congress has given the courts statutory authority to approve covert entries for the purpose of installing electronic surveillance equipment; and (3) the Fourth Amendment does not require that a Title III electronic surveillance order include a specific authorization to enter covertly the premises described in the order.

Audio surveillance is an investigative technique about which appellate courts have rendered many decisions. Fortunately, the U.S. Supreme Court, in *Katz v. U.S.*, 389 U.S. 347 (1967), consolidated judicial thinking in this area and established the doctrine that such eavesdropping may properly be conducted under court supervision similar to procedures now available to police in securing search warrants and warrants of arrest.

The U.S. Supreme Court reversed Katz's conviction: "Wherever a man may be, he is entitled to know that he will remain free from unreasonable searches and seizures." In this decision the court slashed away at a confusing collection of previous decisions in this area, involving, among other things, whether or not a physical penetration or a technical trespass occurred, by pointing out that the trespass doctrine is no longer controlling "for the Fourth Amendment protects people, not places." The final words for the decision suggest that antecedent court review of the probable cause for eavesdropping and a court order similar to a search warrant would have resulted in the court's sustaining Katz's conviction. (See Appendix A: Case Briefs for a digest of *Dalia* and *Katz*.)

Consensual electronic surveillance (as opposed to nonconsensual) is also known as **participant monitoring.** Its primary use is to secure a record of a conversation in which the person wired for sound is a participant. Undercover police agents and cooperative informants, such as accomplice witnesses, can provide police with a record of conversations in which they participated. This record proves exactly what was said and is important when the substance of the conversation is later disputed by one of the other participants. Since electronic surveillance that is carried out with the consent of one of the parties to a conversation is not a "search" within the meaning of the Fourth Amendment, this type of surveillance does not require previous judicial authorization. Telephone conversations that are recorded with the consent of one participant are in this class of consensual electronic surveillance.

Since a collateral purpose of consensual electronic surveillance is to expose wrongdoing, particularly in relation to an ongoing investigation, it is important that police investigators know that the Fourth Amendment does not shield a suspect–defendant from a misplaced belief that a person to whom he or she voluntarily confides wrongdoing will not reveal it.[2]

Investigators contemplating the use of audio surveillance should avoid it unless the means–end factor justifies its use. Because of the overtone of being dirty business, any results obtained by this technique are often mitigated or negated by the means used.

Any electronic eavesdropping technique may be subject to counter-measures. Technicians skilled in surveillance countermeasures make extravagant claims about **debugging.** An electronic device (bug) that is wired to its receiver is difficult to detect, as is a properly connected wiretap, or the installation of a device to record the numbers to which outgoing calls are directed. If an electronic transmitting device is used, however, its radio transmissions can be detected by other electronic devices that are commercially available.

Countersurveillance activities may also include deliberate conversations intended to be heard and recorded, such as (1) incriminating statements involving innocent persons, (2) exculpatory conversations transferring or excusing guilt or guilty knowledge, and (3) scenarios intended to reveal or "blow" the surveillance by confirming the target suspect's belief in police eavesdropping. Fortunately, police investigators carefully screen incriminating or exculpatory conversations for their basic worth, and they avoid acting on any conversation calling for police response (search, arrest) unless confirmed by other independent information.[3]

CONTACT SURVEILLANCE

Contact surveillance techniques are based on the capability of certain fluorescent preparations to stain a person's hands or clothing upon contact and thus to offer observable proof of a connection between the stained person and the object under surveillance. It is difficult to deny the connection and to offer a reasonable explanation for extensive and vivid fluorescent stains in blue, orange, or green. Contact surveillance techniques may be used alone or in supplementing a visual surveillance. They are very useful when visual surveillance is not feasible, as in cases of dishonest employees and of transactions involving the payment of money.

Tracer preparations are usually in the ultraviolet spectrum and become visible only under ultraviolet light. Persons who make contact with the object under surveillance are not aware of the treated surface nor of the transfer to their clothing or hands until questioned about the contact and examined under ultraviolet light. Tracer paste is available for objects exposed to the weather, and a marking powder is available for putting tracer powder on money or any object not exposed to weather. Felt pens are available for tracer marking of objects such as money or merchandise.

Ultraviolet light is not the only option for contact surveillance. A dye powder is available that is also invisible when dry but becomes visible when wet, although it is difficult to wash off. The powder is convenient in cases of petty theft investigated in schools and business offices because a school or office supervisor can monitor the surveillance without ultraviolet light equipment.

These tracers are available from police equipment suppliers, and most police agencies have an assortment in stock from which an investigator can select the appropriate dye, powder, paste, crayon, or pen. The selected preparation should be applied liberally to the object likely to be contacted by the suspect or suspects. It should be tested before field use for its invisibility, its ability to blend in normal light, its adhesiveness, the life of its application, and the difficulty of removing the stain by ordinary washing with soap and water.

A variation of this contact surveillance is the technique of adding a tracer substance to objects or liquids commonly subject to theft. The U.S. government has added various dyes to gasoline at federal garages to enable the ready identification of government gasoline in privately owned vehicles; state agencies have marked containers of foodstuff for state institutions (when unauthorized possession is suspected); and department stores attach tracer tags to merchandise, which alert personnel at store exits unless removed by a salesclerk upon purchase.

SEARCH WARRANTS

The issuance of a search warrant is guided by the Fourth Amendment to the U. S. Constitution. This amendment states the following:

> The right of the people to be secure in their persons, houses, papers, and effects, against unreasonable searches and seizures, shall not be violated, and no Warrants shall issue, but upon probable cause, supported by Oath or affirmation, and particularly describing the place to be searched, and the persons or things to be seized.

Meeting the standard of probable cause requires a demonstration to the judge or magistrate that a crime has occurred, or is occurring, and that evidence relative to that crime will be found at a particular location. The investigator must swear under oath that the information establishing this probable cause is true to the best of his or her knowledge. The application for the search warrant must describe in detail the place to be searched and the items or person to be seized.

In 1968, Congress codified the requirements for obtaining court authority to intercept oral and wire communications in Title III of the Omnibus Crime Control and Safe Streets Act (Title III). This act was subsequently amended in 1994 when Congress passed the Communications Assistance for Law Enforcement Act (CALEA). Most states have enacted similar legislation regarding the issuance of search warrants for electronic surveillance. The courts and Congress have long considered any form of electronic surveillance extremely invasive. Because of this view, the prerequisites for obtaining a warrant authorizing electronic surveillance of oral, wire, and electronic communications, as well as silent video, are quite strict. Investigators must comply with the requirements of the Fourth Amendment regarding probable cause and particularity. In addition, Title III requires that the surveillance must be confined to only relevant conversations or activities; must specify the length of time the technique will be used; and must certify that normal investigative techniques have been tried and failed, are reasonably unlikely to succeed, or are too dangerous to attempt. These requirements are designed to ensure that electronic surveillance is not used as a first resort when other standard, less intrusive investigative techniques would expose the crime.[4]

POLICE INTELLIGENCE: CRIMINAL INVESTIGATION INFORMATION

Intelligence is the secret or clandestine collecting and evaluating of information about crime and criminals not normally available to investigators through overt sources. The detection and investigation of crime and the pursuit and apprehension of criminals require reliable intelligence; otherwise, the investigator is limited to overt acts and volunteered information and thus is severely handicapped in many cases.

The collection and analysis of information discovered by undercover police agents or confidential informants usually is channeled to a special unit within a police department. There the data are analyzed and evaluated so that they may be used in current or future investigations. To a certain extent, intelligence is warehoused until it is needed.

The police intelligence process is cyclical: a series of linked activities beginning with the needs of users (consumers) and ending with intelligence reports to specific users (Figure 7–1). The following are the six stages of the police intelligence process:

1. *Needs.*   Clear needs for information develop as police investigate unsolved crimes and attempt to block the commission of planned crimes. Police personnel demonstrating such needs are the users of police intelligence.
2. *Collection.*   The gathering of information on matters of interest, in response to user needs, is investigatory reporting: raw intelligence (information) is reported along with a field evaluation of the information, its source, and how access to the information reported is gained. The **overt collection** of information is conducted by public sources or nonintelligence police personnel; **covert collection** of information is conducted by sources such as undercover police agents and confidential informants, or it is acquired through various types of surveillance of unaware targets.
3. *Evaluation and Collation.*   The **evaluation** of information screens out useless, incorrect, irrelevant, and unreliable informations. **Collation** of evaluated information consists of its orderly arrangement, cross-indexing, and filing so that meaningful relationships can be developed between apparently unconnected bits and pieces of information.
4. *Analysis–interpretation.*   This is the core area of the police intelligence process. This activity converts information into intelligence. Unanalyzed

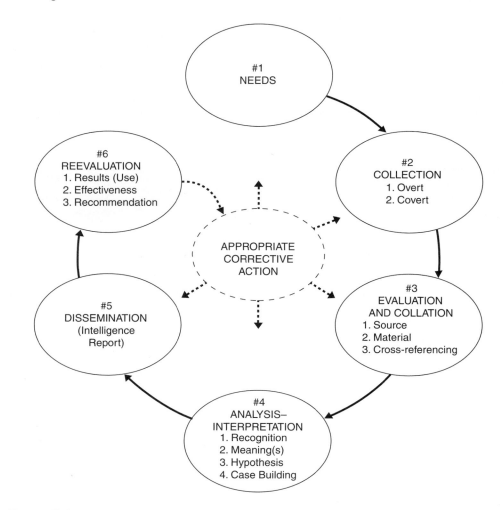

FIGURE 7–1   Six stages of the police intelligence process.

raw information gives little data about a developing pattern of criminal activity or a target suspect. As a result of **analysis**, a new recognition of the significance, meaning, and interrelationships of incoming
information can be developed. **Interpretation** is an inseparable part
of analysis—it is how collated information is related to problems
requiring solutions. Interpretation also encompasses development of
a hypothesis and a tentative statement about the meaning of the
information involved.

5. *Dissemination.*   Police intelligence reports are only released to users
   with a legitimate need for such intelligence. This need-to-know factor
   must be credibly established and strictly enforced. Unused or mis-
   used police intelligence reports sabotage a criminal investigation
   technique that is unique and often the only means of disclosing to
   police information as to ongoing and planned crimes.

6. *Reevaluation.*   This is a postmortem review of the effectiveness of police intelligence reports and of subsequent action likely to improve the
   process and its effectiveness.[5]

Criminal investigation information is police intelligence oriented to the solution of ongoing investigations. A **Criminal Investigation Information Center (CIIC)** within a police agency can assist investigators in clearing assigned cases by doing the following:

1. Reviewing and collating items of information common to police reports
2. Providing information in response to requests by investigators
3. Organizing information on criminal activities in other jurisdictions to connect it to local crime activities
4. Arranging for information "sharing" between investigators and investigative units[6]

PROACTIVE INVESTIGATION

Proactive investigation is new and innovative and moves into an attack mode long before any arrest. Cases begin with a "quiet" investigation and often move into the "hustle" mode. Proactive investigations should be based on information provided by informants, co-conspirators, and intelligence-gathering activities or on data about ongoing crimes.

Link analysis is ideal for profile work and assists in showing the relationships between a number of people and organizations in a visual form. Charting techniques have proven to be extremely valuable in clarifying or visually illustrating relationships that exist among individuals and organizations. The types of charts drawn are limited only by creativity and the needs of the user of the chart. Chart types include, but are not limited to, link charges, time line, telephone toll, case correlations, modus operandi (MO) comparison, and chronology.

UNDERCOVER POLICE AGENTS

Use of police personnel as **undercover agents** is an ethical approach to the problem of securing information about criminal operations from the inside. It is surveillance from a position of advantage. It is dangerous work but is often preferable to using an underworld informant—probably the only other source of such information. Undercover agents make excellent witnesses. Unlike underworld informants whose credibility can be attacked because of criminal histories, the police agent is a person of good reputation and character. Jurors recognize the hazards of this work and tend to accept police undercover agents as very credible witnesses.

Investigators often go underground in searching out the operations of criminals. In one case, a covert investigator arranged with an underworld informant for an introduction to a gambling operator. The agent had a good cover story of being interested in gambling, and he posed as a man who had been arrested and sentenced to prison. A few weeks later, this agent was able to identify thirteen members of a gambling syndicate operating illegally and extensively and to offer legally significant evidence against them at their trial.

Many police units use young recruits fresh from police academy classes for this work because they are not known to local members of the underworld and can uncover meaningful information of help to the investigator. Statewide narcotic and alcoholic beverage control units use their young trainees during their first year or two of employment in undercover work. Federal agencies transfer suitable personnel to areas in which they are not known to facilitate the clandestine collection of information.

LINEUPS

The **lineup** has been the traditional identification procedure used to focus a case against a suspect when eyewitnesses are available. Investigators use three different types of lineups to identify those responsible for the commission of crimes.

The **field lineup** is conducted shortly after the crime has occurred. Such lineups begin when the police have a potential suspect detained and need an eyewitness to confirm that the person being detained is responsible for the commission of the offense. Procedurally, the witnesses are brought to the suspect's location. To bring the suspect back to the scene of the crime has been held to be too prejudicial.

The witnesses to a field lineup are asked whether or not the person they are observing is the person responsible for the crime. Based upon the witnesses' responses, the suspect would be either released or held for further investigation.

A **photographic lineup** is conducted by showing a witness a number of photos, usually four to six. The photographs used in this display must be of individuals whose appearance is similar to that of the suspect's. All of the photos must be of persons of the same sex, race, approximate age, hair color, and facial characteristics, including eyeglasses, mustaches, and beards, if appropriate.

Due to the inherent suggestibility of this process, the investigator needs to advise the witness that the person responsible for the crime may or may not be among the persons present in the photographic display. The investigator should not comment when or if the witness makes a selection. The investigator should only take notes as to the witness's selection or lack thereof.

The **physical lineup** is very similar to those seen on TV and in the movies. Usually four to six persons are allowed to select their own numbered position against a wall marked clearly to indicate their height. The viewing area is well lighted while the witness viewing area is dark, which prevents the suspects from seeing the witnesses. The individuals in the lineup may be asked to speak for identification. As in photographic lineups, great care must be given to the selection of the persons participating in the lineup. All participants must be similar in appearance, and a separate lineup must be conducted for each witness.

In 1972 the U.S. Supreme Court determined, in the case of *United States v. Wade*, 388 U.S. 218 (1967), that a lineup is a critical stage of the proceedings against the defendant and that the defendant has a right to counsel at these lineups. The presence of counsel prevents the taint of an improper lineup, and the defense counsel's role is to ensure a fair lineup. The defense counsel will request that others in the lineup be of the same general age, build, and appearance as the accused. Counsel will note the physical procedure of the lineup, should request that a photograph be taken of the lineup viewed by each identification witness, and may suggest that the accused person be allowed to change positions after each witness has viewed the lineup. He or she will request a separate lineup for any other accused persons. Counsel may object to any voice identification but, if overruled, will insist that all persons in the lineup say the same words.

Counsel will insist upon being present when each witness views the lineup and says whether he or she does or does not identify any person there. Counsel also will note any comments made by the investigator in front of the witnesses.

The presence of an attorney representing a suspect is not akin to the interrogation of suspects during which an attorney representing a suspect is likely to advise a client not to talk at all or not to answer certain questions. An attorney in this bystander role should be welcomed and used by police to strengthen their identification procedures and thus strengthen their eyewitness case at trial by foreclosing the charge of unfairness or of suggestion heretofore often raised by defense counsel.

CASE STUDY

The Brown Case

In the Brown case, the identity of the perpetrator was not known at the time the investigation was started, and only extensive work by assigned investigators disclosed the identity of the suspect and led to prompt apprehension. A known identity case is likely to be underinvestigated, but the work commonly necessary in a serious felony investigation in which the perpetrator is unknown develops the type of evidence structure necessary in any prosecution of an accused person.

Although the killing of this liquor store proprietor might be considered accidental, it was legally classified as murder because it was a homicide committed in the course of committing a felony (robbery).

Synopsis

At approximately 3:20 p.m., March 12, officers on patrol received a call to proceed to the Bank Bottle Shop, a liquor store. The first patrol officer arrived at 3:25 p.m. and walked into the scene of a murder. The scene survey showed the appearance of a struggle and robbery and a victim apparently dead from massive wounds and extensive bleeding. The officer checked the body for signs of life, looked for other occupants, then called for detectives and the coroner. A neighborhood inquiry by the responding police officers located two witnesses. One witness, an adult, observed what was believed to be the killer's automobile in the parking area immediately in front of the liquor store. Another witness, a child, observed what was believed to be the killer and his automobile leave the parking area immediately in front of the liquor store. This witness also saw the automobile scrape the curb in front of the liquor store. Two nights later, evidence was found in a ditch near a golf course along a nearby street. Among the items in the ditch was a hammer that later proved to be the murder weapon. A witness who observed the automobile from which the items were thrown obtained its license number, and this led police to the defendant. This witness also identified the defendant as the driver of the car at a later lineup. In a jury trial, the defendant was found guilty and sentenced to death.

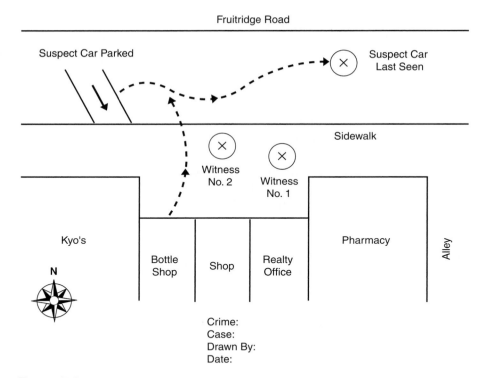

FIGURE 7–2   Brown case crime scene area—position of witnesses.

The Investigation

Sketches and diagrams were prepared by the police to depict the crime scene. Photographs of the crime scene and the extension of the scene were taken. In conjunction with the sketches (1) a written report was developed to describe the items depicted on the sketches and (2) measurements were taken to show the exact location of the evidence illustrated (Figures 7–2 and 7–3).

Recovery of physical evidence at the crime scene included a hat, hair samples, paint scrapings from the area of the parking lot curb in front of the store, and glass particles from the floor. Physical evidence recovered at the extension of the crime scene (the ditch) included clothing in a bundle and, separated from the bundle, a wheel weight tool (hammer) and hair samples from the clothing.

At the time the suspect was arrested, the shoes of the suspect and a hair sample of the suspect were secured. At the suspect's home after the arrest, a sample of the suspect's dog's hair and a sample of paint from the tire of the suspect's automobile were taken for comparison tests.

Interviews of two witnesses at the scene developed the following evidence at the trial.

Witness No. 1. (Previous questioning elicited testimony that established the age and identity of the witness.) The questioning included a number of leading questions, which are sometimes necessary and permissible when the witness is quite young. This witness was eleven years old. The prosecutor phrased the questions.

Q: Do you know the shopping center that is located on the corner of Fruitridge Road and 24th Street?
A: Yes.
Q: On March 12, a Sunday afternoon of this year, were you in the area of that shopping center?
A: Yes.
Q: What was your purpose for going there?
A: Had to get something at the grocery store.

FIGURE 7–3   Brown case crime scene sketch. Numbered locations indicate items of evidence (listed on crime reports).

Q: What were you going to get?
A: Some milk.
Q: And that was at which store?
A: Raley's.
Q: Raley's Market located in that shopping center?
A: Yes.
Q: Which way did you come from when you approached Raley's?
A: By Fruitridge Road.
Q: Do you know where the Bank Bottle Shop is?
A: Yes.
Q: Did you walk past that?
A: Yes.
Q: Do you know where Kyo's is?
A: Yes.
Q: Did you walk past that?
A: Yes.
Q: You passed Kyo's before you approached the Bank Bottle Shop?
A: Yes.
Q: Did you look in the Bank Bottle Shop as you passed?
A: Yeah.
Q: Did you see anything?
A: Saw a pair of legs lying on the floor.
Q: Did you see anything else?
A: Blood.
Q: Where did you go then?
A: I went to the store.
Q: And what did you do?
A: I just got the milk, and I left after I paid for it.
Q: Did you go back past the Bank Bottle Shop again?
A: Yes.
Q: How long did it take you between the time you passed the Bank Bottle Shop on the way to the store and the time that you passed it on your return?
A: About five minutes.
Q: Would you tell these ladies and gentlemen what you saw?
A: Well, I saw a man coming out from the store. I didn't see him run out from it, but he was coming from that direction. Then he got in his car and drove away.
Q: What did you notice about the man, if anything?
A: He had blood on him, a lot of blood, and he was carrying something in his hand.
Q: What was he carrying in his hand?
A: A small hammer.

The witness continued to relate that the man appeared as if his leg was injured and that when he started to drive away his car scraped the curb in front of the liquor store. (When arrested, the defendant had a broken leg.)

Witness No. 2. This was an adult witness who saw the car used by the robber and killer while it was parked in front of the liquor store, the Bank Bottle Shop. After giving testimony concerning his identity, he was questioned by the prosecutor as follows:

Q: Are you familiar with the shopping center at the southeast corner of Fruitridge Road and 24th Street?
A: I live in that area.

Q: Did you have occasion to be in front of that area, the shopping center, on Sunday, March 12, in the afternoon?

A: Yes, I walked down the sidewalk past the Bottle Shop.

Q: Are you referring to the Bank Bottle Shop at 2346 Fruitridge?

A: Yes.

Q: Where were you going at that time?

A: I was going to Kyo's right next door.

Q: What time was it?

A: Approximately three o'clock or a few minutes after.

Q: Did you see any automobiles in that area?

A: There was one car parked out in front.

Q: Would you describe that automobile, please.

A: It was a light, cream-colored, two-door Thunderbird with chrome down the side, and curved fenders, and it had "Thunderbird" written across the side on the front fender. (This described the defendant's automobile.)

Medicolegal (Autopsy) Evidence Developed from the Autopsy Report

Countless wounds were found about the scalp, ears, forehead, and eyes (Figure 7–4). These lacerations are generally sharp in character and are made by a relatively sharp instrument. They show a bruising along the edge and vary in size from 3 to 4 inches in length to virtual puncture wounds. There is one virtually continuous laceration across the entire frontal area from right temporal bone to left temporal bone. Both ears have been partially divided, again by a sharp instrument. There are innumerable other smaller marks, approximately six around the left eye, approximately six to eight around and under the right eye. There is extensive bruising in these areas. These wounds are basically small and appear to be virtual gross puncture wounds. Through one of the lacerations over the left frontal area, there is palpable fracture.

Extremities   There are several small bruise lacerations about the left upper arm, left forearm, and left hand. There are similar lacerations over the right hand. There are two or three superficial abrasions and lacerations over the left lower extremity and a laceration over the right heel. All these wounds—head, arms, and lower extremities—appear to be made by basically the same type of instrument.

Head   There are three areas of fracture involving the skull. The first is in the left frontal area, the second is in the right posterior temporal area, and the third is in the right occipital area. All of these are relatively undisplaced fractures, the intracranial depression being approximately 5 to 10 millimeters in each case. The most severe of these is the right temporal bone fracture, and even in this area there is little or no underlying hematoma. No trace of glass fragments was found in the head area.

I had occasion to reexamine the subject for the purpose of comparing the wounds inflicted with a weapon supplied by the coroner's office. This weapon was a hammer with a green composition handle and a peculiar type of head. There was a flat surface at the front, a side extension resembling a screwdriver, and in the rear a two-pronged structure, one prong being relatively straight and the other being curved, somewhat on the order of a bottle opener. The sutures over the left frontal area were removed and the area of peculiar dual penetration of the skull was exposed and, upon examination, was found to fit perfectly with the end of the hammer described above as two pronged. In addition, multiple lacerations over the hands and face demonstrated virtually perfect conformity to the small screwdriver-like side arm on this hammer. It was my impression, after examining the wounds again, and the hammer supplied by the coroner's office, that this instrument or one very similar to it inflicted said wounds. The skull fracture in the left frontal area appeared to be made by the pronged end of the hammer; the two other skull fractures appear to have been made by the flat end of the hammer. The hammer was then returned to the custody of the coroner's officer (Figure 7–5).

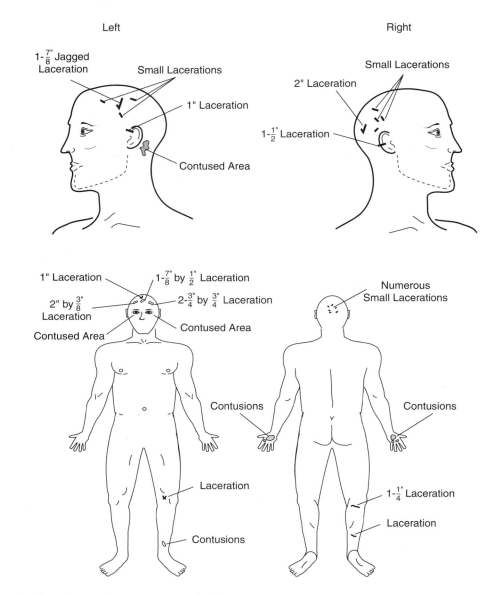

FIGURE 7–4   Coroner's report—wounds of victim in Brown case.

FIGURE 7–5   Murder weapon in Brown case.

Cause of Death   Cerebral concussion due to multiple skull fractures with multiple lacerations of the head.

Laboratory technicians in criminalistics tested the physical evidence and reported their findings as follows:

1. The hair samples from the hat recovered at the scene were similar in appearance and physical characteristics to the hair samples taken from the suspect.
2. Hair samples found on clothing recovered at the scene extension (ditch) were traceable and similar to the hair samples of the suspect's dog.
3. Glass fragments from the crime scene and glass fragments in the soles of the suspect's shoes could not be differentiated one from the other.
4. Paint scrapings from the curb in front of the crime-scene store appeared similar in color and type to the paint transfer found on the tire of the suspect's car.
5. Blood on the hammer and blood on clothing found at the scene extension (ditch) were both human and the same type as that of the deceased.

Critique

The success of the prosecution was ensured by the following:

1. The careful documentation and recovery of physical evidence at the crime scene.
2. Location and interview of the two witnesses at the scene.
3. Careful documentation and recovery of physical evidence at the scene extension (ditch).
4. Initiative of the witness at the scene extension (ditch) in recording the automobile license number and his ability to identify the driver.
5. Postarrest documentation and recovery of physical evidence from the suspect and his home and car.
6. Successful comparison of physical evidence connecting the suspect to the crime scene.

Source: Sacramento, California, Police Department and Public Defender's Office.

CHAPTER REVIEW

KEY TERMS

analysis   *142*
audio surveillance   *137*
bugging   *137*
bumper beeper   *135*
collation   *141*
contact surveillance   *139*
covert collection   *141*
Criminal Investigation
    Information Center
    (CIIC)   *143*
debugging   *139*

evaluation   *141*
field lineup   *144*
fixed visual
    surveillance   *134*
global positioning system
    (GPS) device   *135*
interpretation   *142*
lineup   *144*
link analysis   *143*
moving visual
    surveillance   *135*

overt collection   *141*
participant
    monitoring   *138*
photographic lineup   *144*
physical lineup   *144*
stakeout   *134*
surveillance   *134*
tail (shadow)   *135*
undercover agent   *143*
visual surveillance   *134*

REVIEW QUESTIONS

1. The observation of people and places by investigators to develop investigative leads is known as:
   a. Monitoring
   b. Intelligence
   c. Proactive investigation
   d. Surveillance

2. The use of undercover police officers is a preferred method of securing information about criminal operations because

   _____.

3. A mobile surveillance technique that uses multiple persons or vehicles rotating to the "close contact" position is known as what kind of procedure?
   a. Leapfrogging
   b. Hijacking
   c. Tailing
   d. Shadow tailing

4. Electronic surveillance conducted with the consent of one party to the conversation is known as:
   a. Visual surveillance
   b. Participant monitoring
   c. Contact surveillance
   d. Bugging

5. This type of surveillance is useful when visual surveillance is not feasible, as in the case of dishonest employees and transactions involving the payment of money. This type of surveillance is known as:
   a. Visual surveillance
   b. Participant monitoring

   c. Contact surveillance
   d. Bugging

6. _____ is the information about crime and criminals not normally available to investigators through overt sources that is secretly or clandestinely collected and evaluated.

7. The covert collection of information is from sources that are:
   a. Known
   b. Unknown
   c. Either known or unknown
   d. Neither known or unknown

8. The type of lineup that is held shortly after the commission of a crime and involves bringing the witness to the suspect's location is known as a:
   a. Field lineup
   b. Photographic lineup
   c. Physical lineup

9. The type of lineup that is similar to those seen on TV and in the movies where the suspect and others stand against a wall clearly marked to indicate their height is known as a:
   a. Field lineup
   b. Photographic lineup
   c. Physical lineup

10. The U.S. Supreme Court determined in the case of _____ that a lineup is a critical stage of the proceedings against the defendant.

See Appendix D for the correct answers.

DISCUSSION QUESTIONS

1. Explain the public's approval of visual surveillance and its rejection of electronic eavesdropping.
2. Why is collected police intelligence vital to the success of investigation into the operation of organized crime?

3. What restrictions exist as to the surreptitious entry of homes or places of business by police to install hidden microphones (bugs)?
4. Under what circumstances is it likely that a court would authorize police to enter a home or office surreptitiously for the purpose of installing hidden microphones?
5. How does consensual electronic surveillance differ from nonconsensual electronic surveillance?
6. What is the common scope of countermeasures used by the targets of police electronic surveillance?
7. Justify the sequential arrangement of the six stages of the police intelligence process.
8. Are undercover police agents useful? Is their work ethical?
9. Regarding the case study, how would the presence of a surveillance camera affect the outcome of this investigation?
10. What cases can you think of that have gained nationwide attention because of the presence of a video camera?
11. What effect will surveillance equipment have on the future of criminal investigation?

RELATED WEB SITES

Interested in a surveillance camera concealed in a pair of glasses or in a necktie? Check out the latest in video security at *www.scx.com*.

A full line of surveillance equipment can be seen at *www.spybase.com*.

Think your home or office is being bugged? Information on counterintelligence, bug sweeps, and surveillance countermeasures can be found at *www.tscm.com*.

chapter **eight**

Interviewing and the Detection of Deception

CHAPTER OUTLINE

After reading this chapter you will be able to:

- Define the rapport-building process and its importance in conducting a successful interview.
- Explain the competency and credibility issues involved with interviewing victims and witnesses.
- Discuss the four-step interviewing structure used in interviewing witnesses at crime scenes.
- Recognize the physical signs displayed by people who are being deceptive.
- Evaluate the methods available to investigators to refresh a witness's recollection of an event.

An **interview** is a person-to-person conversation for the purpose of obtaining information about a crime or its circumstances. Interviews should be conducted in private. The actual interview only begins after the investigator has made the person to be interviewed comfortable and has established rapport. While establishing rapport, the investigator must make assessments regarding the potential witness's competency and credibility.

The type of interview conducted at the scene of a crime is a four-step process designed to elicit complete and accurate information from the person being interviewed. These types of interviews are nonstructured and used to determine exactly what happened at the crime scene. Follow-up interviews are more structured and designed to address specific areas of concern.

While conducting an interview, the investigator must listen well. This is an interactive process that involves the interpretation of both visual and verbal input. During the interview, the investigator should be mindful of the possibility of deception on the part of the person being questioned. Clues to deception can be obtained from the suspect's body language, demeanor, and comfort level during the interviewing process. A polygraph examination can be scheduled when it must be determined whether or not the person is being deceptive.

Persons who cannot recall specific details of an event can often have their recollections refreshed. When employed by a trained practitioner, investigative hypnosis can be useful in recalling memories. Another technique used to refresh a witness's recollections is the cognitive interview process. The final step in the interview process consists of transcribing the witness's oral statement to written form.

INTERVIEW ESSENTIALS

PRIVACY

Ideally, interviews should be conducted at the police station, but that is not always possible or practical. About 80 percent of all interviews are informal and take place outside of an office setting.[1] Even interviews conducted at the scene of a crime or at a person's home or place of work must be conducted in private. Privacy can be obtained by conducting an interview inside a patrol vehicle, in another room of a house, or any place where other witnesses or outsiders cannot overhear and possibly be drawn into the discussion.

Privacy is important as it insulates the witness from the input of others. It would be unacceptable for a witness to give a vehicle or suspect description and to have another person join the conversation to try and aid the witness's recollection. Knowing that discrepancies in testimony and differences of perception commonly occur among witnesses, it is important that the investigator obtain the independent recall of each witness. Conducting interviews in private also guards against the possibility of **reverse transference** or **retroactive interference,** which occurs when a witness overhears others witnesses discussing their observations and then takes on some, if not all, of their information as his or her own.[2]

Interviewers should not lose sight of the fact that a witness is much more likely to reveal any secrets in private rather than in the presence of additional persons.[3] Another important reason interviews are conducted in private is that privacy enhances the bonding process between the witness and the interviewer. This bonding process, known as **rapport building**, is essential if an investigator is to obtain the maximum amount of information.

RAPPORT BUILDING

Rapport is defined as developing a harmonious relationship with another person. This process begins by making the person to be interviewed comfortable. The investigator should introduce himself or herself and explain the reason or purpose for the interview. The investigator should be mindful of the witness's stress due to being a victim or a witness to a crime. As a result, this person may need reassurance as to their personal safety and also may need to have their anxiety and personal comfort issues addressed. The goal of rapport building is to make the person being interviewed feel comfortable with the interview process and with the investigator. To accomplish this, the person being interviewed should always be treated with respect and the investigator should be sympathetic and empathic when necessary. A person who is comfortable with the investigator and the interview process is more likely to become an active participant and to supply more information than someone who wants to terminate the experience as soon as possible because he or she is uncomfortable.

Prior to beginning the interview, the investigator should take a few minutes to discuss subjects unrelated to the crime. A well-rounded interviewer can always find a subject about which the witness is willing to talk. Most people like to talk about themselves, so a discussion regarding where they were born is always appropriate, as is a discussion about the weather or current events. Although this may seem like a meaningless waste of time, this step is very important. This conversational process makes the person feel comfortable talking with the investigator and more likely to answer questions. The investigator also should use this step to observe the witness when he or she is not under stress and is answering questions truthfully. This is that person's norm for truthful responses, and any deviations from this norm may be indicative of deception.

COMPETENCY AND CREDIBILITY ISSUES

Another benefit of the rapport-building process is that it allows the investigator to make some assessments of the person being interviewed. The investigator should be aware of competency issues as he or she relates to the person's age, intelligence, mental state, and possible intoxication. For example, no minimum age limit is set to testify in court, but a very young person must know the difference between right and wrong and that it is wrong to tell a lie; the issue for an elderly person would be soundness of mind, which can be addressed with a few questions to determine if this person is rooted in reality and if his or her answers to questions are responsive.

Like the age issue, no minimum intelligence requirements are set for a witness to a crime. However, the potential witness should be able to focus and not be easily confused. A person's mental state will affect his or her ability to testify in court. A person who hears voices or is delusional will not make a good witness, and this state should be apparent to the interviewer after a few questions. The question of intoxication is a matter of degree. Obviously a person who is intoxicated is not going to be a competent witness, but the person who has had one or two drinks might be. The standard here would be whether or not the person's speech is clear or slurred and whether or not his or her answers are responsive to questions being asked.

Credibility issues involve considerations that would make the witness's testimony unbelievable. The witness's relationship to either the victim or suspect would affect their credibility, as testimony driven by love or hate is rightly suspect and often unbelievable. Biases and prejudices are another factor that would affect credibility. If a witness used racial slurs or other hateful epithets during the interview, this information should be noted in the official police report. Bringing a witness's biases to the attention of the prosecuting attorney will be appreciated as these officials rarely like surprises when it is time to go to trial. Other credibility issues that should be brought to the attention of the prosecutor and the defense could be any physical impairments that might affect the ability to observe an event, such as eyeglasses or hearing aids, and if they were in use at the time; conditions existing at the time of the crime, such as weather or lighting conditions that could affect a person's ability to perceive an event; and the witness's reputation for being truthful, since a person with a long criminal history is not as believable as other members of society.

INTERVIEW STRUCTURE

The interview of witnesses contacted at the scene of a crime is a four-step process. The first step starts with the basic open-ended questions, such as "What happened?" or "What did your see or hear?" Once the question is asked, the witness should be allowed to answer without interruption. No notes or audio or visual recording is conducted at this point. Taking notes only slows down the witness and interrupts his or her concentration. Notes and recordings are also intimidating to most witnesses and will motivate them to choose their words very carefully, which is exactly what the investigator does not want.

Once the witness has told his or her story and the interviewer has a good grasp of the information given by the witness, it is time for the second step: having the witness repeat his or her story while the interviewer takes notes or records the conversation. Since the witness has already given the information to the interviewer, the taking of notes or recording will not be as intimidating to the witness. In this step, the interviewer also asks appropriate questions addressing any competency or credibility issues that might arise, such as "Do you wear eyeglasses, and were you wearing them at the time?", "Were you under the influence of alcohol or drugs at the time?", "What is your relationship to the victim or suspect?" and so on.

An officer interviewing a victim of a crime.

The third step of the interview process involves the interviewer going over his or her notes with the witness. This step ensures that the interviewer accurately records or paraphrases what the witness actually said. Since this step involves action on the part of the interviewer, the pressure is off the witness. This step allows the witness to think about his or her testimony and to fill in any areas he or she might have missed.

The fourth and final step in the process involves thanking the witness for cooperating and asking for any additional information the witness wants to give at this time. The witness should be given a business card as a means of contacting the investigator in the event he or she remembers something important that was not mentioned during the interview.

Follow-up interviews are not conducted at the scene of the crime and are more structured. They occur after the event, when the investigator has a good idea of what happened and the type of questions that need to be asked of the witness.

LISTENING

Being a good listener is not easy. Most people speak at a speed of about 125 words a minute, which is extremely slow compared to how fast a person can think. As a result, a poor listener's thoughts drift away into daydreams or outside thoughts and fail to hear crucial spoken words. To aid concentration, a listener should use any extra thinking time to stay ahead of the talker, formulate ideas on where the talker is headed, and connect that information to what has already been said.

Words alone convey only part of any message. Sixty-five percent of our conversation with one another is nonverbal. Therefore, the interviewer must think beyond mere words and gather meaning from tone of voice, eye contact, facial expression, hand gestures, and body language. Remember, it is not what is said but how it is said that is important.

Being a good listener requires active involvement. The interviewer's own body movement, eye contact, hand gestures, head nodding, facial expressions, and tone of voice must convey to the witness an interest in what is being said and an interest in the witness as a person. Leaning toward the witness conveys the nonverbal signal that we are interested, even enthused, about the information being given. On the other hand, the interviewer's tone of voice, facial expression, and body movements can convey emotions of disgust, boredom, disbelief, and contempt, which can make a witness defensive or evasive.[4]

DETECTION OF DECEPTION

Repeated studies have shown that traditional methods of detecting deception during interviews succeed only 50 percent of the time, even for experienced interviewers.[5] In spite of this, investigators still need to test the veracity of those they interview.

PHYSICAL SIGNS OF DECEPTION

An alternative paradigm for detecting deception is based on four critical domains—comfort/discomfort, emphasis, synchrony, and perception management—and can increase the odds in the interviewer's favor.

Comfort/Discomfort.   A person's level of comfort or discomfort is one of the most important clues interviewers should focus on when trying to establish veracity. People who tell the truth more often appear comfortable because they have no stress, nor do they have guilty knowledge to make them feel uncomfortable. People who are being deceptive, on the other hand, first display discomfort physiologically. Their heart rate quickens, hairs stand up, perspiration and breathing increase, all of which are autonomic responses. Nonverbally, they tend to move their bodies by rearranging themselves, jiggling their feet, fidgeting, or drumming their fingers. Deceptive people tend to distance themselves from those with whom they feel uncomfortable. They will lean away from the interviewer or create artificial barriers either with their shoulders and arms or with inanimate objects in front of them. Other clear signs of discomfort include rubbing the forehead near the temple, squeezing the face, rubbing the neck, or stroking the back of the head with the hand. Research also has shown that when people are nervous or troubled, their blink rate increases, which is a phenomenon often seen in liars under stress.

Emphasis.   When people speak, they naturally incorporate various parts of their body—such as eyebrows, head, hands, arms, torso, legs, and feet—to emphasize a point. Liars, for the most part, do not emphasize with nonverbals. They will think of what to say and how to deceive, but rarely do they think about the presentation of the lie.

Synchrony.   In an interview setting, the tone of both parties should mirror each other over time. A certain amount of harmony occurs in speech patterns, sitting styles, touching frequency, and general expressions. An interview that is out of sync or lacks harmony indicates that the person being interviewed is uncomfortable and possibly being deceptive. The lack of **synchrony** often occurs when people say "I did not do it" while nodding their heads up and down as if to say "Yes, I did it," or when asked "Would you lie about this?" their heads again bob up and down. Synchrony should occur between what is being said and the events of the moment. The information and facts should remain pertinent to the issue at hand, the circumstances, and the questions. When the answers are asynchronous with the event and questions, the investigator may assume the possibility that something is wrong or that the person is stalling for time to fabricate a story.

Perception management.   Liars will try to influence their intended targets of deception with verbal and nonverbal behavior designed to demonstrate the implausibility of their involvement in committing a crime. They may use **perception management** statements, such as "I could never hurt someone," "Lying is beneath me," or "I have never lied," all of which should alert the interviewer to the possibility of deception. Statements such as "To be perfectly frank," "To be honest," "To be perfectly truthful," or "I was always taught to tell the truth" are solely intended to influence the perception of the interviewer. Nonverbal behavior, such as yawning, indicating boredom, or stretching out on a couch, as if to demonstrate comfort, are examples of perception management.[6]

POLYGRAPH TESTING

A technique useful in investigation is the instrumental detection of deception. With a cooperating subject, it is a valid investigative technique.

Modern polygraphs have three components or channels—that is, three separate capabilities for recording anatomical responses to the questioning situation. These devices and their action are as follows:

1. The **pneumograph** records respiration (breathing rate and depth).
2. The **galvanograph** records electrodermal response (skin electrical resistance changes).
3. The **cardiograph** records changes in pulse rate and blood pressure.

Generally, the cardiograph is considered to be the most reliable indicator of deception. The **galvanic skin response (GSR)**, which is measured by the

A polygraph test being administered to a subject.

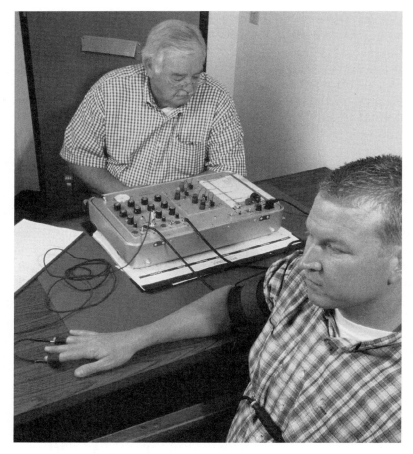

resistance of the skin to the passage of a small electric current, is the least dependable.

Instrumental detection of deception is based on human anatomy. The **sympathetic division** of the **autonomic nervous system**, when stimulated by reactions such as anger and fear, mobilizes the body and its resources for emergencies. The effects are similar to those produced by adrenaline. Sugar is released from the liver for use by the muscles, the heart rate increases, and the coagulability of the blood is heightened.

Because the autonomic nervous system reacts automatically to threat in this fight-or-flight reaction, a subject cannot hide his or her involuntary responses to a situation. If the subject is threatened, fear will occur, and when a person is fearful, an involuntary, animalistic preparation occurs within the body for fight or flight—a prehistoric form of survival insurance.

A guilty subject fears relevant questions during an examination. He or she is in a stress situation: fear of telling the truth that would expose him or her as the guilty person and fear of lying that may be revealed by the measuring instrument, exposing him or her as a liar and, therefore, as a suspect in the case.

If these tests of deception are to succeed, cooperation between investigator and examiner is necessary. Just as the investigator must do an effective job of collecting evidence and delivering it to the criminalist at the police laboratory if he or she is to secure an adequate examination from the criminalist, so too must the investigator guard against contaminating the subject of a lie detection test by any action before the testing session that will make it difficult or impossible for the examiner to administer an effective test. The investigator should not discuss the lie detector or the possibility of such tests with a suspect until a decision has been made to request tests. The reason is not so much that silence is a safeguard against the subject's use of tranquilizers, since a drugged response level will be apparent when the subject is initially tested on the instrument, but rather it is a safeguard against any future allegations that the subject had been threatened with the use of this scientific device. When talking with possible subjects about the use of tests, investigators also should avoid any mention of key facts of the crime and its circumstances. Examiners use these facts for questions at the peak of tension. For example, in larcenies this might include the exact amount of money taken or perhaps the denominations of the larger bills in cash thefts, and in assaults and homicides it might include the type of weapon used or some detail about it.

The procedure in lie detection sessions may vary slightly with the examiner, but it is similar to interviews and interrogations in that these sessions have an introductory period, the actual testing phase, and a closing. During the introductory period, the examiner explains the operation of the instrument and its ability to detect bodily responses. The use of questions calling for a simple "yes" or "no" response is also explained, and the subject is instructed to remain silent if he or she does not understand the question and to reserve explanations for the period after the questioning. The subject is put at ease and allowed to ask questions to which the examiner replies in an easily understood conversational style. The transition to the testing session for suspects in criminal cases usually is accompanied by an assurance that questions will be asked only in relation to the event under investigation. The questions may even be shown to the subject before the test. Some operators believe this to be a more effective procedure. This reassures the subject that the testing period will not dig into an entire lifetime, and it validates responses as emanating from the present situation and not from any past feelings of guilt or fear about other crimes.

The testing begins after the subject is comfortably seated, and the various tubes and wires are attached securely and without discomfort. The first round of questioning contains irrelevant questions to establish a normal level of response for the individual being questioned. After these questions have established a response level, the examiner may demonstrate the capability of the machine by asking the subject to select a card from a deck of cards. The examiner directs the subject to answer "no" to questions about the value of the card. Then, by examining the graph, the examiner determines the identity of the card and tells it to the subject. The examiner is cued to its identity by the subject's reaction, which is shown on the graph made by the instrument when the subject lied by giving the required "no" response.

The core area of the testing session follows this display of the device, and the relevant questions are interspersed with irrelevant questions. The so-called "peak-of-tension" questions relate to the actual circumstances of the crime; the remaining relevant questions may relate to events shortly before or after the crime.

No suspect can be forced to take a lie detection test. The privilege against self-incrimination, guaranteed to individuals by the Fifth Amendment to the

U.S. Constitution, protects against such coercion. However, psychological coercion is percent merely in asking a suspect to take a lie detection test, and this is likely to negate any claim of voluntariness. That is, this testing has "damned if you do" and "damned if you don't" overtones.

The process of lie detection by use of instruments and a skilled examiner has not gained the general acceptance in its field needed to warrant court acceptance of the process as scientifically valid. In *Frye v. United States*, 293 Fed. 1013 (1923), this doctrine of general acceptance was established: "While courts will go a long way in admitting expert testimony deduced from a well-organized principle or discovery, the thing from which the deduction is made must be sufficiently established to have gained general acceptance in the particular field to which it belongs" (p. 1,014).

One of the major criticisms of lie detection is that the examiner's role and the mechanics of testing jeopardize the scientific aspects of the instrument. The relationship of the examiner to the instrument in the detection of deception has been compared to that of a pilot to an airplane. The emphasis on operating skill brings the entire process into question as a way to detect truth or lies.

RECOLLECTION REFRESHMENT

It is not uncommon for a witness to forget some critical details of a crime. The response "I don't remember" can be overcome by refreshing the recollection of the witness through investigative hypnosis or the cognitive interview process.

INVESTIGATIVE HYPNOSIS

Hypnosis is a state resembling normal sleep. A person may be placed under hypnosis by the suggestions and operations of a **hypnotist**—a person who has studied the science or art of inducing hypnosis. Hypnosis in one form or another has been practiced for centuries, but its use in criminal investigation is a relatively recent phenomenon.

The use of hypnotically aided recall to enhance the memories of persons who have witnessed a crime but are unable to recall critical facts about the event is based on the belief that human memory is like a videotape machine that (1) faithfully records, as if on film, every perception experienced by the witness; (2) permanently stores such recorded perceptions in the brain at a subconscious level; and (3) accurately "replays" them in their original form when the witness is placed under hypnosis and asked to remember them.

This "videotape recorder" theory of law enforcement hypnotists, however, is not supported by a survey of professional literature in this area. Highlights of these writings are the following: (1) hypnosis is by its nature a process of suggestion, and one of its primary effects is that the person hypnotized becomes extremely receptive to suggestions that he or she perceives as emanating from the hypnotist; (2) the person under hypnosis experiences a compelling desire to please the hypnotist by reacting positively to suggestions, and hence to produce the particular responses that he or she believes are expected; (3) during the hypnotic session, neither the subject nor the hypnotist can distinguish between true memories and pseudomemories; and (4) neither the detail, coherence, nor plausibility of the resulting recall is any guarantee of its veracity.

The California legislature, in response to California's Supreme Court banning the testimony of witnesses who have been hypnotized to aid in recollection, enacted legislation that allows such a witness to testify under very limited circumstances. In part, the substance of the prehypnotic memory of the witness must be preserved in written, audiotape, or videotape form prior to the hypnosis session; the session must be extensively recorded; and the hypnosis can be performed only by a licensed medical doctor or psychologist experienced in the use of hypnosis and independent of and not in the presence of law enforcement officers, the prosecution, or the defense. Finally, the testimony of a witness who has undergone a memory-jogging hypnosis session is limited to "those matters which the witness recalled and related prior to the hypnosis."[7]

It is, therefore, risk-taking behavior for a criminal investigator to use investigative hypnosis. In some cases, the importance of discovering the identity of the person or persons responsible for a crime is so overriding that an investigator is justified in suggesting a hypnosis session for a witness whose recall of events appears to be blocked. Kidnappings in which the victim is still under the control of the kidnapper(s), terrorist acts, and serious crimes such as rape and murder are examples of instances in which hypnosis may be justified. In effect, the investigator sacrifices any future value of the witness in court to gain information about the identity of the criminal and associates, if any.

COGNITIVE INTERVIEW

Cognitive interviewing is an investigative technique used to enhance a witness's ability to recall events. This technique has proven to be as effective as hypnosis but does not jeopardize the witness's credibility in court. The witness's ability to recall events is improved by taking one or more of the following steps: reinstating the context of the event, recalling the event in a different sequence, and looking at the event from a different perspective.

Reinstating the context of an event involves having the witness recall all of his or her experiences before, during, and after the event. Instead of asking what happened, the interviewer would ask that the witness relive that part of the day surrounding the crime: how the witness got to the scene, what route was taken, what the weather was like, what was being done during and after the event, and such. This process enhances a person's retrieval of stored information: the witness can see the details of the crime in the proper sequence and context.

Changing the sequence involves having the witness recall the event in reverse order or out of order. Normally a witness is asked to recall events in chronological order, a logical sequence of events from beginning to end. By recalling the event out of order, the witness is asked to view each segment of the event independently. This process keeps the witness more focused and may reveal details that might otherwise be missed.

Changing perspective requires that the witness recall the event from the perspective of another person, such as the victim or another witness, or of an object such as a camera mounted on the wall. This technique gives the witness the opportunity to recall more of his or her experiences, and it also serves to lessen the trauma of the event.[8]

WRITTEN STATEMENT OF A WITNESS

Statements are an excellent means of documenting the story told to the investigator by the witness. They usually consist of little more than ruled forms on which a summary has been recorded of what the witness has seen and heard and of how he or she happened to be in a position to make this observation. Investigators are expected to exercise judgment as to the number of statements taken if witnesses are numerous.

When a statement is taken, it should be accurate about both what the witness has said and what the witness is prepared to testify to, under oath, about his or her observations. If any contradiction exists, defense counsel may seize it as an opportunity to destroy the credibility of the witness.

The purpose of taking a statement from a witness is generally threefold:

1. Provide a written record that will allow a prosecutor to evaluate the case and plan its presentation at trial
2. Enable the prosecutor to monitor the testimony of the witness in court
3. "Hold" a witness—that is, discourage surprise testimony by providing a possible base for impeaching the witness

If statements are taken, or if the interview develops as a situation in which a statement should be taken in accordance with standard local operating procedures, a note of the taking of a statement, or the failure to do so when a statement is warranted, should be made part of the investigator's field notes and report to the investigation.

CASE STUDY

Robbery Interview

Victim Terri Shaw, age 34, was contacted on July 3, at her place of employment, The Mini Mart, 3751 Shore Road, at 22:15 hours (10:15 p.m.). The following is a summary of her statement.

I have been working for the Mini Mart for about two years now; it will be two years in August. I work the swing shift, from four to midnight. Today I arrived at work at about 3:45 p.m. to relieve Tom, who works the day shift. It was a pretty busy shift, with the holiday tomorrow and all. I had to keep running to the back to stock the beer cases, as well as waiting on customers. I am the only one working tonight, as the other clerk called in sick.

At around 9:30 p.m., it began to slow down and I had three customers at the counter and one in the back of the store near the beer case. I waited on the customers at the counter and then when they left, the remaining customer approached the counter. He was carrying a six-pack of beer and placed it on the counter and asked for two packs of cigarettes. When I reached up to get the cigarettes, I noticed that he was reaching for something under his shirt. I thought he was getting his wallet, but when I looked back I saw that he had a small gun in his right hand.

He told me, "Keep your mouth shut and you won't get hurt. Give me the money and place it in a bag." I did as I was told and opened the register and placed the money in a small bag. There was a lot of money in the register because it was busy and I didn't get a chance to make a drop. He had me lift the tray, and I placed that money in the bag also. He then had me put the cigarettes in the bag, and he told me to get on the floor and to count to 1,000 before I got up and called the cops. He told me that he would come back to check on me to make sure I was still counting. I got on the floor and counted slowly to 1,000, and because I was afraid that he might come back, I counted to 1,500 before I got up and called the police. When I got up I noticed that the bag and the beer he placed on the counter were gone.

The guy was a white male, about 20 to 25 years of age, 5'10" to 6'0" tall, thin build, about 150 lbs., clean shaven, with brown eyes and hair. He was wearing blue jeans and a white T-shirt. I didn't see any writing on the shirt. The gun was dark blue in color and appeared to have a short barrel. I think it was a semi-auto. I would be able to identify him if I saw him again. That desperate look on his face was unforgettable.

End of statement.

CHAPTER REVIEW

KEY TERMS

autonomic nervous
  system   *162*
cardiograph   *161*
cognitive inter-
  viewing   *165*
galvanic skin response
  (GSR)   *161*

galvanograph   *161*
hypnosis   *164*
hypnotist   *164*
interview   *156*
perception
  management   *161*
pneumograph   *161*

rapport   *157*
rapport building   *157*
retroactive
  interference   *156*
reverse transference   *156*
sympathetic division   *162*
synchrony   *161*

REVIEW QUESTIONS

1. When interviewing a subject, the investigator notices that the person uses racially biased comments and slurs. The investigator should take note of these comments as they relate to that person's:
   a. Competency
   b. Credibility
   c. Varsity
   d. Truthfulness

2. When interviewing a person, the investigator should be aware that the person's age, intelligence, mental state, and level of intoxication could all affect that person's ability to testify at trial. These issues relate to the person's:
   a. Competency
   b. Credibility
   c. Varsity
   d. Truthfulness

3. Interviewing is a four-step process. At which step should the investigator begin taking notes or start recording the interview?
   a. First step
   b. Second step
   c. Third step
   d. Fourth step

4. At what step in the interview process should the investigator begin the probing process that would address any competency or credibility issues that might arise?
   a. First step
   b. Second step
   c. Third step
   d. Fourth step

5. Words alone convey only part of any conversation with another individual. What percentage of our conversations are nonverbal?
   a. 45 percent
   b. 55 percent
   c. 65 percent
   d. 75 percent

6. During the course of an interview the investigator notices that the person being interviewed begins to move around in the chair, jiggles his or her feet, and fidget. These are all signs of a lack of:
   a. Comfort
   b. Emphasis
   c. Synchrony
   d. Perception management

7. During the course of an interview, the investigator asks the subject who is responsible for the crime being investigated. The subject states that he does not know who might have committed the crime, while at the same time he nods his head up and down. This combination of words and body movement is indicative of deception and an example of the lack of:
   a. Comfort
   b. Emphasis
   c. Synchrony
   d. Perception management

8. During the course of an interview, the investigator notes that the subject has stated several times that "Lying is beneath me" and has also said "To be honest" several times. Such phrases are indicative of deception and an example of:
   a. Comfort
   b. Emphasis
   c. Synchrony
   d. Perception management

9. Polygraphs have three major components that record a body's autonomic responses. Which of these components measures respiration or breathing?
   a. Pneumograph
   b. Galvanograph
   c. Cardiograph
   d. Synchronograph

10. One major criticism of the lie detector is that the _____ role jeopardizes the scientific aspects of the instrument.

See Appendix D for the correct answers.

DISCUSSION QUESTIONS

1. In reference to the case study, is there any other information you would have included or questions you think should have been asked? Does this witness need to be reinterviewed?
2. Is it a good practice to interview persons at their place of employment? In the case study, were any options apparent? If so, what are they?
3. Think back to the professional contacts you have had with your doctor, dentist, or lawyer. How did that professional build rapport and make you feel comfortable in his or her presence?

4. In addition to the issues addressed in this chapter, what issues affect a person's credibility as a witness?
5. A crime occurs in a bar and all the potential witnesses have been drinking. Discuss how you would handle this situation and determine which, if any, of the witnesses is competent to testify in a court of law.
6. Explain the difficulties inherent in being a good listener.
7. Discuss why you think you are a good listener.

RELATED WEB SITES

Interested in becoming a polygrapher? For more information on this career choice, contact the American Polygraph Association at *www.polygraph. org*.

For answers to frequently asked questions regarding the polygraph, consult the following Web site: *www.polygraphplace.com*.

For information regarding the shortcomings of the polygraph, see *www. antipolygraph.org*.

chapter **nine**

Interrogation of Suspects

CHAPTER OUTLINE

After reading this chapter you will be able to:

- Realize that a number of Supreme Court decisions over time have led to the existing legal standards for conducting interrogations.
- Identify the legal procedural safeguards established by the *Miranda* decision and how and when these safeguards apply during an interrogation.
- Distinguish between the two types of offenders involved in the commission of a crime, and determine the best approach to be used on each during an interrogation.
- Explain what is meant by the "suspect's dilemma" and how this dilemma can assist investigators during the interrogation process.
- Discuss the various methods available to document a confession, and discuss the strength and weaknesses of each method.

An **interrogation** is defined as the adversarial questioning of a suspect with the goal of soliciting an admission or confession of guilt. Due to the adversarial nature of interrogations, confessions have been challenged in the courts over time. These legal challenges ultimately led to the *Miranda v. Arizona* decision that established procedural safeguards for in-custody questioning of a suspect.[1] An interrogation can only be conducted in an in-custody environment when the suspect voluntarily waives these safeguards.

Unlike an interview, an interrogation is highly structured. Prior to the interrogation, the investigator must thoroughly investigate the crime and its circumstances. As a result of this investigation and during the rapport-building process with the suspect, the investigator must make an assessment as to the kind of person to be interrogated. This assessment will determine the approach for the investigator to take during the interrogation. During the course of the interrogation, the suspect may admit guilt, give a full confession, or invoke his or her **Miranda rights** and terminate the interrogation.

INTERROGATION LAW

In the case of *Brown v. Mississippi*, the defendant was suspected of murder and was picked up by sheriff's deputies and taken to the sheriff's office. Once there, Brown was stripped to the waist and forced to bend over a desk. The deputies then repeatedly whipped him with their belts until he confessed. This confession was then used to convict him of the charge of murder, and he was sentenced to death. Upon appeal to the U.S. Supreme Court, the Court determined that confessions were an essential part of the investigative process but that the confession must be made voluntarily. Accordingly, Brown's confession was invalidated and the case was returned to the state courts.[2]

Other cases dealing with police procedure include *Ward v. Texas*, which was decided in 1942. In this case, the defendant was a suspect in a murder case. He was picked up for questioning and taken out of the county. He was transported from county to county more than a hundred miles from his home over a three-day period and was not allowed to contact family or friends. He finally confessed and was found guilty of murder. Upon appeal, the Court found that holding a person incommunicado was inherently coercive.[3] In the case of *Fikes v. Alabama* (1957), the defendant was held in solitary confinement for a period of ten days until he confessed.[4] In the case of *Ashcraft v. Tennessee* (1944), the defendant was questioned for thirty-six straight hours until he confessed.[5] In both of these cases, the Court found these practices to be coercive and the confession to be involuntary.

The Court also examined the characteristics of the accused. In the 1948 case of *Haley v. Ohio* the court determined that the questioning of a fifteen-year-old from midnight to five in the morning until he confessed was coercive.[6] In the case of *Davis v. North Carolina* (1966), Elmer Davis was a suspect of several burglaries and a homicide. He was questioned once or twice a day for sixteen straight days until he confessed. Throughout the questioning Davis was not told of the true reasons for the questioning: that he was a suspect in the homicide. Due to his low level of intelligence, having only completed the third or fourth grade of school, such questioning was determined to be coercive.[7]

The Court also examined the physical condition of the suspect. In the case of *Mincey v. Arizona* (1978), the defendant was involved in a shootout with police. One officer was killed, and the defendant was seriously wounded in the exchange of gunfire. The defendant was taken to the hospital and admitted to the intensive care unit. A short while later, a detective began to question the defendant even though a tube had been inserted in his throat to help him breathe. To answer, the defendant responded by writing his answers on pieces of paper. During questioning, the defendant lost consciousness several times and questioning was delayed for medical treatment. After four hours, the defendant finally confessed and was convicted of murder. On appeal, the Court found that the defendant's will was weakened by pain and shock and, therefore, his confession was not voluntary.[8]

In the case of *Townsend v. Sain* (1963), the defendant was a suspect in a robbery and murder. He was a heroin addict and during questioning began exhibiting symptoms of withdrawal from the drug. The detectives summoned a doctor who administered medication to alleviate the discomfort of the withdrawal symptoms. Unknown to the detectives, the medication had the effect of a truth serum and the defendant confessed. Upon appeal the Court determined that the confession was not the product of the defendant's free will and was, therefore, not voluntary.[9]

In 1964 the Court heard the case of *Escobedo v. Illinois*. The defendant's brother-in-law was fatally shot, and the following morning the defendant was taken into custody and questioned. He did not make a statement and was released that afternoon on a writ of habeas corpus obtained by his lawyer. A few days later his crime partner confessed and stated that Escobedo had fired the fatal shots. Escobedo was again picked up for questioning and transported to the police station. En route to the station he requested to speak to his attorney and the request was denied. Shortly after Escobedo reached the police station, his attorney arrived and was denied his request to speak with his client. After about four hours of questioning, Escobedo confessed to the crime and eventually was convicted of murder. Upon appeal, the Court held that when "the investigation is no longer a general inquiry into an unsolved crime but has begun to focus on a particular suspect, the suspect has been taken into police custody, the police carry out a process of interrogations that lends itself to eliciting incriminating statement, the suspect has requested and been denied an opportunity to consult with his lawyer, and the police have not effectively warned him of his absolute constitutional right to remain silent, the accused has been denied 'the Assistance of Counsel' in violation of the Sixth Amendment to the Constitution."[10]

Two years later the Court expanded the procedural safeguards established in the *Escobedo* decision. In the case of *Miranda v. Arizona* the court held that when a person is taken into police custody, in which his or her freedom of movement is lost,[11] and he or she is being interrogated with questions designed to elicit an incriminating response,[12] then the police must advise the suspect of the following points of law, known today as Miranda rights:

1. You have the right to remain silent.
2. Anything you say can be used against you in a court of law.
3. You have the right to talk to an attorney and have an attorney present before and during questioning.
4. If you cannot afford an attorney, one will be appointed free of charge to represent you before and during questioning, if you desire (Figure 9–1).

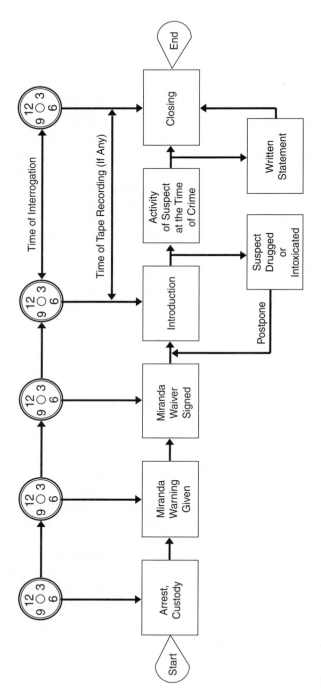

FIGURE 9–1   The process of custodial interrogation.

The Court established that, procedurally, if a person indicates in any manner that he or she does not want to talk to the police, then the interrogation must stop. If the suspect indicates that he or she wants an attorney, then the interrogation must stop until the suspect has had the opportunity to consult with an attorney. The suspect may waive these procedural safeguards; however, the prosecution then has a "heavy burden" to prove that the waiver was freely and knowingly given.[13]

THE WAIVER

Police are routinely seen in the movies and on TV advising a suspect of their so-called Miranda rights while they are in the process of handcuffing a suspect. While this may be acceptable procedure, it is not required by the *Miranda* decision, and it is doubtful if anyone would agree to being questioned at this time. The so-called Miranda rights need only be given when the two-prong test of custody and interrogation come together. A suspect may be interrogated and not be in custody, as in questioning over the telephone, or be in custody and being asked questions not designed to elicit an incriminating response. In these situations Miranda is not required. As in an interview situation, an investigator needs to build rapport prior to beginning an interrogation. Although small talk with a suspect might not be appropriate, obtaining background information is. Questions such as place of birth need to be asked and offer opportunities for other informal questions. Such questioning, which does not meet the definition of interrogation per *Innis*, allows the investigator to build rapport with the suspect.

Ernesto Miranda, whose rape conviction was appealed to the U.S. Supreme Court and resulted in the now famous "Miranda Warnings."

Miranda Warning

Report #_____

1.   You have the right to remain silent.

2.   Anything you say can and will be used against you in a court of law.

    a.   Do you understand that you have the right to remain silent?

       ❏ YES_____   ❏ NO_____

    b.   Understanding that right, do you wish to talk to me now?

       ❏ YES_____   ❏ NO_____

3.   You have the right to talk to an attorney and have an attorney present before and during questioning.

4.   If you cannot afford an attorney, one will be appointed free of charge to represent you before and during questioning, if you desire.

    c.   Do you understand you have the right to talk to an attorney?

       ❏ YES_____   ❏ NO_____

    d.   Understanding that right, do you wish to talk to me now?

       ❏ YES_____   ❏ NO_____

SIGNED_____

OFFICER:_____   BADGE: _____

OFFICER:_____   BADGE: _____

TIME: _____   DATE: _____

The suspect should initial the appropriate answer to each question (yes, no) and sign the waiver. The officer should then sign and date the form.

FIGURE 9–2   Miranda warning—action indicating a suspect about to be questioned by police while in their custody has thoughtfully waived his or her Miranda rights. (See Appendix A, Case Briefs, for a digest of the *Miranda* case.) Source: Sacramento, California, Sheriff's Department.

After building rapport, the suspect should be advised of his or her Miranda rights (Figure 9–2). The Court determined that the prosecution has a "heavy burden" to prove that this waiver was freely and knowingly given. This burden can be met by the use of the Miranda Advisement form used by most police agencies in this country. However, this form is not required by the decision, and other means such as audio or video taping can be used to meet this legal burden.

INTERROGATION ESSENTIALS

PRIVACY

Interrogations, like interviews, should be conducted in private. A suspect is more apt to reveal secrets, such as involvement in a crime, in the privacy of a room occupied only by himself or herself and the investigator. The room should be free from outside noises and off limits to anyone not directly involved in the interrogation. The interrogation room should not contain any ornaments, pictures, or other objects that would in any way distract the attention of the person being interrogated. Even small, loose objects, such as paper clips or pencils, should be out of the suspect's reach so that they cannot be picked up and fumbled with during the interrogation. These tension-relieving activities can detract from the effectiveness of the interrogation, especially during the critical phase when a person may be ready to confess.[14]

PRIOR TO INTERROGATION

Prior to conducting an interrogation, the investigator needs to know as much as possible about the crime in question. What do the victim and witnesses have to say about the suspect's involvement in the crime? What evidence exists that implicates the suspect, and how does this evidence apply to the suspect? The investigator's goal here is to know as much about the crime as the suspect does. In many cases, especially homicides, the suspect may be the only person alive who knows what actually happened during the commission of the crime.

A thorough investigation is important because the suspect is going to know if the investigator is not prepared and only on a "fishing expedition." Such a lack of preparation allows the suspect to lose respect for the investigator's abilities and provides another reason to lie. To prevent this, the investigator wants to know the answers to the questions before asking them.

APPROACH

During the investigative phase and while building rapport, the investigator needs to make an assessment regarding the person to be interrogated. The investigator needs to consider the suspect's personal characteristics, the type of offense, the probable motivation for the commission of the crime, and the suspect's initial response to questioning. Based upon this assessment, the investigator could determine if the person to be interrogated is an emotional or nonemotional offender.

An **emotional offender** is a person who experiences considerable feelings of remorse and mental anguish as a result of committing the offense. This individual has a strong sense of moral guilt—in other words, a troubled conscience. Typically these offenders tend to commit personal crimes, such as homicides, rapes, and physical assaults, or they are first-time offenders. A sympathetic approach that uses expressions of understanding and compassion is appropriate for these offenders.

A **nonemotional offender** refers to a person who ordinarily does not experience a troubled conscience as a result of committing a crime. This offender may have developed an antisocial personality disorder—a conditioned response to repeated prior success in escaping punishment through lying—or may be the career criminal who perceives committing crimes as a business. In the latter case, the suspect approaches arrest, prosecution, and possible conviction as an occupational hazard and experiences no regret or remorse as a result of exploiting victims. The most effective tactic to use on this offender is the **factual analysis approach**. This approach appeals to the suspect's common sense and reasoning rather than emotions and is designed to persuade the suspect that his or her guilt is established and, consequently, the intelligent choice to make is to tell the truth.[15]

WHY PEOPLE CONFESS

You would think that when suspects are taken to the police station to be questioned concerning their involvement in a particular crime, their immediate reaction would be a refusal to answer any questions. It would also seem that once a suspect senses the direction in which the interrogation is heading, the conversation would come to an end. However, for various psychological reasons, suspects continue to speak with investigators. In most cases, suspects commit crimes because they believe that it offers the best solution to their needs at the moment. If investigators are able to convince suspects that the key issue is not the crime itself but what motivated them to commit the crime, they will begin to rationalize or explain their motivating factors.

Investigators must conduct interrogations with the belief that suspects, when presented with the proper avenue, will use it to confess their crimes. Research indicates that most guilty persons who confess are, from the outset, looking for the proper opening during the interrogation to communicate their guilt to the interrogators. However, before confessing, a suspect must feel comfortable in his or her surroundings and must have confidence in the interrogator, who should attempt to gain this confidence by listening intently and allowing the suspect to verbalize his or her account of the crime.[16]

THE SUSPECT'S DILEMMA: THE CRIME PARTNER

When a suspect committed the crime with a partner he or she has a problem: an accomplice. The suspect must decide whether or not to sacrifice a crime partner for some mitigation of his or her own involvement in the crime and must make the decision before the crime partner does. This dilemma is often thought of simply as "Better him than me."

Advising a person being interrogated that a crime partner has talked is a practice that may taint an interrogation if done to persuade a suspect to waive his or her right to remain silent. If done honestly, it can, at times, be an effective technique. The offensive–defensive character of an interrogation session is replete with covert communication. The threatening aspect of the experience may be perceived with little outward awareness, but subliminally the person being interrogated experiences a strong anxiety response. The interrogator does not need to comment; the worry and concern about whether a crime partner has talked provoke a natural form of anxiety. Many offenders assume that their partner has talked or is about to talk and that the only smart thing to do is to talk first—or better, to tell everything.

Interrogators should be alert to situations in which the person about to be interrogated is a professional criminal who has an amateur crime partner. The

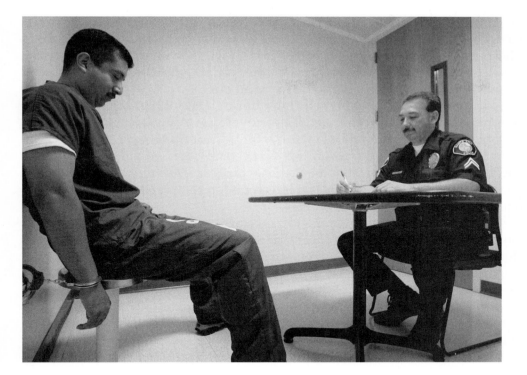

An officer interrogating a subject in private in an interrogation room.

pro may be the "torch" of an arson ring, the hired killer of a heavily insured partner in commerce or industry, or the burglar and thief with a businessperson receiver who buys all the thief can steal.

DOCUMENTING THE CONFESSION

Three methods are used to document a suspect's confession: video recording, audio recording, and writing. Each method has its own strengths and weaknesses.

The strength of video recording is that it captures exactly what happened during the interrogation process. These video recordings can help meet the burden of proof required to demonstrate that a waiver of Miranda rights was freely and knowingly given and that no coercion was used to obtain the confession. As the video records not only what was said but how it was said, the triers of facts can view firsthand any deception on the part of the suspect.

Video recording that is done surreptitiously allows the interrogation process to be viewed by others without the suspect knowing that it is being recorded. State or local law may bar surreptitious taping. However, the U.S. Constitution should not be a bar since a suspect would be hard pressed to prove that he or she had a "reasonable expectation of privacy" while under police interrogation in a station-house interview room. Indeed, the Miranda warning makes explicit that anything suspects say can and will be used against their interests.[17]

The covert recording of an interrogation allows other detectives to watch the interrogation and be a resource to the interrogator regarding areas of concern, deceptive movements, and officer safety issues. Such covert recording allows for the removal of two-way mirrors in interrogation rooms. These mirrors are well known by everyone who watches crime dramas on television. These mirrors work against the concept of privacy and do not aid the rapport-building process because the suspect is aware that other persons are on the other side of the mirror monitoring everything happening in the interrogation room. Another benefit of covert recording is that suspects can be left alone in the room while their activities continue to be monitored. In such situations it is not unusual for suspects to begin to talk to themselves and make incriminating statements. This tactic is even more effective when crime partners are left alone in the interrogation room and allowed to talk to one another.

One of the weaknesses of video recording is that it can be edited or altered. To guard against this allegation, the interrogation room should have a clock on the wall that is included in the recording. Any edits would be apparent to the viewer as the time would change if the tape were to be edited. Interrogation sessions often last for hours, and a drawback of using this technology is that the prosecuting attorney, the defense attorney, and the jury do not want to have to view the entire contents of the video tape of an interrogation. Another problem is that suspects, especially emotional offenders, may begin to sob or cry during the interrogation and are, therefore, difficult to understand when they are making a confession. These problems can be overcome by reducing the confession to writing.

The strength of audio recording is that this technology is available for field use for those interrogations that occur outside of an interview room setting. This technology can be used to capture the voluntary nature of the Miranda waiver, as well as the confession itself. To guard against the allegation that these tapes can be easily edited, the investigator should state the date and time the interrogation begins and ends. The lack of any time difference ensures that the tape has not been edited. However, while taping the interrogation, the investigator must not turn the recorder off and on. Taping an interrogation ensures that the investigator correctly records what the suspect has to say.

On the negative side, tape recorders have a tendency to be intimidating to some people if not used surreptitiously. Once again, the overt use of a tape recorder will work against the concepts of privacy and rapport building. The issues of using a tape recorder surreptitiously are the same as those with video recording.

The third method of documenting an interrogation is to acquire a written confession supplied by the suspect. This captures the words spoken by the suspect but not the suspect's unspoken body language. A written form documenting the waiver of Miranda rights and the written statement supplied by the suspect comprise a very effective means of documenting the voluntary nature of a waiver and confession. In the final analysis, the confession documented by video recording or audio recording must be memorialized in writing. Reducing the confession to writing allows the confession to be condensed to a concise statement of what happened, which can be included in the police report.

CASE STUDY

Interrogation of a Robbery Suspect

Detectives question a suspect in an armed robbery of a credit union and obtain the following statement:

Statement of Suspect

DEROSE: I am Detective Bob DeRose and this is Lieutenant Jacob Saylor. The time is now 1532 hours, the date is August 24. We would like to interview you regarding the offense today. Before doing so, I will advise you of your rights, which I will read to you from this form: "I acknowledge that I have been advised by officers Lieutenant J. Saylor and Detective R. DeRose, that I have the right to remain silent and that anything I say can and will be used against me in a court of law. I have the right to a lawyer and to have him present with me during questioning, and a lawyer will be appointed to represent me before any questioning if I cannot afford to hire one and desire to have a lawyer. Each of these rights has been explained to me, and I understand them. Having these rights in mind, I nevertheless waive them and consent to talk to the officers." Do you understand that?

STRAUS: I understand them, and I waive them.

SAYLOR: You understand and you want to waive and talk to us?

STRAUS: Yes.

DEROSE: How far did you go in school?

STRAUS: Just about finished the second year of college.

DEROSE: Concerning the robbery that occurred at the credit union, could you first describe what happened from the time you got up this morning?

STRAUS: Concerning the robbery? Well, I got up, I thought, well, should I go to work? Today's the 24th and the railroad gets paid on the 24th, and people will be cashing their paychecks at the office, at the credit union office. So having made up my mind to touch and go, I called into work and told them I had a doctor's appointment and wouldn't be there until approximately 10:00 or 10:30. And I proceeded to arrange a pair of blue coveralls, a ski mask, gloves, and the piece—the pistol, the thirty-eight.

DEROSE: Where did you get the coveralls and the other stuff?

STRAUS: I bought them on the 9th of this month at the Emporium, I believe. I bought the ski hat at a sporting goods store next to Allen's Shoes on Temple Boulevard. The thirty-eight is registered to my brother-in-law, and I took it without his knowledge, hoping to return it today.

DEROSE: Then what happened?

STRAUS: Then I got into the car and went down to the credit union. It is sort of hazy from there. I circled the block a couple of times. I parked the car in a loading zone and went to see if they were open, and the door was unlocked, from which I figured they were open at the time. So I had the coveralls on and the hat on my head—I didn't have it over my face, and I had my fist in my pocket. And I heard loud noises in there—people talking—so I figured there was someone in there. I chickened out and I went back to the car and started to leave, and I said if I don't do it now, I won't do it. So I went back and parked in the parking place I showed you. Then I got out of the car. I walked over to the credit union. I went in the door and I heard the same loud male voices. There was two females. There was a couple female clerks in there. So I chickened out again, and I walked halfway back to the car. I say well, if I don't do it, I'll never do it again. And so I went back and got inside the building. I locked the door, the front double doors, behind me, went in and opened the inner door. And there was a man standing at the counter. He didn't turn around, and I put the gun—pointed the gun at the man and I said, "This is a holdup." I believe—I don't know exactly what I said.

DeRose: Do you remember what the man looked like?

Straus: No. I only saw the back of his head. And I told him, "Keep quiet and everything will be all right." I said to the girl behind the counter, "Give me the money." And I had a paper bag in my hand, and I put the bag on the counter. And the man said, "Do as he says." And I was holding the gun on him.

DeRose: Before you committed this robbery, did you anticipate what could happen?

Straus: No.

DeRose: Did you ever think about getting caught?

Straus: No. I didn't worry about getting caught because I figured if I got caught—I got caught.

DeRose: Well, all of the foregoing statements you have made have been given voluntarily and we haven't promised you anything?

Straus: No. Not yet.

DeRose: And everything has been given of your own free volition in this statement?

Straus: Yeah.

CHAPTER REVIEW

KEY TERMS

emotional offender   177
factual analysis
   approach   177

interrogation   172
Miranda rights   172

nonemotional
   offender   177

REVIEW QUESTIONS

1. In what U.S. Supreme Court decision did the Court decide that confessions were an essential part of the investigative process but that the confession must be made voluntarily?
   a. *Brown v. Mississippi*
   b. *Ward v. Texas*
   c. *Escobedo v. Illinois*
   d. *Miranda v. Arizona*

2. In what U. S. Supreme Court decision did the Court first decide that the police must advise the person being interrogated that he or she has a right to remain silent and to have the assistance of counsel?
   a. *Brown v. Mississippi*
   b. *Ward v. Texas*
   c. *Escobedo v. Illinois*
   d. *Miranda v. Arizona*

3. The Court has established a two-prong test that determines when the so-called Miranda warnings must be given. This two-prong test is met when _____ and _____ occur.

4. Prior to conducting an interrogation what must an investigator do?
   a. Interview
   b. Investigate
   c. Analyze
   d. Theorize

5. A/an _____ offender is a person experiencing a considerable

amount of remorse and mental anguish as a result of committing the offense.

6. A person who does not experience a troubled conscience as a result of committing a crime is known as a/an _____ offender.

7. The factual analysis approach during an interrogation works best on what type of offender?
   a. Youthful
   b. Emotional
   c. Nonemotional
   d. Hardened criminal

8. The overt use of a tape recorder during an interrogation will work against the concepts of privacy and rapport building. As used in this context, what does the word *overt* mean?

   a. Surreptitious
   b. Hidden
   c. Open to view
   d. Clandestine

9. A sympathetic approach that uses expressions of understanding and compassion is appropriate for what type of offender?
   a. Youthful
   b. Emotional
   c. Nonemotional
   d. Hardened criminal

10. A suspect is more apt to reveal secrets, such as involvement in a crime, if the interrogation is conducted in _____.

See Appendix D for the correct answers.

DISCUSSION QUESTIONS

1. What has been the impact upon criminal investigation of the U.S. Supreme Court's *Miranda* decision? What are its future implications?
2. Is the offensive–defensive situation common to all interrogations?
3. Explain the similarities and differences between interviewing witnesses and interrogating suspects.
4. Is it likely a case would cease being a general inquiry into the circumstances of a crime when a person is taken into custody and questioned by police as a suspect?
5. Describe the Miranda warning. What are its related procedural safeguards?
6. What is meant by *adversarial nature of interrogations*?
7. Explain the sympathetic approach used during an interrogation, and discuss the type of person with whom this approach works best.
8. When advising the suspect of his or her rights in the case study, the detectives do not quote the exact wording of the *Miranda* decision. Could this be a problem for the prosecution?
9. At the start of the case study interrogation, why did the detective ask the suspect about his schooling?
10. How would the fact that this subject is an admitted heroin addict affect the interrogation process?
11. What is the importance of asking the suspect about promises?

RELATED WEB SITES

To research U.S. Supreme Court cases, consult the following site: *www.findlaw.com*.

To learn more about the Supreme Court of the United States, visit the Court's Web site at *www.supremecourtus.gov*.

chapter **ten**

The Arrest of the Accused Person

CHAPTER OUTLINE

After reading this chapter you will be able to:

- Appreciate the need for urgent action in the preparation of a broadcast alarm for wanted persons who have just committed a crime.
- Understand the progression from the broadcast alarm to the use of wanted notices in the search for wanted persons.
- Discuss the various public sources of information that are available to investigators in their search for wanted persons.
- Explain the concept of an arrested person's "pedigree."
- Discuss the options available to an investigator to close an investigation without making an arrest.

T he accused person may be known and easily located. On the other hand, the suspect's name may not be known, and he or she may have no known address or may be in hiding or in flight. Early in the investigation, an alarm or pickup order containing only fragmentary identification is broadcast locally. Its purpose is to apprehend the perpetrator in flight. When the initial hue and cry alarm has failed, the investigators must collect and publish more detailed information about the perpetrator. This is the means by which other officers, distant in time and space from the crime, locate and identify a person in flight from justice.

The tracing of fugitives depends a great deal on the expertise with which sources of information are exploited for adequate and meaningful information about the wanted person. Although the crime and its circumstances provide the basic information, data about the suspect as a person also are available to a diligent investigator in the records of criminal justice agencies, credit reports, telephone records, employment histories, and public records. Basic research often rewards the investigator with meaningful information.

An arrest brings the investigation into close focus. The prisoner can be searched and booked, and, in the process of recording facts, fingerprinted for positive identification. Evidence that can be collected at this time will be collected, recorded, and preserved. The prisoner may be anxious to talk to the police and may deny or admit to being the criminal. This is the time to warn arrested persons of their constitutional rights to silence and legal counsel, and it is the time to ascertain if the accused person will waive such rights and participate in an interrogation session by cooperating with the investigator.

THE BROADCAST ALARM, OR PICKUP ORDER

The initial hue and cry in pursuit of the perpetrator of a crime emphasizes the distinctive identifying characteristics of the person, vehicle, or property wanted. Transmission of **broadcast alarms**, or orders to pick up a suspect, which alert other police units to the recent crime, usually are done first by radio and then by Teletype, fax, or computer. The first police officer on the scene of a crime or the investigator receiving the report of a crime has the responsibility to obtain the best possible physical description of the criminal and his or her car, if any. A broadcast alarm detailing a want is most effective when it is sent promptly.

Despite the urgency for broadcasting the alarm or pickup order to alert other officers, accuracy must be emphasized. Law enforcement agents no longer ask leading questions to obtain descriptions, and they emphasize in their reports that the description is a composite inasmuch as it usually is secured from both victim and witnesses. Officers do not change the composite description once it is entered in their field notes or other records, nor do they change the composite description when the wanted person is arrested or when a wanted vehicle is recovered and found to differ from the composite description.

Identifying characteristics that make a person or a vehicle different from other persons or vehicles are the basis for success in the apprehension of suspects. Partial descriptions, if distinctive, such as a damaged fender on a vehicle coupled with a fragment of the registration number, have resulted in apprehensions. In cases involving juveniles, a painted identification or other marking on the car may be very distinctive. Several weak, general descriptions that are individually insufficient for identification of suspects often total up to significant identifying characteristics when broadcast as the occupants of a vehicle.

The content of wanted notices at this time in the investigation is oriented toward characteristics that are observable and that will guide searching police. Although a brief description of the crime (including the proceeds of a theft) is included, the major content usually is limited to describing persons, vehicles, and weapons.

The brief description of the crime is no more than the offense the offender is suspected of committing and the date, time, and location of occurrence. Stolen property is not described, but a few details of the amount of currency taken or the kind of item stolen are included. If a weapon was used, its type and description are included in the broadcast to alert police that the fleeing suspect is likely to be dangerous.

When more than one perpetrator is described, a listing by number (Suspect No. 1, Suspect No. 2) is recommended. The following characteristics, in the order listed, are standard for these notices: race, sex, adult or juvenile, age, height, weight, build, hair color, eye color, distinguishing characteristics. A suspect's height and weight are usually reported in blocks or ranges: upward from 5 feet in 3-inch intervals, and from 100 pounds in 20-pound intervals.

Clothing is an observable characteristic that affords excellent opportunities for recognizing a wanted person. In the "How Dressed" section of a wanted notice, the clothing of each suspect is described, and the color, cloth, and design of the outer garments are noted. The absence of garments normally worn by others in the area is also noted. The following items, in the order listed, are standard in such alarms or pickup orders across the nation: bareheaded; hat (color and design: black, gray, porkpie, skimpy brim); cap (color); overcoat (color, cloth, design); jacket (color, cloth, windbreaker); suit (color, cloth, design); shirt (color, dress or sport); trousers or shorts (color); dress, slacks, or shorts (color, cloth, design).

Vehicle descriptions in these alarms or pickup orders generally are limited to the following: year, make, model, color, state license number, damage or suspected damage, number and sex of occupants.

The usual categories of sedan, station wagon, van, convertible, and sports car have been supplemented by pickup, "crew" pickup, jeep, and pickup with camper.

The direction of flight, if it is known, is also included. Roadblocks may be set up, and buses and other public transportation vehicles may be searched. A surveillance of the area may be conducted for criminals who seek refuge temporarily by hiding in yards, basements, hallways, and on roofs along the escape route.

The initial notices usually are concluded with a statement of the authority for the alarm or pickup order—at the local level, the name of the investigator and assignment; at other levels, the name of the issuing police department.

All broadcast alarms are distributed locally, but their coverage is expanded as the interval from the time of the crime indicates the possible enlargement of areas of flight. An **all points bulletin (APB)** is justified when adequate descriptive information is available. The geographical coverage of an APB depends on the locale and may extend to neighboring states.

As facts become available to investigators during the search, it becomes urgent to add information to what was originally broadcast. This added information may be simply a notice that the vehicle, when located, should be protected but not processed until the evidence technicians can visit the scene and search the vehicle for fingerprints and other evidence. Additional facts on the identity of a vehicle, such as the full license number and the name and description of the registered owner, may relate to information secured from the state's Department of Motor Vehicles. Additional knowledge about the suspect may relate to no more than a fragment of information about appearance, but it may be a full name and description of the perpetrator when a prompt and specific identification has been made. The objective of broadcasting facts as soon as they are available is to provide searching police with enough identification to pick out a fleeing person or vehicle with some certainty that the person or vehicle being stopped is the subject of the alarm.

RECORDS AS SOURCES OF INFORMATION

Agencies that may provide an investigator with information useful in locating a fugitive range from criminal justice agencies that might have processed the suspect at some previous time to the vast data banks of agencies providing credit or telephone service.

Investigators develop a knowledge of where to look for useful information. It may be found among records systems common to all localities, but it also may be in the records native to a specific locality. For instance, in Reno, Nevada, the records of the county clerk contain data on every divorce granted in this mecca of unhappy spouses, and these records are dated and cross-referenced with the names of wives, children, parents, and witnesses. Public records in the section of Florida from Miami to Hollywood have been a source of information about husbands "on holiday" and their girlfriends when they were arrested on some minor charge. In every section of the country, a local record system contains unusual information generally known only to investigators who have stumbled upon it or have been advised of its existence by friends or associates.

Investigators should develop their own ready-reference file as to sources of information. In working on an investigation, the assigned investigator has a general idea what he or she is looking for, and a ready-reference information sources file will provide information as to where such information may be found, the form in which it may be found, and how to gain access to it.

A suggested form for a file of this type includes type of information, source, name, and other identification data of a "contact" (for example, telephone number).[1]

Among the sources of information are the following:

1. *City and County.*   Vital statistics; tax, welfare, courts, schools, jurors, and voting records; prosecutor and public defender.
2. *State.*   Tax and corporate records; courts and alcohol beverage records; consumer affairs data; motor vehicle license and registration files.

3. *Federal.*   Federal Bureau of Investigation, and other federal law enforcement agencies such as the Secret Service, Immigration and Customs Enforcement, Postal Inspection Service, Securities and Exchange Commission, and military investigative agencies.
4. *Private.*   Moving companies; telephone company (public directory and directories on file at company office) and other public utilities; credit reporting agencies; banks and finance companies; Better Business Bureau, Chamber of Commerce, business (trade) directories, industry and trade associations, professional associations, etc.[2]

WANTED NOTICES

A **wanted notice** should provide full information about the fugitive and about areas in which he or she is likely to be found. Copies are sent to police in neighboring areas and mailed, faxed, or sent electronically to police in areas that the fugitive is likely to visit, usually large cities and resort centers in adjacent states. The basic content of a wanted notice is a photograph or sketch of the fugitive, his or her fingerprints, and an extensive personal description (Figure 10–1).

The standard mug shot taken at the time of a previous arrest is made part of the wanted notice. When this is not available, any close-up photograph from public records or from associates of the suspect may be substituted. Full-length shots of the suspect alone or with a group of associates can be used to supplement the standard front and profile photographs. Ideally, color photography and printing should be used in wanted notices because they offer a lifelike image of the wanted person.

The fingerprint classification of a fugitive in the wanted notice is a major point of identification. Often these notices contain a facsimile of the fingerprints of a suspect, and a comparison can be made by the local agency making the arrest. In recent years, the fingerprinting of persons not charged with a crime has increased, and these records are available to police agencies preparing wanted notices. It is the classification and comparison of fingerprints that guarantee against the apprehension of the wrong person. Any other type of identification always includes the possibility of error. For this reason, investigators should search diligently for a fingerprint record for the wanted notice.

Observable and distinctive characteristics are used in describing a person. Identifying physical characteristics are necessary to locate the fugitive and to offer some positive identification for an arrest.

The standard base of details for describing wanted persons is race, sex, age, height, weight, color of eyes, and color of hair. Racial appearance or national origin are also identifying characteristics. Many police units use a standard listing and suggest that the most descriptive designation applicable to the fugitive be used. The usual list is White, African American, Mexican, Indian, Chinese, Japanese, and other.

Observable physical characteristics found useful by police in tracing fugitives have been codified in a "relevant matter" listing of key items for a

ARMED ROBBERY SUSPECT

Date: **2/23/2005**

Case # **00-0070**

Height: **5 Feet 9 inches**

Weight: **160**

Age: **20**

Sex: **M**

Race: **White**

OTHER INFORMATION BELOW

On Monday, 2-14-05, approximately 11 P.M., a university professor was robbed on the pathway between Green and Gray Halls at Valley University. The suspects assaulted the victim with a stun gun and departed with his wallet. The suspects are described as follows:

1. White male, early 20s, 5'9" to 5'10", 160 to 180 lb., sparse, straggly beard. He was wearing a dark blue sweatshirt with some type of writing on it. (A composite of the suspect is shown above.)

2. White male, early 20s, no further description.

3. Hispanic female, early 20s, 5'0" to 5'2", 100 to 105 lb., described as "petite."

The University Police at Valley University are asking the public's help in identifying the suspects.

University Police Department, Valley University
(555) 555-5555

TRAK (136:1.6.48) This flyer produced on a TRAK system. For more information about TRAK see www.trak.org

FIGURE 10–1 Typical wanted notice.

personal description. The following are the items of identity believed to be important:

1. *Face*—shape
2. *Hair*—color, type, and cut
3. *Eyes*—color, type, and defects
4. *Nose*—shape and size

5. *Mouth*—shape, size, and unusual characteristics
6. *Chin*—shape, size, and if dimpled
7. *Ears*—type, size, and defects
8. *Eyebrows and beard*—appearance
9. *Scars and marks*—location and type
10. *Amputations and deformities*
11. *Speech*
12. *Peculiarities*

In using these relevant characteristics, a person may be described in great detail—for example, round faced with long, red, wavy hair; blue, bulging, crossed eyes with hooded lids; a broken nose; a wide mouth with full lips; a receding chin; flaring ears; bushy eyebrows meeting in the center; long sideburns, mustache, and light beard; a forehead scar about one inch long over the right eye; needle marks on the left arm; and walking with a pronounced limp.

A fugitive's occupation, associates, friends, relatives, habits, and hobbies are often significant factors in a police hunt. A person's occupation or profession is often a form of habituation. Known criminal associates are likely to offer promising leads, and data on relatives and friends may suggest promising areas of inquiry. Habits and hobbies are related to places frequented or areas in which the fugitive is likely to be found. Amusement and resort areas may offer promise; theatrical and cabaret districts may also be indicated. This field is wide open to innovative practices by both the investigator preparing the wanted notice and police seeking the fugitive.

A final segment of the description of a fugitive concerns whether he or she may resist arrest. All investigators seeking the apprehension of a fugitive have a duty to specify in every wanted notice whether the fugitive is armed, whether a weapon has been used in crime, and whether the fugitive has used weapons on previous occasions to avoid capture or to escape from custody. "Armed and dangerous" may seem a cliché, but the unnecessary injury and death of arresting officers are not routine and can be avoided by adequate notice. Officers staffing roadblocks and stopping suspicious cars on the highway late at night usually are prepared for any aggressive action initiated by the occupants of a vehicle. However, on many other occasions officers likely to be met in the pursuit of a fugitive are not always as alert to possible aggression unless they are warned in advance.

Armed with the knowledge that a person is wanted, all police seek fugitives as part of the general police role. Traffic officers making so-called routine stops have apprehended fugitives. Police on patrol, in responding to a call for help or in handling a minor crime investigation, have encountered fugitives and taken them into custody. Investigators allow some time daily for inquiries about wanted persons.

Investigators, however, must exercise care in questioning people about a fugitive. They may encounter a person who knows the whereabouts of the suspect but who is more friendly with the fugitive than with the police. A warning to the suspect of the inquiries being made may result in flight, and an excellent chance for capture will be lost forever.

Traditionally, a wanted notice has always been aimed solely at locating and apprehending the fugitive. It now has an additional purpose: to discover, to collect, and to preserve evidence at the time of the arrest. The four purposes of a modern wanted notice for a fugitive from criminal justice are these:

1. To provide sufficient identifying characteristics (constituting reasonable grounds for belief) to allow other law enforcement agents to provisionally identify the fugitive upon initial contact and to make positive identification when the suspect is taken into custody
2. To alert other law enforcement officers to the nature and character of the fugitive, his or her criminal history, and if armed and dangerous
3. To suggest activities and areas in which a search or surveillance may locate the fugitive
4. To delineate the crime in sufficient detail to alert arresting officers to potential legally significant evidence available at the time of arrest

THE ARREST

Investigators no longer believe that legally significant evidence can be developed after an arrest has been made. Investigators today assemble evidence—beyond the strong-suspicion or probable-cause level basic to any lawful arrest—before they attempt to arrest the major suspect in a case. Of course, a great deal of meaningful evidence may be collected at the time of the arrest that will connect the prisoner with the crime, the crime scene, the victim, or other crimes and other criminals. The arrest is also an excellent time to guard against faulty identification of the arrestee.

All arresting officers should be alert to the nature and type of evidence that might normally be encountered at the time of arrest. In collecting evidence at this time, the finding officer must exercise the same care he or she would use if the evidence had been discovered in a crime scene search. The officer finding the evidence should make an appropriate entry in his or her field notes and in the records of the arrest, mark it for identification, and protect its integrity.

The search incidental to an arrest may not only recover the proceeds of a theft but may also produce transfer evidence that will link the suspect with the crime, the scene, or the victim. The search should be confined to the person of the arrested individual and to the vicinity of the arrest.[3] A complete body search is made at the time of booking. In serious crimes, it is not uncommon to seize the suspect's clothes for processing by a vacuum cleaner in an effort to collect dust and debris for analysis and to search the clothes for blood and other stains that may connect the defendant with the crime scene or victim.

The search of a person should not verge on conduct that shocks the conscience, as in the 1952 case of *Rochin v. California*, in which an offender's stomach was pumped in order to recover two capsules of heroin.[4] The search should fulfill the obligation of an arresting officer by protecting the officer from harm by removing any material that might aid in the escape of the arrested person and by avoiding the destruction of evidence or the failure to collect evidence.

The doctrine of **immediate control** indicates the area in which a search is justified. If the arrest is made on the street when the suspect is walking, his or her person and the immediate public area may be searched. If the arrest takes place in a parked or moving vehicle, the vehicle may be searched. If the arresting officer witnessed the jettisoning of some article just before the arrest, he or she should search for such article. If the arrest is made inside a premises, the search usually is restricted to the area over which the arrested person has control. (See Appendix A: Case Briefs, Chimel.)

The police department issuing the wanted notice is notified of an arrest, cancels the want by issuing a Teletype notice of the arrest, and makes the necessary arrangements to pick up the prisoner. If the locale of the arrest is outside the state in which the crime was committed, extradition proceedings, unless formally waived by the fugitive, are required.

When a perpetrator is arrested locally, the search incidental to the arrest may involve the home of the prisoner if it is the place of arrest. Burglars and thieves in possession of recently stolen property often conceal it in their homes. Experienced detectives know there is a great deal of promise in inspecting the residence of a suspect in burglary and theft cases. The current doctrine is to seek search warrants when looking for evidence in any building during the postarrest period unless the search is incidental to the arrest. The investigator, citing the fact that an arrest has been made, should be able to establish probable cause for a search of a specific location for particular items of evidence. The investigator can arrange for surveillance of the premises to be searched, which will secure it from disturbance while the warrant is being obtained. The search warrant prevents the tainting of evidence. It is a straightforward matter to conduct a search pursuant to a warrant and to fully report the results to the court.

An investigator may ask the arrested person to consent to a search of an office or residence. If another person has dual or joint control of such premises, consent also should be requested of such individual. Landlords and managers of multiple housing or office structures can consent to a search only of the so-called public portions of such buildings and cannot consent to the search of a room, apartment, or office under the sole control of a tenant. Since the *Miranda* decision, the compelling atmosphere of police custody has been delineated as inherently in conflict with the intelligent waiver of any constitutional right. Therefore, the waiver should be formal, should state it is a voluntary act, and should be signed by the prisoner and by a witness. Ideally, the police should discuss with the prisoner the nature of the evidence and where in the premises it will be found. A postarrest consent to search is not illogical conduct if the arrestee is cooperating with police, and it should be requested.

PEDIGREE

At the time of arrest the booking process either begins the prisoner's criminal history file or adds to it. The police apprehension process has concentrated on identifying a logical suspect as the perpetrator and, after ascertaining sufficient information about the appearance of the suspect for a pursuit, locating and arresting him or her. In these pursuits, the searching police are advised of the suspect's name and whereabouts when these are available. Sometimes, however, pursuits for wanted persons are based on little more than an eyewitness description and a sketch. Therefore, when an arrest has been made, positive identification of the arrestee is required.

The arrest record should reflect as much information about an arrestee as possible. Such basic information should include the following:

1. Name (including alias, a.k.a., and nickname)
2. Sex, race, age
3. Residence, employment
4. Social condition, next of kin
5. Physical description:
    a. height and weight
    b. hair color and style
    c. eye color and any defects
    d. ears, nose, lips, chin, teeth
    e. complexion and general build
    f. facial hair
    g. tattoo marks, amputations or deformities, visible scars, moles, birthmarks, needle tracks
6. Speech
7. Peculiarities
8. Habits (known to . . . , frequents . . . , hobby is . . .)
9. Type of crime, area of geographic operations
10. Associates (neighborhood, crime partners, other)

The fingerprints and photograph of every person arrested should be taken, unless forbidden by local laws stating that they may not be taken in minor cases. Sufficient copies of fingerprints should be taken for circulation to other records systems, and both front and profile pictures should be made. The basic records systems for a fingerprint search are the files of the arresting agency, the state criminal justice files, and the huge records system of the FBI. The search determines whether the fingerprints of the prisoner are on file. The fingerprints taken at the time of arrest are matched against the base files of these agencies, a report of the search is made to the police agency forwarding the prisoner's fingerprints, and the fact of this arrest is filed in all these records.

The report of the records search may be a simple "no record." However, it bears a date and a person's name, and it is evidence that a records search in that agency, based on a set of fingerprints of an arrestee, was made and failed to disclose any record. The search may also yield a report that is several pages long and lists arrests and imprisonments in various sections of the United States—this is the **rap sheet** of a person with a criminal record. (Prior arrests and other contacts with police and criminal justice agencies were once referred to as *raps.* The name is synonymous with criminal record or criminal history. The term *bum rap,* signifying a false charge of crime, is quite common in the argot of criminals.)

Concurrently, the criminal justice status of the arrested person is reviewed by the agencies searching their fingerprint files. When warranted, the arresting agency is notified if the arrestee is wanted by police in other jurisdictions as a suspect in a crime, as a fugitive from justice, as an escapee from a correctional institution or mental health facility; is under the supervision of a probation or parole officer; or is out on bail pending trial upon a previous arrest and charge of crime.

The criminal histories of persons are numbered serially in the local agency, state, and FBI records systems. In effect, the arrestee is given a lifetime identification (ID) number. In some areas, a letter prefix reveals the grade of the crime: serious—usually a felony but sometimes a "high" misdemeanor, and minor—usually a misdemeanor, sometimes not including minor offenses such as traffic violations. In New York City, the prefix is B for serious crimes and E for lesser crimes. In state records systems, the number usually has a simple prefix of letters representing the name of the agency; in California it is CII, for the California Bureau of Identification and Investigation. At the federal level, the prefix is FBI.

If an arrestee has never been arrested within the jurisdiction of the local police agency in which he or she is being booked, a local number will be assigned. If previously arrested locally, the arrestee is booked under a previously assigned ID number.

The collection of data about the prisoner at the time of the arrest does not relate primarily to the offense but rather to the **pedigree** of the offender. *Pedigree* is an odd word for this, yet the questions asked and the information sought at the time of booking an arrestee provide just that: complete information about a person. When an arrested person is in contact with law enforcement agencies as an arrestee for the first time, the facts of the pedigree may be minimal. As a criminal prosecution moves from arrest to trial to sentencing, a great deal of information is collected and filed under the arrestee's ID number. This record becomes more than a personal description; it delineates a person against the background of the crime charged and sometimes provides a record of behavior when in prison and on parole. When another arrest occurs, similar data are collected and integrated with the base file, which is probably why it has persisted as a reference: the criminal history of a person is a pedigree.

For an investigator, compiling an offender's data sheet upon a first arrest is a routine that should be serviced in full recognition of the future use of such data as an investigative aid by other investigators.

CASE PREPARATION

Case preparation is organization. It is the orderly array of information collected during an investigation: all the reports, documents, and exhibits in a case. It is also the preparation of a synopsis of the individual material in the case, an abstract written without personal conclusions, opinions, or facts. A so-called final report is undesirable; the collected reports and other data constitute the final report—the package forwarded to the prosecutor. The investigator does not intrude. The case synopsis is no more than a summary of the package contents. In the evaluation of a case in this pretrial period, investigators must discriminate between evidential material and personal conclusions and opinions, between potential evidence and facts. In a criminal action, fact leads to truth, and courts admit relevant evidence at trial to determine fact.

Case preparation is the round-up time of an investigation. The investigator collates the work of the entire investigation, confers with associates, prepares the case folder and its synopsis, forwards the case to the prosecutor for preparation of the formal accusatory pleading and the legal development of the case before trial, and marks the case closed by arrest.

THE DEFENDANT'S IDENTITY

The identification of an individual as the person accused of the crime leads to an array of witnesses and evidence. Identification usually results from some combination of testimony and other evidence. This evidence structure is sometimes supported by a pretrial statement made by the accused person and is oriented toward proving the identity of the person responsible for the crime alleged in the indictment or information, the **accusatory pleading**.

Guidelines to evidence likely to have legal significance in establishing the identity of the person or persons responsible for a crime can be summarized as follows:

1. A witness (or witnesses) who has seen the suspect commit the crime or some part of it
2. A witness (or witnesses) who has seen the suspect at the crime scene at or about the time of the crime
3. A witness (or witnesses) who observed the suspect in the neighborhood of the crime at or about the time of occurrence
4. Physical evidence discovered in the crime scene search that indicates the suspect was at the crime scene or in contact with the victim
5. Physical evidence found on the suspect or among his or her effects at the time of arrest, or secured by other lawful means, that indicates that the offender had been at the crime scene or in contact with the victim
6. Connect-ups:
   a. the suspect possessing the vehicle that witnesses will testify was used in this crime
   b. the suspect having the proceeds of the crime (in theft and burglary cases)
   c. the suspect having an unexplained injury (in assaults and homicides)
   d. the suspect having the weapon used in the crime
   e. the suspect having been interviewed by an officer at or near the crime scene at or about the time of the crime (the officer having reported it in the regular course of business and being available to so testify)

These guidelines appear to embody a potentially formidable array of witnesses and evidence, but they must be evaluated against the background of the possible defenses the accused person might raise, such as the following:

1. Variances in the original descriptions and the actual description of the accused person
2. Other errors in evidence or variances in statements of witnesses
3. A well-supported claim of **alibi**—being elsewhere at the time of the crime
4. A widespread distrust of eyewitness identification because of the many publicized mistakes in such identifications

THE DEFENDANT AND THE CORPUS DELICTI

The accusatory pleading must show that at a specified time and date in a specific place, the named person committed an act or omission in violation of a particular law specified by both name and section number and in force at the time of the act or omission. Therefore, the first major area of case evaluation is the affirmative evidence of a real-life **corpus delicti**—the classic "body of the crime" plus the identity of the person charged with it:

1. Time and date of the crime and the territorial jurisdiction in which it happened (the **venue**)
2. Name by which the accused person has been identified
3. Essential elements of the crime charged
4. Specification of the criminal agency used to accomplish the crime and of the name of the victim

This process of affirming the corpus delicti is a combining of "what happened" and "who did it" with the knowledge that the happening as reported violates a specific law and that the offender has a legal responsibility to answer to the violation.

NEGATIVE EVIDENCE

The second major area of case preparation concerns **negative evidence** and is oriented to countering defenses to the crime charged. The following are standard negative-evidence defenses:

1. The defendant did not commit the crime. The defense allegation is that the accused person is the victim of mistaken identification, faulty police work, or pure coincidence and was somewhere else at the time.
2. The defendant did commit the crime, but
   a. it was excusable (usually a claim of self-defense or provocation).
   b. it was an accident.
   c. it was the result of legal insanity.
   d. mental factors diminished the defendant's responsibility for the act.

3. No crime was committed:
    a. attack on the sufficiency of the corpus delicti
    b. attack on the sufficiency of the evidence
    c. attack on one or more of the essential elements of the crime charged (intent, proximate cause, etc.)

If any essential element of the crime charged is not proved beyond a reasonable doubt, the defendant is entitled to acquittal.

LAWFUL PROCEDURES

The third major area of case preparation concerns procedural foundations in the securing of evidence. This requires affirmative proof to dispel any allegations of unlawful activity by police that may be presented to a court. The investigator must point out the procedural lawfulness. In most cases, such evidence will show one or more of the following:

1. Nothing suggestive or otherwise improper in locating and interviewing witnesses
2. The reasonableness of the search and the integrity of collecting and preserving evidence
3. A reasonable surveillance that meets the requirements of due process
4. The voluntariness of a confession or admission, together with other due process requirements

THE ARRAY OF EVIDENCE

Evidence must be tabulated in some orderly array. A suggested outline includes the name and a summary of the background of each witness, a synopsis of the story told, and a reference to the name of one or more witnesses who can give corroborating or supporting testimony. The array is usually, in order of importance: the identity of the defendant, relationship to the corpus delicti of the crime, essential elements of the crime charged, and negative evidence likely to block common defenses.

Another means of tabulating testimonial evidence is a timetable of the crime. This chronological exposition of the movements of all persons involved in the crime and brief description of the evidence pinpoint the relevant times and relationships and can be broken into any convenient subdivisions.

This tabulation of evidence in some relevant array helps an investigator avoid disorder in an investigation, facilitates review by others, and permits an overview of the case not possible in any other fashion. This "taking in of the case at a glance" was a principal objective of Hans Gross's "table" of a crime, which allowed the investigator to determine if work on the case was complete or where additional work was necessary.[5]

THE "PACKAGE," OR CASE FOLDER

Police reports and other documents usually are placed in chronological order. The offense or crime report is on top, and the various supplementary or progress reports follow in sequence. Photographic exhibits in the form of color or black-and-white prints or transparencies are integrated with the folder. Physical evidence, if any, may be delivered to the prosecutor or held until requested. The content of the various reports should be sufficient to indicate the physical evidence and its nature.

A synopsis (brief) should accompany each case folder. In preparing a synopsis, an investigator must keep in mind that this is an abstract or digest of the material in the case folder, nothing more and nothing less. It must be brief. It can deal only with the pertinent facts in the complete case folder being forwarded to the prosecutor. Every point covered in the synopsis must be supported by a police report or other document in the case folder being forwarded, and the elements of the synopsis should be organized in the same order as the police reports and documents in the case folder. A quick reading of the synopsis and a scanning of the case folder should inform the prosecutor of the crime committed; the time, date, and place of its happening; and the evidence collected.

A recent innovation is a **face sheet** on all police reports, documents, and exhibits forwarded to the prosecutor. The face sheet is an outline synopsis of the case, which requires only a few notations in appropriate spaces under printed captions. It can be used to serve the same purpose for the transfer of the facts of a case from the prosecutor to the defense attorney under the rules of pretrial discovery.

THE DECISION TO CHARGE

In the office of the prosecutor, the case is reviewed and assigned to a staff member for further investigation and preparation for trial, if warranted. This review of the case by a public official trained in law is a learned review of the work of the investigator. Conferences with the investigator and witnesses usually are scheduled by this legal expert, and the physical evidence and reports of its analysis are examined. If the case is a homicide, the staff of the coroner or medical examiner and their reports may be involved in these sessions. The assigned prosecutor makes his or her decision and moves through the stages necessary for trial or recommends that no action be taken at this time and details reasons for not taking action. The decision to charge is not a function or responsibility of the investigator.[6]

Cases are not moved for trial or rejected as possible trial material solely on the basis of the work done by the investigator and the legal significance of the collected evidence. Tactical factors and the needs of law enforcement may indicate that a trial is not advisable. Prosecutors may waive prosecution in exchange for information or testimony against a more hardened criminal, and the conservation of resources may suggest a negotiated plea of guilty to a lesser charge. For example, in processing first offenders and emotionally disturbed persons, the application of the sanctions of the criminal justice process may not appear justified by the circumstances of the case.[7]

Review by the staff of the prosecutor of case preparation before arrest is not uncommon. Of course, an investigator habituated to the traditional separation of the roles of investigator and prosecutor is reluctant to ask the prosecutor to step into an ongoing investigation. However, when the measure of proof is less than the amount necessary to move the case to the prosecutor, the natural tendency to seek help arises. It is within the concept of the role of the prosecutor to accept a difficult investigation as just that—incomplete and insufficient. In such instances, and in a case with promise, the prosecutor has an ideal investigative device in the local grand jury with its powers of subpoena and the right to administer oaths and take sworn testimony. It is a route for promising cases previously marked by police with the notation "No further results possible."

CLOSING AN INVESTIGATION

An investigation is successful when the crime under investigation is promptly solved and the case closed. Measurable results occur when the case is closed by the arrest of the perpetrator. Cases cleared by arrest are a statistical measure of the efficiency of the criminal investigation function of any police unit. However, case clearance also may be a statistical measure of efficiency when an investigation is terminated without an arrest. A review of reasons given by police executives for closing investigations in this manner shows the following authorized case clearances in lieu of an arrest:[8]

1. The investigation discloses the case is unfounded; no crime occurred or was attempted. However, the return of stolen property, restitution, or refusal by the victim to prosecute does not justify this classification.
2. The offender dies.
3. The case is found to be a murder and suicide; one person kills another person and then commits suicide.
4. The perpetrator confesses on his or her deathbed.
5. Arrest and charge of an identified offender are blocked by an uncooperative victim.
6. A confession is made by an offender already in custody for another crime.
7. The person identified as the perpetrator is located in another jurisdiction, and an unsuccessful attempt is made to gain custody; or the prosecutor does not believe the expense of an attempt to gain custody is justified.
8. Upon the decision of the assigned prosecutor, the person identified as the perpetrator is prosecuted for a less serious charge than that cited at the time of arrest.

If the investigator's case preparation reveals that the identity of the perpetrator has been definitely established, has been located, and that sufficient information and evidence exist to support an arrest and a charge of crime, no valid reason exists not to close the case by arrest if it is not covered by any of the foregoing exceptional clearances. The identification of the perpetrator solves the case and justifies such action.

An investigator should recommend, on a supplementary report, the termination of a case when no further results can be secured. In addition, a follow-up officer should have the authority to file cases in an inactive or hold file when no further results can be obtained despite due diligence.

Therefore, the criminal investigation function can be terminated in the following instances:

1. Results have been obtained in full; the case is cleared by arrest or exceptional clearance.
2. Results have been obtained in part, and no further results can be obtained.
3. No results can be obtained.

Recognition that a bona fide conclusion to a case can be achieved without an arrest is important to the new frontiers of investigation. Such action strips the dead wood from the workload of an investigator, leads to new definitions of responsibility and accountability in the criminal investigation function, and strengthens the concept that arrests are not the primary objective of criminal investigation.

In pursuing truth—the main objective of an investigation—investigators must view all aspects of a case, particularly information pointing to the innocence of the accused person. Presenting a prima facie case and hoping and trusting it will withstand the contradiction of a defense attack are no longer sufficient. The case must be so prepared that legally significant evidence presented in court will withstand attack by the defense and establish guilt beyond a reasonable doubt.

An investigation is a search for truth in which all possible information in a post factum inquiry is searched for, collected, and analyzed. The investigative process examines all the data, both for and against the person accused of crime. Therefore, viewing a case throughout an investigation from the viewpoint of the defense is always appropriate, and particularly so in preparing the case for presentation to the prosecutor. Along with scrupulous accuracy in reporting information, viewing the defense side of a case is the ultimate technique for conducting investigations that exonerate the innocent and discover and identify the guilty.

CASE STUDY

Double Murder—Ms. Wylie and Ms. Hoffert

This case involves a double murder and a lengthy investigation in which George Whitmore, Jr., was arrested and charged with the crime. For clarity, the case is presented in the form of a chronology beginning with the day of the crime.

Wednesday, August 28

The Day of the Crime

Janice Wylie, twenty-one, and Emily Hoffert, twenty-three, were found bound and stabbed to death in Apartment 3-C at 57 East 88th Street, New York City. Their bodies were found by Max

FIGURE 10–2 Janice Wylie and Emily Hoffert were found dead, tied in one of the bedrooms of their two-bedroom apartment.
Source: Weston, Paul B., *Criminal Justice and Law Enforcement: Cases,* © 1972, p. 103. Reprinted by permission of Prentice Hall.

Wylie, father of Ms. Wylie, and by Patricia Tolles, a roommate who shared the murder scene apartment with the two victims.

Ms. Tolles, who had last seen the victims when she left for work at 9:30 that morning, returned from work at 6:40 p.m. and found the apartment in disarray. Shocked and upset, she did not go through the apartment, although she did glance into the bathroom. She called Max Wiley from the telephone in the foyer of the apartment, and he came over directly from his home a few blocks away. They examined the apartment and found the bodies of the two victims in a bedroom—between a wall and a bed. Miss Wylie was nude; Miss Hoffert was fully clothed. Two knives were found near the bodies and another on the basin in the bathroom, which was opposite the crime scene bedroom. The wrists and ankles of both victims were tied, and their bodies were bound together at the wrists and waists. Cloth strips, torn or cut from a bedsheet and a bedspread, were used for this restraint (Figure 10–2). No blood was observed in any room other than the bedroom in which the victims were found. The drawers of dressers and cabinets were open, and their contents were dumped on the floor, on beds, and on dresser tops. Ms. Tolles said that nothing was missing, and that neither the victims, nor she herself, possessed any valuable jewelry or large sums of cash. Preliminary police investigation revealed no sign of forced entry, and no witness who had seen or heard anything suspicious was found. Chief Medical Examiner Dr. Michael Halpern said the bodies of the victims had been mutilated viciously, with no apparent evidence of sexual assault.

Thursday, August 29

1 Day After the Crime

A search of the apartment by police identification technicians revealed numerous fingerprints. All such traces were collected and then processed by the police. The two knives found in the crime scene bedroom had broken blades, but the broken-off portions of the blades were recovered from the floor nearby. The knife found in the bathroom was intact and identified as a standard pointed steak knife. The origin of the knives was apparently the kitchen of the apartment.

Continued questioning of neighbors and building employees failed to locate anyone who had seen or heard anything suspicious or directly related to the crime apartment. One neighbor reported meeting a stranger in the elevator, who he described as of medium build and "baby-faced."

Chief Medical Examiner Halpern said, in a preliminary autopsy report, that the cause of death for both victims was multiple stab wounds in the neck, chest, and abdomen and that Ms. Hoffert had head wounds in which glass was found, indicating blows by a weapon such as a soft-drink bottle. An electric night table clock was found near the bodies. Its plug was out of the wall and on the floor a few feet from a wall outlet, and a good portion of its electric cord was partially under the torso of victim Wylie. The time on the stopped clock was 10:35 a.m.

Max Wylie stated that his daughter Janice had received a threatening phone call on or about August 18, and that she was terrified by it. The caller left a name, Joe Hunter, and a telephone number, Wylie added, but when his daughter called the number, a woman who identified herself as the subscriber for that telephone number said she knew of no man named Hunter or any similar name.

Friday, August 30

2 Days After the Crime

Newsweek, where Ms. Wylie had worked, offered a $10,000 reward for information leading to the arrest and conviction of the murderer or murderers. Continuing investigation revealed that Ms. Hoffert had left the apartment shortly after her roommate, Patricia Tolles, left for work at 9:30 a.m. The victim then drove north to Riverdale to return a borrowed car and pick up her own automobile. She was placed in the Riverdale area up until 1:00 p.m., through contacts with friends and the garage proprietor. The time span of the crime could now be set between 9:30 a.m. and 6:40 p.m. for victim Wylie; and 1:30 p.m. and 6:40 p.m. for victim Hoffert. Police established a public information telephone number and asked for public cooperation in their search for both witnesses and the person or persons responsible for the killings.

Friday, September 6

9 Days After the Crime

No substantial clues were revealed by the continuing investigation, despite a far-reaching search for witnesses and numerous inquiries among relatives, friends, and associates of victims. No motive for the crime was discovered either. Burglary was not believed to be the actual motive, although an attempt was apparently made to create the illusion of a burglary. No cash was stolen, and several pieces of jewelry and a watch were left untouched. Over 100 detectives were assigned to the case by this time. The canvass for witnesses had been concluded without success. All known sex offenders and all known daytime burglars had been questioned by the police, and their activities on August 28 had been investigated—all to no avail.

Friday, September 13

16 Days After the Crime

The report of the fingerprint search and processing revealed that no fingerprints were present on the suspect murder weapons (three knives) and that a total of nine partial sets of fingerprints were found in the apartment. Seven of these sets corresponded with those of the victims, relatives, friends, or occupants of the apartment. The two remaining sets of partial fingerprints did not have sufficient characteristics for overt identification by any search of criminal justice files, but they were marked for possible use as suspects were developed through other information and evidence in the case.

Friday, September 27

33 Days After the Crime

In the continuing investigation of the Wylie–Hoffert murders, detectives had interviewed over 500 persons, but to date no identity of the murderer or murderers had been revealed, nor has any witness been found who observed anyone leaving the apartment or any suspicious person in the building during the time span of the crime. Investigators had been seeking someone who observed a blood-spattered person or someone carrying a bundle or bag. The police believed that the killer's clothing was splashed with blood during the crime, and he then would have had blood-stained clothing when he fled from the scene—unless he had changed clothes at the crime scene. In that case, he would have carried out his bloody garments in a bag or bundle.

Thursday, October 31

64 Days After the Crime

Continuing investigation exhausted all leads contained in telephone and memorandum books of the victims and all other memoranda, such as cards and letters with names, telephone numbers, or other identification that were found in the apartment. Police had also investigated all names and other leads supplied by friends and relatives of the victims, including the "Joe Hunter" lead supplied by Max Wylie. They also followed leads gathered through more than 1,000 telephone calls received by the special public information number. To date, no description or other identification of the murderer or murderers, or of any suspicious person seen leaving the death-scene apartment or its vicinity on the day of the crime, had been secured. The detail of detectives, now reduced to twenty-four, had reoriented the continuing investigation to investigate (1) all previous crimes in which knives were used; (2) all persons moving out of the neighborhood; and (3) persons who left state mental health institutions or prisons just before the crime or who had been admitted or committed since the crime.

Thursday, February 27

183 Days After the Crime

Detectives assigned to the continuing investigation had now interviewed, questioned, and investigated over 1,000 suspects. Most suspects had been fully exonerated. About ten of these individuals required some verification of their activities on the day of the crime. To date, not even one of these persons was classed as a major suspect, and no substantial clue to the identity of the murderer or murderers had been discovered.

Saturday, April 24

240 Days After the Crime

George Whitmore, Jr., age nineteen, was arrested for the Wylie–Hoffert killings. At about 6:00 a.m., Friday, April 23, a Brooklyn police officer who was searching an area in which an assault, robbery, and attempted rape had been committed a few hours earlier spotted a suspect and took him to the police station. The victim of the robbery and attempted rape, Mrs. Ella Borrero, was brought to the police station and identified the suspect, George Whitmore. He confessed to the crime. He was booked for the robbery and attempted rape of Mrs. Borrero. A search revealed no weapon and no drugs, but two photographs were found in his wallet. The suspect said they were "girlfriends." Further questioning led to Whitmore confessing to the murder of Mrs. Minnie Edmonds, age forty-six. Mrs. Edmonds's body had been found in a backyard at 444 Blake Avenue, Brooklyn, on April 14—ten days earlier. Death had resulted from multiple stab and slash wounds from a knife or similar weapon.

Detective Edward Bulger, who was present at the questioning of Whitmore in the Edmonds case, had been assigned to the investigation of the Wylie–Hoffert murders in its early stages. He thought the two photographs found in Whitmore's wallet resembled the blonde, blue-eyed Wylie girl and her roommate–victim. Further questioning resulted in Whitmore admitting to the murders of Ms. Wylie and Ms. Hoffert. Whitmore's formal statement of guilt in the double murder was taken under the direction of Peter Koste, an assistant district attorney in the Manhattan district attorney's office.

Whitmore seemed to know details of the double homicide that had never been made public. In his statement, Whitmore gave the brand name of the broken soft-drink bottle that had been found, and he stated that he broke the blades of two of the knives used in the attack by using his heel and the floor, as in breaking a stick of wood. Last, he admitted that he took the photograph of Ms. Wylie from the dresser of the crime scene bedroom.

Whitmore was arraigned before Judge James J. Comerford in a Brooklyn court. An attorney, Jerome Leftow, was appointed to represent Whitmore when he stated that he was without legal counsel. After a brief out-of-court conference between Whitmore and his new attorney, both returned to court and Mr. Leftow told Judge Comerford that his client had made certain statements to the police but that they were made under duress and stress and that his client now recants and repudiates all the confessions he had made. Whitmore was remanded to jail without bail by Judge Comerford for a hearing on the next Thursday.

Tuesday, April 27

243 Days After the Crime

Jerome Leftow now claimed that his client, George Whitmore, Jr., had asked police to give him a lie detector test when he was arrested. Additional data released by police connecting Whitmore to the Wylie–Hoffert murders was the substance of an unofficial statement published in newspapers. This press story stated that Whitmore knew the location of a razor blade found on the floor of the crime scene bedroom, knew where its wrapper had been found in the bathroom, was able to describe a Noxema jar left on the bloody floor, and told of blood spots that were found on the bedroom window shade.

Wednesday, May 6

253 Days After the Crime

Whitmore was indicted by a Manhattan grand jury in the knife slaying of Janice Wylie and Emily Hoffert. The jury presented a two-count murder indictment to Justice Charles Marks, who ordered Whitmore taken into custody and arraigned for pleading. Whitmore pleaded "not guilty" to the murder charge.

Friday, October 17

317 Days After the Crime

Psychiatrists at Bellevue Hospital found George Whitmore, Jr., sane and able to stand trial for the Wylie–Hoffert murders. The finding concluded the longest study of any one patient in the long history of Bellevue's Psychiatric Center. Whitmore had been committed to Bellevue the previous May by Justice Charles Marks, following his arraignment and not guilty plea in the Wylie–Hoffert case.

Saturday, January 2

393 Days After the Crime

Manhattan's district attorney, Frank S. Hogan, refused comment on the eight-month delay in the trial of Whitmore for the Wylie–Hoffert killings. Police reporters pointed to two factors that might account for the delay: (1) identity of the young blonde girl in the photograph found on Whitmore was in dispute; (2) whether the photograph was really taken from the death scene apartment on 88th Street was also in dispute.

Note: A few weeks after detectives arrested a new suspect in this case, D. A. Frank Hogan quietly asked the Manhattan court to release Whitmore in "the interest of justice." Whitmore was released to the Brooklyn District Attorney for trial in homicide cases in that jurisdiction.

Source: Paul B. Weston, *Criminal Justice and Law Enforcement: Cases.* (Englewood Cliffs, NJ: Prentice Hall, 1972). Reprinted by permission of Prentice Hall.

CHAPTER REVIEW

KEY TERMS

accusatory pleading   *196*

alibi   *197*

all points bulletin
   (APB)   *187*

broadcast alarm   *186*

corpus delicti   *197*

face sheet   *199*

immediate control   *193*

negative evidence   *197*

pedigree   *195*

rap sheet   *194*

venue   *197*

wanted notice   *189*

REVIEW QUESTIONS

1. When a wanted fugitive is apprehended in another state, the fugitive has a right to a legal hearing in which the prosecution must demonstrate the probable cause for the return of the fugitive to the state where the crime occurred. These proceedings are known as:
   a. Extraditions
   b. Extrajudicial
   c. Extrajurisdictional
   d. Exculpatory

2. When a fugitive is arrested, he or she and the area under his or her immediate control may be searched to recover weapons and evidence of the crime. This type of search is known as:
   a. Incidental
   b. Inventory
   c. Incident to arrest
   d. Exculpatory

3. The initial hue and cry in pursuit of a perpetrator of a crime is known as the:
   a. Wanted notice
   b. All points bulletin
   c. Broadcast alarm
   d. All of the above

4. As the coverage area for a wanted person is expanded due to the passage of time, what type of alarm would be distributed?

   a. Wanted notice
   b. All points bulletin
   c. Broadcast alarm
   d. All of the above

5. An abstract or a brief digest of the material in a case folder is known as:
   a. Case summary
   b. Synopsis
   c. Probable cause
   d. Case roundup

6. Police reports are usually arranged in _____ order.

7. The decision to charge a suspect with a crime is the duty of which persons in the criminal justice system?
   a. Judge
   b. Investigator
   c. Prosecutor
   d. Defense counsel

8. When can a criminal investigation be terminated?
   a. When the case is cleared by an arrest
   b. When partial results have been obtained in part, and no further results can be obtained
   c. When no results can be obtained
   d. All of the above

9. An investigation is successful when the crime under investigation is solved promptly and the person responsible is _____ .

10. The collection of data about the prisoner at the time of the arrest does not

relate primarily to the offense but rather to the offender's

_____ .

See Appendix D for the correct answers.

DISCUSSION QUESTIONS

1. Is extensive case preparation necessary when an agency requires its investigators to submit progress reports throughout an investigation?
2. What is the rationale for organizing a final review of an investigation around a theme of witnesses and exhibits of evidence?
3. What is the emerging concept inherent in an exhaustive search for witnesses? An intensive and scientific crime scene search for evidence? The objective and scientific laboratory services for processing physical evidence? Setting limits on suggestibility during interviews with witnesses and lineups for identification?
4. On the basis of available legally significant evidence likely to be admissible in court upon trial, is further action by the prosecutor against George Whitmore, Jr., for the Wylie–Hoffert killings justified?
5. Does the role of prosecutor in making the decision to prosecute an accused involve a preliminary evaluation of evidence on the issue of guilt or innocence?
6. What evidence collected by police, other than Whitmore's confession to the double murder, supports the police theory about this crime and the conclusion about Whitmore's guilt?
7. Present an argument in support of the validity and reliability of reviewing a case from the defense frame of reference—that is, from the point of view of the case for the accused person.

RELATED WEB SITES

Want to know if federal law enforcement is looking for someone you might know? Check out the U. S. Department of Justice Most Wanted Fugitive List. This Web site includes persons wanted by the FBI, DEA, ATF, and the U.S. Marshals Service: *www.usdoj.gov/marshals/investigations/most_wanted*.

The U.S. Marshals Service has a wide variety of law enforcement responsibilities, one of which is fugitive investigations. To learn more about the Marshals Service as a career choice, see the Web site at *www.usmarshals.gov*.

part **two**

Investigating Major Crimes

chapter **eleven**

Physical Assaults

CHAPTER OUTLINE

Homicide

After reading this chapter you will be able to:

- Describe the autopsy procedure and the circumstances that would justify this examination.
- List the various means that are used to establish the time of death of a homicide victim.
- Compare the various types of multicide and define the dynamics of these crimes.
- Discuss and identify the basic patterns of a criminal homicide.
- Explain the telltale signs of physical child abuse and how this abuse is inflicted.

211

P hysical assaults include attacks on the person that produce death or serious bodily injury. These assaults include attacks by others, self-inflicted injury, and physical abuse of children.

HOMICIDE

Criminal homicides, from murder to manslaughter, and common and aggravated assault are major crimes against the person. First the crime scene and then the circumstances of the attack are the focus of investigations of these crimes.

Criminal homicide is usually divided by statute into various degrees. **First-degree murder** is defined as the premeditated killing of another human being with malice, or wrongful intent. If the death occurs as the result of the commission of a felony, such as arson, robbery, burglary, or sexual assault, then the felony murder rule would apply, which makes the killing one of the first degree regardless of the lack of intent or premeditation. **Second-degree murder** involves the killing of another but without the element of premeditation. **Manslaughter** is defined as the unlawful killing of another without malice or premeditation either voluntarily or involuntarily. Voluntary manslaughter involves a killing that is done in the heat of passion. Involuntary manslaughter is the appropriate charge when the death occurs while the perpetrator was involved in the commission of an unlawful act not amounting to a felony, such as driving while intoxicated.

The corpus delicti of all criminal homicide comprises the following:

1. An evidentiary showing of the death of a human being
2. An evidentiary showing of a criminal agency
3. An evidentiary showing that the criminal agency was the proximate cause of the death

The death must be of a human being and must occur within a certain period of time after the act causing the injury. The time may vary in different jurisdictions from one to three years. **Criminal agency** means that the death was caused by another person's unlawful act or omission.

"SUSPICIOUS DEATH" INVESTIGATION

Police investigators conduct a **suspicious death** investigation in all cases in which the circumstances of the death indicate violence or **foul play**—that is, some criminal agency; when death occurs in a place other than the residence of the deceased; or when the deceased is not under the care of a physician at the time of death. From the preliminary investigation of a suspicious death, the facts may result in a decision to close the case because death resulted from natural or accidental causes or was a suicide; or a decision may be made to continue the investigation because the facts disclosed indicate a criminal—unjustified or unexcused—homicide.

The suspicious death concept is more than the traditional "Foul play is suspected" in which the circumstances of a death strongly suggest murder. It is a classification of certain unexplained deaths so that they will be investigated until either the circumstances indicate that death was due to natural, accidental, or self-inflicted causes or the criminal agency is determined and the **criminal agent** is identified.

The **autopsy** is a major method of detecting murder. This postmortem examination of the victim in a suspicious death case is performed by a competent physician, generally a surgeon or pathologist specializing in this field, who determines the cause of death. If the autopsy surgeon reports that the nature of death is natural, accidental, or suicidal, then the death is not classed as a criminal homicide. When the autopsy surgeon's report states that a death resulted from a criminal agency, a criminal homicide has been detected.

Although police investigators can make no contribution to the professional conclusions of an autopsy surgeon as to the cause of death, they can assist such surgeons by supplying information related to the means used to cause death. Current prevailing practices in the detection of criminal homicide have led autopsy surgeons throughout the United States to expect a report from a police investigator before the time of the autopsy that informs the autopsy surgeon of all the facts in the case known to police at that time, including details about the scene of the crime, possible weapons, and other matters that relate to the death. The autopsy surgeon does not participate in the linking of the perpetrator to the criminal agency that caused death; that is the role of the investigator.

Thus, the detection of criminal homicide is based on finding the answers to four classic questions:

1. What was the cause of death?
2. What were the means (agency) that caused death?
3. Was the homicide excusable or justifiable?
4. Who was responsible for causing death (the agent)?

The autopsy surgeon shoulders the major responsibility in determining the cause of death. He or she and the police investigators work together to pinpoint the agency of death and define whether the agency is criminal, excusable, or justifiable. The police accept sole responsibility for identifying the person responsible for the killing.

THE AUTOPSY AS AN EXTENSION OF THE CRIME SCENE

In homicide cases, the autopsy performed on the victim is an extension of the crime scene and offers an additional opportunity to search for clues and evidence useful in the investigation. For instance, the victim's body may contain bullets, the suspect's hairs, and fibers, all of which can be useful in identifying the perpetrator. This is also true, to a lesser extent, of medical testimony about examination of the wounds of a victim or injuries that occur in a rape or other sexual assault. The investigator searching the scene and the evidence technician lack the professional knowledge, skills, and experience of the medical examiner, the pathologist, and the toxicologist. Therefore, any examination of the victim in homicide cases by the investigator searching the scene must be a superficial one.

Many coroners and medical examiners consider an examination of the clothing of the victim to be a segment of the postmortem inquiry and require the same laboratory personnel processing the vital organs of the deceased to examine the clothing carefully. However, in suspicious death cases, it is the duty of the police investigator to make certain that an examination is conducted in a police laboratory.

MEDICOLEGAL LABORATORY SERVICES

Most local laws governing investigative jurisdiction in cases of suspicious death require that the coroner or medical examiner be notified promptly and that the body of the victim not be moved without permission of this official. The basic medicolegal service is to determine whether a death was caused by criminal agency and to identify the deceased person and the cause of death.

The report of the postmortem examination contains the autopsy surgeon's findings. Following are the five parts of this report:[1]

1. The preamble (date, place, and identity of the deceased and of witnesses to identification)
2. External appearance (site, character, and dimensions of any wounds or marks related to the cause of death)
3. Internal examination (description of brain, spinal column, organs, and contents of body)
4. A reasoned opinion of the cause of death based on the facts found
5. Signature of examiner (title and qualifications).

Autopsy technique utilizes external examination and dissection. During this work, the pathologist may dictate his or her findings to a stenographer, an assistant, or a recorder. When transcribed, these notes, along with any sketches, diagrams, or photographs, constitute the raw notes of the examination.

The autopsy surgeon investigates all of the body cavities and makes incisions on the side of the neck to expose the neck organs for examination. A knife, saw, and chisel are used to open the head; the brain is removed and examined. The spinal cord and extremities also are examined. A microscopic examination of substances is used to search for any appearance of abnormality. The pathologist must be systematic and thorough. Recognizing the cause of death is his or her professional responsibility.

External postmortem appearances are very informative when a criminal agency is involved in the death. The areas of the body showing lividity indicate the position after death. Wounds and their appearance are particularly significant as they often assist in reconstructing the circumstances of a crime, as well as the nature of the murder weapon and the manner of its use. Significant data include an accurate description of where the wounds are situated and their shape, size, and direction.

Generally, pathologists classify and report the nature of wounds as follows:

1. *Incised Wounds.*   Spindle-shaped in stabbing, linear in cutting
2. *Lacerated Wounds.*   Irregularly edged, some tearing

3. ***Contusions.***   Bruises, discolorations, hematoma
4. ***Abrasions.***   Scratches, trivial wounds
5. ***Gunshot Wounds.***   Shotgun: "rat hole" to dispersion; rifles and pistols: contact, entrance, exit
6. ***Antemortem*** or ***Postmortem***
7. ***Age of Wound.***   Signs of healing or decay
8. ***Opinion about Wound.***   Accidental, suicidal, or homicidal; "hesitation" wounds in suicides, and "defense" wounds in homicide

A practitioner skilled in medicolegal procedures can define the shape of the striking area of the weapon used and the degree of force in relation to the weight and striking surface of the weapon. This can mean a possible matching of a murder weapon when found and, if the offender has not been identified, possibly an estimate of the sex and size of the perpetrator.

Body temperature, lividity, and rigor mortis indicate the time of death in on-the-scene examination, but the general appearance of the body and its stomach contents afford the pathologist a means of fixing the time of death within reasonable limits (see "Time of Death"). The clinical history of the case and its revelations about persons who were the last to see the victim alive and the victim's activities assist the pathologist in determining the time of death.

Classically, the autopsy report should provide information on the following:[2]

1. Cause of death
    a. Natural causes
    b. Accident
    c. Suicide
    d. Homicide
    e. Undetermined origin
2. If a weapon or substance caused death, the nature of the fatal wounds or injuries
3. Time of death in relationship to wound
4. Whether the scene where the body was discovered was the death scene; whether marks and signs indicate the victim was mobile or that the body was moved
5. Evidence of chronic illness or other disease
6. Evidence of blood, hair, or skin other than the victim's
7. Evidence of sexual knowledge or deviancy

In suspected poisoning cases, the pathologist must correlate his or her clinical postmortem findings with the history of the deceased, if available, and suggest the most promising area of investigation to the **toxicologist**, who specializes in the detection of chemical, physical, and biological toxins. The history in a medicolegal autopsy includes all available information about the circumstances of a case: (1) manner of death, (2) preceding manifestations of illness and pain, and (3) investigation at the death scene if foul play is suspected. After the toxicologist's report has been received, the pathologist first evaluates the significance of the toxicologist's findings with regard to the body conditions at autopsy and against the background of the clinical history of the deceased and then bases an opinion of the cause of death on these three types of facts.

Identification after death is determined by characteristics that distinguish the deceased from all other individuals. The usual police investigation attempts to disclose the name of the deceased to find responsible persons (relatives or friends) to view the body and identify it. The deceased person frequently is fingerprinted, and the inked impression may be forwarded through the criminal justice information system for identification or verification.

Teeth provide leads to identification, and dentists can elicit valuable clues to identity. A wealth of dental information is now in the hands of the dental profession and can be useful in the identification of deceased persons.[3]

Sex, age, marks and scars, and other physical features such as old bone fractures or deformities are also identification factors.[4] Death masks are sometimes made, photographed, and included in police bulletins when identification is a problem. These flyers are circulated in the same manner as wanted notices. Unrecognizable remains of a human body present problems. Fire, water, explosion, mutilation, and exposure to the elements and to animals often make it difficult or impossible to arrive at an identification. Nevertheless, pathologists almost always can establish some clues to identity. By correlating all available data, they may arrive at a determination of race, sex, age, and approximate height and weight.

SUICIDE, ACCIDENT, OR CRIMINAL HOMICIDE?

Persons who kill themselves adopt methods similar to techniques used in criminal homicides. Many suicides do not leave classic notes explaining their reasons for self-destruction and do not foreshadow their intent to commit suicide in any observable fashion. Even when the circumstances of a suspicious death reek of murder, a comprehensive investigation may indicate that the death was suicidal.

Circumstances of a suspicious death often invite an investigator's conclusion of self-destruction. However, a great number of murderers attempt to hide their crimes by cloaking them in clues and traces that will indicate suicide. The greatest problem exists when the circumstances of death show that someone has a motive, or could have a motive, for murder. An investigation into the background of a victim may indicate strongly that an apparent suicide is out of character with the victim's lifestyle—a fact that must be weighed heavily before closing a suspicious death case as a suicide.

The techniques of criminal homicide are similar to accidental causes of death. Death can result from being pushed out of a high window or from accidentally falling out of the window. It can result from being shot by another person or accidentally while cleaning a firearm. Death can be caused by another's plunging a knife into a vital area or an accidental fall on a bottle driving shards of glass into the same vital area and causing similar fatal injuries. A fatal dose of poison can be administered by another or can be taken by mistake. A skull can be crushed with a blunt instrument or can result from falling down a flight of stairs.[5]

This victim was strangled, shot, and then set on fire.

IDENTIFICATION OF THE VICTIM

In most homicides, identifying the victim is not a problem. He or she is known and can be identified by relatives and friends. Identifying a victim becomes a problem when death occurs in a public place, a hotel, or a place other than the domicile of the victim. This is particularly true when the victim is a member of the large transient population in the United States. Although homeless men make up most of the transient population, the drug scene has contributed a great number of runaway girls and boys to the ranks of those who move about from place to place in the United States.

A major problem of victim identity occurs when the killer attempts to avoid detection by doing away with the remains of his or her victim through burning, sinking the victim in a substantial body of water, cutting up the victim, or destroying the victim's remains by chemical means. Sometimes the killer does not seek complete destruction of the body but may attempt to destroy only portions of the remains to prevent or delay identification. Scientific means for identification of the partial remains of victims in suspicious deaths include the following:

1. *Fingerprints.*   If the victim had been fingerprinted in his or her lifetime, this is a positive means of identification.
2. *Dental Work.*   This is a comparison identification, with the dental work of a victim being matched with the dental work of a person who has been missing from home or is otherwise unaccounted for.
3. *Bones.*   Bones serve as a broad index of identification when other means are not available because of the condition of the victim's remains. They may indicate sex, height, and age and sometimes time of death, cause of death, and other features of identification.
4. *Surgical Procedures.*   Surgery that took place during the lifetime of the victim may also aid in identification.

Estimates of the size, age, sex, and race of a homicide victim are possible from the study of the victim's remains, but identification of the unknown victim must depend on finding a sufficient number of unique physical characteristics for comparison with records that were made during the victim's lifetime. Insofar as skeletal remains are concerned (no fingerprints), dental records and body X-rays are the most likely means of identification. Dentists can be queried and identification made from dental records. Bone injuries severe enough to suggest hospitalization during the victim's life can lead to existing X-rays in hospital records and result in a positive identification.[6]

TIME OF DEATH

Criminal homicide investigations have a built-in time clock keyed to the time of death. Methods for establishing this vital time, or period of time, range from the testimony of witnesses (the person who saw the killing or who last saw the victim alive, or the person who discovered and reported the crime) to the testimony of autopsy surgeons as to the condition of the body of the victim when found or examined.

The time of death connects the events that happen before the crime with the actual killing in homicide cases. The important questions related to this time-clock sequence are twofold:[7]

1. What activity was the victim engaged in at the time of the fatal assault?
2. What activity did the victim engage in immediately before death (twenty-four to forty-eight hours, and longer if warranted)?

Inasmuch as the only certain time element in the beginning phases of a homicide investigation is the time the crime was discovered, the witness or witnesses who can testify to this aspect of the case are carefully questioned as to the circumstances that first aroused their interest or suspicions, as well as the time of that event; the time of the discovery of the victim; how the victim was found and if he or she was found dead; and the circumstances and time of reporting this discovery to police.

As a homicide investigation continues, witnesses are located who talked to the deceased victim prior to the fatal assault, either in person or over a telephone. Such witnesses can give information about the content of the conversation and its time. Sometimes the activity in which the victim was engaged prior to or at death can be timed within reasonable limits. This process is known as establishing the **window of death**.

When a homicide has no witnesses, the time of death within the window of death may be established by the forensic scientist and pathologist. Estimating the time of death is important in determining opportunity to commit the crime. These estimates are based upon the postmortem, or after-death, changes that occur in the body and the activity of insects that may attack the body.

After death the body begins to cool through the process of **algor mortis**. The body temperature falls until it reaches the ambient air temperature, which usually occurs within eighteen to twenty hours. Algor mortis is considered to be one of the more reliable indicators of time of death. However, due to a number of variables, including the body temperature at the time of death, clothing, surface temperature, humidity, and air movement across the body, these estimates are not exact.

Biochemical changes in the body after death produce stiffening of the muscles, or **rigor mortis**, which usually appears within two to six hours after death. The process begins in the jaw and neck and proceeds to the trunk and extremities and is complete within six to twelve hours. This rigidity remains for two to three days and disappears in the same order in which it appears.

Due to gravity, when the blood stops circulating, it begins to settle to the lowest portion of the body. This process, **postmortem lividity**, is noticeable approximately within one hour after death and is fully developed within three to four hours. Lividity appears as blue or reddish marks on the skin. Fresh livid stains are not produced by a change in position twelve hours after death. Lividity discoloration provides two types of information. The degree of discoloration is an indicator of the time of death and can indicate a change of position or movement of the body after death.

Decomposition, or **putrefaction**, begins at the time of death as a result of two processes: autolysis and bacterial action. **Autolysis** occurs by a chemical breakdown of the body that results in the softening and liquefaction of body tissue. **Bacterial action** converts body tissue into liquids and gases. Within twenty-four hours, a discoloration of the skin is noticeable. This greenish-red or blue-green color change is pronounced within thirty-six hours. Bacterial action produces gases that cause the body to swell and produces an unpleasant odor. The environment affects the rate of decomposition: colder temperatures tend to impede the process while warmer temperatures will increase it.

Various kinds of insects feed on dead bodies. These insects lay their eggs, which develop into larvae, or maggots. They can reduce a body to skeletal remains in less than two months under favorable conditions. The life cycle of these insects is constant, and the forensic entomologist, a specialist in insects, can determine how long a body has been exposed to the action of these insects.[8]

EXHUMATION

A court order must be secured for **exhumation**—the removal of the body of a deceased person from its place of burial—for a medicolegal examination to disclose the presence of a previously unknown or improperly identified injuries, or to reveal the presence of a poison or other noxious substance that would indicate a criminal agency caused death.

Examination after burial is rarely as satisfactory as an autopsy before burial. However, full autopsy procedures should be carried out, and before and after the autopsy the body should be fully X-rayed and photographed in both color and black-and-white film.

CHECKLIST FOR THE INVESTIGATION OF CRIMINAL HOMICIDE

A checklist for a criminal homicide investigation should be divided into stages to allow for the orderly progression of the investigation from its beginning to its focusing and then to the arrest of the perpetrator and crime partners, if any (Figure 11–1).

Stage 1: Crime Scene

1. Be alert at the approach to and the entrance to the crime area for the perpetrator and others leaving the crime scene. All persons at or leaving the crime scene should be stopped and identified before they leave. Interviewing of such persons may be done at the scene or later.

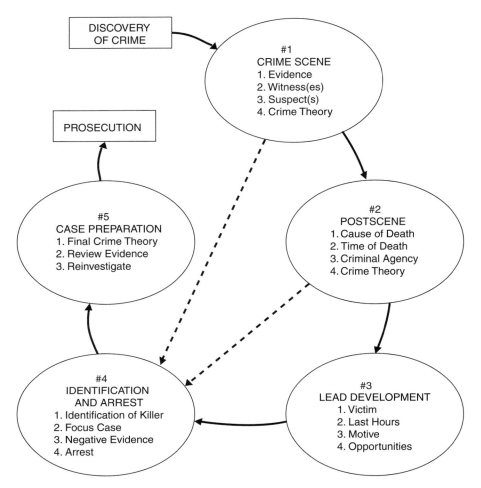

Figure 11–1 Investigation of criminal homicide.

2. Take a good, hard look when entering the crime scene to obtain an overview of the situation.
   a. *The Victim.* Give first aid or summon medical help, if necessary. Note if the victim is apparently dead or pronounced dead by a physician. Take a dying declaration, if possible.
   b. *The Scene.* Check entrances, exits, and extent of the scene. Protect weapons and other evidence. Prevent entrance of unauthorized persons. Call for technicians (if available) to take photographs. Process the scene for fingerprints and other physical evidence.
3. Protect the integrity of the scene by warning all present not to smoke, use any plumbing (sinks, tubs, showers, toilet) or towels, touch any objects or surfaces at the scene, or walk in or otherwise contaminate blood traces at the scene.
4. Identify witnesses, interview them, get a statement of their knowledge of the crime, and begin the search for additional witnesses.
5. If an apparent suspect is at the scene (case is focusing), warn him or her of rights; note appearance, clothing, and physical and mental condition; and record any spontaneous utterances. All present at the

scene are possible suspects until the case has focused. Begin a search for suspicious persons and vehicles that were at the scene before or at the time of the crime.

6. Record the scene.
   a. Photograph the scene.
   b. Measure and sketch the scene.
   c. Make notes.
   d. Collect evidence and record where it was found and who found it. Mark the evidence, transport it, and secure it with the property officer.
7. Seal the scene: do not open it without the previous agreement of associates, technicians, and the prosecutor.
8. Identify the victim.
9. Develop a tentative crime theory.

Stage 2: Postscene

1. Determine time of death; bracket the time period.
   a. Witness(es) who saw victim alive or talked to victim by telephone before his or her death
   b. Witness(es) who discovered victim (the crime)
   c. Medicolegal testimony setting a maximum and minimum limit for time of death (report of autopsy surgeon)
   d. Other evidence
2. Determine the place of fatal assault (when different from the place of discovery of the crime).
3. Determine cause of death.
   a. Apparent cause at the scene
   b. Medicolegal autopsy report
4. Determine the means of death.
   a. Criminal agency
   b. Specific weapon
   c. Weapon recovered
5. Develop a tentative crime theory.

Stage 3: Lead Development

1. Determine the victim's background and activities.
2. Investigate the victim's last hours.
   a. Contacts
   b. Activity at time of death and before death
3. Determine the vehicle(s) used.
4. Interview injured suspects.
5. Interview informants.
6. Locate the weapon.
7. Investigate tie-ups with other crimes.
8. Determine the perpetrator's knowledge of the victim's activity and access to the premises.

9. Establish motive: the "pattern" of the criminal homicide.
10. Determine opportunity to commit the crime.
    a. Persons known to have been at the scene
    b. Persons who may have been at the scene
11. Develop a tentative crime theory to include the identification of one or more prime suspects.

Stage 4: Identification and Arrest

1. Develop evidence that will identify the killer. Review evidence for corpus delicti, identification, and consistency with the crime theory.
2. Focus the case.
3. Exonerate innocent suspects.
4. Arrest the killer and crime partner(s), if any.
5. Gather negative evidence as needed.
    a. Alibi
    b. Self-defense
    c. Intent
        i. Mental state of suspect
        ii. Sobriety of suspect
        iii. Crime record of suspect
    d. Crime or treatment (medical, psychiatric) records of witnesses and victim

Stage 5: Case Preparation

1. Reconstruct the crime.
2. Summarize the physical evidence.
3. Summarize the testimony of witness(es).
4. Review the motive (reason) and intent.
5. Confer with associates and the prosecutor.
6. Reinvestigate the crime as warranted or directed by the prosecutor.
7. Prepare the cover sheet (synopsis) for forwarding with the case records to the prosecutor.

PATTERNS OF CRIMINAL HOMICIDE

The basic pattern of a criminal homicide ordinarily is disclosed in the initial investigation of a suspicious death. Even though a killer may attempt to falsify the facts of a dispute or cast the suspicion of guilt upon another person, a routine investigation should disclose the facts.

Among the basic patterns of criminal homicide are the following:

1. *The Anger Killing.*   The **anger killing** pattern is an extension of the crime of assault. A dispute occurs, and anger develops. The victim is attacked, with or without weapons, and fatally injured.
2. *The Triangle Killing.*   The possibility of an errant husband, lover, or mistress should rarely be ignored. If a wife is dead and another

woman is involved in a romantic triangle, grounds exist for suspecting that the husband wished to rid himself of an unwanted wife. The reverse situation is frequently encountered: the wife is anxious to rid herself of an unwanted husband because of a developing romance. When the person who may have the motive in this triangle was also the last one to see the victim alive, the investigation starts to gather momentum in its development as a **triangle killing**.

3. *The Revenge or Jealousy Killing.*   In a **revenge or jealousy killing,** the initial investigation of who the victim was and the history of the involvement between the victim and suspects usually will disclose the motive of revenge or jealousy, and thus a suspect.

4. *Killing for Profit.*   The elimination of another person because the murderer would gain some benefit has long been a standard motive for murder. Who would profit? This is a splendid avenue of investigation for developing suspects. When the circumstances of a suspicious death show that persons who would profit from the death are among those who last saw the victim alive, a theory of criminal homicide along these lines can be developed. **Murder for profit** is closely aligned with the triangle-killing situation; the victim is eliminated to gain some benefit.

5. *The Random Killing.*   Every killing has a motive, if *motive* is defined as a reason for the slaying. Even the **random killing**, with no previous connection or tie with the victim, has a motive. This type of killing is often termed *unmotivated* because the reason for the killing is clouded and unknown until the suspect is discovered. The killing of a complete stranger is perhaps the most difficult to solve. This pattern of murder may be disclosed by first excluding the usual or common patterns of criminal homicide.

6. *Murder–suicide.*   The **murder–suicide** pattern of criminal homicide is one in which the killer self-destructs shortly after the fatal assault on the victim. In these often "compact" killings, a husband and wife, boyfriend and girlfriend, or parent and child agree that both should die with one taking the responsibility for killing the other and then committing suicide.

7. *Sex and Sadism.*   The **sex and sadism murder** is marked by unusual violence. It may follow child molesting, rape, acts of perversion, or other sadistic acts. It often has bizarre overtones. In one New York case, the two female victims were stabbed repeatedly, undressed, and tied together face to face. The killer rubbed Noxzema face cream on and about the rectums of his victims. In a Nevada case, the victim's vagina and breasts were slashed deeply with a sharp instrument.

8. *Felony Murder.*   In the **felony murder**, the victim's death does not result from an angered attack; a triangle, revenge, jealousy, or profit motivation; random chance; a murder–suicide compact; or sex and sadism. Rather, death results from injuries inflicted by someone in the act of committing a felony. The criminal intent of the original crime carries over to the killing.

The investigator must not close his or her mind or the investigation too quickly. A homicide investigation may appear to fit one of the criminal homicide patterns, and evidence developed in a continuing investigation may reveal sufficient data to change the murder classification to another pattern or combination of patterns. For instance, a criminal homicide case in St. Paul, Minnesota, first appeared to be a burglary gone wrong. Mrs. Carol Thompson was found semiconscious and bloody in her home. She was rushed to a hospital, where she died as a result of bleeding from multiple fractures of her skull. The death weapon was a blunt instrument, and when fragments of pistol grips were found in a pool of blood in the Thompson living room, it was assumed to be a pistol whipping. Evidence of a burglary was apparent at the crime scene in the ransacking of bureau and desk drawers. Continued inquiries developed the fact that the husband of the victim had been intimate with another woman, and a new potential pattern developed: elimination of an unwanted wife. A few days later, when local insurance executives responded to police inquiries with the news that the housewife–victim was insured for over $1 million with the husband as sole beneficiary, the "killing for profit" pattern was added as a possible motive for the crime.[9]

MOTIVE FOR MURDER: RELATIONSHIPS

In a trial for murder, proof of motive is always relevant but never necessary. In a criminal homicide investigation, a motive is necessary and useful. It may surface while following the basic leads of benefit and opportunity or while reviewing the relationships of the victim. Current and former spouses and lovers of the victim promptly become suspects, as friends and relatives, not strangers, are often the killers. These relationships include the following:

1. Spouse (or ex-)
2. Common-law spouse (or ex-)
3. Boyfriend; girlfriend (or ex-)
4. Live-in boyfriend; girlfriend (or ex-)
5. Sister; brother
6. Mother; father
7. Daughter; son
8. Other relative (includes in-laws)
9. Friend of family; relative (specify)
10. Neighbor
11. Business associate (specify partner, coworker, other)
12. Acquaintance
13. Seen before (as "known from neighborhood")

The frequency of the contacts common to a relationship are classified as *live together, see daily, see weekly, see monthly,* or *hardly see at all.*

Mass murderer Andrea Yates in a family portrait. She is now confined for drowning all five of her children. (One is not pictured.)

MULTICIDE

Multicide is the killing of a number of victims by one or more persons working in concert. Mass murder, spree murder, and serial murder are the various types of multicide.

Mass murder is the homicide of four or more victims during a single event at one location.[10] The mass murderer appears to give little thought or concern to his or her inevitable capture or death. Some are killed by police during the attack; others kill themselves once they have completed the massacre. In some cases, these killers surrender to the police and offer no resistance. Most appear to commit their crimes in public places. In cases in which families are murdered, the killer usually leaves ample evidence to lead to his or her arrest.[11]

Spree murder is the killing of three or more persons within a relatively short time frame. Most of these cases last from only a few weeks to as long as a year. The victims may be men, women, or children, and an element of randomness is present in victim selection.[12] The so-called "D.C. Sniper" who killed thirteen persons and wounded six others in five states and the District of Columbia during a three-week period in the fall of 2002 is an example of a spree killer.

Gary Ridgeway, one of the most prolific serial killers in the United States, pled guilty to killing forty-eight women in the state of Washington.

    Serial killers, by contrast, may make special efforts to elude detection. They may continue to kill for weeks, months, and often years before they are caught, if at all. The definition of a **serial murder** is two or more separate murders when an individual, acting alone or with another, commits multiple homicides over a period of time with time breaks between each murder event.[13] Several types of serial murderers have been identified based upon their motivation for the killing.[14]

1. The **visionary serial killer** is propelled to kill by voices he hears or visions he sees. These breaks from reality demand that he kill certain kinds of people. This kind of offender is truly out of touch with reality— a psychotic. This killer's competency to stand trial for his actions is a consideration for the court to decide.

2. The **mission serial killer** feels a need on a conscious level to eradicate a certain group of people. This offender is not psychotic; he is in touch with reality but acts on a self-imposed duty to rid the world of a certain class of people: for example, prostitutes or religious or racial group members.

3. The **hedonistic serial killer**—the **lust killer** or **thrill killer**—is a subtype of this category. This killer has made a connection between personal violence and sexual gratification. These offenders murder because they derive pleasure from the act: killing for them is an eroticized experience. These killings are process focused, taking some time to complete, and include torture, mutilation, and other fear-instilling activities.

Another type of serial killer in this category is the **comfort-oriented serial murderer** who kills for personal gain. Professional assassins and people who kill for personal gain fall under this category.

4. The **power and control serial killer** receives sexual gratification from the complete domination of his victim. He derives his gratification from the belief that he has the power to make another human being do exactly what he wants. By dominating his victims completely, he experiences a sexual pleasure. This murderer is psychologically rooted in reality: a true sociopath who lives by his own personal rules and guidelines.

The crime scene or lack of a crime scene will determine whether the killing was the work of an organized or disorganized offender. **Organized offenders** are usually above average in intelligence. They are methodical and cunning. Their crimes are well thought out and carefully planned. They are likely to own a car that is in good condition. The crime is usually committed out of their area of residence or place of work. They are mobile and travel many more miles than the average person. Fantasy and ritual are important to them. They select their victims, usually strangers. Most of their victims will share some common traits. They are considered socially adept. They use their verbal skills to manipulate their victims and gain control over them until they have them within their "comfort zone." They are likely to follow news reports of the event and will oftentimes take a "souvenir" from the victim as a reminder, which is sometimes used to relive the event or continue with the fantasy.

Disorganized offenders are inadequate individuals who are experiencing intense sadistic sexual fantasies and may suddenly act out these fantasies on a victim of opportunity. The crime scene would be disorganized, and the perpetrator's actions and behavior could be viewed as psychotic. Offenders are usually of below average intelligence. They generally are loners who are not married, and they either live alone or with a relative in close proximity to the crime scene. They experience difficulty in negotiating interpersonal relationships and are described as socially inadequate. They act impulsively under stress and will usually select a victim from their own geographic area. In most instances, such offenders do not own a vehicle but have access to one. They use a blitz style of attack, which catches the victim off guard. This type of spontaneous action, in which the offenders suddenly acts out their fantasy, does not allow for a conscious plan or even for a thought of being detected. This is why the crime scene will be disorganized and clustered. A **clustered crime scene** involves a situation where most of the activities take place at one location: the confrontation, the attack, the assault, and sexual activity.[15]

While knowing the kind and type of serial killer involved will not tell the investigator who is committing these crimes, this information will aid the investigator in determining where to look and the type of person who may be involved. The real benefit of this information is its value at the time of interrogation. Knowing the motivation of such killers will aid in the formation of the proper questions to ask when this serial killer is caught.

The mobility of the organized offender presents a problem for the investigator as this killer may intentionally cross jurisdictional lines of authority to avoid detection. For instance, Ted Bundy, an infamous serial killer, killed twenty-nine victims in five states and was able to avoid capture for several years primarily for this reason. The **Violent Criminal Apprehension Program (VICAP)** administered by the Federal Bureau of Investigation is the clearinghouse for information regarding serial killers. Investigators send in data on their local murders, and when cases are linked the reporting investigators in the local agencies are given each other's names so that they can coordinate their work.[16]

STALKING

About half of the states in the United States now have penal code provisions to combat stalking. For instance, in Kentucky, **stalking** is defined as an intentional course of conduct that does the following:

1. Is directed at a specific person or persons
2. Seriously alarms, annoys, intimidates, or harasses the victim
3. Serves no legitimate purpose

Stalking ranges from phone calls and letters, through personal confrontations, to attempted murder, murder, or rape. A recently developed typology may be helpful to investigators who are suddenly confronted with the activity of a stalker:[17]

1. *Celebrity Stalker.*   Victim known on an impersonal level—actor, sports star
2. *Lust.*   Predatory sex (in which the victim is a stranger to the assailant), escalates to murder
3. *Hit Stalker.*   Professional killer
4. *Love-scorned Stalker.*   Intends violence against known victim
5. *Domestic Stalker.*   Ex-lover or spouse, "get even" violence
6. *Political Stalker.*   Selected victim is a stranger to the assailant

ASSAULTS

An **assault** is an unlawful attempt, coupled with the present ability, to commit an injury on the person of another. In other words, it is an attempt to commit a **battery**: an unlawful beating or other wrongful physical harm inflicted on a human being without his or her consent.

In assaults, the victim is usually alive and willing to cooperate with investigators. In many cases, the assailant is known to the victim and the investigation becomes one in which establishing the identity of the perpetrator is not a problem. When the assailant is not known to the victim, the investigation of assault is closer to a homicide investigation than it is to any other investigation.

Assault without a weapon and in which serious injury is not inflicted on the victim is a relatively minor crime. Assault with a deadly weapon or an assault in which serious injury is inflicted with or without a weapon is **aggravated assault**—a serious crime.

Aggravated assaults are often murder attempts that have failed as a result of the intervention of witnesses, prompt medical treatment, or pure luck. For this reason, the characteristics of assailants in either crime are likely to be similar.

The term **violent injury** is synonymous with force in assault cases. It includes any application of physical force even if it entails no pain or bodily harm and leaves no marks.

The assault scene must be protected and its integrity preserved. Of course, the victim must be given first aid and prompt medical attention, if required, and furniture may have to be moved to care for the victim. The investigating officer at the scene should make note of these changes in the crime scene, and if the victim is moved from the position he or she was in at the time of the officer's arrival, the victim's original position should be noted.

The crime scene is processed for evidence that will assist in reconstructing the crime and identifying the participants as the attacker and the victim; witnesses at the scene are interviewed for the same purpose. The work of investigators at this time concentrates on securing the details of the attack and of the dispute that led to the attack.

When the victim is seriously injured and requires medical care, the investigating officer should accompany the assault victim to the hospital. The situation is flexible, but the objective is to gain as much information as possible from the victim as to the circumstances leading to the attack, the nature of the attack, and the identity of the attacker. The information provided by a victim in periods of consciousness after being seriously injured may be compelling evidence in a future trial. If a victim is in extremis and is aware of impending death, the officer may secure a dying declaration indicating the victim's mental condition and the circumstances of the attack.

If the circumstances warrant, the officer accompanying an assault victim to the hospital should collect, mark, and retain the victim's clothing as evidence. Future processing by criminalists may indicate the direction of force in bullet holes and the damage caused by knives or other sharp instruments, bloodstains and their origin, and similar evidence.

It is particularly important that the weapon or weapons involved in an assault be promptly identified, recovered, and related to a participant in the assault event. The police search of the crime scene should disclose the presence of all weapons at the scene at the time of arrival of police. Interviewing of eyewitnesses should seek disclosure of any weapons used in the attack but not found at the crime scene.

Before an assault, the offender and the victim usually have had some interaction. Generally, this was an **altercation**—a verbal dispute. The dispute's origin may range from domestic difficulties to a pushing-and-shoving situation to prove masculinity among drinking partners. Although intoxication (drugs or alcohol) may not be a factor, the high incidence of assaults during late evening and early morning hours suggests that many disputes arise during, or because of, some leisure-time pursuit. Investigators must seek out the details of the dispute in assault cases to cast some light on the reason for the attack and the roles of both the victim and the assailant.

Sometimes in the preliminary investigation of an assault case the investigating police charge both participants with assault or **disorderly conduct**. Responding police often charge the apparent victim (the one most seriously injured) with **disturbing the peace** until it can be ascertained whether the victim was responsible for the attack upon himself.

Data in assault investigations are usually organized within the following major segments:

1. *The scene.*   Reconstruction of the assault event
2. *Dispute Origin.*   Place, time, participants, witnesses
3. *Weapon or Weapons.*   Existence or nonexistence, identified with user (attacker, victim), recovered at scene, recovered elsewhere
4. *Negative Evidence.*   Whether lawful resistance, victim armed, victim previously in fear of attacker (state of mind)

CHILD ABUSE

Child abuse is the intentional and deliberate assault upon a child in which serious bodily injury is inflicted by a parent, foster parent, babysitter, day-care worker, or other person in a nonparental relationship.

Serious bodily injury is a standard that excludes intervention by police in cases involving only minor assaults that could be described as corporal punishment incidental to disciplining a child.[18] In most areas of the United States, however, cases of child abuse brought to the attention of police—or discovered by them—are more properly classed as **battered child syndrome**.

Signs of physical abuse, in the absence of a reasonable explanation for the injury, include the following:[19]

1. Damage to the skin (burns, bruises, abrasions, lacerations, or swelling)
2. Brain damage (convulsions, coma, retardation)
3. Bone damage (pain on movement, deformity)
4. Internal injuries (shock, abdominal pain, signs of internal bleeding)

Burn injuries make up about ten percent of all child abuse cases. Immersion burns result from the child's falling or being placed into a tub or other container of hot liquid. In a **deliberate immersion burn**, the depth of the burn is uniform. The wound borders are very distinct, with sharply defined edges. Little evidence indicates that the child thrashed about during the immersion, which infers that the child was held in place. **Contact burns** are caused by flames or hot solid objects. Cigarette and iron burns are the most frequent types of such injuries. Cigarette burns on a child's back or buttocks are unlikely to have been caused by walking into a lighted cigarette and are more suspect than burns to the face. Accidental burns are usually more shallow, irregular, and less well defined than deliberate burns. Multiple cigarette burns are distinctively characteristic of child abuse. Purposely inflicted branding injuries usually mirror the objects that caused the burn, such as cigarette lighters and curling irons, and are much deeper than the superficial and random burns caused by accidentally touching these objects.[20]

Shaken baby syndrome occurs primarily in children eighteen months of age or younger because their necks lack muscle control and their heads are heavier than the rest of their bodies. Such injuries are caused by a violent, sustained shaking action in which the infant's head is whipped violently forward and backward and hits the chest and shoulders. The baby begins to show symptoms such as seizures or unconsciousness within minutes of the injury being inflicted. The result may be respiratory arrest or death of the child.

A classic medical symptom associated with shaken baby syndrome is **retinal hemorrhage**, which is bleeding in the back of the eyeballs. Simple household falls and tossing a baby in the air in play are not good explanations for retinal hemorrhage. Not enough force is involved in minor falls and play activities to cause retinal hemorrhage or the kinds of severe, life-threatening injuries seen in infants who have been shaken.

Munchausen syndrome is a psychological disorder in which the patient fabricates the symptoms of disease or injury in order to undergo medical tests, hospitalization, or even medical or surgical treatment. In cases of **Munchausen syndrome by proxy**, a parent or caretaker suffering from this disorder attempts to bring medical attention to themselves by injuring or inducing illness in their children. Common occurrences in these cases include the following: the child only experiences seizures or respiratory arrest when the caretaker is there—never in the presence of a neutral third party; while in the hospital, the caretaker turns off the life-support equipment, causing the child to stop breathing, and then turns the equipment back on and summons help; or the caretaker induces illness by introducing a mild irritant or poison into the child's body.

Sudden infant death syndrome (SIDS) is not a positive finding; rather, it is a diagnosis made when no other medical explanation can account for the abrupt death of an apparently healthy infant. SIDS rarely occurs in infants older than seven months and almost never is an appropriate finding for a child older than twelve months. Before SIDS can be ruled the cause of death, the investigator must ensure that every other possible medical explanation has been explored and that no evidence points to any other natural or accidental cause for the child's death. An investigator's suspicions should be aroused when multiple alleged SIDS deaths have occurred under the custody of the same parent or caretaker.[21]

When child abuse is suspected, the assigned investigator should take the child to a local hospital for examination by a physician. This examination and the physician's report will indicate the nature of the injuries and some age dating, but the reporting physician may be reluctant to diagnose the case as child abuse.

Factors likely to influence physicians to link discovered injuries in a child with child abuse include the following:

1. Delays in seeking medical care
2. Injuries not reported by parent or guardian
3. Bruises or broken bones in an infant
4. Age dating of bruises indicating that they were sustained at different times (Figure 11–2)

<table>
<tr><td colspan="2">**Determining the Age of a Bruise by Its Color**</td></tr>
</table>

Color of Bruise	Age of Bruise
Red (swollen, tender)	0–2 days
Blue, purple	2–5 days
Green	5–7 days
Yellow	7–10 days
Brown	10–14 days
No further evidence of bruising	2–4 weeks

FIGURE 11–2   Age dating of bruises. From U.S. Department of Justice, Office of Justice Programs, Office of Juvenile Justice and Delinquency Prevention, *Recognizing When a Child's Injury or Illness Is Caused by Abuse* (Washington, DC: U.S. Department of Justice, Office of Justice Programs, Office of Juvenile Justice and Delinquency Prevention, 2002), 5.

5. Characteristic wraparound bruises caused by whipping with a belt, rope, or electrical cord

6. Discrepancies in the story of a parent or guardian as to how the injuries happened: described circumstances inconsistent with the nature of the injuries

When the report of child abuse originates in a hospital, the examining physician may have been alerted by one or more of these preceding factors or simply because the parent or guardian bringing the child to the hospital can be classified as a "hospital shopper" for bringing the child to a hospital outside his or her own community when a local hospital was readily available.

At this time, the investigator must make a decision as to whether or not to take the child victim into protective custody. The action taken should be in the best interest of the child. A person in the home environment of a child being a suspect in the abuse is adequate cause to remove the child from this environment. (It also warrants action as to other children in the same household, if they have been abused or may be the subject of abuse.)

During the initial contact with a child victim, while present in the hospital or following the physician's examination, the investigator must gather what facts he or she can from the child. This may be difficult when the child is very young (two to four years old) or the child has been instructed by the person responsible for the injury either not to talk to anyone about how it happened or to repeat a false story. Once a child realizes that the investigator is truly interested in finding out the truth, the details of the assault are usually forthcoming.

The when, where, and what happened factors in these cases may cover a broad time period, several different locations, and different assaults. Once these factors have been correlated, the investigator can determine if a crime was committed, what crime, and the person or persons responsible for it.

CASE STUDY

Autopsy Surgeon

The witness, a physician, has been qualified at the beginning of her testimony, which has just ended the direct examination on how long the victim lived after being stabbed.

Direct-Examination Prosecutor

Q: Doctor, can you tell us what then would in your opinion be the maximum time that it could have been?

A: Well, he could not have lived an hour, I am sure, but all outside limits—I mean it could possibly be, but in my opinion it would be less than that.

Q: Less than an hour?

A: Oh, yes.

Cross-Examination Defense Attorney

Q: How long did the autopsy take?

A: About an hour and a half.

Q: Was that consistent work, or were there lapse times in the hour and a half?

A: It was consistent work going over the body, yes, sir.

Q: What did your autopsy consist of, Doctor?

A: External examination of the body.

Q: As to the external examination of the body, would you tell us what that consisted of?

A: Examining the wounds, examining the depth of the wounds, examining the positions of the wounds.

Q: You examined those by probes?

A: Yes, sir.

Q: How long did that part of your examination last, your external examination?

A: Approximately thirty minutes.

Q: How many actual—how many wounds actually penetrated into and through the lung wall into what you call "where the air would be in the lung"?

A: There were nine of them.

Q: All nine penetrated actually?

A: Yes, sir.

Q: Were those large wounds, sir?

A: They were approximately three-eighths of an inch—approximately three-eighths of an inch in width. None greater. They were still of the stab-wound type.

Q: There were some less?

A: Yes, sir, there were. The more distant ones, there were two that were approximately a quarter of an inch. But there were nine little wounds going right down in this medial border of the lung, and each of them would have been enough to let some air into the chest cavity.

Q: Would that depend upon the position the person was in? Would that at all be a factor?

A: I don't think position would have so much—

Q: Well, would the position tend to either close or open the wounds?

A: You mean when he was standing up or lying down?

Q: Not only lying down—or curled up, or any other position.

A: I don't think position would have so much to do as possibly activity from breathing, and activity—muscular activity.

Q: But as you move, and your chest cavity moves, don't your internal organs also tend to move or contract?

A: Well, see, your lungs—when you breathe, your lungs contract and expand, the diaphragm comes up and your chest muscles contract, and there is a pumping action, like a bellows on the lung. Now, a lung that is punctured, and a lung cavity where the—instead of being a vacuum, has atmospheric air in it, and where there is a loss of blood, a rush of blood into it, that lung just contracts right down.

Q: Let's get back now to your external examination in the detail that we started with before we got off on this track—which took half an hour. Your external examination, you probed, you say, to determine the depth of the wounds, right?

A: Yes, sir.

Q: Also, Doctor, what other examinations did you make with your external examination?

A: Looking for other wounds, looking for fractures, looking for signs of trauma, and the general configuration of the body, and looking into the mouth and checking the eyes, and I was looking for any extraneous marks or anything that would give me any more of a clue as to the cause of this man's death.

Q: Did you find any except the puncture wounds and the two marks on the neck?

A: No, sir, I did not.

Q: There were no other signs of trauma?

A: No, sir.

Q: By "trauma" you mean a blow of some kind?

A: Yes, blows, bruises, any other types of mark that would, you know, have a bearing on the death of this individual.

Q: I presume you examined very closely for those kind of things.

A: Yes.

Q: You gave an opinion as to the time between the injury and death. What factors are involved to determine that particular thing?

A: The factors involved, of course, are the wounds, the number of wounds.

Q: How do you mean the wounds? That is rather a general thing.

A: Let me put it under classification of wounds, then your subheading of that would have the number of wounds, number two under that you would have the size of the wounds, number three you would have the location of the wounds, and number four you would have to figure the rate of bleeding. Then there are variable factors under that: there would come blood pressure, coagulability of the blood. That is about all, I believe, under those factors.

Q: All right, any other factors?

A: I believe that would cover just about everything, I mean when you figure time of death.

Q: Are there any others? You say just about all of them, and are there any other factors that would be important?

A: Not that I think of extemporaneously here.

Q: On what facts do you base your opinion?

A: On the above.

Q: Well, that is pretty general. Would you detail that for us, please?

A: All right, and in doing that, of course, I would have to describe the wounds again.

Q: What I want is your detailed basis for your opinion.

A: The detailed basis of the opinion would be a description of the wounds as just described. First of all, I believe I described an incised wound, four inches long in the neck going through the skin and superficial fascia of the neck.

Q: Did that have something to do with the time of death, that particular wound?

A: Yes, it would have something to do with bleeding.

Q: All right, go ahead.

A: I would then take into consideration the wounds on the rest of the body, namely, the extremities, which, as I said before, were supplementary and contributing factors of death but not actual causes of death. Then I would take into consideration the stab wounds of the chest. And I would take into consideration the multiplicity of those wounds, their location, nine in number. Relatively an educated guess from what I have seen before, and what I know about medicine, yes.

Q: But it still would be a guess, wouldn't it?

A: Yes, sir.

CHAPTER REVIEW

KEY TERMS

aggravated assault   *229*

algor mortis   *218*

altercation   *229*

anger killing   *222*

assault   *228*

autolysis   *219*

autopsy   *213*

bacterial action   *219*

battered child
   syndrome   *230*

battery   *228*

child abuse   *230*

clustered crime
   scene   *227*

comfort-oriented serial
   murderer   *227*

contact burn   *230*

criminal agency   *212*

criminal agent   *213*

deliberate immersion
   burn   *230*

disorderly conduct   *230*

disorganized
   offender   *227*

disturbing the peace   *230*

exhumation   *219*

felony murder   *223*

first-degree murder   *212*

foul play   *212*

hedonistic serial
   killer   *226*

lust killer   *226*

manslaughter   *212*

mass murder   *225*

mission serial killer   *226*

multicide   *225*

Munchausen
   syndrome   *231*

Munchausen syndrome
   by proxy   *231*

murder for profit   *223*

murder–suicide   *223*

organized offender   *227*

physical assaults   *212*

postmortem lividity   *219*

power and control
   serial killer   *227*

putrefaction   *219*

random killing   *223*

retinal hemorrhage   *231*

revenge or jealousy
   killing   *223*

rigor mortis   *218*

second-degree
   murder   *212*

serial killer   *226*

serial murder   *226*

serious bodily
   injury   *230*

sex and sadism
   murder   *223*

shaken baby
   syndrome   *231*

spree murder   *225*

stalking   *228*

sudden infant death
   syndrome (SIDS)   *231*

suspicious death   *212*

thrill killer   *226*

toxicologist   *215*

triangle killing   *223*

Violent Criminal
   Apprehension
   Program (VICAP)   *228*

violent injury   *229*

visionary serial
   killer   *226*

window of death   *218*

REVIEW QUESTIONS

1. The major method of detecting murder is the postmortem examination of the victim by a/an _____ physician.

2. The cooling of the body after death is a fairly constant process and can be used to establish the time of death. This cooling process is known as:
   a. Algor mortis
   b. Rigor mortis
   c. Autolysis
   d. Lividity

3. Biochemical changes in the body that occur after death produce a stiffening of the muscles known as:
   a. Algor mortis
   b. Rigor mortis
   c. Autolysis
   d. Lividity

4. As a result of gravity, when the blood stops circulating it begins to settle to the lowest portion of the body. This pooling of blood is permanent and is useful in determining a change of position of the body after death. This process is known as:
   a. Algor mortis
   b. Rigor mortis
   c. Autolysis
   d. Lividity

5. After death a chemical breakdown begins that results in the softening and liquefaction of the body tissue. This process is useful in determining time of death and is known as:
   a. Algor mortis
   b. Rigor mortis
   c. Autolysis
   d. Lividity

6. The removal of a deceased person's body from its burial place so that a medicolegal examination can be conducted to disclose the presence of previously unknown or improperly identified injuries or reveal the presence of poison or another noxious substance is known as:
   a. Autopsy
   b. Antemortem examination
   c. Postmortem examination
   d. Exhumation

7. The homicide or killing of four or more victims during a single event, usually at one location, is the definition of what type of multicide?
   a. Mass murder
   b. Spree murder
   c. Serial murder
   d. Hedonistic murder

8. The homicide or killing of two or more victims as a result of separate murders when an individual, acting alone or with another, commits multiple homicides during a period of time, with time breaks between each murder is known as:
   a. Mass murder
   b. Spree murder
   c. Serial murder
   d. Hedonistic murder

9. The killing of three or more persons within a relatively short time frame is known as what type of multicide?
   a. Mass murder
   b. Spree murder
   c. Serial murder
   d. Hedonistic murder

10. Parents or caretakers who attempt to bring medical attention to themselves by injuring or inducing illness in their children suffer from the psychological disorder known as:
    a. Sudden infant death syndrome
    b. Munchausen syndrome
    c. Munchausen syndrome by proxy
    d. Battered child syndrome

See Appendix D for the correct answers.

DISCUSSION QUESTIONS

1. Define a criminal homicide.
2. What is the role of the medical examiner (autopsy surgeon) in evaluating suspicious deaths?
3. List and describe the common patterns in criminal homicides. What patterns in criminal homicide are often related?
4. What are the possible routes (techniques) for identifying victims in suspicious deaths?
5. Why is the determination of the time of death of important in the investigation of criminal homicide?
6. What procedures should be followed to protect the integrity of an autopsy in exhumation cases?
7. List five major segments of the on-the-scene phase of a criminal homicide investigation.
8. What are the similarities and differences between the investigation of criminal homicides and the investigation of criminal assaults?
9. How can a pattern of serial murders be established? Why are they difficult to close out with an arrest?
10. What circumstances are likely to indicate physical child abuse?
11. What is the goal of cross-examination in the case study?
12. The time of death is vital to this case. Why?

RELATED WEB SITES

To view homicide trends in the United States visit the Bureau of Justice Statistics at *http://www.ojp.usdoj.gov/bjs/homicide/homtrnd.htm*.

For information regarding homicide in the workplace, see *http://cdc.gov/niosh/topics/violence*.

Researching serial murderers? If so you might want to take a look at *Court TV's* crime library at *www.crimelibrary.com*.

chapter **twelve**

Sexual Assaults

CHAPTER OUTLINE

After reading this chapter you will be able to:

- Distinguish the differences between forcible rape, date rape, and statutory rape.
- Identify the various types of rapists and their personality profile.
- Explain the common defenses a suspect is likely to offer when charged with the crime of rape.
- Recognize the various types of child molestation and discuss the molester's motivations.
- Describe the major obstacle in prosecuting child molestation cases and how investigators deal with this challenge.

RAPE

Forcible rape is an act of violence. It is not a crime of sexual desire but an act of brutal violence, as in murder with intent and **malice**. It should be investigated in the same manner as criminal homicides and just as thoroughly.

In common law, **rape** was defined as the carnal knowledge (sexual intercourse) of a woman with force and without her consent. Consent induced by fear of violence is not consent, and it is against the woman's will if her male attacker uses an array of physical force to overcome the victim's mind so she dare not resist. Of necessity, since force or fear is an essential element of the crime of rape, evidence should be developed of the victim's resistance or that her resistance was overcome by force or that she was prevented from resisting by threats to her safety.[1]

The means used to overcome the will of the female victim is of major importance in rape investigations:

1. Force or the threat of the use of force
2. Administration of drugs (including alcoholic beverages)
3. Incapacity to consent (victim's physical or mental condition or age)

In the terminology of state legislatures, rape is said to be **aggravated rape** when the rapist is armed with a dangerous weapon, kidnaps the victim, inflicts bodily injury, or is in a position of trust in regard to the victim such as official authority (custody or control) or a familial relationship.

Date rape or **acquaintance rape** is male sexual aggression in which the female half of a twosome is forced to have sexual intercourse. Sexual coercion by dates or acquaintances is really rape. This is not the blitz rape without previous interaction between offender and victim in which the offender immediately threatens or employs force to overcome his victim. In date or acquaintance rape, a previous relationship exists between the offender and the victim but the victim has been forced to have sex without her consent.

The prevalence of forced sex among dates and acquaintances may be increasing, but what is more likely is that victims are now more aware of their basic rights. This so-called simple rape, after years of underreporting, is now being reported for what it is: **forcible rape**.[2]

Although most sexual assault victims are women, a man can also be victimized sexually. However, depending on the jurisdiction, the crimes involved when a man is a victim are usually sodomy, forcible oral copulation, or both, rather than the crime of rape. The investigative protocol is the same, regardless of the victim's sex.

INITIAL ACTION

The initial task of police upon receipt of a report of a forcible rape is to aid the victim (Figure 12–1). The injured victim may require immediate transportation to a local hospital that provides emergency services; apparent shock—known as **rape trauma syndrome**—should also warrant medical attention. Men and women taking rape reports must do their best to avoid contributing to the

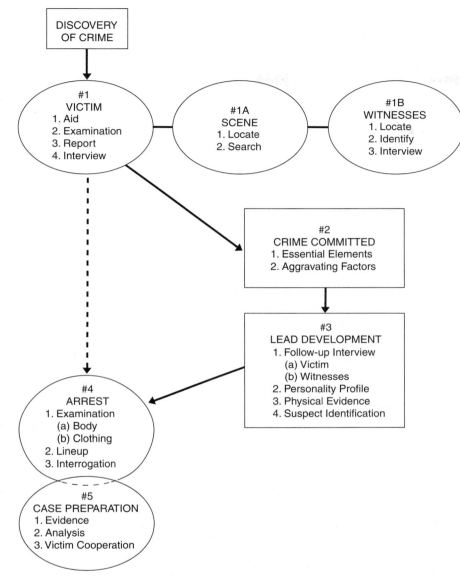

FIGURE 12–1   Investigation of forcible sexual assault.

victim's mental distress. The professional reporting officer realizes that the person reporting a forcible rape has just been through an emotionally shattering experience and acts accordingly.

Depending on the condition of the victim, the next step is the initial interview in which the victim is asked about the circumstances of the crime and the identity of the rapist. If the victim requires medical attention or is in a state of shock, questioning should be very brief and limited to the facts of the crime and a description of the rapist for a radio-broadcast alarm. If the victim can be questioned, this interview should probe all the circumstances of the crime and the identity of the rapist.

At the conclusion of this interview, the victim should be told about the necessity of a physical examination. The victim should be informed that this is

242 Part 2   Investigating Major Crimes

voluntary but that her consent is vital to the collection and preservation of evidence that will reveal and corroborate the acts done to her and contribute to the identification of the rapist.[3]

A medical examination of a forcible-rape victim may be conducted as part of the medical treatment of the victim when hospitalized or by special arrangement with the victim. The report of the examining physician becomes part of the record of the case. It is usually concerned with four specific matters:

1. Bodily injuries of the victim
2. Evidence of force in relation to the rapist's sex act
3. Evidence of the completion of the sex act to the penetration required by rape statutes
4. Evidence likely to identify the suspect

The victim of a forcible rape may not know exactly where she was when she was raped, or she may have been in the rapist's car, and the vehicle is not usually available until the rapist is arrested. If a crime scene has been located, however, it must be promptly secured until properly searched.

Correlated with the victim's telling of what happened, who did it, and where it happened is the search for witnesses. Their identity and where they can be located are important at this time in the investigation. What they observed can be secured later.

When the reporting officer believes the circumstances of the attack spell out the elements of forcible rape (lack of consent, use of force or fear, and penetration), the case will be so classified and emphasis placed on identifying and apprehending the rapist.

When the victim identifies the suspect by name or as having been seen before the rape, the emphasis will be on locating this suspect. This is also true when the victim provides information as to the color, design, or license number of a vehicle used by the rapist.

Unless the rapist is promptly identified by information supplied by the victim or witnesses or is arrested in the hot-pursuit phase of the police apprehension process, discovering the identity of the rapist is likely to be the major problem in rape investigations. Identification of rapists is a problem because, as a general rule, informants are not helpful, modus operandi files do not supply any leads unless the rapist is a repeater (serial rape cases), photographs of rape suspects are not usually available, and field interrogation reports are usually nonproductive.

Leads to the identity of an unknown rapist may be developed from the same areas as in criminal homicide investigations:

1. The victim's background
2. Persons in contact with the victim or places visited by her in the hours immediately preceding the rape
3. Weapons found at the scene
4. Persons with knowledge or opportunity—access to the victim and scene of the crime, or at or near the scene at the time of the rape

5. Injured suspects (when victim believes he or she scratched or otherwise injured the rapist)
6. Connect-ups with previous forcible rapes

FOLLOW-UP INTERVIEW OF VICTIM

If a suspected rapist is arrested before this interview, the focus of the follow-up interview is identification that will be legally significant in court at the trial of the rapist. Inquiries should concern just how the victim identifies the attacker. A lineup in which the suspect is placed among others to be viewed by the victim is warranted. All of the standard legal safeguards protecting this identification from suggestibility or other invalidating factors must be in operation.

When the victim is unable to identify the rapist at this lineup but police believe they have arrested the correct person, concentration is on other evidence of identity that will be compelling and will overcome this failure to positively identify the suspect in a lineup. Even when the victim does identify the rapist in a lineup, this other evidence of identity is important in the event that the lineup identification is attacked by defense counsel at trial.

If the rapist has not been identified, the focus of the interview is on what the victim can remember of the circumstances of the rape that will contribute to the rapist's identification. What did the rapist look like? How was he dressed? Is a vehicle included in the circumstances of this rape? These and related questions should develop the physical characteristics of the rapist, how the rapist was dressed at the time of the rape, and perhaps some vehicle identification. Investigators must probe the victim's recall of events to uncover any particular physical characteristics or article of clothing that is distinctive or unique. Even the most fragmentary description can be helpful.

Arrangements with a police artist or Identi-Kit specialist may be indicated, with the victim cooperating and approving the final artwork as a reasonable illustration of the rapist.

Computer searches are now available in most state motor vehicle bureaus, and "possibles" may be obtained, indicating vehicles matched to a fragment of a license number or a partial description, or both.

Extensive searches for unidentified multiple rapists (serial rapists) by police in several urban jurisdictions have pointed to the need for information on the rapist's behavior. Therefore, investigators should question the victim as to the rapist's approach, how he exerted control of the situation, the sex acts attempted or communed, and whether or not the rapist made any effort to conceal his identity.

Was the approach friendly with sweet talk, or was it brutal and surprising? What was the victim doing during this initial conduct? What had the victim been doing just before this contact? Where had the victim been? Who had the victim seen there? Who might have witnessed this initial approach? These are some of the questions that will give behavioral dimensions to the first contact of the rapist with the victim.

Rapists control their victims by some combination of the following:

1. Verbal activity, particularly threats
2. Display of a weapon
3. Physical force

Threats and orders are the usual verbal activity, but some rapists are animated conversationalists. The essence of what was said and its pace are important aspects of the rapist's behavior.

What weapon was displayed? How does the victim describe it? What did the rapist do with it? The details of weapon display are also part of the rapist's behavior.

The use of physical force and its extent constitute one of the most important factors in defining the behavior of the rapist during the crime. A precise description of the force used should disclose whether it is minimal, excessive, or brutal. Another important factor is the rapist's reaction to resistance by the victim.

A problem area of these follow-up interviews of the rape victim may occur when the investigator seeks details of the sex acts attempted or committed by the rapist. Perhaps the best technique is to inform the victim that these queries are necessary to determine the behavioral pattern of the rapist and, possibly, to connect the rapist with other rapes.

This in-depth interview of the victim may be postponed because of injuries, mental condition, lack of a suitably private place, or a departmental ruling that such interviews be conducted by specially trained personnel.[4]

FOLLOW-UP INTERVIEWS OF WITNESSES

The police officer accepting the report of a forcible rape has the duty of securing the names and addresses of possible witnesses and, if time permits, of briefly interviewing them as to what they might have observed. Then, when the scene of the crime is located and the time of occurrence firmly fixed, investigators may interview or reinterview these witnesses.

Follow-up interviews of the person to whom the victim reported the rape, or from whom the victim initially sought help following the attack, are mandatory. These persons are primary witnesses to the victim's appearance and condition at the time. Of almost equal importance are witnesses who observed the victim, and possibly the rapist, just before the attack occurred.

Usually, rapists find some area in which they will not be observed when they commit this assault upon their victims. Therefore, investigators are unlikely to find witnesses to a rape. Of course, experienced investigators make every effort to find the chance onlooker who was a witness. Failing in this discovery, investigators depend on those individuals who observed the before and after phases of this crime.

The focus of these follow-up interviews of witnesses is to find evidence supportive or corroborative of the victim's report of the rape.[5]

PERSONALITY PROFILE OF THE SERIAL RAPIST

The victim's description of a rapist's behavior, upon analysis by competent personnel, reflects the personality of the rapist. From data secured in the

Sadistic rapist Ted Bundy is believed to have raped and killed over 40 women.

follow-up interview of the victim, a criminal personality profile may be prepared. These profiles require the services of persons trained in the behavioral sciences who can review the manner in which the rapist behaved and can portray the rapist as a person.[6] Based upon these victim's description of the rapist's behavior, as well as the results of personal interviews with convicted rapists, three major types of male rapists have emerged.

The Anger Rapist.   The **anger rapist** or anger retaliation rapist commits the crime of rape as a means of expressing and discharging feelings of pent-up anger and rage. The assault is characterized by physical brutality. The rapist uses far more force than is necessary to overpower the victim and achieve sexual penetration. This offender attacks his victim— grabbing her, striking her, knocking her to the ground, then beating her, tearing her clothes, and raping her. He may use a blitz style of attack or a confidence-style approach to gain access to the victim and then launch a sudden, overpowering attack. The anger rapist typically finds little or no sexual gratification in the rape. The act is more of a weapon—a means by which he can defile, degrade, and humiliate his victim. These attacks tend to be of short duration and infrequent, as it takes time for his frustrations and aggravation to reach a volatile point again. In summary, his intent is to hurt and degrade his victim; his weapon is sex and his motive is revenge.

The Power Rapist.   The **power rapist** uses sex as a means of compensating for underlying feelings of inadequacy and to express issues of mastery, strength, authority, and control over another person. His goal is sexual conquest, and he uses only the amount of force necessary to accomplish his objective. His aim is to capture and control his victim. He often is armed with a weapon for intimidation. His victim may be subjected to repeated assaults over an extended time. This offender tends to find little sexual satisfaction in the rape for it never lives up to his fantasies. The amount of force and aggression used in the assault may increase over time as the offender becomes more desperate to achieve that indefinable experience that continues to elude him.[7] Power rapists are of two types:

The Power Reassurance Rapist.   The **power reassurance rapist** is the least violent of all the rapists and the least socially competent, suffering from low self-esteem and feelings of inadequacy. The reason he rapes is to elevate his own self-status. This rapist's self-image is as a loser, and by controlling another person he hopes to make himself feel important, if only temporarily. He uses only enough force to control his victims. He may later contact his victim to inquire about her health as if he is concerned about the ill effects of the rape. He may also be convinced that his victim enjoyed being raped and may promise to return.

The Power Assertive Rapist.   The **power assertive rapist** rapes to express his virility and personal dominance. He has a sense of superiority simply because he is a man and he rapes because he believes that he is entitled to do so. This rapist is indifferent to the comfort and welfare of his victim—she is at his mercy and she must do what he desires. He is image conscious and tends to be a flashy dresser. He is a regular at singles bars, and he is known as someone who is always trying to pick up women, and he is continually trying to validate his image as being macho.

The Sadistic Rapist.   The **sadistic rapist** finds the intentional maltreatment of his victim intensely gratifying and takes pleasure in her torment, anguish, distress, helplessness, and suffering. The assault usually involves bondage and torture and frequently has a bizarre or ritualistic quality to it. In extreme cases—those involving sexual homicide—grotesque acts may take place, such as the sexual mutilation of the victim's body or necrophilia. Usually, the victims are strangers who share some common characteristic, such as age, appearance, or occupation. They are symbols of something the sadistic rapist wants to punish or destroy. The assault is deliberate, calculated, and preplanned. The offender takes precautions against discovery by wearing a disguise or blindfolding the victim. The victim is stalked, abducted, abused, and sometimes murdered. The sadistic rapist has made a connection between the infliction of pain and sexual gratification, which results in abuse and torture of the victim.

In examining the incidence of these primary patterns of rape, it appears that power rapes are the most prominent. More than half (55 percent) of the cases constitute a power rape, approximately 40 percent are anger rapes, and about 5 percent are sadistic rapes.[8] In essence, the crime of rape is primarily about anger and power and not about sexual desire. While this information may not be considered a basic investigative lead in the identification and apprehension of the rapist, it is useful information for the interrogation of the suspect when he is eventually caught.

ARREST OF THE SUSPECTED RAPIST

Time is of the essence in arresting suspects in forcible rape cases. If the arrest is made within a reasonable amount of time after the rape, medical personnel at a local hospital should conduct a full body examination of the suspect. Most hospitals with emergency treatment facilities have kits containing the medical equipment and supplies used in rape examinations. The report of the medical personnel conducting the examination becomes part of the total investigation report. Since this report is nontestimonial evidence, no legal problems should be encountered. Delays incidental to securing a court order could result in the destruction of evidence. If the arrestee consents to this examination, appropriate forms should be prepared for his signature.

Examiners search for and report scratches, bites, bruises, and other wounds; they describe scars, moles, and tattoos; and they secure physical evidence associated with the crime of rape. In addition, samples of the suspect's blood, urine, and hair (head and pubic) are taken.[9]

If clothing worn by the suspect at the time of arrest is believed to have been worn at the time of the rape, it should be seized and sent to the forensic science laboratory for examination. If it is apparent that the clothing was not worn at the time of the rape, a prompt search should be instituted for such clothing. A search warrant may be required. All suspect clothing should be promptly forwarded to the forensic science laboratory for examination. Reports of these examinations also become part of the investigation record.

The time of arrest is when investigators search for associative evidence that will corroborate the testimony of the victim by placing the arrestee at the crime scene or in contact with the victim.

CASE PREPARATION

Investigators assigned to a forcible rape investigation must develop and hold the victim as a cooperative witness for the prosecution. The reinterviewing of a victim (which is common in these cases), the time gap between arrest and trial, and the procedural safeguards protecting all accused persons dismay most men and women who have been victims of a serious, violent crime and want the criminal punished.

Lack of victim cooperation may seriously complicate case preparation and make it difficult or impossible to develop evidence proving the necessary elements of forcible rape. This aspect of forcible rape investigations, along with the humanitarian aspects of treating a rape victim decently and exhibiting a sincere concern for the victim's well-being during the postrape period, should motivate an investigator to do his or her best to close the case with an arrest and move it to trial as fast as possible.

To overcome the common defenses of a forcible rape charge, the investigator must prepare a case in which the victim is cast as the most truthful witness in the trial. Confirming and compelling evidence must be available at the trial to depict the victim in this truthful witness role.

PROBLEMS OF PROOF

When a defendant denies any involvement in a rape, the most common defense is mistaken identity plus an alibi for the time of the rape (a claim of being elsewhere at or about the time of the crime).

Identification of a defendant as the rapist is a major problem of proof. Some rapists pull a pillowcase over the victim's head or cover the victim's face with an article of clothing, others wear gloves to avoid leaving conclusive physical evidence, and a few have been known to command their victim "Don't look at me!" In recent years, ski or stocking masks have become popular headgear for blitz rapists. This problem can be overcome by a combination of the victim's identification of the defendant, the testimony about the initial meeting between victim and defendant (the rapist's "approach"), and the transfer of physical evidence linking the defendant to the victim or the scene of the rape.

An investigator must be innovative. In one New York case, the defendant was convicted primarily on a voice lineup. The prosecution proved that this defendant wore a ski mask habitually, and the jurors apparently accepted the idea that the only possible identifier was his voice.

When a suspect admits to sexual intercourse with the victim, the usual defense is that of consent. This is an effective defense when the prosecution is unable to show that the victim's resistance was overcome by an immediate threat or an overwhelming use of force or that the victim did resist and did attempt to flee from the defendant.

In cases involving date or acquaintance rape, the element of consent has been a major problem. The fact of a prior relationship in these cases no longer implies such consent.

Problem-solving assistance is available from the Federal Bureau of Investigation's Investigative Support Unit (ISU), which offers profiles, assessments, and other support and may be able to take the details of the case under investigation and link them with multiple rapes elsewhere. Evidence from these other cases may provide a starting point for case development.[10]

Sperm and blood are the common forms of evidence in rape cases. In fact, this has become such a given that many investigators have developed a mental block with regard to other physical evidence that may be effective in proving guilt or innocence or possibly penetration in rape cases.

As the use of condoms increases, it is likely that rapists will also use them with increasing frequency. Investigators aware of the potential for traces from condoms to associate a suspect with one or more rapes will find that many problems in investigating these sexual assaults will diminish and possibly disappear. This is because of the emerging forensic science procedure for extracting condom lubricant traces from evidence items in sexual assault cases. If condom lubricant traces are to have significant evidentiary value, new collection procedures at crime scenes and in subsequent transport to a crime lab must be developed. This professional how-to is likely to include instructions for the doctor doing the medical examination, the investigator collecting crime scene evidence, and the detective interviewing the victim and suspect.[11]

STATUTORY RAPE

Statutory rape involves consensual sex relations between two persons, in which one of the parties is a minor who by statute is considered incapable of consenting to a sexual act. The California penal code defines a minor as anyone under the age of eighteen. Many other state jurisdictions have set the age of majority lower than California.

Both men and women can be arrested and prosecuted for having sexual relations with minors. These crimes usually come to the attention of investigators when one of the parties becomes pregnant, the couple is caught in the act, or their activities are otherwise discovered. The identification of the perpetrator is usually not an issue as the minor usually knows their partner. When the identity of the perpetrator is unknown, the lines of inquiry are the same as for a forcible rape investigation. The most common defense in these cases is one of mistake in fact as to the victim's true age at the time of the offense. For this defense to be viable, the minor must have presented himself or herself as being an adult at the time of involvement with the perpetrator.

CHILD SEXUAL ABUSE

When children are the victims of criminal activity, they must be treated as persons to be helped (similar to victims of forcible rape). The shock of being a crime victim, particularly when it involves sex acts, is heightened by police inquiry into the circumstances of the crime. Investigators must promptly recognize that the child victim may require medical attention for possible injuries and for the emotional shock of such a crime.

Investigators serve as the community's agent in redressing the harm done to the child victims of crime. The role of investigators in cases involving child abuse, sexual exploitation, or abduction is common to all investigations: (1) reconstruct the event or events; (2) determine if a crime has been committed and, if so, what crime; (3) identify the person or persons responsible; and (4) take appropriate action. The investigator's role is not that of medical practitioner, social worker, counselor, or psychologist. The investigator does, however, have the responsibility to make referrals to such professionals whenever the investigation discloses that the child victim requires such help.

INCEST

A person commits the crime of **incest** when he or she has sexual intercourse with a person known to be within the relationship of parent/child, brother/sister, uncle/aunt, or nephew/niece. Most state laws use a broad definition of incest: any sexual contact between blood-related family members who are not permitted such behavior by social norms.

So-called **psychological incest** is sexual activity between a child and a stepparent, foster parent, or a live-in boyfriend of the child's mother. It also includes such nonrelated family members as stepbrothers and stepuncles.[12] This degrading form of child sexual abuse should be investigated along the same lines as physical child abuse: fact gathering must include when, where, and what happened, the identity of the adult involved, and the adult's family relationship to the victim.

Some important validations of the fact that incest has been committed include these:[13]

1. The acts done were continuing and progressive.
2. The child's story of sexual abuse gives explicit detail in his or her own words.
3. Secrecy was encouraged, and the victim was pressured to keep silent (through gifts, threats, family disgrace).
4. The victim retracts the accusation due to familial pressure.

Child victims should be transported to a hospital for an examination similar to that conducted in cases of forcible rape. A similar examination of the suspect at the time of arrest may be warranted. Both examinations are oriented to discovering and collecting evidence supportive of the victim's story of the sexual abuse.

PEDOPHILIA

A **pedophile** is someone who "loves" children, but this love of children—**pedophilia**—is a sexual interest that ranges from fondling to mutilation and murder. Two types of pedophiles are recognized: the situational and the preferential child molester.

Of the two, the **situational child molester** has fewer victims. This type of molester does not have a true sexual interest in children but will experiment with them when the opportunity presents itself. Following are the three types of situational child molesters:

The **regressed child molester** experiences a situational occurrence that impels this pedophile to turn to children as a temporary, not permanent, object for sexual gratification. This molester turns to children as substitute sexual partners in response to something that has occurred in the molester's life that challenges his or her self-image and results in poor self-esteem. Normally this molester would be involved with adults in normal relationships.

The **morally indiscriminate child molester** is an abuser of all available persons; children are just another category of victim. This offender has a basic motivation toward sexual experimentation and is willing to try anything; nothing is taboo for this offender.

The **naïve or inadequate child molester** includes those persons who are suffering from some form of mental disorder that renders them unable to make the distinction between right and wrong, including sexual practices with children. This type of offender does not physically harm the child and is more likely to experiment with children with sexual practices that include holding, fondling, kissing, and so forth but not sexual activity.

The **preferential child molester** views children more intensely as providers of sexual pleasure. This group prefers children as sexual partners and is the true pedophile. The preferential child molester prefers children over adults as providers of sexual satisfaction. This person's interest in children is persistent and compulsive. A large number of pedophiles can be classified as preferential child molesters, and these offenders are the most likely type to be very dangerous to children. Two types of offenders fall under this category:

The **fixated child molester** is often childlike in lifestyle and behaviors. This offender selects children as sexual objects because youths are less demanding, more easily dominated, and less critical. The fixated offender is not interested in physically harming the child but rather loves children and does not want to harm them. Young boys are the preferred sexual target of this offender.

The **sadistic child molester** has made a vital connection between sexual gratification and personal violence. Typically, the child will be a stranger, and the offender may stalk the child rather than use any form of seduction. This offender will often abduct a child from places where children gather, such as playgrounds, schools, and shopping centers. This type of pedophile has no "love" for the child victim and is interested only in causing harm and death to a vulnerable victim compared to whom the offender feels great superiority. [14]

Diligent inquiry will disclose a network of other incidents, victims, and pedophiles. This **mushroom factor** links activity likely to identify a previously unknown child molester. Evidence available upon the arrest of a suspect (address book, identity of friends and associates) will often disclose the full details of a network of pedophiles and their victims. Common to this organization of pedophiles and child victims are registered sex offenders.[15]

Victims are good sources of information about pedophile networks, particularly those boys or girls who have participated in this activity voluntarily either because of their friendship with the molester or because they were paid for their services. Teenage runaways of both sexes have admitted to this type of prostitution as a survival technique in a hostile environment.

Many molesters operate in their own home or business neighborhoods, sometimes using one victim to recruit others in the age group of the molester's sexual preference. Others gain access to victims by seeking leadership positions in church or community child-centered programs. The mushroom factor in these cases takes little more than simple queries to develop: Who are the victim's friends in the neighborhood, and what children's group is involved?

Pedophiles (a.k.a **chicken hawks**) use computers and online services to locate potential child victims. They pose as another youth and begin their conversations (drugs, girls, school, parents) with teenage subjects. As the "friendship" develops, they suggest a meeting. Child exploitation through computer bulletin boards and online information services is a rapidly growing problem.[16] Investigators can learn more about this when they make their first arrest, questioning the offenders about their activities. When their acts do not imply guilt, but merely a displayed interest in the area, these offenders are likely to talk—and teach.

Police investigators have a great responsibility to detect and discover child sexual molestations. Detection may originate in a casual inquiry of a runaway child encountered in other police activity as to how they survived on the street, in the investigation of an unrelated crime, or in the willingness of a knowledgeable defendant in a case awaiting trial to reveal significant information as to child molestation in exchange for help with his or her plea negotiations.

A medical examination of the victim in these cases is more than warranted, as is a similar examination of the suspect upon arrest. This examination should be aligned with the reported sexual abuse and be focused on discovering urogenital or anal injuries, pain, irritation, and evidence of a venereal disease or any other illness related to child molestation.

Investigators should send clothing worn by the victim at the time of the attack and clothing belonging to the suspect and seized as evidence at the time of arrest or in the postarrest period to the forensic science (crime) laboratory as physical evidence. It may contain trace evidence linking the suspect to the victim or place of occurrence of the attack, or it may contain evidence of the sexual contact or contacts.

When it happened, where it happened, what happened, and who did it are the classic inquiries likely to uncover the circumstances of these crimes (Figure 12–2). If the collected evidence indicates child sexual molestation, the investigator should act promptly to identify and arrest the adult responsible. The investigator must work hard to link the suspect with other victims and other cases of child sexual abuse from evidence developed at the time of arrest or in the postarrest period.

THE CHILD AS VICTIM–WITNESS

Children may testify in court in a variety of cases, but they are most likely to be classed as key witnesses in child-abuse trials. In such cases, the child is the victim and the only eyewitness. Moreover, in these criminal proceedings, police and court personnel suspect that attention is focused on protecting the constitutional rights of the defendant(s)—not because the rights of the child victim–witness will be disregarded but because the child's competence as a witness will be examined in depth and the testimony given in court will be sharply scrutinized.

Investigators usually operate on the assumption that the child is telling the truth. This behavior is desirable in any first-line agent—parent, teacher, neighbor, physician, or police officer. However, the assigned investigator must work beyond this assumption and critically appraise the story of the child during interviews and postinterview periods when evidence supporting the child's story is sought. Linked to this appraisal is an ongoing demand that the investigator in charge of carrying the case offer an opinion as to the competency of the child victim as a future key witness.

Supporting evidence of a child's story of physical or sexual abuse should develop evidence in total at the probable-cause level, along with basic leads likely to upgrade the case when fully developed. The investigator needs this for his or her decisions during the investigation; the child victim needs such

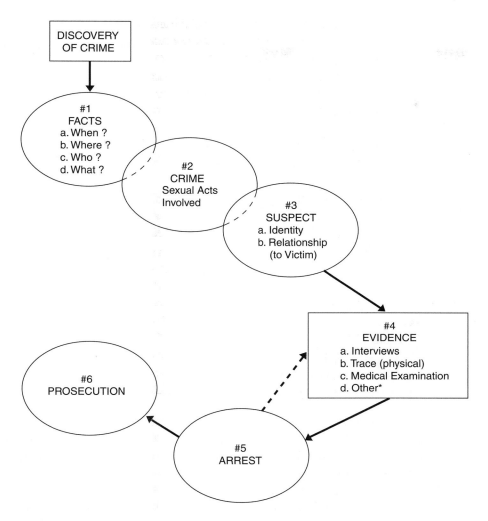

*Includes Network Development–Sex Abuse.

FIGURE 12–2   Investigation of child sexual abuse.

support for his or her testimony in court. In forming an opinion about the child's competency, investigators should be mindful that the child must be observant and articulate, know truth as opposed to lies, and understand that a witness must testify truthfully.

California's McMartin preschool case was long and costly and a revelation to criminal investigators regarding deficiencies in their inquiries. Police investigators attempted to jump-start their investigation by sending a letter to nearly 400 parents of children enrolled in this school. This letter encouraged parents to question their children about any sexual abuse by their teachers. However, many parents promptly mentioned it to one or more of the suspect teachers, alerting them to the threat of an ongoing investigation. The case went on for several years to a very unsatisfactory conclusion: no one convicted, no truth of the accusations proved in court.[17]

Investigators need to learn the how-to of securing information from children. A nonsuggestive interview is likely to be more productive and characterized by a basic integrity. The basic structure of this interview should contain several "don'ts": (1) don't suggest anything to the child—or to his or her parent(s)—or even appear to suggest; (2) don't reveal the allegations of other children involved in the same investigation; (3) don't use dolls of any kind until subsequent interviews, and then only with good reason; and (4) avoid news releases until the crime and its facts are clear and focused.

MISSING CHILDREN

Any young person under the legal adult age (unemancipated) who, without permission of parent or guardian, remains away from his or her home for twenty-four hours or more is generally termed a **runaway** by local police.

Police in large cities often field a **diaper squad** to patrol local bus stations and "gut" areas containing such occupancies as adult theaters and adult bookstores, the "stroll" section in which local prostitutes operate, and the "meat rack" frequented by boys and young men catering to older men.

When runaways spend the money they carried with them when they left home, they find it difficult to replenish their funds through legitimate employment. **Hustling** is an aggressive reaction and is generally focused on sex for sale. Less aggressive runaways are picked up by pimps or sexual **deviants** and sometimes forced into prostitution.

Unfortunately, despite the work of police officers to locate missing children and return them to their parents or guardians, the number of runaway children in the United States provides pedophiles with recurring opportunities to find child victims.

The great number of runaways creates a major obstacle to searching for and finding a missing child. In addition, local police have to depend on police from other jurisdictions in this search-and-identify task. Runaway programs operated by various youth organizations are a resource for runaways, getting them off the street and encouraging them to contact their parents or guardian. These programs may also become a resource for investigators seeking missing children, particularly when some evidence suggests that the child has fled to a particular city.

When some aspect of a child's disappearance indicates abduction, local police will generally make an effective and timely response. The 1982 Missing Children's Act placed federal resources at the service of local police. The Missing Person File of the FBI's National Crime Information Center is being used in searching for missing children believed to have been abducted.

The first step in the investigation of child abduction is to make certain that the child has not been kidnapped by a parent or grandparent. Once it is ascertained that the child is not a pawn in a family dispute, every reasonable means should be used to broadcast the facts of the case and a description of the missing child. Since many child victims are murdered, this description should contain the child's dental chart, medical information, and fingerprints whenever available. (Emerging police programs fingerprint local children and provide parents with the prints in case the child becomes a victim of an abductor.)

The investigation into an abduction generally follows the outline of any criminal homicide investigation. Since the victim is not available for interviewing, the investigator must concentrate on securing data about the victim's movements just before his or her disappearance. As facts are gathered, data are added to the published alarm. Collaterally, investigators probe among registered sex offenders, suspected pedophiles disclosed as part of a network in child sexual abuse investigations, and suspect persons or vehicles seen in the neighborhood of the child's disappearance.

Investigators must move promptly along two general lines: (1) find the child and (2) identify and locate the suspect. One experienced detective has described this type of investigation as "frantic," which is also a graphic description of the fast-breaking and aggressive investigation likely to produce results in these cases.

CASE STUDY

The East Area Rapist

The first rapes occurred in the eastern part of the county—hence the name "East Area Rapist". In all, fifty-five rapes were reported to the police in five different counties. However, many more rapes may have been committed but not reported. The rapes started in northern California and eventually ended ten years later in southern California. It is now believed that this rapist made the transition to serial killer and may be responsible for as many as ten murders. Despite investigating and eliminating 5,000 possible suspects and spending in excess of $2.5 million on the investigation, investigators have no clear picture of the armed man in a ski mask who terrorized his victims.

The rapist cased his victims with eerie diligence, which led some to believe he had military or law enforcement training. Sometimes he would first slip into their homes, swiping a photograph or other small items that barely raised suspicion. He would gather details, like the floor plan, how the garage door operated, how an outside light timer worked, or the names and schedules of occupants. At one home, he removed bullets from a gun tucked under a mattress, then put it back. Then, he would come back during the night, armed with a gun or knife, carrying shoelaces to tie up his victims. He started with women living alone but soon moved to couples.

For up to three hours, he would administer terror. He kept the men from moving by putting dishes on them, threatening to kill if he heard anything break. He would then attack the women, disappear quietly in the house—eating pumpkin pie at one place—then come back again. The victims never knew for sure when he was gone. In later rapes, he grew more violent, more forceful in his threats. He was bold. He would telephone victims after the attack and would seem to know which lines were tapped. At town hall meetings set up by the authorities, as many as 700 people would jam inside. At one meeting, a couple spoke, raised doubts about the rapist's methods, and questioned his existence—and became the next victims: investigators are sure the rapist was in the audience, watching.

In southern California, this offender also invaded quiet neighborhoods. He would sometimes prowl beforehand, then slip in through unlocked windows or doors. He would bring his own cord to tie up victims. He would sexually assault the women before bludgeoning them to death. Because of the similarities in these attacks, investigators, using long-shelved DNA evidence, have connected these crimes together. With this new evidence investigators are optimistic that it will lead to an identification of a suspect.

Source: Adapted from M. S. Enkoji, "New Hope in the Hunt for Rapist," *Sacramento Bee,* May 24, 2001.

CHAPTER REVIEW

KEY TERMS

acquaintance rape   *240*
aggravated rape   *240*
anger rapist   *245*
chicken hawks   *251*
date rape   *240*
diaper squad   *254*
fixated child
   molester   *251*
forcible rape   *240*
hustling   *254*
incest   *249*
malice   *240*
morally indiscriminate
   child molester   *250*

mushroom factor   *251*
naïve or inadequate
   child molester   *250*
pedophile   *250*
pedophilia   *250*
power assertive
   rapist   *246*
power rapist   *245*
power reassurance
   rapist   *246*
preferential child
   molester   *251*
psychological
   incest   *249*

rape   *240*
rape trauma
   syndrome   *240*
regressed child
   molester   *250*
runaway   *254*
sadistic child
   molester   *251*
sadistic rapist   *246*
situational child
   molester   *250*
statutory rape   *249*

REVIEW QUESTIONS

1. The person reporting a forcible sexual assault has just been through an emotionally shattering experience and may be in shock, known as the

   _____

   syndrome.

2. What type of rapist is on a mission to get even with women for all the injustices, real or imaginary, he has suffered in his lifetime, using far more force than necessary and exceptional physical brutality?
   a. Anger retaliation rapist
   b. Power assertive rapist
   c. Power reassurance rapist
   d. Sadistic rapist

3. What type of rapist is very image conscious and believes he has a right to rape a woman because he is a man expressing his virility and personal dominance?
   a. Anger retaliation rapist
   b. Power assertive rapist

   c. Power reassurance rapist
   d. Sadistic rapist

4. What type of rapist finds the intentional maltreatment of his victims intensely gratifying and takes pleasure in tormenting his victims?
   a. Anger retaliation rapist
   b. Power assertive rapist
   c. Power reassurance rapist
   d. Sadistic rapist

5. What type of rapist uses a minimal amount of force and is trying to elevate his own self-status because he believes he is a loser and that controlling another person will make him important?
   a. Anger retaliation rapist
   b. Power assertive rapist
   c. Power reassurance rapist
   d. Sadistic rapist

6. What type of child molester is an abuser of all available adults and

children, is basically motivated toward sexual experimentation, and does not have a preference for children?

a. Morally indiscriminate child molester
b. Naïve or inadequate child molester
c. Regressed child molester
d. Fixated child molester
e. Sadistic child molester

7. What type of child molester has made the connection between sexual gratification and personal violence, has no love for children, and is only interested in harming or killing the child?

a. Morally indiscriminate child molester
b. Naïve or inadequate child molester
c. Regressed child molester
d. Fixated child molester
e. Sadistic child molester

8. What type of child molester typically has normal relationships with adults but has experienced a situational occurrence that impels him to turn to children as a temporary object for sexual gratification?

a. Morally indiscriminate child molester
b. Naïve or inadequate child molester
c. Regressed child molester

d. Fixated child molester
e. Sadistic child molester

9. What type of child molester includes persons who are suffering from some form of mental disorder that renders them unable to distinguish between right and wrong, including sexual practices with children, and finds children to be nonthreatening, which allows them to feel more in control?

a. Morally indiscriminate child molester
b. Naïve or inadequate child molester
c. Regressed child molester
d. Fixated child molester
e. Sadistic child molester

10. What type of child molester is often childlike, selects children as sexual objects because they are less demanding and more easily dominated, is not interested in physically harming the child, truly loves children, and does not want to harm them?

a. Morally indiscriminate child molester
b. Naïve or inadequate child molester
c. Regressed child molester
d. Fixated child molester
e. Sadistic child molester

See Appendix D for the correct answers.

DISCUSSION QUESTIONS

1. What is the major responsibility of the first police officers at the scene of a forcible rape?
2. What are the aggravating factors in these cases?
3. Is the medical examination of a forcible rape victim necessary? When should it be conducted? What is its scope?
4. Outline the major factors to be covered by investigators during the follow-up interview of a victim.
5. What is the focus of the follow-up interview of a witness in forcible rape cases?
6. Does the previous relationship between victim and rapist in date rapes create a problem for the police–prosecutor team?

7. Describe network development in child sexual abuse cases.
8. Can police detect child sexual abuse? How?
9. How do child molesters use computers to find potential victims?
10. Which type of rapist is discussed in the case study?

RELATED WEB SITES

Interested in knowing the sexual assault statistics for the United States? Then visit the Men Against Sexual Assault Web site at *www.sa.rochester.edu/masa.*

For information regarding what is a sexual assasult and preventive measures, contact *www.sao.co.st-clair.il.us/sexalt.asp.*

chapter **thirteen**

Robbery

CHAPTER OUTLINE

After reading this chapter you will be able to:

- Define the elements of robbery and the distinction between the various degrees of this offense.
- Explain the various tactics or styles of robbery.
- Describe the different persons who may be involved in the commission of a robbery and their roles.
- Discuss the signature aspects of robbery and how this is an aid to investigators.
- Appreciate the methodology a robber uses in the selection of a target to be robbed.

COMPONENTS OF ROBBERY

To substantiate charging a suspect with robbery, the investigation must uncover legally significant evidence that a crime was committed, that this crime was robbery, and that the defendant committed it. In such investigations, the basic evidence must range through each of the essential elements of the crime of robbery. The essential elements of **robbery** are these:

1. Taking of personal property from the person or presence of a possessor
2. Taking against the possessor's will
3. Taking by force or fear

Taking "from the person" means from the victim's body or his or her clothing, and "from the presence of a possessor" means within sight or hearing of the victim. It is in the nature of robbery that an offender not only takes personal property with intent to steal but also carries it away. Taking a possession away from the victim and into the control of the robber is sufficient. Control by the robber rather than the distance moved is the issue. "Against the possessor's will" is implied in the force and fear element of robbery, which must be adequate to frighten the victim and make the victim part with his or her property against his or her will.

Robbery is generally divided into degrees to express the legislative intent that armed robberies are more serious than unarmed robberies:[1]

1. *First Degree.*   Robbery while armed with a dangerous or deadly weapon likely to cause death or serious wounding
2. *Second Degree.*   Robbery accomplished by physical force or its threat but without a weapon, including purse snatching.

Robbery is a felony-level crime likely to result in a convicted robber receiving a lengthy sentence. It may be aggravated robbery (leading to a longer sentence) when the robber has an armed crime partner at the scene and either of them inflicts serious bodily injury against the victim or any witnesses.

Related crimes, such as kidnapping, must be substantiated in a similar manner. However, larceny and assault merge with robbery. Kidnapping, on the other hand, may not merge with the robbery. In 1969, the top court in California repudiated the doctrine that any movement of the robbery victim amounted to kidnapping. In *People v. Timmons*, the court held that the true test was whether the movement of the victim substantially increased the risk of harm beyond that inherent in robberies.[2] If it did, kidnapping would be added to the charges against the robber or robbers; if not, the "movement" would be considered part of the robbery activity.

During the robbery investigation, the investigator need not decide whether these crimes join with the robbery or are separate crimes; the investigator's role is simply to collect all available evidence and develop the existence of related crimes from the array of collected evidence.

Another area of concern is the difference between robbery and extortion. One of the essentials of robbery is consent resulting from force or fear; in **extortion**, the victim consents more willingly. Consent may be induced by

A video surveillance camera picture of a robbery in progress. From Sacramento, California, Sheriff's Department.

persuasive threats that are related to future harm or disgrace rather than here-and-now harm. A close call for investigators is a **scam** described in 1890 by Chief of Detectives James Byrnes of the New York City Police Department as the **badger game.** This is an extortion scheme in which a woman places a selected victim in a comprising position (nude, in bed, in a hotel room) and then victimizes him by demanding money. Next, her male accomplice breaks in and pretends to be an outraged husband threatening violence, scandal, or the like. The harassment of the victim is the key to the success of this scheme. It has been successful over the years with only minor changes.

The identification in an armed robbery case often relates to the tactics or style of the robbery. Robbery has been categorized as having three styles: (1) the ambush, (2) the selective raid, and (3) the planned operation. The **ambush robbery** is the least planned of all and is based on the element of surprise. The **selective-raid robbery** involves a minimum of planning but involves some casing of the robbery scene. The **planned-operation robbery** is carefully structured: the robbery group examines all aspects of the situation and plans for all foreseeable contingencies. In fact, the group may engage in practice runs in this style of robbery.

Crime partners in a robbery group form a loose partnership that provides the skills for the various tasks necessary to carry out different types of robberies. They participate in planning the robbery, including the basic decision about whether or not a certain target can be successfully robbed. Crime partners usually are associates from spontaneous play groups in the underworld: persons who live in or frequent the same neighborhood, who purchase drugs from the same source, or who have served sentences together in juvenile or adult institutions.

New York's notorious "Robert's Lounge Gang" was composed of customers frequenting a small bar near the cargo area of John F. Kennedy International Airport (JFK). This was a gang of varying size—depending on the availability of targets—but in total its membership was drawn from the **spontaneous play group** that assembled daily in this popular drinking place. Seven members of this gang carried out a robbery at the Lufthansa air cargo terminal at JFK. Their loot totaled $8 million in cash, jewels, and gold. Investigators were frustrated in their probing, until one of the suspects led them to Robert's Lounge and the gang associates.[3]

Investigators assigned a single robbery or series of robberies should search for **link-ups** or **connect-ups** that will indicate the operations of a group. In many instances, a gang of two to six robbers will not allow more than two robbers to be on the scene of a robbery. A Chicago robber, whose robbery group specialized in ambushing lone pedestrians late at night in streets and alleys, explained this switching of the group's membership in various robberies: "Now we never did nothing with the four of us together, always two. I'd be with George when we'd get one guy, and next I'd be with Percy."[4] Linking or connecting several robberies may lead to the identification of four or five members of a gang, and such data may lead the investigator to some clues about the style of a particular robbery gang.

The fact that a robbery mob may be involved in a robbery or series of robberies can be developed by the investigator through a study of the style of the robbery: if it was a selective raid or a planned operation, whether a getaway driver aided the robbery, and whether backup people were present at the scene. Inquiry may develop data identifying one or two persons who are not similar in description to the armed robber or robbers who committed the crime but were loitering about the premises and inquiring about employment or making other inquiries that would permit them access to the premises and that would allow them to scan (case) the scene of the crime before the robbery.

The presence of a getaway driver may be established from witnesses who can offer data as to how the robber or robbers who committed the actual robbery fled the crime scene. A **getaway driver** is a specialist who remains in the escape vehicle until the robbers have completed the robbery, then picks them up and flees the scene.

A **backup person** is a member of the gang who remains in the background unnoticed and, in case of trouble, supports the members of the gang who are actually committing the robbery. The presence of a backup person may be more difficult to discover because he or she often does not flee from the scene in the same car as the armed robber or robbers. Since the backup person has not been identified with the crime, he may stay at the scene for some time and then walk away to meet with his crime partners at some prearranged location. The role of the backup person in modern robbery gangs is to protect his or her crime partners from the unexpected. He or she is "buried" in the store (when customers are not the victims) or outside the robbery scene, from

Although most robberies are committed by men, women also commit this crime. From Sacramento, California, Sheriff's Department.

where the crime scene and its approaches can be viewed. The backup person's job is to fight off police who might chance on the scene or respond to a silent alarm.

Some signature aspects are typical of robberies. These trademarks are part of the modus operandi of a crime and distinguish it as work of a specific robber or robbery group who have committed previous crimes in which the same identifying circumstances occur. The investigating officers pick out from the modus operandi the most likely identifying signature characteristic and develop their investigation to lead to the identity of the robber group. For instance, the "paper bag robber" carried a brown paper bag to the scene of the robbery and told the victims to put their money and valuables in it. The "lover's-lane robber" frequented lover's lanes and always victimized a boy and girl. The "Mutt and Jeff" robbers were always described as a tall man and a short man.

Traditionally, weapons indicate violence, but violence is used in robberies only as a tool of the robber in carrying out the robbery itself. Only in recent years has a new measure of violence in robberies indicated some hostility on the part of the robber. Such hostility can serve as a signature characteristic to identify suspects because it is unusual among robbers. Most robbers view the employment of violence to overcome resistance only as a self-defense measure, but today the number of wanton pistol whippings or shootings of victims is increasing. This use of force is beyond what is necessary to control the robbery victim or victims. As one convicted robber expressed it, "The last thing you want is trouble. If you gotta shoot somebody you gotta run, and you don't get any money. The thing is to get in and get what you are after and get out with the least trouble possible."[5]

The use of addicting and dangerous drugs by a robber is indicated when the modus operandi reveals restricted drugs are part of the proceeds of a robbery. Even when restricted drugs are not acquired during a robbery, an investigator can identify the robberies of a drug addict by the time span between robberies and the proceeds of each crime. This assumption is based on (1) other modus operandi information identifying a series of robberies as the work of one or more robbers, (2) the amount of money stolen, and (3) the date of the next robbery of the robber or robbers under investigation. The time gap between the robberies is extended when a good score allows the robber to buy sufficient drugs for a specific habituation level ($100-a-day habit; $200-a-day habit). A characteristic of the addict–robber is that robberies are not committed when the addict is high on a drug but rather when he or she needs money to purchase drugs.

Robbery investigators must realize the potential for conflict between data contained in police reports and the testimony of witnesses in court. Accuracy in recording the statements of witnesses is of primary importance. Investigators should not encourage a witness to guess or record a guess as a fact and should not suggest facts to a witness who is unsure but rather should let the witness describe the person, car, weapon, clothes, disguise, marks, hair, speech, and the like in his or her own terms. Investigators should record the description in the witness's terms and not interpret them. Mistakes will be made, but the investigator should not compound them by adding to or interpreting the witness's descriptions.

THE TARGET IN ROBBERIES

The determination of a criminally oriented person to rob a specific and predetermined person or place, when and how to do it, and whether he or she cruises to find a place to rob are mental processes of considerable interest to an investigator. The selection of a target in robberies offers clues about who did it. In planned robberies, whatever was done before the crime can suggest suspects or indicate persons in the suspect group who are unlikely suspects. In the unplanned robberies of the cruising criminal, an investigator can develop a theory of who did it solely on the basis of the target selection.

In planned robberies, the offender considers not only the victim of the robbery but also such operational facts as the number of accomplices necessary, the weapons selected, the number of persons likely to be present during the robbery, and the escape route. In unplanned robberies, the offender acts on impulse, generally selects a weapon based on its availability, and haphazardly cruises an area in search of a victim.[6] Nevertheless, the "cruiser" does avoid victims likely to be armed or places that might be wired for a silent alarm that will alert police to a robbery in progress.

In using the target aspects of a crime to further an investigation, the investigator first attempts to determine if the robbery was planned or unplanned.

Beginning with information about the victim and whether he or she was alone at the time, plus information about where the crime occurred, the investigator tries to evaluate the need for precrime planning. The cruising robber seeks out victims who will present little or no operational problem, such as resistance or activating an alarm. Lone victims are symptomatic of unplanned robberies, although the location of the robbery may offer a more substantial clue to target selection and to the planning of the crime.

Residence (**home invasion**) robberies were always considered planned crimes until the advent in recent years of **cruising robberies** in above-average-income residential areas and secluded hotel rooms. Bank robberies also were considered planned until the emergence of the **single-teller bank robbery** in which persons armed with a note and some threat of force victimized only one teller. Businesses are still the victims reserved for most planned robberies. Residence and bank robberies can be placed in the same class as each other when the residence victim has a local reputation for having large sums of cash at home or when the bank robbery extends to more than one teller. Airport cargo areas also are the targets of planned robberies, with information coming from dishonest air cargo employees and indicating the best time for the robbers to strike for maximum profit.

Markets, liquor stores, and other retail establishments are targets that are categorized between planned and unplanned robberies. A cruising robber will enter such premises and appraise their vulnerability within a few minutes of shopping or browsing and then make a decision.[7] The circumstances of the robbery may offer meaningful clues that are illustrative of planning, such as a fast entry and an apparent knowledge of either the routine or the personnel, or both, or of the timing to coincide with an unusual amount of cash on hand.

Automated teller machines (ATMs) are now popular as robbery targets for younger and potentially violent robbers. The robbery of ATMs, service stations, taverns, drive-in facilities, on-street victims, and victims in vehicles usually are the work of cruising robbers. The cruising of an area by a robber seeking victims appears to be a nocturnal activity. The lone service station attendant and the little-patronized drive-in or motel offer targets of opportunity, as do the isolated tavern and café. Pedestrians and victims who are accosted in vehicles when stopped at a traffic signal, picking up a hitchhiker, accepting a taxi passenger, operating a bus, or responding to a telephone order to deliver food are victims by chance.

IDENTIFICATION EVIDENCE

In robberies in which the victim is not killed, identification is made through facial characteristics, identifying natural marks or tattoos, hair line and color, race, clothing, speech characteristics, and unusual habits or nervous spasms. In robberies in which the victim is killed or is unable to see the robber's face, identification can be made by general physical build, fingerprints, footprints, type of disguise, recovery of the loot, means of escape (automobile license, model, or year, if an automobile is used), and type of weapon. A sufficiently compelling combination of these factors will convince a court or jury of the identity of the robber. Facial characteristics, fingerprints, or an auto license may be sufficiently persuasive without additional factors.

Grounds for attacking the credibility of the identification evidence may be any of the following:

1. Suggestive use of photographs
2. Failure to safeguard the rights of the accused in placing a suspect or arrestee in a police lineup (see Appendix A for a case brief of *U.S. v. Wade*)
3. Conflict between the physical description given by witnesses and the actual appearance of the defendant in court
4. Conflict between the weapon described by witnesses, or "constructively described" by the nature of injuries inflicted on victim, and the weapon presented in court as the robbery weapon
5. Conflict between the vehicle, if any, involved in the robbery as described by witnesses and the actual vehicle used in the robbery

Fixed TV surveillance cameras have become an increasingly important tool in the identification of robbers. This photographic surveillance frequently captures identifiable photographs of persons engaged in a robbery. Such photographs are used in identifying suspects, in their apprehension, and as identification evidence at trial. Banks pioneered the use of overt, fixed surveillance cameras, but the rise in robberies of stores and other businesses has expanded the use of these cameras in both overt and covert installations.[8]

CHECKLIST FOR THE INVESTIGATION OF ROBBERY

A prompt response by police to the scene of a robbery, a fast-breaking search for the robber or robbers, and a continuing investigation aimed at identifying the person or persons responsible are the basic routine for successful robbery investigations (Figure 13–1). The following is a checklist for the investigation of robbery:

1. Assume the suspect is present and make an arrest.
2. Ascertain if the suspect has left the scene and, if so, how; obtain descriptions of the suspect and any vehicle.
3. Provide a description of the suspect to the dispatcher; also provide the following information:
   a. Nature of the offense
   b. Weapon involved
   c. Direction of flight
   d. Description of vehicle
   e. Loss, if any
4. Search for the suspect.
   a. Escape route
   b. Refuges (theater, tavern)

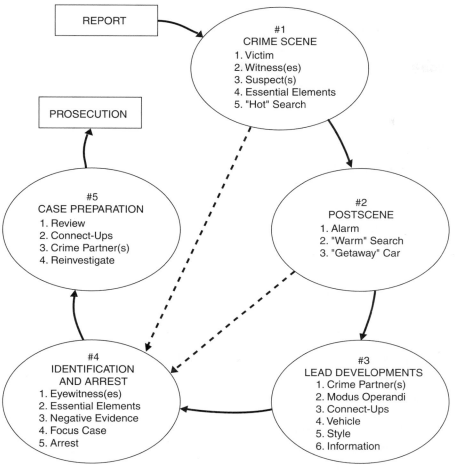

FIGURE 13–1
Investigation of a robbery.

　　c. Hiding places (stairways, cellars, yards, trash bins)
　　d. Prowler calls
　　e. Stolen cars
5. Search the crime scene for evidence.
　　a. Protect the area.
　　b. Call in a technician.
　　c. Extend the crime scene to the "discard" area where masks and clothing may be discarded.
6. Search the scene for witnesses.
　　a. Include latecomers and onlookers.
　　b. Canvass the view area and the neighborhood.
7. Advise the superior officer of the following:
　　a. Details of offense
　　b. Identification of victim and witnesses
　　c. Personnel at scene and assignments
　　d. Progress of preliminary investigation

8. Prepare a report on the preliminary investigation.
9. Compile a physical description of the suspect(s) and vehicle, if any.
10. Ascertain the modus operandi.
    a. Target
    b. Bindings (tape, wire)
    c. Weapon(s)
    d. Plus rape
    e. Plus kidnapping
    f. Narcotics taken
    g. Signature traits
11. Locate and interview informants.
12. Identify robbery groups.
    a. Number in group
    b. Connect-ups
    c. Spontaneous play groups
       i. Prison
       ii. Neighborhood
       iii. Same drug dealer
       iv. Same teen center
    d. Presence of getaway driver
    e. Presence of backup person or people
13. Identify the style of the robbery.
    a. Ambush
    b. Selective raid
    c. Planned operation; inside information
14. Identify other basic leads.
15. Identify and arrest the offender(s).
16. Prepare the case.

REPEAT-OFFENDER CASES

Career criminals are offenders who have had previous arrests, have one to two cases pending in the local courts, and are on the street on some form of conditional release at the time of their latest arrest. While other violent serious crimes may be committed in a series of two or more, the series assailant or rapist is not usually a career criminal.

Career criminals comprise a high percentage of armed robbers. Aggravated robbery is the violent crime favored by repeat offenders. As a result, many prosecutors have established special units to concentrate on the prosecution of recidivists, particularly armed robbers. From a crime-control standpoint, priority for such repeat-offender cases is now established as an appropriate strategy for prosecutors.

In the past, prosecutors expended effort based on the strength of the evidence in a case, the probability of conviction, or the leverage of plea bargaining. More recently, prosecutors have been realizing that repeat offenders are inherently more convictable. Witnesses are generally more cooperative in repeat-offender cases, and the factors leading to the frequent arrests of such robbers also contribute to the weight of evidence indicating guilt.[9] Of course, investigators must make every effort to build a strong case against a repeat offender to maximize the probability of conviction, but they must also do so as rapidly as possible to get repeat offenders off the street and into an effective corrections program.

CARJACKING

Carjacking—the theft or attempted theft of a motor vehicle by force or threat of force from the person or the immediate presence of the victim—is armed robbery and a felony-level crime. Even when the carjacker has not displayed a weapon, the force and fear required for robberies is present (a forced entry of the driver's-side door, followed by a rude command to leave the car). When the circumstances and conditions of the robbery lead to a reasonable belief in the victim's mind that he or she may suffer injury unless he or she complies with the robber's demand, the fear required in such a robbery is present. The most common carjacking is described as one committed by an assailant in his or her twenties with a pistol or revolver and a crime partner. Auto thieves, on the other hand, commit crimes of stealth without violence and without the owner's presence. When the thieves no longer need the car, they abandon it. Investigators in police agencies should stop treating carjackings as they would auto theft (by closing out the case when the car is recovered) and should treat them as crimes of violence primarily against the person, not against property.

OUTLINE OF A CARJACKING INVESTIGATION

The carjacking investigation is structured around a multiscene routine focused on using the recovery of the car not as a goal but as an aid in the identification of the offender. When the offense runs true to form, the carjacking has taken place, the first officers and associates have secured a physical description of the carjacker from the victim along with data on his or her car, and the investigation is turned over to an assigned detective or detectives. The outline of investigation suggested is the following:

1. *The Crime Scene.*   Investigation of a carjacking crime scene is the same as for a robbery crime scene, plus an expanded canvass for witnesses to the offender's and possibly the crime partner's, precrime activity; the vehicle used; and the offenders' conduct while selecting a victim.

2. *The In-Progress Crime Scene.*   An in-progress crime scene includes places such as the gas station where the fleeing offenders purchased gasoline and the area in which the offenders were involved in a traffic accident. Likewise, if the car was equipped with a cell phone, calls made on the phone should be investigated.

3. *The Dump Scene.*   Prior notice should be given to patrol units to secure the car where it is "dumped" and to not touch it. The finder

should be asked to notify the assigned detective or command. Arrangements should be made to tow the car to the crime lab, where fingerprint examination of the interior and exterior of the car should be requested. Any damage to the car and any other possible physical evidence should be noted.

4. ***The Prearrest Scene.***   A modus operandi search for "similars" in the past year should be conducted, and incoming crime reports on carjackings, ATM heists, and fast-food restaurant robberies should be scanned hourly. Composite sketches and photo spreads should be arranged. Inquiries should be made in line with relevant basic leads. (The investigator's hunch should be used as a guide to the suspect's home neighborhood and why the crime scene location was selected—for example, the suspect might have been a former employee of fast-food restaurants in the crime scene area.)

5. ***The "Receiver" Scene.***   The receiver scene is where the car parts are sold. The investigator should trace the car parts to buyers and thus seek the offender's identity.

6. ***The "Fraud" Scene.***   If the victim had a handbag in the car at the time of the crime, the carjacker may use the victim's credit cards, pass them to family or friends, or sell them on the street. Each transaction should be traced to determine the offender's identity.

7. ***Postarrest.***   The investigator should try to develop the crime partner, if he or she was arrested with the carjacker, receivers of car parts, and credit card abusers as witnesses against the carjacker at trial.

PROBLEMS OF PROOF

The first major problem of proof in robbery cases concerns the defendant: identifying him or her as the robber. The second major problem is how to show conclusively that the crime committed is a robbery in which the victim was separated from his or her valuables through force or against the victim's will.

The victim is expected to testify as a major identification witness. After all, the confrontation in robberies is between robber and victim. If a victim's testimony is weak and inconclusive, supporting witnesses need to be positive in their identification of the robber. Often, the defendant not only denies the act done but also claims mistaken identity and offers an alibi in support of this claim. If the alibi has strength and the identification evidence is weak, many jurors will think that this constitutes reasonable doubt.

The victim of a robbery is also mandated by the elements of the crime of robbery to testify that he or she handed over to the robber money and other valuables out of fear. Threats alone are not legally significant unless the victim testifies that he or she believed the robber had the intent to carry them out, as well as the apparent ability to do so promptly.

CASE STUDY

This is a Holdup!

A case summary written by assigned detectives details the circumstances of an armed robbery.

Case Summary

0900 Hours.   A WMA (white male adult), armed with a revolver and wearing a ski mask, coveralls, and gloves, entered the State Credit Union office and confronted two clerks and a male customer. The armed suspect demanded money after placing his weapon to the head of the male customer. Demand was met by Anne O'Brien, employee of the credit union. She placed approximately $8,600 in paper monies in a paper bag given to her by the suspect. The suspect then ordered one of the clerks to lie on the floor and then fled through the front door of the credit union, where he had made his initial entry.

0930 Hours.   Detectives Robert DeRose and Lieutenant Jacob Saylor arrived at the scene. Investigation was made and it was determined that witness O'Brien believed she recognized the robber as being a former borrower whose name she could not recall; but she recognized him by his build, eyes, and voice. She advised that she believed the suspect had recently applied for a loan at the credit union. The investigation was completed at the scene, and the officers returned to the Detective Division after advising Mrs. O'Brien to come to the Detective Division as soon as possible.

1100 Hours.   Mrs. O'Brien called Detective DeRose and advised that she now recalled the robber's name as being Herbert C. Straus. She stated she obtained this information from a credit application she had on file. She also supplied other pertinent information regarding the suspect.

1120 Hours.   Detective DeRose arrived at DMV (Department of Motor Vehicles) and picked up a Soundex photo of the suspect: Straus.

1210 Hours.   Mrs. O'Brien arrived at the Detective Division and viewed five driver license photos of like appearance, one of which was that of the suspect Straus. Without hesitation, Mrs. O'Brien picked the photo of Straus and advised that she was positive that this was the person who had robbed her this date.

1245 Hours.   Det. R. Phelps, Det. R. DeRose, Sgt. D. Migliorini, and Lt. Saylor arrived at 402 12th Street after a determination had been made that the suspect lived at that address. Lt. Saylor rang the doorbell and a male voice from within inquired, "Who's there?" Lt. Saylor replied, "Police." The door was opened by suspect Straus, and he was immediately taken into custody. He was handcuffed and seated on the couch in the front room. After being apprised of his constitutional rights, the suspect was advised of the circumstances that brought the officers to his residence. A consent to search his home was also obtained at this time.

The suspect became very cooperative. He admitted that he was the robber. Det. DeRose found a coffee can in the southeast bedroom that contained what appeared to be a considerable amount of money. Suspect then told officers that the gun he used in the robbery was under the cushion on a chair in the front room and pointed out the chair. Gun, a .38 caliber Smith & Wesson 2-inch "Chiefs Special," was discovered.

1330 Hours.   Identification unit arrived and arrestee's residence was processed.

1510 Hours.   Arrestee was brought to Detective Division. There he again was apprised of his constitutional rights, and he gave a free, voluntary, and complete statement. In his statement, the suspect made admissions that he and he alone was responsible for this offense.

1600 Hours.   The suspect was booked as Herbert C. Straus into the County Jail (Arrest #1068) as the person responsible for this robbery. Monies and gun booked as evidence.

1730 Hours.   Arrest #1068 clears this report. Recovered was approximately $8,600.

CHAPTER REVIEW

KEY TERMS

ambush robbery   *261*
backup person   *262*
badger game   *261*
carjacking   *296*
connect-up   *262*
cruising robberies   *265*
extortion   *260*

getaway driver   *262*
home invasion   *265*
link-up   *262*
planned-operation
    robbery   *261*
raid robbery   *261*
robbery   *260*

scam   *261*
single-teller bank
    robbery   *265*
spontaneous play
    group   *262*

REVIEW QUESTIONS

1. Residential robberies are known as _____ robberies.

2. Crime partners are usually associates from _____, such as persons who live in the same neighborhood, purchase drugs from the same source, or have served time together.

3. A member of the robbery group that remains in the background unnoticed and whose job it is to fight off the police who might arrive on the scene is the:
   a. Robber
   b. Getaway driver
   c. Backup person
   d. Decoy

4. Lone victims of a robbery are symptomatic of _____ robberies.

5. A person armed with a note and some threat of force that victimizes one teller is known as the _____ robbery.

6. The type of robbery that is based on the elements of surprise and is the least planned of all types of robbery is the:
   a. Planned operation
   b. Ambush
   c. Scam
   d. Selective raid

7. The most carefully planned robbery is the:
   a. Planned operation
   b. Ambush
   c. Scam
   d. Selective raid

8. The type of robbery that involves a minimal amount of planning, such as casing of the scene, is the:
   a. Planned operation
   b. Ambush
   c. Unplanned operation
   d. Selective raid

9. The single-teller bank robbery is what type of robbery?
   a. Planned operation
   b. Ambush
   c. Scam
   d. Selective raid

10. The most common defense in a robbery case is one based on:
    a. Alibi
    b. Improper lineup procedures
    c. Mistaken identification
    d. Improper Miranda waiver
    See Appendix D for the correct answers.

DISCUSSION QUESTIONS

1. What are the styles of robbery?
2. Relate the styles of robbery to robbery targets.
3. What are the essential elements of robbery that distinguish this crime from theft?
4. Describe the role of a backup person in a robbery.
5. What facts likely to be disclosed in a robbery investigation can serve as identification of a robber?
6. Why are ATMs a popular target in robberies?
7. Which of the basic leads should be used to develop evidence of identification in robbery investigations?
8. Discuss the groups from which robbers generally recruit crime partners.
9. What are the signature aspects of the modus operandi of robbers?
10. Why is it useful to determine whether a robbery suspect may be addicted to restricted drugs?
11. What is the role of fixed surveillance cameras in the investigation of robbery?
12. What are the similarities and differences between a serial rapist and a repeat offender (robber)?
13. Is it a violation of a suspected robber's constitutional rights to give priority to the investigation and prosecution of career criminals (repeat offenders)?
14. Discuss the physical evidence involved in the case study.
15. What kind of evidence was most useful in solving the case study?
16. Discuss the cooperative nature of the suspect after being placed under arrest. What brought about this level of cooperation?

RELATED WEB SITES

For charts and tables about robbery trends in the United States, consult this Web site: *www. ojp.usdoj.gov/bjs/glance/rob.htm.*

To view robbery surveillance photos and robbery prevention tips, check out the Colorado Association of Robbery Investigators Web site at *www.co-asn-rob.org.*

chapter **fourteen**

Arson, Bombings, and Hate Crimes

CHAPTER OUTLINE

After reading this chapter you will be able to:

- Distinguish between the legal concepts of arson and aggravated arson.
- Explain the distinction between a naturally occurring fire and a suspicious fire.
- Discuss the motivation that compels a pyromaniac to set fires.
- Describe the methods used by arsonists to set fires and the use of incendiary fire-setting devices.
- Evaluate the problems investigators face in proving arson and bombing cases.

ARSON AND ARSON LAW

Fires set by arsonists and explosives placed to damage property and kill or inflict injury on people are crimes against both person and property. Because great secrecy usually surrounds the fire setting or the placing of explosives, these crimes create problems for investigators.

The great eighteenth-century British jurist Sir William Blackstone, in his *Commentaries on the Laws of England*, defined **arson** as the "malicious and willful burning of the house or outhouse of another man."[1] In common law, arson was considered an offense against the home (habitation). It was defined as the malicious and willful burning of a dwelling (house or outhouse) of another, and extended to structures within the curtilage (enclosed space around building) of the dwelling.

Arson law in the United States has taken many twists—depending on the individual state law examined. Arson may include the burning of buildings other than houses or outhouses, personal property, and crops. The law may distinguish between burning in the day and at night and between vacant and occupied buildings. The degree of arson may depend on the value of what is burned. Such laws generally make the burning of one's own insured property, with intent to defraud, a crime within the general scope of arson. Common, however, to all arson or arson-type crime is the element of burning and the malicious intent of the person setting the fire.

The corpus delicti in arson cases requires that the burning be the result of a criminal agency and that there be actual burning—a consuming-type fire—although the fire need not in fact consume, for a charring is usually sufficient.[2] Thus, the facts that must be proved in any prosecution for arson are as follows:

1. The fire occurred—a burning, a charring.
2. The burning was not accidental; its origin was the result of a criminal agency.
3. The person who appears as a defendant in court in an arson case is identified as the person who set the fire, or caused it to be set, or otherwise acted in furtherance of a criminal plan for the fire setting.

The term **aggravated arson** reflects public and legislative concern with arson as a crime against people as well as property. It is best described as any arson in which the following are true:

1. Explosives are used.
2. People are present or at the site or are placed in danger.

Aggravation occurs when explosives are used to injure or harm people or property or, if at the time of fire or explosion, a person other than the arsonist is within or upon the structure damaged. Inherent in the present or placed-in-danger element of aggravated arson is the fact that actual physical harm can result from the fire or explosion. Some states use aggravation as essential to first-degree arson; others cite it as adding to the seriousness of arson and, if proven at trial, as calling for additional years to be added to the sentence linked to basic arson.[3]

Although motive is an important element in the continuing phase of an arson investigation, it is not necessary to prove motive in an arson prosecution in order to convict the defendant as long as the defendant can be identified as the fire setter and his or her intent to set the fire is established.

THE SUSPICIOUS FIRE CONCEPT

In investigating a burning, the investigator must first seek evidence to prove whether the fire was of natural or accidental origin. When little or no evidence can be secured to identify the fire as accidental, the second step is to seek evidence to eliminate all possible causes except **incendiarism**. The investigator must evaluate the possibility of persons smoking in bed, of spontaneous combustion, of a pilot light igniting fumes from flammable liquids, of electrical storms, or of faulty construction or maintenance of a building (electrical wiring, motors, space heaters, furnaces, and flues). Next, the investigator must review the possibility of small children, elderly persons, intoxicated individuals, and the mentally ill being involved in a noncriminal incendiary fire through carelessness or misfortune.

The third step is to seek evidence that will prove that the fire was of incendiary origin. Investigators seek such evidence as separate and distinct fires in different areas of the premises: the residue of inflammables; the odor of petroleum and like fire starters; holes in plaster walls; windows and doors shaded and locked to prevent discovery and retard entry of firefighters; removal of personal effects before a fire; owner or occupant not present, or absent when normally present; excessive insurance; and the presence of ignition devices or **fire sets.**

Once the suspicious nature of the fire has been revealed, the investigator attempts to classify the burning as a rationally or irrationally motivated fire. Rational motivation is based on either hate, profit, or the desire to conceal a crime. In rationally motivated fires, the suspects are those people who would want the fire. Irrationally motivated arsonists are pathological fire setters.[4]

Hate fires are set because of some dispute. The work of the investigator is to question the victim as to his or her suspicions and any recent arguments. Landlords may need questioning to help recall a dispute over an unfulfilled tenant request. Querying employers about recently discharged employees or customers with complaints may help them recall a few names. Persons who set hate fires have emotional problems. An unimportant event to an average person may be overemphasized by these individuals and serve to trigger a fire in spite or for revenge. Religious, racial, and political disputes may be involved. Although the identity of the **arsonist** or **incendiary** is not as apparent in these disputes, suspects may be identified in the opposition group involved in the dispute if the investigator probes and pries.

For-profit fire setters are not difficult to expose once hate has been eliminated as motivation. The first step is a general inquiry about the company insuring the building and its contents, followed by a more specific inquiry into the insurance and the record of the policyholder. Collaterally, a general inquiry as to the financial status of the insured and his or her business is appropriate and often rewards the investigator with information that the insured "needed" a fire.

Representatives of the national crime syndicate have been linked to arson with great frequency in recent years. They buy into a legitimate business and turn it into an illicit operation. The general procedure in these cases is for the new owners to manipulate the firm's operations to gain full control from the previous owners; to take all readily available assets in merchandise, services, and credit from the business; and then to set a fire for the insurance money.[5]

A fire may have originated as an attempt to conceal a major crime. This is not a difficult evaluation. What crime could be involved? Was a human a victim of the fire? Was murder involved? Was any property missing? Did a robbery occur? Were the record books destroyed, found partially burned, or tented (spread half open with the bound edge up and the leaves spread out for burning)? Is tax fraud an issue? What about embezzlement? Sometimes the seriousness of the basic crime does not appear to warrant arson, but people in trouble do strange things.

Pyromania is the obsessional impulse to set fires or a preference for arson as an instrument of damage. **Pyromaniacs**, the "firebugs" who terrorize entire neighborhoods by their fire-setting activities, repeat their crimes unless they are apprehended and placed in a correctional setting oriented to their needs. These individuals may claim rational motivation, but they set fires for no practical reason and receive no material profit from their incendiarism.[6] Motive in these cases is some sensual satisfaction resembling an irresistible impulse—the act of setting a fire solves the fire setter's problems more efficiently and often more pleasurably than any other means available.[7]

The pathological fire setter usually does not have any relationship with the victim or the place of burning. A "pyro" fire is similar to a "psycho" murder case in this respect. The fire scene search may reveal a clue to personal identity. The suspect may attract attention by his or her overt and suspicious conduct in the crowd watching the fire. These irrationally motivated incendiaries have a tendency to act out the role of hero at the fire scene. In seeking a solution to these fires, it is possible to develop suspects by reviewing records of suspicious juvenile vandals, sex psychopaths, known pyromaniacs, and others with a history of weird behavior or bizarre acts. When fires occur in a series within reasonable geographic limits, the technique of working out the pattern of the fire setter and organizing a surveillance for his or her apprehension is sometimes successful.

BURN PATTERNS: STRUCTURAL FIRES

Structural fires form a pattern that is determined chiefly by evaluating the physical layout of the building involved, the available combustible material, and ventilation. Simply stated, the fire burns upward from its original ignition in an inverted conical shape with the apex of the cone at the place of origin—where the fire was ignited. Physical characteristics of a building may retard a fire or change its direction. Ventilation will cause a fire to spread away from this conical fire pattern: open doors, open windows, chimneylike

FIGURE 14–1   Normal fire path in structural fires. Arrows indicate spread of fire from origin in kitchen.

physical characteristics (stairways or elevators), and holes in a floor, wall, ceiling, or roof (either caused by the fire or some other means) contribute to the spread of a fire and its rate of burning (Figure 14–1). Another variation of the classic fire pattern is caused when the fire encounters highly combustible materials that burn more vigorously and thus radically modify the direction of a fire.[8]

Combustibility in structural fires usually is defined in terms of ignitability, rate of heat release, and total heat release. It is a function of the physical characteristics of the furnishings and building materials at the fire scene, their spatial relationships, and the structural features of the place of occurrence.[9] A little-known aspect of structure fires is room **flashover**—a rapid development of the fire that occurs when the volume of active fire becomes a significant portion of the room volume. At flashover, all the previously uninvolved combustibles in a room suddenly ignite. The rate of the heat release at this time is high and usually a flaming spreads across the ceiling of the room.[10] A basic key to determining the pattern of a structure fire is to determine the approximate time between ignition and flashover in the room in which the fire originates.[11] A fire initially may be classified as suspicious when its pattern suggests more than one place of origin, when an inexplicable or unexplained deviation from a fire pattern is common to the structural characteristics and ventilation of the place burned, or when a rapid buildup of a room fire is not in harmony with the known combustibility of the room and its contents.

BURN PATTERNS: NONSTRUCTURAL FIRES

In outdoor fires in which a structure is not involved, a predominant horizontal spread characterizes the fire, rather than the typical cone pattern of structural fires. The factors that influence fire patterns in outdoor fires are the wind and terrain. On level ground—in the absence of wind—a fire will spread from the point of origin in all directions. In the absence of a strong wind, the partial vacuum created by the fire, which permits air to flow into the fire's base, has a tendency to retard the spread of the fire. Wind spreads the fire in a fan shape with the apex of the fan closest to the source of the wind. On terrain with an uphill slope, the fire will burn uphill from the point of origin. The combination of wind and terrain may produce a fire that burns uphill and is canted to the left or right because of the direction and velocity of the wind at the time of the fire. A strong wind sometimes can overcome the influence of terrain and cause a fire to burn laterally across a sloping hillside. In some cases, fires have been spread downhill by a very strong wind.[12]

A wind condition in southern California known as the **Santa Ana winds** contributes to the ignitability of forest-fire fuels. These winds, by their strong airflow associated with very low humidity, quickly dry out forest fuels. When a fire is started in the presence of these conditions, the increased ignitability of these fuels accounts for a rapid spread in all directions and, due to wind-driven embers, the occurrence of many spot fires ahead of the main fire. Under Santa Ana conditions, fire can spread quickly and violently in any direction. A surge or slackening in the airflow or a sudden change in wind direction, rapid heat release, and the mountainous southern California terrain, characterized by numerous canyons that act as chutes or chimneys, all contribute to sudden changes in the pattern of the fire.[13]

FIRE IGNITION AND PLACE OF ORIGIN

One of the major differences between an accidental fire and an incendiary fire is that accidental fires frequently burn themselves out because of a lack of proper ventilation or combustible material. On the other hand, the set fire is planned. The fire setter places his or her fire so that it will burn vigorously after being ignited. He or she may use a fire **accelerant** or may depend on ventilation and the combustible material normally at the fire scene.

Sparks, matches, mechanical lighters, friction, radiant heat, hot objects, and chemical reactions can cause fire. The primary source of ignition can be manual, as in striking a match; mechanical, as in a spark device used by welders; electrical, as in faulty wiring or defective appliances; or chemical, as in spontaneous combustion.

When matches or other simple devices are used to set a fire, little evidence points to the means of ignition. However, many arsonists construct various mechanical delay devices to afford themselves a few hours in which they can establish an alibi of being elsewhere at the time the fire was started. Candles provide another delay factor for the arsonist. The time lag depends on the diameter and height of the candle above the **plant**, which is the fire-boosting material such as newspapers used to spread the fire. An alarm clock is another common mechanical device used to start fires. Both clocks and candles leave traces at the fire scene—when the debris and rubble at the fire scene are searched, some evidence of their use is often located. Electrical fire starters often make a fire appear to be accidental because faulty wiring and careless handling of electrical appliances often cause fires. Spontaneous combustion from items such as oily rags is often claimed as a cause of fire, but ideal conditions are needed to generate enough heat for self-ignition. In some industrial fires, however, spontaneous combustion can result from the chemical reaction of various volatile oils with air.[14]

Where a fire was ignited is classified as the place of origin. Fire setters set fires in more than one place to get a rapid buildup of the fire. **Trailers** are often used to spread fires from a point of ignition and can be considered a secondary incendiary device, carrying the fire from the original place of ignition to other parts of the room or building. The trailer may be nothing more than a rope or a ropelike string of toilet paper, newspaper, or rags soaked in fire accelerant. Sometimes a fire accelerant is simply poured across the floor in a pattern similar to the spokes of a wheel, with each trail radiating outward from the original source of ignition.[15] The major indication of a set fire is the fact that the source of ignition is such that the fire spreads rapidly, indicating the use of a trailer and a fire accelerant or that several different places constitute the points of origin.

The investigator should study the lower regions of a fire for the place or places of origin. However, the place of origin may be higher than some of the burned portions of a building because the fire accelerant that spread the flames from the original place of ignition might have dripped downward through holes or crevices in the floor before the fire secured enough heat to change the fire accelerant from its liquid state.

THE FIRE SCENE

The best-case scenario in arson investigation is when the investigator arrives at the fire scene while the fire is still in progress. All the firefighters are still on the scene then, and occupants of the premises (or the owner of the land on which the fire started), onlookers, and other witnesses are also available at this time. Under these circumstances, the investigator can conduct on-the-scene interviews of persons knowledgeable about the fire and its circumstances (Figure 14–2). These interviews should point toward securing the following data:

1. Who reported the fire
2. The color and volume of flames and smoke
3. Whether anyone reported the odor of gasoline or other fire accelerant
4. Where and when the fire started
5. The movements of occupants and others involved in the fire
6. Anything unusual at the fire scene

After the fire is over and the investigator can enter the fire scene—which is when most investigators arrive at the fire scene—the onset of the fire and its

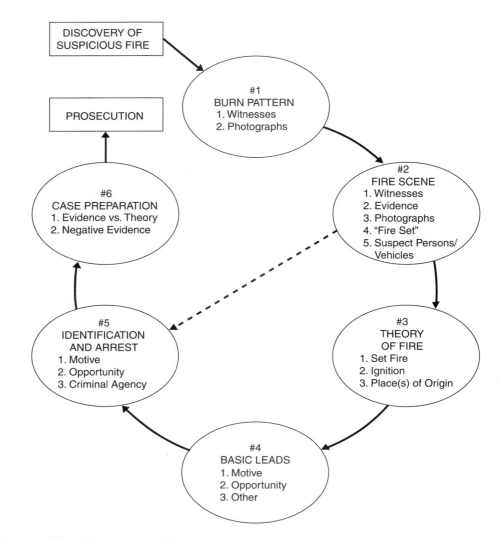

FIGURE 14–2 Investigation of arson.

circumstances can be reconstructed. Unfortunately, fire investigators usually are faced with various disturbances or changes in the original fire scene caused by the need of firefighters to overhaul after extinguishing a fire. **Overhauling** is the examination and search by firefighters for hidden flames or sparks that might rekindle the fire. To accomplish this, firefighters often throw the contents of a room outside the building and frequently rip cabinets and paneling from walls to expose the space between the studs.

Tracing the root of a fire by examining the manner and direction of burning from the point of origin is the primary means of reconstructing the fire scene.[16] Basically, reconstruction of a fire scene requires the investigator to secure data on how a fire started, how it burned, and whether it was accelerated.

Once an investigator has reconstructed a fire, he or she can develop a theory about it. This theory may be backed up by various items of evidence, such as empty containers of flammable fluid found at the scene, traces of fire accelerants, or the remains of a fire-setting device in the rubble of a fire. It is

The color of the smoke in a suspicious fire is an important investigative lead.

primarily concerned, however, with the pattern of a fire: how it was ignited, the point of origin, and the source and direction of its burning.

Searching a fire scene is similar to searching any crime scene, with the exception that a lengthy period of freezing the scene is necessary to protect physical evidence until the searchers can find it among the rubble and debris of a fire. Although the fire scene search is pointed toward discovery of the means of ignition and the point or points of origin of a fire, the searchers also look for anything unusual or foreign to the fire scene, evidence that will connect a suspect to the scene by revealing his or her presence at the scene (the opportunity to set a fire), clues to the motive of a fire setter, or evidence of the fire setter's intent to set a fire.

Items of evidence suspected of containing volatile substances commonly used to accelerate fires must be found and sealed quickly to prevent loss by evaporation. Such items must be transported to the crime laboratory in airtight containers.

Liquid fire accelerants (e.g., kerosene, gasoline) can and do survive fires. The areas most likely to contain residues of these accelerants are the low points at the fire scene: floors, carpets, or soil. When a suspect is arrested shortly after the fire at or near the scene, the suspect's outer clothing and shoes may contain residual traces if the fire setter used a liquid fire accelerant. The human nose can detect the distinctive odor of a liquid fire accelerant at the scene or on a suspect, but it is best supplemented by detectors of flammable vapors. These "sniffers" operate on several principles. The most common type operates on the catalytic combustion principle. However, the recovery and individualization of fire accelerant residues require the services of forensic scientists in a crime laboratory and the use of solvent extraction devices.[17]

Arson crime scene.

One popular method for separating flammable and combustible liquid residues from fire debris is the **passive headspace concentration method.** In this method, an adsorbent material such as activated charcoal is used to extract the residue from the static headspace above the sample, then the adsorbent is eluted with a solvent. Results of studies have demonstrated that multiple separations can be performed without jeopardizing the recovery and identification of volatile residues.[18] The headspace concentration method is best used when a high level of sensitivity is required because of a low concentration of ignitable liquid residues in the sample. Several variations on this method have also been developed and are effective for separating residues from fire debris.

Solvent-extraction devices support the work of fire scene searches by recovering flammable fluids from fire rubble (wood, cloth, and paper). The searchers find and recover the material suspected of containing residues of a fire accelerant and transport it to the crime laboratory for processing by criminalists. Later, the report of these laboratory technicians may contribute to the development of the case, and their expert evidence in court at the trial of the offender offers testimony in support of the prosecution's case.

PHOTOGRAPHS OF THE FIRE SCENE

Fires and fire scenes are ideal subjects for photo essays that communicate otherwise undetectable facts about a fire, its origin, and its pattern of burning. In-progress photos are seldom taken by assigned investigators, but they are taken by the news media, fire personnel, and amateur photographers and can be secured by investigators. Such in-progress photographs, particularly when in color, identify the location of a fire, reveal its spread and intensity, and detail the mixture of smoke and flames. In addition, such photographs sometimes reveal the presence of a suspect at the fire scene, identify one or more vehicles parked at or entering or exiting from the scene, and reveal signs of forced entry, attempts to bar firefighters from the structure, or methods used to prevent prompt discovery of the fire.

Investigators and assisting personnel assigned to process the scene of a suspicious fire should take both color and black-and-white photographs of the fire scene and of items of evidence found at the scene. Inasmuch as the corpus delicti of arson is the burning (charring) of a portion of a structure, this burning should be photographed from its place of origin to wherever the fire caused damage to the structure or its contents, both in overall views and in close-ups. Overall pictures reveal a fire's patterns and offer some clues to its ignition and origin, but it is the close-up photography in the area or areas of the origin of the fire that is of particular importance in revealing any ignition device and the use of a fire set with trailers and accelerants. Although the ignition device itself may have been consumed in the fire, mute evidence of its use to set the fire may be developed from such photographs.

Photographs taken during the postfire processing of the scene of a suspicious fire may exonerate innocent suspects or serve as the only corroboration of an investigator's testimony as to things found, or not found, at the fire scene and their application to the prosecution's theory of the fire, the criminal agency, and the identity of the defendant on trial as the fire setter.

THE CONTINUING ARSON INVESTIGATION

The preliminary investigation of a suspicious fire is complete when the fire scene examination is recorded and the theory of an incendiary fire has been developed, and when it can be proved by available evidence that the fire was not accidental.

The investigator assigned to the continuing investigation uses the following lines of inquiry as to motive and opportunity (presence at crime scene):

1. Who would want or benefit from the fire?
2. Who would have the opportunity to set the fire?

The specific lines of inquiry suggested by the basic investigative leads are not exhausted until the dual inquiry as to motive and opportunity is fully developed. The specific areas of inquiry in the continuing investigation of an arson case depend on the individual characteristics of each case, but the following major areas of inquiry should be explored in developing an arson investigation:

1. Burn pattern (whether in harmony with structure and contents)
2. Fire scene
   a. Examination for source of ignition
   b. Determination of place or places of origin
   c. Physical evidence
3. Witnesses
   a. Person discovering fire
   b. Fire personnel

    c. Eyewitnesses

    d. Occupants (and owner of premises or place)

    e. Others (onlookers, neighbors, and relatives of person discovering fire)

4. Suspicious Persons

    a. At fire scene

    b. At fire scene but left before arrival of investigators (e.g., children playing, strangers in area, transients or homeless persons, former occupants, discharged employees)

5. Suspicious Vehicles

    a. At fire scene

    b. Usually parked at fire scene but not present now

    c. At fire scene but departed before arrival of investigators

6. Theory of Fire

    a. Rationally motivated

        i. Hate

        ii. Profit

        iii. Concealment of a crime

    b. Pathological fire setter

        i. Lack of rational motive

        ii. Fire in series

        iii. Neighborhood involved

        iv. Known pyromaniacs

    c. Criminal agency

        i. Not caused by accident

        ii. Means of ignition

        iii. Place of origin(s)

        iv. Proof fire was set

            a. Physical evidence

            b. Witnesses

            c. Other (e.g., motive, opportunity)

7. Identification of Fire Setter

    a. Scene

    b. Witnesses

    c. Suspicious person or vehicle

    d. Inquiries—basic leads

8. Review of evidence disclosed by the following:

    a. Burning pattern

    b. Examination of fire scene

    c. Witnesses

    d. Suspicious persons and vehicles

    e. Basic leads

9. Compatibility of Evidence—Identifying Fire Setter

    a. Burning pattern

    b. Evidence at fire scene

    c. Testimony of witnesses

    d. Results of investigation

10. Case Preparation; Compatibility of Identification of Fire setter with Theory of Fire
    a. Criminal agency
    b. Motive (rational, irrational)
    c. Review of negative evidence (block common defense of accident, alibi, mistaken identification, or lack of motive)

BOMBINGS

Many fires result from explosions. Criminal investigation techniques used in arson investigation can be applied to bombings despite the fact that a fire may not result from the explosion.

The investigation of bombings takes place in six stages (Figure 14–3):

1. ***Determination of Cause.*** An accidental origin, such as a gas explosion or an explosion resulting from the misuse of chemicals, must be eliminated as the cause of the explosion.

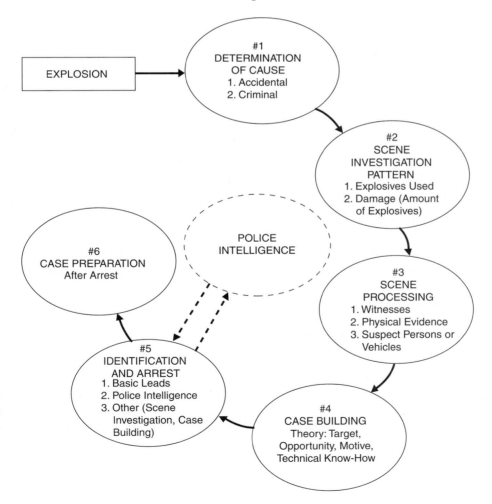

FIGURE 14–3   Investigation of bombings.

2. *Scene Investigation Pattern.*   The pattern of the explosion must be determined—high or low explosive; approximate amount used (damage).

3. *Scene Processing.*   The bombing scene is processed by police (responding officers and bomb squad personnel, if available) to locate and interview witnesses and victims, to find and preserve physical evidence, and to identify any suspicious persons or vehicles.

4. *Case Building.*   The investigator develops a theory of the bombing target, opportunity, motive, and technical know-how.

5. *Identification and Arrest.*   Inquiries are initiated to exploit any basic leads, police intelligence, and other clues and traces (scene investigation and processing, case building) likely to result in the identification and arrest of the person or persons responsible for the bombing.

6. *Case Preparation.*   The case is prepared immediately after the arrest of the bomber and any associates.

Because the nature of an explosion destroys traces of the explosives used, explosive **tagging** offers future promise that the scene investigation of a bombing will hold identifiable traces of the explosives used. An explosives tagging program developed at the federal level involves the addition of coded microparticles or **taggants** to explosives during their manufacture. The taggants survive detonation, can be recovered at the bombing scene, and can be decoded by crime laboratory examination to show where and when the explosives were made.

The use of police intelligence reports may be the most important factor contributing to the success of a bombing investigation. These reports can provide information that will link suspects to prior bombings and provide data on the associates and possible whereabouts of suspects and associates. In addition, a police intelligence unit may initiate preventive intelligence operations to disclose the identity of persons involved in the planning of future bombings (see Chapter 7).

Individuals or groups who use explosives as the ultimate weapon against persons or property may be linked to any of the following:

1. Politically motivated groups (extremists, radicals) (see Chapter 18)
2. Organized crime (bombings involving known criminals, informants for police, and witnesses or potential witnesses against members of crime syndicates)
3. Mentally ill persons (including bombers motivated by hate, anger, and revenge).

PROBLEMS OF PROOF IN ARSON AND BOMBING CASES

Two common defenses create problems of proof in prosecuting arson cases: (1) a claim that the fire resulted from an accident, a misfortune, or a natural cause and (2) if the fire did result from a criminal agency, the defendant was not that agent.

To prove that a criminal agency was responsible for the fire, the police prosecutor team must foreclose all possibilities that the fire resulted from any other cause (accident, misfortune, natural cause) by a strong showing of evidence linking the fire to a single cause: someone set it.

Identifying the defendant as the fire setter is a problem that is generally attacked along the dual lines of motive and opportunity. The prosecution must, at the least, produce evidence showing that the defendant wanted the fire or would benefit from it, and that by his or her presence at the fire scene, not only had the opportunity to set the fire but did so, or that the defendant contracted with a crime partner to set the fire.

While cases involving explosive devices may be linked to fires, their investigation is hampered by the fact that the explosion usually destroys most of the physical evidence at the bombing scene. When these cases are prosecuted, the motive and opportunity factors are important. In political bombings, anyone proven to be a member of a terrorist group is assumed to have a motive for the bombings of that group.

HATE CRIMES

Hate crimes are committed by individuals or organizations of people who engage in antisocial and illegal behavior and pose a danger to agents of the criminal justice system and to the general public. Add to this definition the fact that the hate–violence is commonly directed at African Americans, Asians, Hispanics, Jews, gays, and even at the U.S. government itself—for example, the Oklahoma City bombing.

Hate groups include organizations such as the Ku Klux Klan (KKK), Aryan Nation, and **skinheads**. In some locales, various militias demonstrate against the government for a specific reason.[19]

Alan Berg, a controversial talk-show host, was shot dead not far from his home on the outskirts of Denver. His killers were members of a neo-Nazi group aligned with the Aryan Nation. Berg was Jewish and openly challenged neo-Nazi and other hate groups. Killing Berg was murder—but also a hate crime. He was killed because he was "different" in the eyes of his murderers.

A hate crime is not usually so closely identified with a **community threat group**. It is usually a single offender acting out his or her particular hate. Arson and bombing are common, and often fires and bombings occur in a series a few days apart. Although the motivation is irrational, suspects can be found and evidence can be developed for a trial.

Cults range from groups preaching revolution or resistance to taxation or similar governmental activity to those preaching from the Bible and performing good works among the sick and the poor. These groups may have other problems linked, for example, to the children of the group or the lifestyle of the group. Some cults have been targeted for allegations of **mind control**, which is the use of undue influence and unethical means to recruit and retain members.

Despite the negative public perception of groups labeled as cults, police investigators must remember that the United States has a longtime commitment to religious tolerance and freedom. Investigators should not probe and pry into any such group unless a crime has been reported or discovered and unless there is strong probable cause to warrant police action.[20]

CASE STUDY

Motive for Arson

The defendant was convicted by a jury of the crime of arson. In April 1995, defendant secured fire insurance in the sum of $141,000 on a home located in Corona (comprising rooms numbered on a diagram in evidence at trial as 1 to 10, inclusive). Title to the property was formerly in the name of defendant's son, who, with defendant, was one of the co-beneficiaries of the policy. The house was leased to a Mr. Keys, who resided in it from April 1995 to November 1998. During that period, defendant listed the property for sale at $160,500.

On January 5, 1998, defendant came to Corona from her home in Santa Clara where she lived with her husband. She stayed in the Corona house on the nights of January 5 and 6. On January 7, defendant's insurance agent received a telephone call from defendant informing him that she wanted $10,500 additional insurance. The agent notified the head office to increase the insurance accordingly, effective January 7, 1998. Defendant spent the night of January 9 with a friend in Corona.

A neighbor, living next door to defendant's property, testified that he saw defendant carry an amber-colored gallon bottle into the house on January 7 and saw her again at the house on the morning of January 10; that he saw lights in the back part of the house about 6:00 p.m. that night; that he retired about 9:00 p.m.; and that at 2:30 a.m. on January 11 he was awakened by flames coming from the gabled ends of the defendant's house. The fire department was called. The firemen forced open the back door and saw no flames in rooms 8, 9, 3, or 4. One fireman saw evidence of separate fires in rooms 5, 6, and 10. In room 1, other firefighters found an open-faced gas heater on which the valve was open and gas was coming into the house. After the fire was subdued, the fire chief discovered that one of the back doors had been left open.

On January 11, a deputy state fire marshal and others investigating the fire discovered that the heaviest fire occurred in room 10—a closet—which was separated from room 1 by a door. The fire in that area had burned down through the floor and up through the ceiling, resulting in considerable fire damage to the house and roof. Directly across from room 10, in room 1, an area about 36 inches wide had been burned on the wall. Apparently, the fire at that point started from the floor and burned up because the baseboard was entirely gone.

Prosecution

The district attorney focused on the incendiary origin of a fire, which is generally established by circumstantial evidence, such as the finding of separate and distinct fires on the premises. Evidence of four separate, simultaneous, and unrelated fires was found in the house in question; holes were found in the plaster behind two of the fires; boxes of combustibles were in front of the holes; papers were stuffed between the laths in one of the holes; and debris smelling of petroleum products was near another hole in the plaster. The facts amply justify an inference that the fire was of incendiary origin and that it was neither accidental nor from natural causes and that the jury could reasonably infer that the fire was willfully and maliciously set for the purpose of burning the house.

In the opinion of duly qualified experts who testified at the trial, there was no communication or connection between the fire causing the charred condition in room 5 and the burned areas in rooms 10 and 1, nor between the burned area in room 6 and the burned area in rooms 10 and 1, nor between the fires causing the burns in rooms 5 and 6.

Defense

Counsel for defendant contended that the evidence of the corpus delicti was insufficient because it had not shown that the defendant was present when the fire was set, nor that the defendant was the means by which the fire occurred. No evidence connects the defendant to the crime.

The identity of the defendant as the person who committed the crime may be proved by circumstantial evidence connecting her to the crime, but circumstantial evidence must consist of proof of the defendant's motive and conduct that connects her with the crime and statements that show a consciousness of guilt.

Comment

The jury was justified in believing the defendant had offered the house for sale and that it had not been sold. This fact and evidence of several points of origin, coupled with the fact that defendant had secured an increase in the insurance on January 7, three days before the fire, justify the inference that she had a motive in burning the building and collecting the insurance.

CHAPTER REVIEW

KEY TERMS

accelerant   *280*
aggravated arson   *276*
arson   *276*
arsonist   *277*
combustibility   *279*
community threat
  group   *289*
cult   *289*
fire set   *277*
flashover   *279*

hate crime   *289*
hate fire   *277*
incendiarism   *277*
incendiary   *277*
mind control   *289*
overhauling   *282*
passive headspace
  concentration
  method   *284*
plant   *281*

pyromania   *278*
pyromaniac   *278*
Santa Ana winds   *280*
skinhead   *289*
taggants   *288*
tagging   *288*
trailer   *281*

REVIEW QUESTIONS

1. _____ is any arson in which explosives are used and people are present or placed in danger.

2. When investigating a burning, the investigator must first seek evidence to prove whether the fire was _____ or _____.

3. A fire that is started due to some real or imagined dispute with another person is an arson motivated by _____ reasons.

4. A person who has an obsession to set fires or has a preference for arson as an instrument of damage is known as a/an _____.

5. At _____, all the previously uninvolved combustibles in a room suddenly ignite. At this time, the rate of the heat release is high and flaming spreads across the ceiling of the room.

6. Factors that influence patterns of outdoor fires are _____ and the _____.

7. _____ are often used to spread fires from a point of ignition.

8. Coded microparticles are added to explosives at time of manufacture. These _____ survive detonation, can be recovered at the bombing scene, and can be decoded to indicate where and when the explosives were made.

9. _____ crimes are committed by individuals or organizations of people who engage in antisocial and illegal behavior and who pose a danger to agents of the criminal justice system and to the general public.

10. Pathological fire setters are motivated by _____ reasons to set their fires.

See Appendix D for the correct answers.

DISCUSSION QUESTIONS

1. Define a suspicious fire.
2. How does the burning pattern in structure fires differ from the burning pattern of nonstructure (field and forest) fires?
3. What is a fire set? A fire trailer? A fire accelerant?
4. What basic factors should be considered in investigating fires set because of hate (revenge or jealousy), for profit, or to conceal a crime?
5. What are the basic characteristics of fires set by pyromaniacs?
6. What are the similarities and differences between arson and bombings?
7. Define combustibility.
8. What information is sought by investigators in on-the-scene interviewing of witnesses in the investigation of a suspicious fire?
9. How is the ignition and spread of a fire reconstructed at the crime scene? What is the primary objective of this reconstruction?
10. What special care must be taken with evidence suspected of containing residues of a fire accelerant?
11. Outline the major phases of the continuing investigation in arson cases.
12. What are the six stages of a bombing investigation?
13. What are the essential elements of stage 3 in the investigation of a bombing (scene)? Of stage 4 (case building)?
14. What individuals or groups may be involved in a bombing?
15. What is explosives tagging?
16. Has the corpus delicti been established in the case study?
17. How was the fire in the case study started?

RELATED WEB SITES

For information regarding arson investigation, recent events, and related sites, consult *www. firehouse.com.*

Arson facts and statistics for the United States can be found at. *www.emergency.com/arsonrpt.htm.*

Statistics on hate crime in the United States can be found at this Website: *www.fbi.gov/hq/cid/ civilrights/hate.htm.*

chapter **fifteen**

Property Crimes

CHAPTER OUTLINE

After reading this chapter you will be able to:

- Ascertain the legal distinctions among the various types of property crime.
- List the various methods burglars use to enter buildings to commit a felony or theft.

- Explain the three types of employee theft and how these crimes are investigated.
- Identify the more common swindles or con games used to defraud unsuspecting victims.
- Explain how the disposal of stolen merchandise obtained in the commission of property crimes can be an important investigative lead.

Property crimes are committed for the personal gain of the perpetrator. These crimes include burglary, theft, and fraud. While **burglary**, by definition, is the entering of a structure for the purpose of committing a felony or theft therein, the crime of burglary is almost predominantly a crime wherein the object of the crime is the breaking and entering of a structure for the purpose of committing a theft.

BURGLARY

In the past, conviction of common-law burglary required the proof of six essential elements:[1]

1. A breaking
2. An entry
3. In the nighttime
4. Of a dwelling house
5. Belonging to another
6. An intent to commit a felony

In most jurisdictions today, conviction for burglary requires only three basic or essential elements:[2]

1. Entry
2. Of a building (or other structure, place, or thing described by the particular penal code section)
3. With intent to steal or commit another felony

Burglary is usually separated into first-, second-, and possibly third-degree burglary. Some of the old essential elements of common-law burglary are used to divide the modern crime of burglary into degrees. The division into degrees may be based on whether the crime occurs in a dwelling house; whether such a dwelling is inhabited by a person actually present at the time; whether it is entered in the nighttime; or whether the act is committed by a person who is armed with a deadly weapon or who, while in the commission of a burglary, arms himself or herself with such a

Burglars often gain entry by prying or kicking doors open.

deadly weapon, depending upon the state in which the crime is committed. In recent years, the use of explosives has increased the degree of burglary.[3]

The allied misdemeanor offense of possession of burglar tools assists police in apprehending burglars and in preventing burglaries. Any person who has on his or her person or in his or her possession a picklock or other instrument with intent to feloniously break into or enter any building is guilty of a misdemeanor in California. So is any person who knowingly makes or alters any picklock or other instrument so that it can be used to open the lock of any building without the specific consent of a person having control of such building.[4]

Burglary is a crime of opportunity, a crime of easy opportunity. Although many burglars limit their activities to a certain area and thus reduce the scope of their burglaries, every area has many easy opportunities.

Investigators should try to develop some insight into how a burglar selects a site for his or her crime. Why the choice of one area? Why the selection of one house as opposed to a neighboring house? The probability of profit and safety are perhaps at the core of this site-selection process, with burglars having a large physical area in which they evaluate (by search) the opportunity for a successful burglary.[5] If this insight can be developed, a roving stakeout of an area may be successful in apprehending the burglar.

Burglary is usually a passive crime in that the burglar normally tries to avoid contact with victims. The chances of getting caught in an unoccupied structure are lower than the chances of being apprehended in an occupied structure. Persons who are not present at the scene of a burglary can never be eyewitnesses to the identity of a burglar in court. Without an alarm to alert police of a crime "in progress," no "hot" search can take place. In more public crimes, when a criminal has fled the scene shortly before the arrival of police, the victim may give the police a physical description of the criminal, of a vehicle, and of the direction of flight, thus giving the police the opportunity for a "warm" search. This is not possible when the victim does not even know that his or her premises have been burglarized until some time after the burglar has fled the scene. This restricts the police apprehension process to the "cold" portion of this crime-solving process, commonly termed the **investigative phase**. In other words, burglars usually are not apprehended at the scene of their crime or in flight but must be apprehended as a result of an investigative process (Figure 15–1).

The objective of burglars may be something other than theft. It may be assault—usually rape. Sometimes theft and assault are joint goals. Both

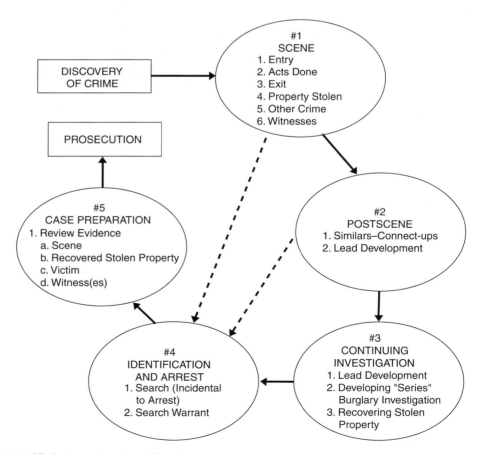

FIGURE 15–1 Investigation of burglary.

larceny and rape or any other crime involved is investigated along with the basic burglary. The investigator must be alert to obtain evidence of each essential element of the additional crimes, as well as the essential element of the burglary.

TYPES OF BURGLARS

For years, police schools have taught about two general types of burglars: (1) the amateur and (2) the professional. **Professional burglars** are defined as those persons who work at burglary as a trade, making their living by burglary and larceny alone and having no other means of income. Other burglars are loosely grouped beneath this plateau of "professionalism." The **amateur burglar** includes the burglar who commits crimes primarily to secure money for drugs.

   Because burglary is probably the most common serious crime in the United States, it is timely to reconstruct a typology of burglars that will encompass skill levels. This typology categorizes the skills of a burglar on two levels:

1. The ability to gain entry to a premises
2. The business sense of the burglar in regard to the selection of loot and the method of disposing of the proceeds of the crime (i.e., selling the stolen property)

The skill required to gain entry to a premises may be limited to forcing open a door or window, but it can extend to the use of lock-picking tools, which keeps pace with the art of the locksmith in providing security against thieves, and to the skill that opens locked containers such as safes. The business sense of a burglar depends on his or her ability to distinguish between valuable and worthless items at the time of the burglary, the burglar's contacts with receivers of stolen property, and whether he or she needs desperately (common with drug addicts) to sell the stolen property.

   This new typology of burglars describes a burglar as being in one of the following categories:

1. Unskilled
2. Semiskilled
3. Professional

   The fact that such a typology of burglars exists does not mean that investigators should discount the classic modus operandi criteria used to describe various types of burglars. These specifies have served as a working typology for many years, as follows:[6]

1. Type of premises entered
2. Means of entry
3. Type of loot (stolen property)
4. Time of operation
5. Presence of crime partners

It does mean, however, that these basic items of modus operandi information should be reviewed from the viewpoint of discovering the skills demonstrated in gaining entry to the premises and the business sense demonstrated to some extent by the nature of the property taken at the time of the burglary, its quantity, and its value.

The **means of entry** differ in various burglaries and are related to the skill of a burglar. The various known **means of entry** include the following:

1. *Open Door or Window Entry.*   The burglar roams residence areas, apartments, and hotels looking for open doors or windows.
2. *Jimmy Entry.*   The burglar forces a door or window with a tool such as a tire iron, screwdriver, or small crowbar or box opener.
3. *Celluloid Entry.*   The burglar forces open a door's spring lock with a small piece of celluloid.
4. *Stepover or Human Fly Entry.*   The burglar is an aerialist; the **stepover burglar** steps from a fire escape, balcony, or other building to a nearby window; the **human-fly burglar** can progress upward or downward on the sides of a building to a selected point of entry.
5. *Roof Entry.*   The burglar breaks into a premises through a skylight or air conditioning duct on the roof or by cutting a hole in the roof of a building.
6. *Hide-In Entry.*   The burglar hides in a commercial premises until all employees have left, then breaks out with the stolen property.
7. *Cut-In Entry.*   The burglar uses tools of various kinds to cut through the floor, ceiling, or wall of a store or office to another store or office.
8. *Hit-and-Run Entry (Smash and Grab).*   The burglar breaks a window of a ground-floor store and takes property from a window or nearby portions of the premises, then flees before police can be alerted to the crime.
9. *Key Entry.*   The burglar uses a key. The key may have been given to him or her by an informant, it may have been stolen, or the burglar may have obtained a duplicate or master key by various means.

It is apparent that most unskilled or semiskilled burglars are prowlers who enter a residence and search very rapidly for cash or property that is easily transported and quickly converted into cash. Whether they succeed in finding it or not, they will leave without any loss of time, taking with them the portable wealth of the householder—usually stereo systems, VCRs, computers, and other items that are easily sold to individuals seeking bargains or to persons who deal in and sell drugs and are willing to exchange the drugs for the stolen merchandise.

The semiskilled and the professional burglars also deal in articles of value, but those articles are not as easily converted into cash and generally require the services of a **fence**, a receiver of stolen property. The loot of such thievery ranges through jewelry, furs, clothing, liquor, tobacco, meat, and textiles.

BURGLARY AS A BEHAVIORAL CONCEPT

Burglarizing is the behavior of committing a burglary and, most likely, another and another and another. Burglaries usually are crimes in a series.

Like all behavior, burglary involves needs and the opportunity to satisfy these needs. It also involves a common decision about whether or not to take advantage of opportunities. The five-step **behavior cycle in burglary** is as follows:

1. Needs
2. Opportunities
3. Means (skills)
4. Satisfactions
5. Choice

To understand the elements in this burglary cycle is to understand the behavior of burglars. Among burglars whose goals are theft (profit), the economic needs are met through successful burglaries, the successful taking away of stolen property, and its profitable disposition. The opportunity to commit a burglary is perceived; the burglary and its profit will meet the needs of the burglar; the burglar has the necessary "technology" to enter a premises successfully to take away the proceeds of a crime and to sell it. The individual with these needs who makes a choice of burglary over other possible activities to meet unmet needs not only receives satisfaction from the work but also a reinforcement of this behavior, thus increasing the probability of the recurrence of this behavior—more burglaries and theft.[7]

Many years ago burglars stole primarily for economic reasons. Today, the same economic reasons may be complicated by an addiction to drugs. Although the need for funds to buy drugs is an economic need, a more urgent compulsion is related to the need for the drugs and their effect on the drug user.

Rapist–burglars exhibit needs to satisfy various psychological and physical desires. These burglars are abnormal in selecting forcible rape as an outlet, but they follow the burglar's typical cycle of behavior—and each successful crime is reinforcement for continuing this pattern of behavior.

SAFE BURGLARS

Burglars often demonstrate skill at opening locked desks, file cabinets, safes, and other containers. It may be that such entry to locked containers will be made by basic tools such as a jimmy or screwdriver or tools picked up on the premises and used by the burglars. Most safe burglars, however, will bring to the crime scene whatever special tools they need: torch, sectional crowbar, and so on.

Force used to attack safes generally follows one of the following patterns:

1. *Punching.*   In the **punching** manner of entry, a sledge hammer and a drift punch are used to knock the combination dial from the safe and drive the spindle back into the safe. This makes the release mechanism of the lock accessible and allows the safe to be opened.

2. *Pulling.*   In **pulling**, a device similar to a gear or wheel puller is used to pull the dial or spindle completely out of the safe door, thus allowing the safe to be opened (similar to punching).

3. *Peeling.*   **Peeling** involves prying off the outer surface of the safe door so that the locking mechanism of the safe is exposed and can be pried open, allowing entry to the safe.

4. *Ripping.*   **Ripping** is a battering of the top, bottom, or sides of a safe with a chisel or other metal cutter such as a ripping bar (burglar's tool) or the hydraulic ramming device used in a body-and-fender shop.

5. *Drilling.*   In **drilling**, one or more holes are drilled in the door of the safe to expose the lock mechanism, allowing the safe breaker to align the lock tumblers manually and open the door of the safe.

6. *Burning.*   In **burning**, the safe is attacked with an oxygen-acetylene torch, and a section of the safe is burned out to allow entry. When bank vaults are involved, a variation of this burning technique is the use of a thermal-burn burning bar that makes the original oxygen-acetylene torch much more efficient so that it is possible to burn through 6-inch tempered steel in 15 to 20 seconds.

7. *Blasting.*   **Blasting** is the use of explosives to open safes.

8. *Carrying Away.*   **Carrying away** occurs when the burglar removes a safe in order to open it at a more convenient location.

Intruders often open a safe without force, by means of its combination. It may be that the burglar found the safe open, but when no physical force is used to open a safe, investigators assume it was opened by using the combination. In such cases, the burglar may have found the combination written on the side of a drawer in a nearby desk, in an account book, or in another convenient place, or he or she may have been given it by a dishonest employee.

THE BURGLARY SCENE INVESTIGATION

The purpose of the burglary scene investigation is to ascertain what clues or traces at the scene may identify the burglar and crime partner(s). The burglary scene investigation has three major phases:

1. The means of gaining entry
2. What the burglar did while in the premises
3. How the burglar exited the premises

The place of entry and toolmarks are the classic identifying characteristics found at the scene of burglaries. The burglar's ability to break into any locked containers at the scene is a demonstration of a skill in the use of tools. Various identifying toolmarks may be discovered.

Acts done while at the crime scene may be no more than necessary to accomplish a theft. On the other hand, the acts of a rapist–burglar spell out the essential elements of a second major crime. In addition, some acts may aid in identifying the burglars. The property stolen is another useful factor in identifying the burglar.

The burglar's means of exit rounds out what can be gleaned from a burglary scene by investigators. The burglar may simply have exited from a rear door after a roof entry. In the course of determining this fact, however, investigators may find significant clues or traces in and about the place of exit.

However, none of the evidence likely to be found at burglary scenes will actually identify a burglar by name or as a person. Factors related to the burglar's modus operandi may contribute to developing one or more suspects. Therefore this on-the-scene evidence should be preserved for future use. When suspects are uncovered, the clues and traces can be related to these suspects by the investigator.

If the investigator has good reason to believe that a suspect is still in possession of stolen property from one or more recent burglaries, and the investigator can secure reliable information describing this stolen property and where it is located, such data can be tied to the victim's reports of what was stolen and developed into an application for a search warrant. The execution of the search warrant and the recovery of the stolen property in premises controlled by the suspect will support other evidence identifying him or her as the burglar.

THE POSTSCENE INVESTIGATION

The postscene investigation is the development of leads from connect-ups and a comparison of modus operandi with other crimes either solved or unsolved, which tends to identify one or more suspects as the offender in a series of crimes of which the burglary being investigated is the latest. It often involves the use of informants or identification through recovery of the stolen property and a tracing back to the burglar.

Although connect-ups and the use of informants are classic avenues of investigation to identify suspects in burglary investigations, they offer little or no admissible prosecution evidence that a particular suspect committed the particular burglary under investigation.

The identification of the seller of stolen property through a questioning of the receiver of stolen property has a more promising potential as evidence. When a person is known to be in possession of stolen property, a search warrant can be secured. The resultant seizure of stolen property is lawful, and such evidence can be used in court against the receiver or against the person who sold the stolen goods to him or her—if there is testimony or other evidence that connects the seller to the stolen property.

KNOWN BURGLARS

When an investigator has developed a suspect known to police to be a burglar but is unable to develop evidence likely to serve as probable cause for an arrest, then he or she must continue the connecting-up of subsequent burglaries until sufficient evidence is accumulated to supply probable cause for the arrest of the suspect.

Innovative surveillance procedures have been used in recent years in many police departments to clear burglary cases when a known burglar is identified as the suspect in a series of burglaries. An around-the-clock surveillance of the known burglar (and usually a crime partner or partners) is established and continued until such time as the burglar enters a building under circumstances that indicate intent to commit a crime. This type of arrest is opportune and timely.

THEFT

In common law, *larceny* was defined as a trespassory taking and carrying away of personal property belonging to another with an intent to deprive the owner of such property permanently. Currently, **larceny** (theft) is defined in most states as the unlawful taking or stealing of property or articles without the use of force or violence. It includes shoplifting, pocket picking, purse snatching without strong-arm tactics, thefts of and from vehicles, and taking property or cash from a home.

New terms used in criminal justice statistics describe the scope of common larceny:[8]

1. *Household Larceny.* Theft or attempted theft of property or cash from a residence or the immediate vicinity of the residence is **household larceny**. The thief must have a legal right to be in the house—as a guest or maid, for example.
2. *Personal Crimes of Theft (Personal Larceny).* **Personal larceny** is the theft or attempted theft of property or cash by stealth, in either of the following manners:
   a. with contact but without force or threat of force
   b. without direct contact between the victim and the offender
3. *Personal Larceny with Contact.* **Personal larceny with contact** is the theft or attempted theft of property or cash directly from the victim by stealth but not by force or the threat of force.

Thieves steal money, vehicles, and other property from rightful owners. They sell it to individuals (bargain seekers) or criminal receivers of stolen goods (fences). The profit motive in thefts is too general to offer any promising leads. The solution of these crimes begins with a prompt alarm for the stolen property and an examination of the crime scene to determine the circumstances of the crime and to search for and collect physical evidence. Victims are interviewed to develop suspects, and witnesses to some preparatory or postcrime activity are sought and their help solicited. Extensive modus operandi comparisons are made. Information about the work of known thieves suspected of operating locally is correlated with the facts known about the crime being investigated. Thieves can be traced when the proceeds of the crime are sold and recovered by police. Persons who buy stolen property quite frequently reveal the identity of the thief. However, thefts are difficult to solve because of the lack of eyewitnesses. They generally are unknown-identity investigations characterized by the absence of a named suspect (Figure 15–2).

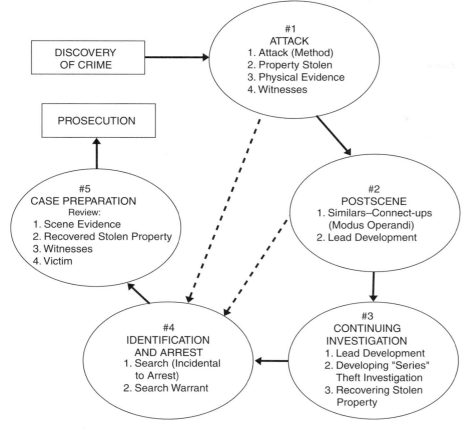

FIGURE 15–2   Investigation of thefts.

Before the recovery of the stolen property, investigators attempt to identify the perpetrator by seeking a characteristic signature in the modus operandi of the crime or a basic lead from field interview reports and tips from underworld sources of information. The value of physical evidence found and collected at the scenes of thefts has a growing importance. It is not likely that such scientific evidence will serve to name a suspect, but it can serve as an identifier when the foregoing techniques bring together a group of persons who are all equally suspect.

Most investigations of thefts involve past thefts. The police patrol force sometimes detects a thief at work or responds to a theft-in-progress call. Quite often when investigating prowler calls, the responding officers discover a thief, but usually the victims of these crimes do not discover the prowler until after the crime has been attempted or is completed. One of the unfortunate aspects of thefts is that police have to bracket the occurrence between the time of discovery and the time at which the stolen property was last seen or otherwise noticed.

Time is likely to favor a criminal. It may blur the focus of an investigation and can aid escape and safe disposal of stolen property. The time element in past crimes does not encourage the assigned investigator and probably serves as a passive means of discouragement. Crimes of violence have an inherent motivation for any investigator. In thefts, the investigator must seek motivation within his or her personal experience and occupational goals for effective work.

THE ATTACK

Money and valuable property are usually safeguarded. To steal either or both requires planning, direction, and operating skills. This is the attack of the thief. To be considered are the premises attacked, the method of the attack itself, and the means used to dispose of the proceeds of the crime—the loot or swag. In fact, the proceeds of a crime are the objective of the attack, and they are an important highlight in viewing the attack as an event.

The property stolen is a major clue. The broadcast and Teletype alarms that announce to all cooperating law enforcement agencies the fact of the crime and identifying data on the property taken begin the tracing that often leads to recovery of the property and a backtracking to the thief. The stolen property is listed by quantity, kind, material, physical description, serial numbers, and value. Many investigators at crime scenes have discovered that victims cannot describe the stolen property. Therefore, investigators often must question the victim about the stolen property item by item—what each item is used for, what it is made of, whether it is a man's or woman's item, what marks are on it, and its value (cost and estimated current value).

The characteristics of the stolen property have long been used as part of modus operandi searches, but they are gaining new significance as indicative of the routine decision making of a particular thief. The property stolen is now recognized as part of the attack event that can serve to name a suspect. It is part of the criteria used to evaluate a target. Some thieves steal money only, which is not grossly incriminating even minutes after a theft. Other thieves consider a proposed theft and reject it because of the difficulty of disposing of the property that will be the proceeds of the crime. Thieves who have an established disposal route with customers such as housewives, employees of gas stations and drive-ins along a highway, and small merchants in nearby towns and villages reject all proposals unless the property is suitable for their customers. Other thieves use wholesalers of the underworld—the fences—and tend to specialize in property that can be legitimized by removing all identifying marks. A few professional thieves have the necessary friendships among members of the organized crime syndicate to dispose of jewelry, furs, bonds, electronics, and other merchandise with retail values in the tens of thousands of dollars and higher.

MODUS OPERANDI SEARCHES

Modus operandi searches are rewarding in theft investigations because thieves are known as single-pattern offenders. Modus operandi searching will identify a group of suspects as persons actively engaged in committing property crimes and will produce a number of suspects for the crime being investigated. Computerized record searches allow the scanning of a huge number of past crimes for the purpose of modus operandi identification.

A great deal of personal satisfaction can be gained by solving a theft in the early stages of a continuing investigation before the proceeds of the crime have been recovered and the process of tracing back has been initiated. It is a possibility that is not being exploited to its fullest extent; the lack of a named suspect often relegates a theft investigation to a category of "no results possible" until there is some feedback about the stolen property being recovered.

The key to an early break in property crime investigation is the expanded modus operandi search to include the decision-making processes exhibited by the criminal in his or her operations. By developing an understanding of how thieves make decisions and the nature of the thought processes that underlie this decision making, an aware investigator can learn a great deal about these criminals. Interpreting selected modus operandi data of a theft under investigation provides clues about a thief's decision routines for dealing with each of the components of the overall task. Then it is the role of the investigator to develop an "identifier" based on the thought streams of individual thieves. Each person's decision making exhibits a pattern because each person learns how to deal with a particular aspect of any task in an individual way. The investigator's use of this decision pattern may disclose the who, when, where, or how, making it possible to identify, trap, or find the thief before or during his or her next crime.

THE UNIVERSE OF SUSPECTS

Each member of a criminal investigation division should be able to recognize information that is of importance to all members of the division and to advise coworkers of possible suspects in current or future crimes. In solving thefts, unlike the pursuit of a named suspect in crimes of violence, one must engage in a battle for information, and every investigator needs the help of associates. Although mainly concerned with general information about individuals who are suspected of earning the major portion of their incomes from criminal operations, this information can sometimes isolate a number of persons as suspects in a specific crime.

Field interview reports placed into police records systems may hold meaningful data about persons and vehicles stopped and questioned by police officers on patrol. However, a great deal of data about people living and working in a patrol sector is stored in the minds of the officers working the sector with some regularity. Often, this useful information never gets into the police records system. At one time, local police communicated this type of information to federal agents and uniformed police supplied local detectives with similar data about persons considered suspects because of their activity. More recently, the upward supply of information from local levels has been noticeable in its absence. An investigator must work to correct this situation, allocating time on a daily basis to developing liaisons with local sources of information among fellow police officers, to finding out the names and descriptions of persons known to be well supplied with money but without a known source of income, to noting the automobile make and license number of a newly arrived hoodlum or a recently released felony parolee, to learning the consensus in regard to a merchant suspected of buying and selling stolen property, and to hearing about a host of seemingly unimportant items shared among police officers in friendship and appreciation of mutual occupational objectives.

Work also must be devoted to remedying current practices about credit and reward for information received. Entries should be made in the service records of the helping officers when such leads assist in breaking a case. More important, such fellow workers may be assisted when their ambition is to step up into investigative work. Willingness to help an investigator is a good recommendation about a person's basic worth for this type of duty.

Investigators also must allocate time regularly to frequent the haunts of known thieves. Taxi drivers, waitresses, cocktail hostesses, bartenders, and tavern owners in such areas are potential sources of information about persons who are new to the area and apparently well supplied with money. Persons in these occupations are less reluctant to talk about thieves than they are about people who rob and are assaultive. Underworld informants interviewed clandestinely can give supplementary information for a better understanding of data already collected, they can assist in interpreting information, and they can offer leads that may be developed by inquiries in the known hangouts of these criminals. This is necessarily a discreet inquiry in order not to compromise any ongoing investigation. The investigator's relations with such sources of information are guarded ones, quite different from the friendships necessary to develop information from among local police officers.

Learning to appreciate the significance of an apparently minor item of information is a developed skill. However, it is a learned skill that will enhance the value of other information collected during an investigation. It will also increase the universe of suspects and the probability that the group of suspects will contain the person responsible for the crime under investigation. Because of the lack of eyewitnesses in crimes against property, the ability to solve a crime is likely to rest on the necessary information getting into the police system without loss or distortion and being used to the best advantage.[9]

CRIMINAL RECEIVERS OF STOLEN PROPERTY

Theft investigators would be seriously handicapped if the proceeds of all thefts were cash or its equivalent. Most thefts are of various goods and merchandise. Unfortunately, the market for stolen property is stable and continuous.

The real success in stealing is not the completion of the crime itself but the disposal of the stolen property at a profit—without leaving the trace that so often identifies the perpetrators of these crimes. Criminals who commit property crimes are repeaters. It may be that they are fatalistic about this Achilles heel of property crimes and consider it a permanent occupational hazard, but not many of them blithely pawn their loot or sell it to someone likely to identify them to police.

Initially, the receiver of stolen property insulates the thief from identification and arrest. As soon as the property transfer is made, the thief can no longer be caught with the stolen property in his or her possession. However, when police detect and apprehend a receiver with stolen property, the potential for tracing it back to the thief is always present. This tracing from receiver to thief is an effective investigative technique for theft. It is the only method to use when a thief does not leave any fingerprints or "signature" (modus operandi) at the crime scene, when the thief is not observed or apprehended while crime is in progress, or while the thief is in possession of recently stolen property.

When the stolen property is purchased by an individual seeking a bargain, this tracing is relatively easy. The receiver is informed of the possible criminal implications of possessing stolen property. Usually, the price and the circumstances of purchase create a reasonably probable cause to assume the purchaser knew the property was stolen. In disclaiming any criminal responsibility, this type of receiver either identifies the seller–thief or gives sufficient information about the purchase to enable the investigator to identify the thief.

When the stolen property is purchased by a professional receiver (a fence), tracing from receiver to thief becomes a problem. Fences with long-standing business dealings with a thief are unlikely to reveal the circumstances of how they received the stolen property.

Fences are the intermediaries of larceny. They buy and sell stolen property regularly. They are in direct contact with thieves and with possible purchasers. Most of them have acquired a reputation ("rep") on both sides of this business loop, and depend on this "goodwill" for third-party referrals of new business. This rep is that the fence will not, under any circumstances, inform police of the identity of a thief or a purchaser of stolen property.[10]

The **storefront or 'sting' technique** is an investigative technique in property crimes aimed at the wholesale identification and apprehension of thieves. Police investigators pose as fences for the purpose of "buying" stolen property.[11] Since the prices paid to thieves by a real fence are copied by the police, the cost of this technique is not a real problem. The problem is whether such police activity may encourage local thieves to take more and more—as long as a thief has the ability to convert merchandise into cash will the thief be encouraged to steal more.

AUTO THEFT

The theft of passenger cars, trucks, and motorcycles is common throughout the United States. **Auto theft** is the term generally used by police in describing this form of larceny. The universe of auto thieves is comprised of both amateurs and professionals.

1. *The Joyriding Juvenile.* Joyriding juveniles are usually host to several other juveniles. They abandon the vehicle when it runs out of gas or they tire of it.

2. *The Transportation Thief.* The transportation thief "borrows" a car for transportation, sometimes to cross state lines or for a lengthy period and abandons the vehicle when it has served the thief's purpose.

3. *The Use-in-Crime Thief.* Use-in-crime thieves steal a car for the sole purpose of using it in the commission of another crime, such as a robbery. Again, this type of thief abandons the vehicle when it has served its purpose.

4. *Insurance-Fraud Swindlers.*   Insurance-fraud swindlers abandon automobiles in ghetto areas where they know they will be stripped promptly for parts, or they have an automobile dismantled or "squished" in a junkyard or will arrange for its burning. The vehicle owner claims—and usually receives—the current *Blue Book* value of the vehicle from the insurance company.

   In a spin-off of this fraud, the swindler registers and insures a "paper" car (forged title to a nonexistent vehicle), reports it stolen, and puts in a claim to the insurance carrier for the current *Blue Book* value of the phantom car.

5. *Strippers and Dismantlers.*   **Strippers** usually attack a parked car, taking a variety of parts readily disposed of on the local black market. Stereos, CDs, batteries, bucket seats, transmissions, rear ends, generators, wheels and tires, and even motors have been stripped from automobiles in public places. **Dismantlers** steal a car, tow or drive it to a "chop shop," and have it cut up for most of its parts. The stolen car's body (sometimes even minus fenders, doors, headlights, front grill, and motor hood) is abandoned some distance from the shop, usually in a remote area. These thieves work fast. A parked car can be stripped in place in less than an hour, and dismantlers can chop up a car, dispose of the leftover body, and move the parts to be sold to another location all within an hour or so.

6. *Professional Auto Thieves.*   The "pro" auto thief steals late-model automobiles and resells them. Sometimes the stolen car is transported to another state and registered in that state with forged or fraudulent papers prior to resale. A contemporary practice is to ship the stolen car out of the country (Mexico and South America are favorite destinations) and sell it on arrival. Some of these professional thieves have developed a new trade: stealing cars to order for "chop shops."

Many auto thieves now use weapons to gain possession of a car. **Carjacking** is the armed robbery of a person in possession of an automobile or other motor vehicle. One or more thieves confront a car's driver with a gun, knife, or other weapon and demand the car's keys, then drive off.

While amateur car thieves (joyriders and transportation thieves) sometimes seek automobiles with the keys in the lock or the car doors unlocked, the pros use tools such as dent pullers and slide hammers or a set of master keys to enter a locked car and defeat the ignition lock. Of course, many amateur thieves are as skilled at hot-wiring a car's ignition as are the professionals.

An auto theft investigation has the following stages:

1. *Preliminary Investigation.*   The preliminary investigator accepts the report of a stolen vehicle from the owner or his or her representative. The report must contain the name, address, and telephone number of the owner; a full description of the vehicle, including registration number and public and other identification numbers; the time and place of the theft and the location of the vehicle when stolen; and assurance that the vehicle was not repossessed by a finance company or other legal owner. Anything distinctive about the stolen vehicle (e.g.,

design, color, damage) will be entered on this report to aid in its location as promptly as possible.

2. *Alarm.*   Information from the preliminary investigation report—particularly the distinctive characteristics of the stolen vehicle—is transmitted to all members of the police agency and sent to cooperating agencies, by Teletype or other means, and reported to state and national computerized records systems.

3. *Recovery.*   Auto thefts for convenience or joyriding are usually identified by prompt recovery of the stolen auto without any evidence of stripping. This is also true of the use-in-crime theft, with the time of recovery usually occurring shortly after the crime. Citizens often notice these parked vehicles and assist the patrol force in locating them.

      The recovery of a stripped or "chopped" vehicle identifies the work of strippers and dismantlers. The nonrecovery of the stolen vehicle tends to identify the other types of auto thieves.

4. *Continuing Investigation.*   Arrest of an auto thief while in possession of the stolen vehicle or its recovery are usually what prompt a probing into the circumstances of an auto theft. When the vehicle is not recovered within a reasonable time, investigators prowl auto accessory and salvage yards and body and fender shops proactively to locate stolen vehicles. Local laws usually require proprietors to allow police inspection.

5. *Case Preparation.*   Cases involving the theft of a *single* vehicle closed out by arrest are simple: the appropriation of another's property to the thief's own use without permission of the owner. Cases involving *multivehicle* thefts require extensive evidence not only to show the larceny but possibly to assemble a conspiracy case against all offenders involved. In either event, inquiries along the basic leads common in property crimes give initial direction to any continuing investigation of auto theft.

The reality of auto theft is that the current high prices for vehicle accessories and components contribute to the growth of "hot parts" dealers. This ready market for the proceeds of crime assures strippers and dismantlers of better-than-average prices in comparison with thieves stealing other goods and merchandise. In fact, the growing market for such goods has attracted many segments of the national crime syndicate to this lucrative field.

In preliminary or continuing investigations of auto theft, primary identification of a stolen vehicle is made by the public vehicle identification number (PVIN), motor number, and confidential vehicle identification number (CVIN) at various hidden locations on the vehicle. (Vehicle manufacturers and the National Automobile Theft Bureau supply police agencies with information about the location of such numbers on passenger cars, trucks, and motorcycles.)

THEFT BY EMPLOYEES

Businesses in this country lose billions of dollars annually as a result of employee theft. **Shrinkage** is the term business uses for the loss of inventory from employee theft. The resulting loss is transferred to the consumer in the form of higher costs for products and services. Many large firms employ security personnel who are trained in employee theft investigations. However, the criminal investigator may be involved when the loss is extensive and criminal prosecution is desired or when the business does not have access to an investigative staff. A thorough investigation is required in these cases because the suspected employee may be fired and subject to criminal prosecution. Generally, employee theft falls within three categories: incidental, situational, and continual theft.

Incidental theft involves those instances when employees consume the employer's product while on the job or take home items such as pens and pencils at the end of the day. The cost to the employer is relatively minor. Most businesses deal with this type of employee theft through disciplinary measures and assume the loss as the price of doing business.

Situational theft involves those instances when the employee is presented with an opportunity for theft that, in the employee's mind, must be acted on. Truck drivers, for instance, who at the end of their route have extra merchandise that has not been charged out to them, have an excellent opportunity to take that merchandise. The restaurant manager who is called away to handle an emergency while counting the previous day's receipts inadvertently leaves the office door open. An employee acts on the opportunity, and the manager returns to find that some or all of the money is missing. In both of these instances, the criminal investigator may become involved and presented with the challenge of having a number of potential suspects. The missing merchandise could have been put on any one of a number of trucks, and any of the restaurant's employees could have entered the manager's office while he or she was gone.

The initial goal for the investigator is to reduce to a manageable total the number of possible suspects who will ultimately be interrogated or asked to submit to a polygraph examination. To accomplish this task requires that each suspect be interviewed individually. Each suspect is asked a predetermined set of questions designed to evaluate their reaction to each question. An example of the type of questions the investigator might ask would include the following:

> Do you know why I am talking to you?
> Do you have any idea of who may be responsible for the loss?
> Is there anyone you would eliminate as a suspect?

The guilty and innocent employees have different motivations concerning the responses to these questions. The innocent employee wants to aid the investigation and knows he or she is there to help the investigator. The innocent employee wants the responsible person caught so that the innocent employee will no longer be a suspect and life at work will return to normal. The innocent person, therefore, will identify the most likely suspects for the investigator and will eliminate those above suspicion. In contrast, the guilty person will want to expand the list of possible suspects as much as possible. The missing merchandise could have been put on anyone's truck or could have been a clerical error; anyone in the area at the time could have access to the manager's office and the missing money. The guilty would not eliminate anyone from suspicion; after all, everyone could use some extra cash. The guilty would pretend not to know why the investigator is talking to them, since he or she would not want to be considered to be a suspect. When the employee's reactions indicate guilt, the investigator may switch to an interrogation mode or, possibly, may schedule the suspect for a voluntary polygraph examination.

Continual theft involves ongoing, constant acts of theft by an employee. This type of theft is usually motivated by the need to support a vice of the employee, such as gambling, drugs, or alcohol. In California, the theft of money, labor, or real or personal property valued at more than $400 in any twelve-month consecutive period is a felony.

The investigator usually starts the investigation by charting the known dates and times of the losses and comparing this information with employee attendance records. A reasonable match, over a sufficient amount of time, of a specific employee who was on the job when the losses occurred would qualify him or her for closer scrutiny. Trusted supervisors and managers should also be consulted to determine any reason that the suspected employee may be responsible for the losses. Finally, the suspected employee would be subjected to surveillance, either by visual or contact method, until a loss occurs. Once the surveillance confirms that the employee is the responsible party, the employee should be confronted while still in possession of the money or merchandise and then questioned.

FRAUD

Fraud is nothing new. It is defined as a nonviolent crime involving elements of intentional deceit, concealment, corruption, misrepresentation, and abuse of trust to gain the property of another, and it is often facilitated by the willing cooperation of unaware or unknowing victims.

The guile, deception, and trickery common to frauds often silence the victim. Either the victim does not realize a theft has occurred or is unwilling to report it for fear of being involved in a crime or of publicly admitting to being a "sucker" who has been duped. In addition, police frequently fail to discover unreported frauds because fraud is a covert scheme with a lower profile than overt thefts or violent crimes.

Fraud in the United States is on the increase. Swindlers use simple bunco or complex confidence (con) games to steal from unknowing victims. Fraudulent check writers menace the integrity of banks. White-collar criminals operating in both the marketplace and the workplace abuse the trust common to merchant–customer and employee–employer relations.

Fraud investigations usually begin with a citizen's complaint or a police probe. A preliminary investigation should disclose whether the act or acts done to further the objective of the fraud are a crime under state laws. Such investigation should spell out the time, place, and modus operandi of the fraud, along with data on the victim, property lost, witnesses, and suspects.

Continuing investigations are the action phase in which suspects are identified, pursued, and apprehended, and the case is prepared for criminal prosecution. When a fraud case reveals substantial economic loss to a victim

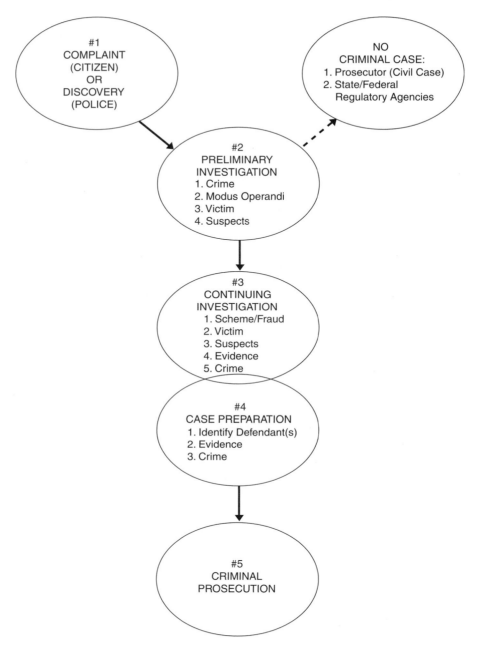

Figure 15–3   Investigation of fraud.

but cannot be developed for criminal prosecution, it is best referred to state or federal regulatory agencies for possible civil action, a cease-and-desist order, or other appropriate remedial action (Figure 15–3).

Fraud auditing is a new occupational specialty in commercial and industrial employment. Fraud auditors are assigned the task of detecting and preventing frauds in commercial transactions. Job descriptions in this role call for the skills of a well-trained auditor and an experienced criminal investigator. Fraud auditors examine the covert aspects of employee behavior and the barriers established to prevent fraud. Can the barriers be breached? When? How? By whom?[12]

ELEMENTS OF FRAUD

Investigators must seek evidence of four common characteristics of fraud:

1. Criminal intent (mens rea)
2. Wrongful objective (deprive true owner of property)
3. Disguise or concealment of objective (wrongful)
4. Reliance on victim's cupidity, carelessness, or compassion

The criminal intent is to achieve the wrongful objective of the scheme. The act or acts done to implement the scheme spell out the disguise or concealment of the scheme's unlawful objective. Thieves who profit from fraudulent schemes must induce the victim to part voluntarily with his or her property. This may be accomplished by the signing of a contract or the actual payment of money or transfer of property ownership.

BUNCO SCHEMES AND CON GAMES

Bunco schemes and **con games** are frauds based on promises of unusual returns: something for nothing, double your money, or income for life. The false hopes of the victim are fostered by assurances that the risk is minimal. The scheme is usually described as a "sure thing."

Some of the more common swindles classed as bunco or con games are (1) pigeon drop, (2) payoff, and (3) carnival bunco. The **pigeon drop, or pocketbook drop** (Figure 15–4), is street bunco that requires a minimum number of "props": pocketbook or envelope and a sizable amount of cash. The **pigeon** is the victim, and no more than two or three swindlers participate in this crime. This is a scheme in which a victim is conned into withdrawing a large sum of money from a bank account to show financial responsibility. In the presence of the potential victim, one of the swindlers apparently "finds" a pocketbook or envelope filled with money (from $500 to $2,500 usually). The approach to the victim is disarming, combining happiness at finding the money along with the query, "What do I do now?" As the victim starts to discuss the swindler's apparent good fortune, the second swindler shows up. Assuming the role of a stranger who just happened to witness the "find" and wants to be part of it, the second swindler joins in the excited talk that makes the victim a partner in a plan to withhold the money from its owner until the origin of this amount of cash can be determined. Since this will take time, the two swindlers team up to convince the victim that he or she should hold the find, but to assure them of the victim's good faith, they ask the victim to show cash equal to the amount found (or close to it). Faced with the possible loss of one-third of the found money, the gullible victim goes to a bank, gets the cash, and reveals it to the swindlers. They go through the motions of counting it, advising the victim of their satisfaction, and bundling the found money with the victim's cash and arranging to meet again with the victim the next day. After this parting, the natural curiosity of the victim leads to an examination of the bundle of

487 PC PIGEON DROP

Date:	**6/22/2005**
Case #:	**01-6956 / 01-7010**
Name:	**UNKNOWN**
Height:	**5 Feet 8 Inches**
Weight:	**180**
Age:	**40**
Sex:	**M**
Eyes:	**BROWN**
Hair:	**BLACK**
Complexion:	**CLEAR**
Race:	**BLACK**

OTHER INFORMATION BELOW

On 6-20-2005 at 1400 hours, (S) took up conversation with Asian (V) at Valley Shopping Center. (S) told victim he was new in the U.S. and stated he was not trusted since he was black. (S) asked (V) to withdraw money ($6,700) from (V)'s bank account to prove his point. The (V) withdrew the money. The (S) then asked (V) to trust him to walk around the block with the (V)'s money. (S) told (V) that if he did that and if the (S) returned, the (S) would give the (V) double his money. The (V) agreed and the (S) left with the money and never came back.

On 6-21-2005 at 1446 hours, the same (S) made another attempt at the Cheapcost Store. In that crime, a second suspect (BMA) was used. Police were called by the (V) while he was in the bank conducting the withdrawal. (S)s fled the area prior to police arrival.

Please BOL and contact me with any similars.

Officer John Smith   Valley Department of Public Safety
(555) 555-5555

TRAK (59 -> 131:1.70.66) This flyer produced on a TRAK System. For more information about TRAK see www.trak.org

FIGURE 15-4   Pigeon drop con game wanted notice.

money. It turns out to be paper cut to size. The swindlers switched the bundle just before they parted from the victim.[13]

The **charity switch** is a variation of the pigeon drop used by swindlers who have a potential victim unlikely to be motivated by greed. The pitch in the charity switch is to a victim's compassion. The swindlers convince the victim (often a clergyman or nurse) to hold money ($500 to $2,500) for a sick or dying person. If the owner of the money does not recover, the victim can use the money for his or her favorite charity. However, to show good faith, the victim is asked to show financial responsibility. At this point, the routine of the pigeon drop occurs, with the swindlers taking off with all of the money.[14]

The **payoff** is a swindle in which the swindler claims to have access to information regarding fixed horse races. In its simple street bunco form, the swindler acts out the role of **tout**. Three or four bettor–victims place large bets on horses that the swindler believes will win a selected race. If one of the swindler's horses wins, the winning bettor shares the winnings with the swindler. In its more elaborate form, victims are identified by **ropers** and are put in contact with men who pose as representatives of the fixed-race conspiracy. Another man poses as the manager of the bogus horse room used in this swindle. In a carefully orchestrated scheme, the **sucker, or mark,** is allowed to win at first, but he or she loses the final large bet. In breaking away with their loot, the swindlers "cool" the victim by implying that he or she is equally guilty of violating federal or state communications laws or participating in a criminal conspiracy.[15]

Carnival bunco is street bunco in which each victim may only be "taken" for small amounts of money, but the overall profit to these swindlers is huge. Customers pay a 10- to 50-cent fee to play these games, hoping to win one or more of the better-quality prizes exhibited, but they cannot win those better prizes. Customers are encouraged to try and try again by allowing them to win minor prizes (cheap merchandise) and fast counting their scores: operators total up a customer's score above what has been achieved to convince the victim that he or she is really close to winning a better prize. Of course, the games are rigged so that these scores can never be attained. Trick balls, weighted dolls, underinflated balloons, and oversized marbles are some of the mechanical aids used to defraud gullible carnival goers.

THE BANK EXAMINER FRAUD

Bank examiner fraud is an ego-building swindle based on the hidden desire of many people to serve as a secret agent for the police. Victims are located through telephone books or pseudosurveys. The first telephone call to the victim is double-talk, alleging some problem with his or her account at the local bank. The next call is allegedly from an officer of the bank. The story told is that one of the bank's employees has been tampering with accounts of depositors, they want to catch him, and they need the victim's help to do so. Cooperative victims are then informed they should go to the bank, withdraw a specific sum (usually just short of the victim's total deposited funds), and bring it home. The victim is assured that the withdrawal will be watched secretly by an armed agent who will follow the victim home to make certain the money is safe. A few moments after arrival at home with the money, the victim is visited by the swindler posing as the armed agent. After some double-talk, the swindler counts the victim's money, gives him or her a signed deposit slip, and takes the money. Hours, days, and even weeks later, the victim finds out that the name on the deposit slip is fictitious, the bank knows nothing of any dishonest employee, and the money given to the swindler is a total loss.

FRAUDULENT CHECKS

Passers of forged checks have always concerned police forgery squads. However, it is the unusual fraudulent check writers who attempt to pass off a signature as genuine. It is true that they sign names other than their own, but this is just the first step in a fraud that also involves (1) false or stolen identification cards, (2) a story that overcomes a merchant's reluctance to cash a check upon presentation of minimal identification, and (3) a bunco or a con artist's sense of the right time, place, and victim to conclude this fraud successfully. Fortunately, the modus operandi of these check passers identifies them to investigators. Sometimes, a victim will assist in identification, but since the identification documents are spurious and the contact at the time of check cashing is short, victims have recall problems.

NSF (not sufficient funds) check writers are overt thieves, signing their name to a worthless check and cashing it. Willingness to repay the loss to the victim and an active checking account can overcome the perception of fraud. So-called "occasional" fraudulent check writers can postpone criminal prosecution on a promise of restitution. The true fraud investigation in this area focuses on the "chronic" fraudulent check writer and the extent of his or her theft when more than one NSF check has been cashed.

CREDIT CARD FRAUD

Credit card fraud is emerging as a popular form of theft. Fraudulent use of credit cards provides the thief with various goods and services, and credit cards can easily be converted into cash by sale on the street—the illegal marketplace. Thieves obtain credit cards by theft (from mail, the person to whom the card belongs, a residence, an auto, a place of business, a hotel, or other location), by fraudulent application to the issuing firm, or by counterfeiting. Credit cards stolen from the mail, intercepted en route to the legitimate receivers, are sought on the illegal market because they have not been reported as lost or stolen. If the card requires a signature, the illegal owner can sign the card in the name of the legitimate card owner and in a style he or she can readily replicate (despite disguising the handwriting).

Credit card thieves may be discovered on the complaint of merchants who call for an authorization because of the amount of a purchase and discover that the card is on the "hot card list," on the complaint of those who become suspicious because of alterations on the card itself, during legal searches, or in the course of other investigations. In one Los Angeles case, the investigation of a group forging motor vehicle driver's licenses led to several credit card thieves who bought forged licenses to show additional identification when "running a card."

CONSUMER AND BUSINESS FRAUD

Consumer and business frauds are marketplace swindles in which the buyer or investor is defrauded by the swindler's misrepresentations.[16] Common consumer frauds include these:

1. *Bait and Switch.*   In **bait and switch**, advertised merchandise bargains lure customers into a merchant's place of business. Sales personnel then run down the advertised merchandise and switch the customer to a higher-priced item of allegedly better quality.
2. *Repair Fraud.*   **Repair fraud** includes overcharging for services performed; charging for services not performed or parts not replaced; failing to provide labor and materials as agreed; and charging for labor or materials not needed or discussed with the customer, or within the scope of the customer's agreement.
3. *Misrepresentation.*   **Misrepresentation** is failing to give the true facts about product performance, warranties, credit charges, or other hidden costs.

The **Ponzi scheme, or kiting,** is the base of all investment frauds; securities frauds are get-rich-quick schemes; land frauds have a similar scheme along with the promise of a future home in a desirable climate; and advance fee swindles offer assistance in securing huge loans to poor-risk credit applicants.

In a Ponzi scheme (named after its originator) the swindler uses money invested by new victims to pay a high interest on the investments of earlier victims—whose money the swindler has appropriated to his or her own use, rather than investing it as claimed in the sales pitch given the victim. A Ponzi scheme collapses when the swindler runs out of victims.

Securities frauds are based on promises to victims of rapid capital growth and a high and quick rate of returns in dividends, as well as special advantages such as tax shelters. Victims are selected on the basis of their liquid or convertible assets. High-income professionals and persons approaching the threshold of retirement are common victims.

Land-sales frauds are based on the swindler's misrepresentations about the value and future development of worthless, unimproved land. Fraudulent land sales have involved the sale of property at inflated prices in which the swindler had no existing title or interest. Undeveloped property owned by the swindler, but without roads, water, or other improvements, is sold because of false statements of current or future development (e.g., roads, water) that does not exist and that the swindler has no intention of providing.

Advanced-fee frauds victimize businesspeople who are having problems securing loans from local banks or other lending institutions. The swindler claims to have access to loan officers or out-of-town banks or the mortgage loan officials of a labor union pension fund. The advance fee is up-front money to motivate the loan arranger (swindler) to arrange the loan. The swindler has no intention of performing as promised but will make any misrepresentation to secure the victim's money. This swindle is common in the United States because the reality of securing loans by poor-risk applicants is that up-front money has been used to influence bank loan officers and officials of union pension funds.

Home-improvement frauds victimize homeowners by false claims that the work is necessary or that the cost of the proposed work is much below its real worth and will add to the homeowner's basic equity. Gangs of home-improvement swindlers move from town to town, transferring their accounts payable to a local bank at a discount and moving to new areas. These frauds include one or more of the following characteristics:

1. Misrepresentation of the need for labor or materials
2. Poor workmanship
3. Substandard materials
4. Gross overpricing
5. Failure to provide paid-for labor and material
6. Concealment of the cost of credit, as well as the fact that failure to pay will result in a lien on the victim's home

Bankruptcy frauds involve false claims of insolvency. The planned bankruptcy or scam has been used by organized crime personnel to loot the assets of a business. In bankruptcy fraud, the swindler either conceals or diverts to friends and associates the major assets of a business so that they cannot be sold to pay off creditors or uses previously established credit to secure huge amounts of merchandise and then conceals or converts such merchandise to his or her own use just prior to the bankruptcy—and without paying the supplier's bills.

Insurance frauds are not uncommon in the world of commerce and business. They are in a class by themselves because the swindler must be the insured, and the victim is the insurer. The swindler may have crime partners, but only the insured can profit from defrauding an insurance company. The filing of false claims is the fraud. In some fraudulent fire cases, sham mortgages are used fraudulently to raise the value of a building. As a result, insurance policies are issued in amounts far in excess of the true value of the insured building. An arson investigation into a series of fires in an urban ghetto area found that the insured owner had engaged in selling to friends and business associates a number of times, with little or no cash involved in the transfer of ownership. Each time, the seller took a new second mortgage to artificially inflate the building's value.[17]

WORKPLACE FRAUD

Major frauds in the workplace are embezzlement and computer frauds. Investigations are usually initiated upon discovery of the fraud, with investigators following leads about the identity of employees having the necessary access to the funds or the computer.

Embezzlement is the conversion of another's property over which the thief has custody or control. Victims are the employers of these dishonest employees, with the scope of the theft depending on the position held by the employee and his or her ability to conceal the theft or thefts. Investigators should be alert for money losses reported as armed robberies to cover up embezzlement.

The newest fraud in the workplace involves computers and has frightening potential for victimization. The Equity Funding fraud exemplifies use of a computer as an essential tool for accomplishing a theft that totaled a $100 million loss to customers, stockholders, and others. To sustain its image as a successful insurance company, Equity Funding produced fake insurance policies, which were recorded in the computer as new business and sold for cash to reinsurance firms. In this case, the computer was also programmed to conceal the fraud: a special code was used to skip the usual premium procedures on the fake policies. At least seventy-five employees served as accomplices and participants in this crime. So-called "creative" accounting covered up this fraud for many years until a fired employee talked about it.[18]

ATM FRAUD

Thieves find automated teller machine (ATM) cards in the wallets and pocketbooks of their victims. They also find driver's licenses, sometimes checkbooks, and, often, photographs or papers with the names of family members. All this material used to be worthless; today, it has become the basis for finding the personal identification number (PIN) that validates the ATM card. ATM card holders seem to have a subliminal fear of forgetting their "secret" PIN numbers and use easily remembered numbers, such as birth date or anniversary date, a fore-and-aft series of numbers from their bank account or driver's license number, a simple 1-2-3-4 code based on their name or the names of children or grandchildren, or a transposition of a home or office telephone number.

Now in possession of the ATM card and the correct PIN number, the thief tries to get to the machine before the rightful owner of the card contacts the bank and cancels his or her card. Withdrawing whatever the cash limit is for a single transaction, thieves have hit an ATM, walked away, come back for another withdrawal, continuing until the account is empty or the card is reported stolen and the machine retains the card.

Thieves are aware of the surveillance cameras at these machines but knowingly discount any in-court identification at trial and openly scoff at the possibility of arrest. However, police and bank fraud investigators struggle with the "gotcha" problem in these cases:

1. They move fast upon a stolen card cancellation notice, study the rhythm of the withdrawals by the thief from the ATM transaction record, and, as long as funds remain in the account, wait until the thief arrives to hit the machine again.
2. When credit cards from the same source have been used successfully, they interview the salesclerks who wrote up the sales, asking for a good physical description and knowledge of the suspect. They also request the cooperation of one or two of these individuals to help produce a composite sketch.
3. When forged checks begin to appear, they interview the endorser for help in identification of the suspect.
4. They send cards and checks to the crime lab to lift latent fingerprints.

5. If they have partial identity, they seek out ex-lovers, ex-spouses, and former friends or crime partners for help in making a full identification from photos or the composite sketch. If any one of these individuals is in jail awaiting trial, the investigator may have the classic leverage to secure cooperation.

IDENTITY THEFT

The identity thief is an imposter who uses the identifiers of another person to apply for and receive credit cards under their assumed identity. These credit cards are then used to purchase merchandise and services until the theft is discovered. Identifiers are driver's licenses, motor vehicle registrations, and other proofs of identity.

Identity theft is new and is bound to increase as stolen identifiers become readily available to thieves in an area. Such proofs of identity are now being used to buy houses and open bank accounts, all under the assumed identity being used by the identity thief. Victims of this scam are expected to report their losses to the issuing credit card company. (See Appendix C: Identity Theft).

COMPUTER FRAUD

The chief executive officers (CEOs) of large corporations and the managers and owners of smaller businesses have accepted the responsibility for denying access by unauthorized persons to their computer systems. Access codes are guarded zealously to prevent hackers from entering a computer system. Ongoing sales talk from both hardware and software representatives is about "super safety" that not only blocks access but also sets up an alarm mode when attempts at unauthorized access are made—closing down any entry and promptly triggering a trace program to locate and identify the source of the attempted entry.

When someone does break into a system, the response is fast and oriented toward damage control. Computer security personnel of the victim company react to this crisis by joining forces with computer industry representatives who fear unfavorable publicity. When personnel determine who did it, how it was done, and the identity of crime partners, they will terminate with prejudice if an employee of the victim firm is guilty, and they may report to the police.

When a computer fraud is reported to police, the person reporting should be considered the victim or an identified representative of the victim (corporation, firm), and a standard crime report should be filled out with the interviewing investigator as the reporting officer. In addition to the called-for information, the narrative of this form should include (1) what was taken without permission, (2) an estimated amount of the loss, (3) how this successful attack on the victim's computer system was accomplished, and (4) background information on any person listed on the crime report as a suspect. You are likely to need legal assistance (what crime has been committed or attempted; what are its essential elements) and a computer expert (e.g., agency or contract employee) who can help in the here and now of an investigation and later testify in court as an expert witness.

Then, if the case develops well, go to the prosecutor's office and seek help in case preparation. It takes a large support group headed by a cybersleuth to build a case against clever cyber-thieves. Tsutomu Shimomura, a computational physicist and computer security expert, was a leader of a support group comprised of FBI agents, local police, and telephone experts from the network world. Their charge and mission were to identify, arrest, and assist in the prosecution of a world-class hacker who had outwitted authorities for over two years. After his arrest, both parties negotiated a deal that lowered the severe sentence likely on twenty-three counts of computer fraud and related crimes to less than a year in a county jail and gained the cooperation of this offender as a willing witness in the trials of his former crime partners, an important prosecutorial advantage.[19]

INVESTIGATION OF FRAUD

Since crime scenes are usually nonexistent in fraud cases, the investigator must concentrate on securing facts about the crime from the victim and witnesses and from the records or other documents prepared and used by one or more of the participants.

Collected evidence should be organized under the following major headings:

1. *Description of the Offense.*   How was the scheme conceived, what was its nature, where was it placed in operation, and what dates was it in operation?
2. *Victim.*   How was the initial contact made? Subsequent contacts? Where? Who was involved? Who made what representations? What was the victim's reliance on such representations? What was the extent of the loss? How was payment made to the swindlers?
3. *Suspect–Defendant.*   When available, what are the name, address, occupation, date and place of birth, physical description, associates, and criminal history of the suspect–defendant? What is the identity of the suspect–defendant who may cooperate with the investigation, possibly serving as an accomplice witness in a criminal trial?
4. *Evidence.*   What data on witnesses, victim, documentary and other physical evidence are available, and how were they obtained?
5. *Crime.*   What are the essential elements of the crime or crimes that might be charged along with (a) major misrepresentations, false pretenses, false promises used by the suspect–defendant in obtaining the victim's money and (b) presentation of evidence in support of the investigator's conclusion that such evidence supports a belief in the criminal intent of the suspect-defendant and sets out the fraud involved?

Identification should not be a major problem in fraud investigations once a suspect is located and apprehended. The pursuit and apprehension of swindlers is often handicapped by the inability of victims to properly describe the swindler and others involved. Once the swindler is apprehended, however, the victim can usually identify him or her.

The investigation of credit card frauds provides a splendid opportunity to uncover more serious crimes and to apprehend crime partners. A credit card is unusual in that the issuing firm (the theft victim in extensive frauds) will aid the investigation by tracing and reporting the activities associated with the illegal use of the credit card. As a result, investigators may secure the following:

1. Samples of handwriting in the form of signed sales drafts and applications
2. License plate numbers recorded on gasoline sales drafts at service stations
3. Driver's licenses on car rental contracts or on sales drafts for which further identification was requested
4. Credit card imprint on copies of sales drafts, airline tickets, hotel bills, or car rental contracts
5. Description of a rented motor vehicle that the subject had in his or her possession at any particular time
6. Description of merchandise on a sales slip, which could reveal the purchase of guns, knives, or items identifiable by serial numbers, as well as distinctive clothing and wigs

Decoy vehicles and appliances have opened up new horizons for proactive, as well as reactive, investigations of consumer frauds. The **decoy vehicle** or appliance is in good working order except for some minor or easily discovered and repaired fault. When the repair personnel entrusted with the decoy vehicle or appliance lie about needed repairs, or charge for repairs not done or for parts not supplied, the investigator can begin developing a fraud case.

CASE STUDY

The Year My Life Was Stolen

It started in February. I came home about midnight after an evening out with friends, only to see a sight that made my heart drop: the front door, wide open.

Someone had ransacked my house, strange hands pawing through my most private possessions. They stole jewelry, crystal, some electronics. They even took the oak nightstand from beside my bed. A nightstand!?

Then, two months after the burglary, things went from bad to horrific. It was 5:00 P.M., and I'd just gotten off work. There's a bar and restaurant on Broadway that I usually go to, and I was just pulling up on a nearby side street when it happened.

As I turned off the ignition and started to open my door, I looked up to see a man—I couldn't tell if he was African-American or Hispanic—in a knit cap blocking my way. The first thing I noticed were his eyes. They were absolutely black. Black and cruel.

I started to tell him to back off, but he stopped me cold.

"I want your f***ing car," he hissed. "If you say another f***ing word, I'm going to blow your f**ing brains out."

Then he pulled back his coat to reveal a pistol tucked in the waistband of his pants.

I got the message.

Just then, two of my friends pulled up in front of us and started walking toward me. I was thinking "No, no, no," because from the look in the guy's eyes, I think he would have blown us all away and not thought twice.

So I jumped out and ran, yelling for my friends to "Get away, get away, he's got a gun."

Was he just looking for the right victim in the right car to come along, or was he waiting especially for me? The thought sent a chill through me.

It was the worst thing that had ever happened in my life, but as I was soon to learn, my problems were just beginning. Part of it was emotional. I was scared all the time. There were the nightmares, too—the carjacker's face, with those black, evil eyes filling my dreams night after night.

But it wasn't only at night that the incident came back to haunt me. Pretty soon, stores all over town were having checks from my account returned to my bank. Someone else, using my driver's license—yeah, that was in my purse, too—was writing checks like crazy. Hardware stores. Grocery stores. Clothing stores. Auto parts stores.

I wasn't held responsible—it was the store's fault for not properly checking identification. But every time it happened, I had to deal with the store, provide them with police reports and things like that so that my credit wouldn't be affected. It was one hassle after another.

This was around Memorial Day, and by then I was getting pretty irritated by the police department, because as far as I could tell, it had done absolutely nothing. It wasn't like it didn't have any leads. There was my cellular phone bill, for example. Even though I'd canceled within a half hour of my car being stolen, the carjacker still made a few phone calls. When the bills came, those numbers were listed, but I don't know if the police ever did anything with the information.

They did find the car about three days after it was stolen. It had been abandoned alongside the road somewhere, the stereo and dashboard ripped out, the clutch blown, and the body all banged up.

It cost about $7,000 to fix, and I never drove it again. Maybe if it had been stolen from my driveway or something, it wouldn't have been a problem. But the way it was, I was just too scared to ever get back in it. I was just about to make my very last payment on it, too, and I sure wasn't looking forward to all those new monthly payments. But I just couldn't get in my old car again, so I traded it in.

Source: Mari Brendel, "The Year My Life Was Stolen," *Sacramento News & Review*, August 3, 1995. Reprinted by permission of *Sacramento News & Review*.

CHAPTER REVIEW

KEY TERMS

advanced-fee fraud   *317*

amateur burglar   *297*

auto theft   *307*

bait and switch   *317*

bank examiner fraud   *315*

bankruptcy fraud   *318*

behavior cycle in
   burglary   *299*

blasting   *300*

bunco scheme   *313*

burglarizing   *299*

burglary   *294*

burning   *300*

carjacking   *308*

carnival bunco   *315*

carrying away   *300*

charity switch   *315*

con game   *313*

continual theft   *311*

credit card fraud   *316*

decoy vehicle   *322*

dismantler   *308*

drilling   *300*

embezzlement   *318*

fence   *298*

fraud   *311*

fraud auditing   *312*

home-improvement
   fraud   *318*

household larceny   *302*

REVIEW QUESTIONS

1. Burglary is usually a/an _____ crime in that the burglar normally tries to avoid contact with victims.

2. The real success in stealing is not the commission of the crime, but the _____ of the stolen property at a profit.

3. What type of employee theft occurs when the employee takes items home, such as pens or tools?
   a. Situational theft
   b. Incidental theft
   c. Continual theft
   d. Grand theft

4. What type of employee theft occurs when the employee is presented with an opportunity for theft that in the employee's mind must be acted upon?
   a. Situational theft
   b. Incidental theft
   c. Continual theft
   d. Grand theft

5. What type of employee theft is usually motivated by the need to support a vice such as gambling, drugs, or alcohol?
   a. Situational theft
   b. Incidental theft
   c. Continual theft
   d. Grand theft

6. In what type of fraud does the swindler use money invested by new victims to pay high interest rates on the investments of earlier victims?
   a. Bait and switch
   b. Ponzi scheme
   c. Securities fraud
   d. Embezzlement

7. In what type of fraud is advertised merchandise used to lure customers into the place of business where sales personnel then bad-mouth the advertised merchandise and sell higher-priced merchandise to the customer?
   a. Bait and switch
   b. Ponzi scheme
   c. Securities fraud
   d. Embezzlement

8. In what type of fraud are victims promised rapid capital growth, a high and quick rate of return on dividends, or special advantages such as tax shelters on their investments?
   a. Bait and switch
   b. Ponzi scheme
   c. Securities fraud
   d. Embezzlement

9. What type of theft involves the conversion of another person's property over which the thief has custody or control and victimizes employers of dishonest employees?
   a. Bait and switch
   b. Ponzi scheme

c. Securities fraud
d. Embezzlement

10. The intermediaries of larceny, the people who buy and sell stolen property regularly, are known as_____.

See Appendix D for the correct answers.

DISCUSSION QUESTIONS

1. What skills or technology should be taken into account in classifying burglars?
2. What are the characteristics of semiskilled burglars?
3. List and describe five means of entry common to burglars.
4. Describe the behavior cycle in burglaries.
5. List and describe five means of entry used by burglars to open and enter safes.
6. Why does motive offer very little promise as a basic lead in thefts?
7. Why do the proceeds of thefts offer substantial promise as a basic lead?
8. Because a study of modus operandi and a search of police modus operandi files cannot be used in the same manner in thefts as in investigations of crimes of violence, cite the potential of such study and search in this area.
9. Explain the "Achilles heel" of stealing and the bland acceptance of this occupational hazard by thieves.
10. What circumstances may induce a receiver of stolen property to reveal the true circumstances of its purchase?
11. What are the advantages of a storefront or sting program to recover stolen property? The disadvantages?
12. What is a chop shop?
13. What are the four elements of fraud?
14. Describe the bank examiner fraud.
15. Describe two consumer frauds and five business frauds.
16. Define embezzlement.
17. What are decoy vehicles? Appliances?
18. In the case study, cite the modus operandi of each theft or loss and the most likely suspects.
19. Consider the victim's feelings in the case study and focus on the police response.

RELATED WEB SITES

For charts and tables about burglary trends in the United States see *www.ojp.usdoj.gov/bjs/ glance/burg.htm*.

For information about mail fraud, mail theft, identity theft and about becoming a U.S. Postal Inspector contact the Postal Inspection Service Web site. *postalinspectors.uspis.gov*.

To learn more about Internet fraud, such as charity scams, online auctions, and pyramid and other schemes, check out this Web site: *www.fraud.org/internet/intinfo.htm*.

chapter **sixteen**

Dangerous Drugs

CHAPTER OUTLINE

After reading this chapter you will be able to:

- Describe the major kinds of dangerous drugs and the effects these drugs have on the user.
- Identify the organizations responsible for the manufacture or importation of dangerous drugs into the United States.
- Explain how an arrest based upon the purchase of dangerous drugs is conducted to withstand legal challenge.
- Recognize those circumstances in dangerous drug investigations for which a search without a warrant would be appropriate.
- Define the major defense of entrapment as it would apply in cases involving the sale of controlled substances.

T he possession of dangerous and restricted drugs or narcotics is prohibited. Exceptions are made when such dangerous drugs or narcotics are possessed through a lawful medical prescription. Previous conviction of one or more offenses related to possession of dangerous drugs or narcotics generally adds to the basic penalty imposed upon conviction. Many jurisdictions specify that a convicted offender may not be eligible for release on parole or on any other basis until he or she has served a stated minimum number of years in prison. The basic law prohibits the unlawful possession of drugs and narcotics, transporting, importing, selling, furnishing, administering, or giving away of a dangerous drug or narcotic.

The word *possession,* in statutes forbidding the possession of drugs and narcotics, means an immediate and exclusive possession under dominion and control with intent to exercise control.[1] Persons having such control must have knowledge of the presence of drugs or narcotics, and such knowledge must precede the intent to exercise, or the exercise of, such control. Knowledge is a basic element of crimes related to illegal drugs and narcotics. This also means that a knowledge of the character of the substance is essential to the offense of possession of narcotics.

In a prosecution for possession of dangerous drugs and narcotics, the burden is on the prosecution to prove knowledge of the presence of the drugs or narcotics. The prosecution must also show that a defendant charged with possession of illegal drugs and narcotics knew that the objects in his or her possession were drugs and narcotics. However, the burden of proof may be satisfied by facts that infer such knowledge (circumstantial evidence).

The events leading up to a suspect's arrest should show a state of facts amply sufficient to constitute reasonable cause for arrest (Figure 16–1). Reasonable and probable cause for an arrest without warrant, on justified belief that a suspect has committed a violation of illegal drugs and narcotics laws, can be based on an officer's past experience, knowledge of the suspect, and observation of suspicious and furtive conduct.

The following instances are illustrative of evidence sufficient to arrest:

1. Investigators knew of a suspect's previous arrest and conviction for possession of narcotics; learned from the manager of suspect's apartment building that a good deal of suspicious traffic had been going in and out of suspect's apartment; and overheard occupants' references to funnels used in preparation of narcotics and balloons commonly used as containers for narcotics. The officers had reasonable cause for belief that occupants were committing a felony, and an arrest without warrant was proper.

2. In a prosecution for possession of heroin, the evidence indicated that the arresting officer had known the informant for approximately one year, that the informant had given information of a detailed nature and a complete description of the defendant and his or her modus operandi, and that such information had been independently verified in substantial part. This was reasonable cause to arrest the defendant without warrant.

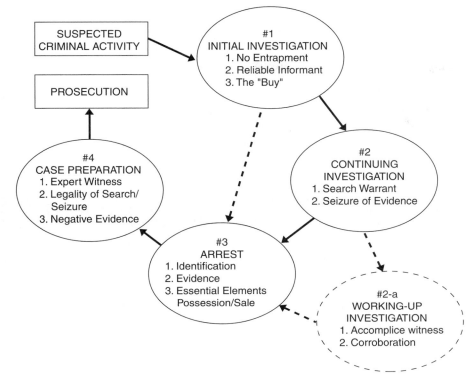

FIGURE 16–1   Investigation of illegal drugs and narcotics.

The fact that a person is a drug addict, a "user" of drugs, does not justify arresting him or her. In *Robinson v. California,* the U.S. Supreme Court ruled that drug addiction is an illness, drug addicts are sick people, and their capacity to form the necessary criminal intent is diminished.[2] Before this case, California had a law that allowed police to arrest drug addicts just for being addicted—for a condition rather than commission of an act. In *Robinson*, the Court ruled the California law to be unconstitutional.

ENTRAPMENT

Any conviction for the possession (or sale or transport) of illegal drugs should be for a wrongful act voluntarily committed and not for an act induced by the investigator or his or her "special employee," which would not have occurred without such urging. It is not simple to determine whether, in a particular case, facts suggest the unlawful **entrapment** of an individual who might otherwise have gone through life without an arrest.

For instance, one defendant charged with the possession for sale of narcotics was not a user.[3] No evidence indicated that he was regularly engaged in the traffic of narcotics, and he did not have previous arrests of any kind. The sale of illegal narcotics, which was admitted, was consummated only after constant urging by a federal agent over a period of three months.

To avoid a defense claim of entrapment, no more pressure or persuasion can be exerted than that ordinarily occurring between willing buyer and willing seller. However, a defense of entrapment is not available to persons charged with possession of heroin when a suspect suggested to the police investigator that he could obtain illegal drugs or narcotics, and where no persuasion or allurement had been used by the officer who had merely furnished an opportunity for the suspect to acquire illegal drugs or narcotics to sell to the undercover investigator.[4] It is not the purpose of the law to prevent the unwary criminal from being trapped in a crime; it is instead the purpose of the law to prevent the police officer from manufacturing crime—that is, from seducing the unwary, innocent person into a career of crime.

THE DRUG SCENE

Numerous restricted drugs and narcotics, from marijuana to heroin, are being used by millions of people. The most common drugs that can lead to drug dependence or addiction fall into four major groups:

1. *Narcotics.*   **Narcotics** are drugs that depress the central nervous system. They usually lead quickly to both psychological and physical dependence.
2. *Sedatives.*   Like narcotics, **sedatives** cause both psychological and physical dependence, but the dependence develops more slowly. They are also central nervous system depressants.
3. *Stimulants.*   Amphetamines and methamphetamines are **stimulants**. These drugs cause a rapid buildup of tolerance so that additional quantities are needed to achieve the same stimulating effects. Stimulant use quickly leads to psychological dependence.
4. *Hallucinogens.*   **Hallucinogens** cause sensory distortions and result in illusions and delusions. They are the psychedelic, or "mind-expanding," drugs.

Eight types of drugs are commonly encountered on the "drug scene." Each is described next.

HEROIN

Heroin is derived from a morphine base to produce diacetylmorphine (the chemical name for heroin), which, when blended with hydrochloric acid, forms into a salt (heroin hydrochloride) that is easily soluble in water. It usually consists of crystals so small as to resemble powdered sugar or flour. Heroin ranges in color from white to ivory, through dull or brownish gray, to tan or brown. Heroin is usually administered intravenously. Narcotics have four main characteristics: First, they kill pain—that is, they have an **analgesic** effect. Second, they are **soporific agents**, which means they induce drowsiness, lethargy, and sleep. Third, used with time, they produce physical and psychological dependency, and, fourth, they generate a sense of **euphoria**—a feeling of well-being and tranquility.

COCAINE

Cocaine is a stimulant, usually derived from the leaves of the South American coca bush, and sometimes from bushes grown in the West Indies, Java, India, and Ceylon. The alkaloid is extracted from the leaves and treated with hydrochloric acid to form cocaine hydrochloride, a salt easily soluble in water. It is encountered as fine, fluffy white crystalline powder, and (depending on the degree of refinement) may resemble snowflakes, camphor, sugar, or Epsom salts. It is sometimes found in tablet form. Cocaine produces feelings of exhilaration and euphoria, and it increases the user's energy level and suppresses fatigue. Cocaine is usually administered by snorting through the nose and produces a psychological dependency. Cocaine is also smoked in two forms.

1. *Freebase.*   When cocaine is freebased, it is dissolved in ether and then heated to boil off the impurities. What remains is a pure form of cocaine which is then ground up and smoked. Because smoking is a more effective means of administration the user feels a more intense "rush," which often leads to heavy chronic use.
2. *Crack.*   Also known as **hubba** or **rock, crack** is made by soaking cocaine in baking soda and water. The mixture then heated until the water is driven off. During the heating process, the mixture makes a crackling sound, hence the name. The resulting crystals—or pea-sized "rocks"—are crushed, heated, and smoked in a crack pipe. This smokable form of cocaine gives the user a "rush" that lasts as long as two minutes, followed by an afterglow the lasts ten to twenty minutes.

MARIJUANA

Marijuana, or **pot**, consists of the leaves and flowering tops of the female hemp plant (*Cannabis sativa, C. indica*) cultivated in many temperate zones of the world. Crude marijuana contains parts of the leaves, tops, stems, and seeds (fruit) of the plant; "manicured" marijuana consists of smaller particles of the leaves and tops, from which almost all the stems and seeds have been removed. Fresh marijuana is dark green and turns brown with age and exposure. It may be packaged in tobacco tins, cellophane, paper bags, tissue paper, or cigarettes. Bricks of crude marijuana are about three inches by five inches by ten inches and weigh about two pounds. The psychoactive agent in marijuana is delta-9-tetrahydrocannabinal, or **THC**. Wild, or uncultivated, marijuana may have a 1 percent THC level. Proper cultivation will raise the THC level to 3 percent. Marijuana grown in Colombia or Hawaii may have a THC level between 4 to 6 percent. Sinsemilla, a hybrid without seeds, may have an 8 to 14 percent THC content. Two derivatives of marijuana are hashish and hash oil:

1. *Hashish.*   The resin of the marijuana flower is dried and compressed to make hashish, which has a THC level of 8 to 14 percent.
2. *Hash oil.*   Amber to dark brown, hash oil is produced by boiling hashish in alcohol. It is sold as a viscous liquid with a THC level between 15 and 50 percent.

A "Bong" used to smoke marijuana. What does the number 420 represent?

AMPHETAMINE AND METHAMPHETAMINE

Amphetamine and methamphetamine are synthetic substances usually produced in clandestine labs. The most common form of these substances is **methamphetamine**, also known as **speed, crank**, and **meth**. It has the same effects as cocaine and is often referred to as **poor man's cocaine**. Injected meth usually produces a "flash" or "rush" and is taken every four to eight hours, which leads to a "run"—a period of wakefulness lasting two to five days followed by a long period of sleep. A chronic user is known as a **tweaker**.

PHENCYCLIDINE

Phencyclidine has the street names **angel dust, dust,** and **PCP**. It was originally developed as a general anesthetic for surgical procedures. However, its use for this purpose was abandoned because of the ability of the drug to produce hallucinogenic side effects. For a while, it was used in veterinary medicine to tranquilize large animals but was removed from the market in 1978 and is now made in clandestine labs. PCP is a white, crystalline powder that readily dissolves in water. It is commonly applied to tobacco or marijuana cigarettes and smoked. In the right dose, PCP will produce hallucinations and in some users will evoke violent suicidal impulses. Because of the anesthetic

Methamphetamine concealed in these statues was smuggled into this country. From Robert Pennal, Special Agent Supervisior, California Department of Justice, Bureau of Narcotic Enforcement.

effect of his drug, the user may display a total disregard for personal safety coupled with a lack of sensation.

LYSERGIC ACID DIETHYLAMIDE (LSD)

LSD is a semisynthetic drug derived from a fungus that contaminates rye bread. Although LSD was first synthesized in 1938, its psychoactive properties were not discovered until 1943. LSD is usually swallowed in the form of impregnated paper, tablets, or thin squares of gelatin. A dose equal to a few grains of salt can produce hallucinations lasting ten to twelve hours. The drug is ambivalent, in that the users experience both good and bad sensations.

ECSTASY

Ecstasy is methylenedioxymethamphetamine (MDMA). First developed in 1912 as an appetite suppressant, it is a stimulant like meth and a hallucinogenic similar to LSD. It produces a warm, fuzzy sense of well-being and the manic energy to dance all night. Most of the drug is produced in Europe, although it can be made in clandestine U.S. labs. It is usually consumed at "raves," where the user spends the night dancing to music.

This clandestine methamphetamine lab was found in the kitchen of this suspect's home. From Robert Pennal, Special Agent Supervisor, California Department of Justice, Bureau of Narcotic Enforcement.

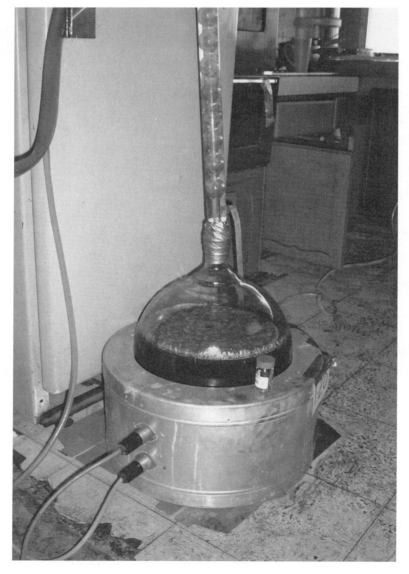

ROHYPNOL

A sleeping pill not licensed in the United States, **Rohypnol** is legal in Europe, South America, and Asia. It is also known as **roofies**. In the United States, the drug is most frequently used with alcohol—the synergistic effect produces disinhibition and amnesia. Because of these effects, Rohypnol is known as the **date rape drug**.

DRUG-SELLING ORGANIZATIONS

Knowledge of the organizational setup of criminals engaged in selling illicit drugs is important to investigators working on the drug scene. The traditional sales–marketing pyramid of manufacturer, importer (source of supply),

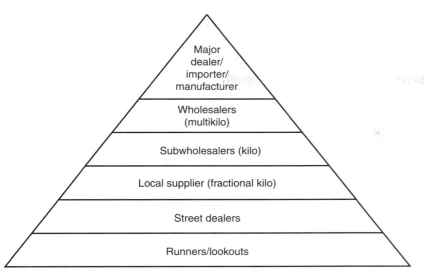

FIGURE 16–2   The marketing pyramid—illegal drugs and narcotics.

distributors, wholesalers and jobbers, and retailers (peddling mobs, or "pushers") has not changed a great deal in the last quarter century.[5] "The boss" is still at the top of the pyramid, whether he or she is a major dealer or importer, or both. Today a few more levels can be found in the distribution network, generally based on the volume of sales (multikilo, kilo, fractional kilo). The formerly lowest level—street dealers—has been augmented by lookouts and runners. **Lookouts** inform about any police presence. **Runners** transport small quantities of drugs from the **stash** of the dealer to wherever the drugs are being sold (Figure 16–2).

Twenty-five years ago, most of these sales–marketing pyramids were headed by the leaders of Italian crime "families" or their "underbosses," and importation of drugs into the United States was mainly in the hands of Europeans (French, Corsicans, Italians). Today criminal organizations have expanded, and importation routes originate in South America, Central America, and Mexico. Cocaine and its derivative crack are immensely popular in the United States, and both are readily sold at high profits. In addition, the pyramid networks have become more sophisticated in their sales–marketing and in avoiding police interference with their daily sales. Currently, the following are the known criminal organizations engaged in major dealings in illicit drugs:

- Mafia (La Cosa Nostra) crime families
- Colombians
- Jamaican ("posses")
- Asian (Chinese, Vietnamese, Korean)
- Motorcycle gangs
- Prison gangs
- Street gangs (Crips, Bloods)

Both the Mafia and Colombians are generally organized along "family" lines, with roles in the sales–marketing pyramid resulting from recommendations from internal sources. The Jamaican "posses" are sophisticated crime mobs dealing primarily in crack in major U.S. cities. Personnel are recruited from Jamaica and other countries in the Caribbean basin. They are a hardball organization characterized by ruthless and extensive violence.[6]

Asian criminal organizations have kept a low profile. Not much is known about the extent of their operations, but a great deal is suspected. Because they operate in their own ethnic neighborhoods, investigators have had little success in developing informants or making buys. Youth gangs are often the source of personnel for these networks.

Motorcycle gangs have been involved in general misbehavior and traffic in firearms for some time. In recent years, they have developed tightly organized drug-selling networks.[7] These are nationwide groups with major dealers in most of the large urban centers. They are disciplined groups, with murder a common form of punishment for violations of gang rules.

Prison gangs originated in prisons and sold drugs to inmates. Released members of these gangs were soon employed as street dealers in illicit drugs. In the U.S. Southwest, the Mexican Mafia is a major prison gang selling drugs both inside and outside prison walls. Various prison gangs (neo-Nazis, Aryan Brotherhood, and others.) operate in other areas of the United States.

Street gangs are a new addition to the drug-selling field. They do not usually buy as a gang but rather as individual members or small groups of gang members. They do sell drugs ("sling dope"), but their manner of purchasing drugs and selling them usually reflects the loose organizational structure of these street gangs.[8]

All these drug-selling gangs commit murder as a business technique to (1) eliminate competition, (2) protect their territory from the competition of rival gangs, (3) discipline suspected informants, and (4) protect their cash and illicit drugs from rip-offs by armed robbers.

DRUG INVESTIGATIONS

PICKUP ARRESTS

In warrantless arrests for the possession of dangerous drugs or narcotics or both, the investigator must act within the legal image of a "reasonable person." The test is this: Would the facts from which the arresting officer acted warrant a person of reasonable caution to believe that a crime was committed? The court usually takes into consideration police expertise from training or experience in determining whether the arrest was reasonable. An important case in this area of pickup arrests is *Draper v. United States*.[9] In Draper, a federal narcotic agent of considerable experience (Marsh) had been informed by a special employee (Hereford), an informant, who had always been found to be accurate and reliable, that Draper was peddling narcotics and that he had gone to Chicago and would return by train with three ounces of heroin on the morning of September 8 or 9. The informant gave a physical description of Draper and said that he would be carrying a "tan zipper bag" and that he habitually "walked real fast."

The agent kept the incoming trains from Chicago under surveillance, and on the morning of September 9 observed a person fitting the description given by the informant walking "fast" toward an exit and carrying a tan zipper bag. This person was Draper, and he was arrested by the officer.

The information about Draper given to narcotics agent Marsh by "special employee" Hereford may have been hearsay to Marsh, but coming from one employed for that purpose and whose information had always been found accurate and reliable, it is clear that Marsh would have been derelict in his duties had he not pursued it. And when, in pursuing that information, he saw a man—having the exact physical attributes, and wearing the precise clothing, and carrying the tan zipper bag that Hereford had described—alight from one of the very trains from the very place stated by Hereford and start to walk away at a "fast" pace toward the station, Marsh had personally verified every facet of the information given him by Hereford except whether the petitioner had accomplished his mission and had the three ounces of heroin on his person or in his bag. Surely, with every other bit of Hereford's information being thus personally verified, Marsh had "reasonable grounds" to believe that the remaining unverified bit of Hereford's information—that Draper would have heroin with him—was likewise true.

In some instances, officers discover contraband in the form of illegal drugs or narcotics in searches incidental to an arrest or in the normal course of executing a search warrant. In such cases, the legality of the basic arrest and search or the search under the authority of a warrant must be demonstrated and supported by evidence before the illegal drugs or narcotics case can be developed for prosecution.

ARRESTS BASED ON "BUYS"

The investigation of cases involving the possession or sale of dangerous drugs or narcotics usually is developed by one or more "buys" of these illegal substances. An undercover police investigator (sworn officer) or an informant (special employee) buys a quantity of dangerous drugs or narcotics from a suspect; the transaction often is witnessed by officers conducting a surveillance of the undercover agent or special employee and of the suspect. The integrity of the informant's buy is preserved by a pre-transaction and post-transaction search of the informant; compelling evidence often is secured by prior registration by the investigators of the serial numbers of the money used for the "buy." The substance purchased is marked for identification and transported to a local police (or state) narcotics laboratory for examination and identification and is retained as evidence of the sale of drugs or a narcotic substance to the informant or employee.

The informant, under supervision, sets up the "buy." The suspect may be identified by police and the informant asked to develop a case, or the informant may identify to the police a suspect known to him or her as a drug seller. After the "buy," the informant details the circumstances of the transaction to his or her police associates, turns over the substance purchased, and returns any unused money advanced for the "buy."

The usual procedure in making a "buy" is as follows:

1. The informant is advised to avoid any taint of entrapment.
2. The informant, under police supervision, makes contact with the subject and arranges the "buy."
3. The police arrange a surveillance of the informant and possibly of the suspect.
4. The police search the informant to make certain that he or she is not carrying any drugs or any substantial amount of money. They also provide the informant with "state" money (serial numbers recorded) for the "buy."
5. The police maintain contact with the informant to the scene of the transaction.
6. The police watch the transaction as closely as possible.
7. When the informant returns to his or her police associates, he or she informs them of the transaction, turns over the purchase and any unspent funds, and is again searched (to allow police investigators to testify that the informant had none of the funds given him or her or any other drugs).
8. The purchased substance is marked as evidence and transported to a laboratory.
9. A laboratory analysis is sought to confirm the illegal nature of the substance as drugs or narcotics, the type of drug, and the amount.
10. The case is prepared for (a) an arrest warrant, (b) an arrest (with or without warrant) on subsequent "buy," and (c) an application for a search warrant.

When an undercover police agent participates in a "buy," he or she conceals his or her identity as a police officer. A crewcut police recruit can become in a few weeks a long-haired participant in the search for drug sellers. The ability to act out his or her new identity without revealing police employment ensures continuation in this undercover role until the officer must reveal his or her identity as the investigation is terminated.

Successful undercover police operations in the drug scene usually require that an informant introduce and vouch for the undercover agent. The undercover agent's identity is revealed only when the agent has developed cases against a number of sellers of narcotics and the department decides to make all the appropriate arrests simultaneously.

SEARCH WARRANTS

A "buy" is a normal prelude to an application for a search warrant in illegal drug and narcotics cases. The purpose of the search warrant is to gain judicial authorization to enter a place in which the suspect from whom the "buy" was made has his or her stash of drugs, to seize these drugs, and to arrest the suspect.

The past criminal record of a suspected person, his or her association with known narcotics users, and the fact that another person (usually the informant) was found to be in possession of a narcotic after leaving the premises of a suspected drug seller may be taken into account in determining whether probable cause exists for issuance of a search warrant (Figure 16–3).

In many instances, the report of an informant in relation to his or her purchase of drugs will identify a specific room, or portion of a room, from which the drug seller procured the drugs. This allows the application for the search warrant to contain the necessary particulars about the place or places to be searched.

To be constitutionally sufficient, an affidavit (accompanying an application for a search warrant) based solely on an unnamed informant's tip must set forth some underlying circumstances that reveal the source of the informant's information pertaining to the criminal activity, and it must present sufficient objective evidence to enable the magistrate to conclude that the unnamed informant is credible or that his or her information is reliable.[10] The report of the chemist examining the substance purchased can be used to establish the fact that before the transaction or transactions ("buys") the suspect had possessed illegal drugs or narcotics.

Unlike an application for search warrants in burglary and theft cases where specific articles of stolen property must be identified in the application, drugs may be described in general terms as contraband and by common names. Although returns to the issuing magistrate must contain a specific inventory of the drugs and narcotics seized under the authority of the search warrant, the drugs or narcotics seized do not need to "match" the drugs or narcotics in the application for the warrant.

An outline of the usual procedure in this major type of investigation follows:

1. The case against the suspect is developed by one or more "buys" and information from a reliable informant.
2. The investigator makes observations supporting the transactions and information as evidence of the suspect's criminal behavior and is prepared to show the reliability of the informant.
3. Application is made to the magistrate for a search warrant, naming the suspect and the place or places to be searched, and citing dangerous drugs or narcotics, or both, as the object of the search.
4. A warrant is executed, the suspect is arrested, and the "return" is made to the magistrate.
5. The substances are seized and analyzed, and the fact that the substances are illegal drugs or narcotics, or both, is revealed and reported to the magistrate in a supplementary "return."
6. The case is prepared against the arrestee for presentation to the prosecutor.

In the investigation of a major drug seller, the "buy" is the preliminary investigation. With this transaction, and any subsequent "buys," accumulating evidence is likely to support an application for a search warrant. In preparing and executing the search warrant, investigators are conducting a continuing investigation that will identify the drug seller as the person in possession of a quantity of drugs or narcotics.

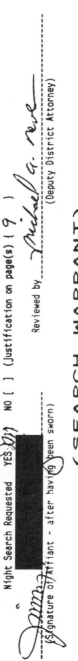

STATE OF CALIFORNIA - COUNTY OF SACRAMENTO

SEARCH WARRANT AND AFFIDAVIT
(AFFIDAVIT)

No. ___

JIMMY ███, being sworn, says that on the basis of the information contained within this Search Warrant and Affidavit and the attached and incorporated Statement of Probable Cause, comprising a total of __14__ pages, he/she has probable cause to believe and does believe that the property described below is lawfully seizable pursuant to Penal Code Section 1524, as indicated below, and is now located at the location(s) set forth below. Wherefore, affiant requests that this Search Warrant be issued.

Night Search Requested YES ❌ NO [ ] (Justification on page(s) (9))

_____
(Signature of Affiant - after having been sworn)

Reviewed by ___Michael A. Neve___
(Deputy District Attorney)

(SEARCH WARRANT)

THE PEOPLE OF THE STATE OF CALIFORNIA TO ANY SHERIFF, POLICEMAN OR PEACE OFFICER IN THE COUNTY OF SACRAMENTO:

proof by affidavit having been made before me by JIMMY ███, that there is probable cause to believe that the property described herein may be found at the locations set forth herein and that it is lawfully seizable pursuant to Penal Code Section 1524 as indicated below by "x" (s) in that it:

------ was stolen or embezzled

--X--- was used as the means of committing a felony

--X--- is possessed by a person with the intent to use it as means of committing a public offense or is possessed by another to whom he or she may have delivered it for the purpose of concealing it or preventing its discovery.

--X--- tends to show that a felony has been committed or that a particular person has committed a felony.

YOU ARE THEREFORE COMMANDED TO SEARCH:

███ Arcade Boulevard located in the City and County of Sacramento. It is a single story, single family residence, beige in color with brown trim and a brown composition roof. The numbers ███ are affixed to the front of the residence and are visible from the street. The single car attached garage is to the right (west) of the residence and the house is on the south side of Arcade Boulevard, between Colfax Street and Edgewater Road. Also to include all attics, basements, rooms, garages, outbuildings, storage sheds, inoperative vehicles, garbage cans and containers located with in the property boundaries.

FOR THE PERSON(S) OF:

███, Dennis Michael aka Dennis Michael ███, DOB: 10-4-54.

340

FOR THE FOLLOWING VEHICLE(S):

A white with blue trim motor home, California license ▆▆▆ and also request authorization to search the 1978 Datsun Pickup, California license ▆▆▆ registered to ▆▆▆

FOR THE FOLLOWING PROPERTY:

Methamphetamine and paraphernalia associated with its use, sales, transportation and manufacture, including: measuring and weighing devices, milk sugar, baggies, paper bindles, funnels, syringes, bent spoons, chemical formulas, phenylacetic acid, phenyl-2-propanone, methylamine, benzyl chloride, acetaldehyde, formamide, ephedrine, ether, acetone, lye, mercuric chloride, magnesium filings, sulfuric and hydrochloric acid, sodium acetate, chloroform, methanol, ethanol, red phosphorus, palladium black, and acetic anhydride, funnels, flasks, distillation flasks, various types of heaters and heating mantles, hot plates, various types of crystallizing dishes, desiccators, distilling apparatuses, extractors, vacuum dryers, beakers, jars, condensers, graduated cylinders, vacuum pumps, shakers and stirrers, thermometers, transformers, ovens, regulators, glass tubing, hoses, scales, filter papers, PH papers, plastic containers, gloves, masks, fans, air conditioners, generators, bills, receipts, ledgers, maps, charts, buyers lists, seller lists and recordation of sales, personal telephone books, address books, telephone bills, papers and documents containing lists of names, addresses and phone numbers, utility company receipts, rent receipts, addressed envelopes, keys and photographs. Searching officers are directed to answer the phone and converse with callers who appear to be calling in regard to drug/narcotic sales and note and record the conversation without revealing their true identity. They are also directed to note and record phone numbers or other messages received on telephonic pagers for the purpose of calling those persons paging the suspect(s) to determine if the page was regarding an intended purchase or delivery of drugs/narcotics.

AND TO SEIZE IT IF FOUND and bring it forthwith before me, or this court, at the courthouse of this court. This Search Warrant and Incorporated Affidavit was sworn to and subscribed before me this ___5___ day of ___January___, 19_89_, at _____ A.M./P.M. Wherefore, I find probable cause for the issuance of this Search Warrant and do issue it.

Night Search Approved YES [✗] NO [_____]
(Magistrates' initials)

_____
(Signature of Magistrate)

Judge of the Superior Court [✗] Municipal Court-Sacramento Judicial District [ ].

Date ___1-5-89___ Hr. ___10:45 P.M.___

Executed by ▆▆▆

FIGURE 16–3 Search warrant issued by a California court in an illegal drug case. The request for this warrant totaled fourteen pages. Magistrates are aware of their responsibility for this prior approval of police action and scan these requests with great care. If they do not understand it or believe it is inaccurate, they will deny the request.

WARRANTLESS SEARCHES

Reasonableness is the constitutional test of any warrantless search. Exigent circumstances are often present in drug cases. Drug possession for the purpose of sale is an ongoing crime; drug sellers do not suspend their activity while police do the necessary paperwork involved with obtaining a search warrant. Evidence that might be sufficient to convict them may be destroyed if police do not take prompt action.

An example of this reasonableness is a case in which a police officer observed a crime in progress inside a building (narcotics "cutting" and packaging operation—a "factory") and contraband (drugs) in plain view.[11] An appellate court ruled that the police were fully authorized under these circumstances to enter the premises, make arrests, and seek contraband. The police officer in this case, acting on an anonymous tip, went to a certain address, looked through a basement window, and saw the major narcotics-packaging operation in progress. He then sought the aid of other police officers. With this additional help, the officer subsequently (within thirty to forty minutes) entered and searched the premises without a warrant. Searching officers found the "cutting" mirror (used for mixing the illegal drugs with cheaper adulterants) on a table, along with plastic bags and measuring spoons and pans. Nearby, the officers found a large quantity of narcotics packaged for distribution. Four persons found on the premises were arrested.

WORKING-UP INVESTIGATIONS

Working up the drug-selling marketing pyramid necessitates both buy-and-bust arrests and arrests and seizures under the authority of a search warrant. An arrest is first made at the sales level of the pyramid (Figure 16–2), the street seller of illicit drugs. Then the supplier of this dealer is arrested, and onward and upward until a major supplier or importer is arrested.

Informants in these **working-up investigations** are arrestees who have agreed to cooperate in revealing their suppliers in return for leniency in drafting the indictment or at the time of sentencing. This is often termed **working off a beef**. However, investigators must be cautious in these cases because many arrestees make a deal with the arresting officer (and prosecutor) but have no intention of informing on their true source of supply. They engage in **lateral snitching**, informing only on drug sellers who are equal or lower than themselves in the drug-marketing pyramid. In this fashion, an arrestee manipulates an investigator, informing primarily on his or her competition.[12]

Lengthy investigations probing upward in a drug-marketing network can develop a case against a manufacturer, a major dealer, or an importer. To be successful, such investigations require (1) a criminal associate of the "targeted" major manufacturer, dealer, or importer and (2) evidence corroborating the expected testimony of the accomplice witness.

Arrestees situated above the street-dealer level in a drug-marketing pyramid are more difficult to "turn" than are lesser network members. When a man or woman close to a major manufacturer, dealer, or importer is arrested, the "boss" commonly provides legal counsel, bail, and other assistance pending trial.

In addition, the past-performance record of informants being murdered while in prison or out on bail is an ongoing deterrent to cooperating with the police. As a result, an investigator needs a strong case against an arrestee to entertain any hope of turning him or her into an accomplice witness.[13] When an accomplice witness can provide data as to the date and time of a future delivery of drugs, an arrest and seizure based on this information and involving the major dealer or importer are most compelling evidence. Usually, corroboration results from an investigator collecting bits and pieces of information from techniques such as the following:

- Physical and electronic surveillance
- Tally analysis of telephone records of outgoing calls from a "suspect" telephone
- A survey of car rental contracts, credit card purchases, hotel and motel registrations, and major cash purchases
- Tracing "laundered" cash

Corroborating the expected testimony of an accomplice witness against a major manufacturer, dealer, or importer is more or less a "paper chase." Ideally, the observations made by investigators of the activities of the suspect will reveal the linkage between others in the drug-marketing network. The observations are supported by these persons contacting the suspect from time to time by telephone. Renting cars, registering in hotels, and buying items—from gasoline to mansions—tend to place the suspect in various locations on specific dates. Finally, money can be traced. The Bank Records and Foreign Transactions Act requires bank officials to report deposits and withdrawals over $10,000. It is difficult to conceal millions of dollars in drug-selling profits.

It is a long and difficult investigation when a major manufacturer, dealer, or importer is targeted for arrest and prosecution. Suspected informants are immediately murdered, both to negate their services to police and to build up a long-time creed of organized crime: "Death to the informer." Confidential police files and operations are compromised by bribery of public employees in order to learn what evidence the police have to date and the scope of their existing plans.[14]

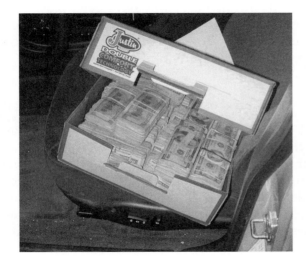

The drug trade is all about money, lots of money. From Robert Pennal, Special Agent Supervisor, California Department of Justice, Bureau of Narcotic Enforcement.

RAIDS

A **raid** in drug-law enforcement is an entry into a building for the purpose of seizing illicit drugs and arresting one or more drug dealers and associates. Entry may be gained by subterfuge (a tale to gain entry without force) or by the use of force (sledge hammer, battering ram, kicking).

Commonly, raids are no longer the combined effort of several investigators. They are now a major action of the investigating unit with a superior officer designated as the overall commanding officer. Most departments now require all members of a raiding party to wear bulletproof vests. In fact, the expectation of a shoot-out during a raid is today integrated with raid planning. Special weapons teams are frequently assigned to back up the investigators, particularly when the place to be raided is a "rock house" from which crack is sold—such premises are heavily armored, and automatic weapons fire from the premises being raided is more than a possibility.

A great deal of responsibility rests with the leadership of a raid on the drug scene. Fears are of "hitting the wrong door," of having a member of the raiding party injured or killed, of failing to identify the major suspect among the occupants, of not finding any drugs at all (or only a small amount), and of not finding the **trap**—a built-in hiding place usually constructed by a skilled carpenter—containing the major stash.

Legally, the authority for a raid is a search warrant authorizing police officers to enter a specific premises to seize illicit drugs believed to be in the described premises. These warrants or local laws will provide for a "no-knock" entry. In past years, the notice-and-demand factor slowed up raiding parties to such an extent that drug sellers and associates had time to get rid of the incriminating evidence, usually flushing the illicit drugs down the toilet. Today, aware jurists and legislators have recognized the need of police for speedy entry.

Armoring the place from which drugs are sold is the drug seller's response to the capability of police to gain speedy entry and to seize drugs before they can be destroyed. Sheet-steel panels are screwed or bolted to entry doors, and windows are covered with steel panels and heavy iron gratings. Drug sellers claim that this armoring is necessary to protect them from rip-offs, but it has a valuable side action in preventing speedy entry by police.

Once entry is made and the occupants have been placed under control (and disarmed, if carrying weapons), the commanding officer of the raiding party supervises a methodical search for illicit drugs and weapons and oversees a thorough scanning of the identity of the occupants.

PROBLEMS OF PROOF

The classic defense claim in drug-selling cases is entrapment: that the investigator or police agent (special employee, informant) urged and persuaded the defendant to sell the drugs and that the sale itself was solely to recover the cost of the drugs to the defendant. This entrapment defense has many variations, but it has been successful in many jury trials. It is likely to continue as a successful defense unless prosecutors can affirmatively show that no coercive persuasion or allurement was used on the defendant.

In cases involving only a small quantity of illicit drugs, a defendant may claim that he or she was **flaked** by the police investigator or his informant partner—this is, that the illicit drugs were planted by the informant or the arresting officer. Unfortunately for the prosecution in these trials, one or more jurors may have heard of the police practice of flaking and may be willing to give greater credence to the claim than to the denial.

The compulsion of immunized testimony by an accomplice witness is an in-court problem of credibility. This person is not a sympathetic witness to whom jurors might relate but rather a person who has turned state's witness to save his or her own skin. The problem is that many jurors are ready to believe that such a witness is prone to lie, and they are repeatedly told this by the defense counsel.

Undercover investigators appear to many jurors to be individuals who have used friendship, deceit, and persuasion in making arrests. Defense attorneys' allegations of entrapment—that their client did no more than "accommodate" a friend by getting him or her illicit drugs—cater to this conscious or subliminal belief. The legal significance of most of the evidence may rest on the prosecutor's ability to somehow insert a "victim" into the case—but this is difficult to do because drug selling is one of the so-called "victimless" crimes.

CASE STUDY

Dangerous Drugs Law Enforcement—Roles and Story Lines

SCENE: Extracts from the testimony of police investigators tell the story of a major investigation into drug selling.

The first witness was a state chemist who testified that the substances examined by him (a bottle of orange tablets and balloons containing a white powder) were dangerous drugs—amphetamines—and a quantity of narcotics—heroin.

The next witness was one of the police investigators, Sergeant Charles Nekola of the City Police.

Direct Examination by the Assistant District Attorney (ADA)

Q: Sergeant Nekola, directing your attention to last April 13, did you have or were you present at an address, 150 "E" Street, here in the city on that date?

A: Yes, sir, I was.

Q: What was the purpose of being out there?

A: We went out there to serve a warrant of arrest on Robert Rodriquez at his residence at 150 "E" Street and a search warrant for the premises.

Q: Was the arrest warrant in relation to the recent grand jury indictment of the defendant?

A: Yes, sir.

Q: Who were you in company with?

A: I was in company with Sergeant James Larson.

Q: Did you approach the door of the residence?

A: Yes, I did.

Q: What did you do, if anything, at that time?

A: I knocked on the front door and waited approximately fifteen seconds. A female I later identified as Alice Rodriquez came to the window just north of the door.

Q: Did you observe her through the window?
A: Yes, sir, I did.

Q: What, if anything occurred at that time?
A: I told her to open the door, and she said, "What for?" I told her we were police officers and we had a search warrant for the house.

Q: Did you in any way identify yourself other than to say you were police officers?
A: Yes, sir. I had my badge in my right hand.

Q: Could you hear her through the window?
A: Yes, sir, I could.

Q: And what occurred, if anything, at that time?
A: I waited a short moment, and then she turned and appeared to run toward the back of the house.

Q: Could you hear noise coming from inside the house?
A: Yes, sir, I could.

Q: What, if anything, happened at that time?
A: Sergeant Larson started kicking the door, and he forced the door open with his foot.

Q: You have been a police officer for approximately thirteen years?
A: Yes, sir.

Q: Did you feel it was necessary to force the door open?
A: Yes, sir. I did.

Q: Would you explain why?
A: Usually, in a case when we are serving a search warrant on a residence and we know that the residents are people involved in the sale of drugs, they will recognize the agents and will flush the drugs down the toilet.

Q: Have you ever had this personally happen to you?
A: Yes, sir.

Q: Approximately how many times?
A: Oh, I'd say more than twenty times.

Q: Did you later enter this residence?
A: Yes, I did.

Q: And this young lady you indicated, who you observed in the window, was she present inside the residence?
A: Yes, sir, she was.

Q: After you entered?
A: Yes, sir.

ADA: No further questions, Your Honor. (Witness was excused.)

Direct Examination of Sergeant James Larson by the Assistant District Attorney

Q: Sergeant Larson, where are you employed?
A: The City Police Department.

Q: How long have you been so employed?
A: Nine and a half years.

Q: Where do you work within the City Police?
A: I'm on assignment to the narcotics detail.

Q: Direct your attention to last April 13. Did you have occasion to be at a residence in the city, specifically 150 "E" Street?
A: I did.

Q: What was your purpose in being there?
A: We were going to make a warrant arrest and execute a search warrant on the residence.

Q: Were you present when a forced entry was made?

A: I was.

Q: Were you through the door first or were you the second one or—

A: (Interposing) I believe I was the first officer through the door.

Q: What did you observe immediately upon entry?

A: There was no one in the front room or in the kitchen, that I could see. I went to the hallway and turned left. As we were entering, I had heard some doors closing in this direction. The door to the bathroom was closed. It opens off this hallway.

Q: Had you ever been in that house before?

A: I had been in it in February.

Q: What, if anything, did you do at this time?

A: I tried to open the bathroom door, and I couldn't get it open. I then knocked on it and pounded on it. I said, "Police officer. Open up." They didn't open up, so I then kicked in the door of the bathroom.

Q: You kicked in the door of the bathroom?

A: I did.

Q: After you kicked in the door what did you find, if anything?

A: Rodriguez was against the wall in the bathroom. He had a bag in one hand, which he dropped to the floor.

Q: Now, let me show you an item marked previously, marked No. 1 for identification. It is a brown manila envelope, and contained within there appears to be a brown leather bag. Does that in any way resemble the bag that you saw Mr. Rodriquez holding?

A: Yes, it does.

Q: When you entered the bathroom did he have it in his hand?

A: He had it in his right hand.

Q: Then what happened?

A: He dropped it to the floor as I entered.

Q: Then what occurred?

A: I then turned him against the wall, searched him, and placed him under arrest.

Q: Had you seen Mr. Rodriguez on previous occasions?

A: I had.

Q: You knew him?

A: I did.

Q: And what was your purpose for being there—in this house at this time?

A: To place Rodriguez under arrest on an arrest warrant we had in our possession, and also to serve a search warrant.

Q: What was the arrest warrant based on?

A: It was two counts of sales of narcotics. We made "buys."

Q: Grand jury indictments?

A: That's correct.

Q: Let me show you this brown leather purse. It is marked No. 1-A for identification. Would you examine the contents contained therein?

A: Yes, sir.

Q: Do you recognize the contents contained therein?

A: Yes, sir. This is the brown leather purse that was on the floor in the bathroom when I arrested Robert Rodriguez, and I seized it as evidence.

Q: How about the other items contained therein. Do you recognize any of those?

A: All of these items were contained inside the purse.

Q: Specifically, would you elaborate for the record what items we are talking about?

A: Yes, sir. This is a bottle of orange tablets.

Q: How about the brown paper bag. Do you recognize this item?

A: Yes, sir.

Q: Let me open up the contents of the brown paper bag. By the way, does it bear your initials?

A: Yes, sir. It has the initials J. L. on it for my name.

Q: How about any of the contents contained within the brown paper bag?

A: All the items have my initials, J. L., written on them.

Q: Just briefly describe what was contained in this brown paper bag.

A: There were thirteen green balloons containing a powdery substance.

Q: What did you do with these items?

A: I retained them in my possession until such time as marked and submitted to the state chemist's locker.

Q: How long have you been an agent with this special squad?

A: A little over one year.

Q: Approximately how many arrests and investigations involving narcotic or restricted dangerous drugs have you participated in?

A: I would have to estimate over a hundred.

Q: Have you personally made "buys" of heroin?

A: Yes, sir, I have.

Q: On more than one occasion?

A: Numerous occasions.

Q: Assuming these items, that is the thirteen balloons, do contain heroin, do you have an opinion as to whether that is an amount sufficient to constitute a possession for sale?

A: Yes, it is.

Q: What do you base that opinion on?

A: On the method of packaging, the quantity contained inside, and the number of balloons.

Q: Have you ever seen heroin packaged in balloons before?

A: Yes, sir, I have.

Q: On numerous occasions?

A: Yes, sir.

CHAPTER REVIEW

KEY TERMS

REVIEW QUESTIONS

1. What controlled substance kills pain, induces drowsiness, produces physical and psychological dependency, and generates a sense of euphoria?
   a. Heroin
   b. Cocaine
   c. Phencyclidine
   d. Ecstasy
   e. LSD

2. What controlled substance produces a warm, fuzzy sense of well-being and the manic energy to dance all night?
   a. Heroin
   b. Cocaine
   c. Phencyclidine
   d. Ecstasy
   e. LSD

3. What controlled substance is commonly applied to tobacco or marijuana cigarettes and smoked, produces hallucinations, and—because of its anesthetic effect—may result in the user displaying a total disregard for his or her personal safety?
   a. Heroin
   b. Cocaine
   c. Phencyclidine
   d. Ecstasy
   e. LSD

4. What controlled substance produces feelings of exhilaration and euphoria, increases the user's energy level, and suppresses fatigue?
   a. Heroin
   b. Cocaine
   c. Phencyclidine
   d. Ecstasy
   e. LSD

5. What controlled substance produces hallucinations lasting ten to twelve hours and is ambivalent in that the user may experience both good and bad sensations?
   a. Heroin
   b. Cocaine
   c. Phencyclidine
   d. Ecstasy
   e. LSD

6. The drug that is most frequently used with alcohol has a synergistic effect that produces disinhibition and amnesia and, because of these effects, is known as the _____ drug.

7. A/An _____ is a normal prelude to an application for a search warrant in illegal drug and narcotics cases.

8. The purpose of the _____ law is not to prevent the unwary criminal from being trapped in a crime; instead, it is to prevent the police officer from manufacturing crime.

9. When cocaine is dissolved in ether and then heated to boil off the impurities, the resulting drug is known as

   _____.

10. When cocaine is mixed with baking soda and water and then heated to drive off the impurities, the resulting drug is known as _____.

See Appendix D for the correct answers.

DISCUSSION QUESTIONS

1. What drugs are common on the drug scene?
2. Briefly describe the drug-marketing pyramid (network).
3. Under what circumstances of investigation is a pickup arrest justified?

4. Name and describe the participants in a buy of illegal drugs.
5. In working-up investigations, what investigative techniques have proven useful in discovering evidence to corroborate the testimony of an accomplice witness?
6. What are the story lines of each witness in the case study?

RELATED WEB SITES

Want to know what our national drug control policy is? If so you should visit the Office of National Drug Control Police's Web site. This site contains information on drug facts, enforcement, prevention and treatment programs: *www.whitehousedrugpolicy.gov.*

To learn more about dangerous drugs as a global problem, visit the United Nations Office on Drugs and Crime Web site: *www.unodc.org.*

chapter **seventeen**

Special Investigations

CHAPTER OUTLINE

After reading this chapter you will be able to:

- Recognize when investigations are conducted on vice and gambling operations and what the implications to law enforcement are for being overly aggressive or inattentive in the enforcement of the laws relating to public morals.
- Describe the operational structure of organized crime in the United States and the problems associated with achieving successful prosecution of these criminals.

- Appreciate the type of crime that can be committed using a computer and the steps being taken to address such crimes.
- Understand the various motivations of the hit-and-run driver.
- Discuss the investigatory process involved in the apprehension of hit-and-run drivers.

Many times during an investigator's career, he or she will be involved in cases that are outside or beyond his or her field of expertise. Even so, the investigator will be expected to contribute to the investigative efforts of these cases. This scenario is often played out in the area of the highly specialized investigations involving vice and gambling, computer crime, and hit-and-run accidents. Investigators should have a basic understanding of the underlying concepts involved in these investigations so they can be contributing members of the investigative team.

VICE AND GAMBLING

Vice laws, which regulate standards for public morals, are not usually aggressively enforced unless someone is offended and lodges a complaint or unless the activity occurs publicly. For example, most of the efforts of vice cops are directed toward the highly visible street-level prostitute. Prostitution that has gone underground, or become invisible, generates little attention. The same is true of gambling and other forms of immoral conduct. The degree to which these laws are enforced can easily bring forth criticism. A department that aggressively pursues enforcement of public morals laws may be criticized for squandering resources that could be used to control far more serious forms of crime. Too little effort in this area is often cited by critics as a graphic example of the corrupt nature of local law enforcement agencies. Somewhere between these two extremes is the fine line that most agencies follow in an effort to control vice and gambling in their community.

GAMBLING

The social harm of gambling has diminished with the added convenience of legal betting and a public awareness of the "fairness" of state-run lotteries, horse betting at tracks with a pari-mutuel setting system—even at "ghost" tracks (without horses but using video systems linked to other tracks with betting hooked to a central computer system and payoff the same as if the races were run locally). Some states offer off-track betting, which also affords the appeal of convenience and track odds.

Sports gambling's main events are professional and college basketball and football games; baseball is a poor second. A new interest is visible in soccer games among fans at local sports taverns. All sports wagering is aided by the local press, which gives the day's **line**, or betting odds for these events. Boxing is a suspect sport since it lacks the basic fairness of team sports.

Some **bookies**, people who take illegal bets on these events, are very quick to take a game **off the board**, or stop taking bets, with the knowledge that a **fix** is in, or the outcome of the event is predetermined. This they consider to be only good business—no morality is involved.

Casino gambling run by American Indian tribal enterprises that are not controlled by crime bosses brings Las Vegas–type table games to the local level. These relatively new gambling establishments establish a new horizon on the question of fairness: Is it better for the local compulsive gambler to be able to satisfy his/her needs at local tables rather than at the hands of the local crime boss?

Illegal gambling is big business, often with interstate connections to organized crime. Investigators need to think big and be proactive in their investigative actions. Once probable cause exists to believe that illegal gambling is occurring, it is time to gather information and evidence, which often involves court-ordered eavesdropping. A task-force approach is an excellent way to gather the necessary personnel and resources to address this problem.

PROSTITUTION

Most cities are large enough to support a variety of prostitutes, including call girls, hotel and tavern pickups, "escort" services, and some alleged massage therapists. The local **stroll**, in which prostitutes will use the client's car as the place to perform the sex act, is another form of this vice.

As long as the client names an act that the prostitute is willing to perform for a specified price and denies being a police officer, and the prostitute acts in furtherance of committing the sex act (such as getting in the client's car), the crime of solicitation for purposes of prostitution has been committed. Typically male undercover police officers are used to arrest a prostitute once the crime of solicitation has been committed. The prostitute, by then in the officer's car, is driven to a staging area where transportation to the local jail facility awaits. Female undercover officers or volunteer decoys are used to arrest **johns**, who solicit females for the purpose of prostitution.

Pimps are men and **madams** are women who live off the proceeds of one or more prostitutes. The activities of these people are a clear sign that someone is testing the no-tolerance rule of local law enforcement. Prompt action to arrest these people for their hustling activities sends a clear message that this behavior will not be tolerated. Similar prompt action should be taken against hotel/motel and tavern employees who act out the role of a pimp or madam on a part-time basis.[1]

ORGANIZED CRIME

Fighting regional organized crime is more than solving a single murder case, raiding a house of prostitution, or exposing an illegal bankruptcy ring. The investigation must be pursued beyond the operational level of the local overlords of crime to their allies in local government who have been well bribed.

Convicted organized crime boss John Gotti listens to opening arguments in his New York State Supreme Court trial for racketeering on January 20, 1990.

The characteristic that most distinguishes the crime syndicate (organized crime) is unity of action. Criminal actions are dictated by executive and management personnel and performed by subordinates in the organization. Little freelanceing takes place; crime is almost always a franchise operation.

The hierarchy of command (the lines of authority) begins with the regional boss or chief, then extends to the underbosses who exercise a functional supervision over a group of activities, and then to the "owner" of an activity, such as a bookmaking enterprise, a ring of prostitutes, or other such activity. Authority is clearly delineated, and orders and suggestions are obeyed without question. The severity of supervision prompts an adherence to direction difficult to attain otherwise.

A second major characteristic of syndicate operations is the corruption of weak and foolish public officials to secure immunity from arrest and successful prosecution. This protection allows the open and notorious operation of both criminal and quasi-legal enterprises.

A third major characteristic of syndicate operations is the extension of the creed of death to the informer to justify the killing of anyone who interferes with the operations of organized crime. As a business technique, this may have originated as the only feasible means of settling disputes and silencing witnesses. Witnesses who have been connected with the syndicate do not talk to police investigators and are unlikely to talk even under the threat of legal action because other witnesses who have talked have died—usually in a very unpleasant manner.

Participant informant Salvatore "Sammy the Bull" Gravano testifies against his boss, John Gotti, in New York State Supreme Court.

NATURE OF OPERATIONS

An emerging characteristic of considerable importance to investigators is the wraparound nature of syndicate operations. Organized crime members involved in prostitution have expanded from the traditional role of madam or pimp—enjoying a profit from the earnings of a prostitute. They also control the booking of prostitutes from one area to another (a change of merchandise for local customers) and provide them with medical and legal talent as necessary. In labor racketeering, the labor unions are infiltrated for the basic enterprise, but the operation of nonunion shops and the control of employee associations provide fringe profits. In the infiltration of legitimate business, in addition to a planned bankruptcy or monopolistic activity, in-plant gambling and assignment of all freight business to syndicate trucking firms are organized until the organized crime operation is wrapped around every possible means for making money.

CHARACTERISTIC ACTIVITY

Unity of action, immunity from governmental action, murder as a technique of business, and expansionistic methods summarize the characteristics that have made the crime syndicate a successful business in which large regional groups operate with nationwide unity.

A significant factor in syndicate activity is whether an enterprise can be operated without interference from law enforcement agencies. The syndicate does not dislike sharing its profits with its allies in government, but corrupt politicians and police officers often make distinctions among different types of corruption. Syndicate members know that they must operate in areas such as their initial business of bootlegging—that is, in activities having a modicum of public approval. This often constitutes a black market of consumer services and sales in which the fixers and hookers of the crime syndicate corrupt politicians and police with the plea that nothing is wrong with a little prostitution, gambling, money lending at high rates of interest, or manufacturing and selling a good grade of untaxed alcohol. Of course, the enterprise has to be illegal to ensure a lack of competition by legitimate business groups, but it cannot be "too illegal" because then immunity is not only costly but may not be purchasable.[2]

The syndicate also operates in other areas of crime, such as selling narcotics, receiving and selling stolen goods, labor racketeering, infiltrating legitimate business, and hidden ownerships in casinos in Nevada and other areas in which gambling is legalized by state or local law.

INVESTIGATIVE ALERTS

A lead alerting an investigator to local activity by members of an organized crime syndicate may originate in a federal or local agency. Personnel of the U.S. Drug Enforcement Agency (DEA) alert the local police when they believe the syndicate has started a new operation—and the locals work closely with informants who have in-depth knowledge of the lower-echelon members of the syndicate. The FBI continuously inventories the operations of organized crime and its allies in government. The work of FBI agents in clearing cases involving the interstate transportation of stolen goods has made this bureau very knowledgeable about the massive fencing operation of the syndicate. Local police intelligence units collect and interpret all incoming information from their own and the foregoing sources and compile their own files on the resident representatives of organized crime and the transients who display interest locally.[3]

In their work on other cases, investigators often encounter facts indicating that organized crime is developing a local interest—the changeover of a cabaret or roadhouse to a strip joint, the opening of an after-hours club, or the expansion of local sales of pornographic material. A little probing may indicate that these places of business are employing persons with police records or that ex-convicts are involved in management through a hidden ownership shield if licenses are required. The investigator has a lead to some of the initial operations of the syndicate when a restaurant owner complains of being pressured into buying meat from one firm or leasing linens from a particular concern, or when a bartender mentions that he or she and the owner of the bar were "asked" to use a certain vending machine firm. These danger signals are probable cause to inquire into the pressure and its origin. The inquiry may reveal the monopolistic control of a legitimate business and isolate and identify some of the resident members of the syndicate.

Arrests for illegal gambling, prostitution, and violations of state laws regulating the sale of alcoholic beverages can be audited by supervisors of the criminal investigation unit for traces that indicate syndicate takeover, such as a new pattern of arrests (mere increase or decrease is not significant) marked by continuing operations and the use of a small group of bail bondsmen and attorneys after arrests. Reports of the patrol force about suspicious persons and premises—whether increasing or diminishing—should be integrated to see what patterns emerge.

Because syndicate members are today closely involved with business, the initial alert may originate with the rank and file of a union, a trade association, or the Better Business Bureau and may be little more than an allegation of unfair treatment or competition or a complaint of in-plant gambling. Quite frequently, syndicate activity can be detected because of a killing, a suspicious fire, or an aggravated assault. Because of the massive fencing operation developed by organized crime, the presence of organized crime in an area may be determined from the activities of burglars and thieves who appear to operate without selling their loot. The alert may result from some suspicion or knowledge that the police agency has been penetrated (for information) or infiltrated (for protection), based on evidence that suspected personnel are living above their wage levels or of other suspicious behavior.

GANG ACTIVITY

Motorcycle ("biker") gangs have an organization similar to regional organized crime (La Cosa Nostra, the Mafia) but tend to specialize in peddling firearms and illicit drugs.[4] The bikers confront police officers with their crimes rather than attempting to conceal them or secure approval for their commission. Police surveillance can easily reveal the bikers' lifestyle.

Asian criminal organizations, made up primarily of Chinese and Vietnamese persons, are ethnic crime groups that closely resemble other "families" of organized crime in terms of their possible relationship to other social business groups of the same ethnic composition, in this case called **tongs.** The crimes of these groups are concentrated on extortion of local illegal gambling groups and legitimate business owners.[5]

Prison gangs operating outside prisons are somewhat similar to organized crime, although they also have a limited range of criminal activities—primarily drug selling—as do other drug-selling organizations, such as those composed of Colombians and Jamaicans.

Ideally, the person to lead a comprehensive investigation into the operations of organized crime is the local prosecutor or U.S. attorney. These public officials can develop a special investigation that combines the interrogation of witnesses with the examination of subpoenaed or seized records. Witnesses can be called before grand juries by prosecutors and placed under oath when they are questioned. Witnesses fearful of the syndicate may talk when granted immunity or threatened with jail for contempt if they refuse to testify or for perjury if they lie when they do testify. Despite the fact that members of the hierarchy of organized crime rarely become informants, this dilemma of cooperation or jail for contempt or perjury can be effective to make otherwise mute witnesses talk. Police investigators do not wield this power, but prosecutors can do so in their role as legal advisor to a public investigative body.

PROBLEMS OF PROOF

Witnesses are the major source of evidence in a case. They are commonly available when none of the defendants have links to organized crime or other crime groups, such as bikers, prison gangs, and other such organizations. Any link to a crime group on the part of a defendant usually means that witnesses will be threatened and intimidated—if they are not previously conditioned by the "death to the informer" stance of most of these groups. Usually, all of the co-conspirators know of potential witnesses who have been killed or so intimidated that they moved out of town without leaving a forwarding address. This disposal of witnesses by death or intimidation tends to silence anyone thinking of becoming a witness for the prosecution.

COMPUTER CRIME

Computer crime, or **cybercrime**, is distinguishable from other forms of crime in that a computer was either the target or the means to commit the crime. Computer crimes were originally limited to theft or vandalism by employees of those businesses using computer applications. With the advent of the Internet in 1993, new opportunities were presented to criminals to expand their activities to a larger scale, including a worldwide basis. Cybercrime now includes the crimes of theft, vandalism, counterfeiting, fraud, child pornography, child molestation, and terrorism.

HACKERS

Hackers are, in essence, trespassers—intruders who enter into another's computer system without authorization. In a survey of businesses and government agencies, 85 percent detected security breaches during the previous year. Businesses have suffered more than $250 million in losses at the hands of hackers—a figure that certainly will grow.[6] Three types of hackers are recognized: crackers, criminals, and vandals. **Crackers** are often antisocial misfits who are more comfortable online in front of a computer than with other people. They tend to be intelligent, curious, and have a high degree of expertise with computers. They rarely have a specific goal in mind beyond exploring another's system. Their ultimate challenge is to get around system firewalls or security protections, such as user names and passwords. The tougher the task, the better. The cracker is into it for the challenge—a test to determine if his or her computer skills are better than the person who designed the system's security protections. One **cyberpunk** was caught after he hacked his way into a computer security firm's Web site, the computer systems of four U.S. military bases, and the antidrug site of the Los Angeles Police Department, where he added a cartoon of Donald Duck with a hypodermic needle in his arm.[7]

Computer criminals engage in fraud, sabotage, industrial sabotage, and theft. They are the mercenaries of cyberspace. Like a cat burglar they hope to gain access, commit their crime, and leave without being detected. The primary threat comes from full- and part-time employees and contract employees, with hackers being a close third. These thieves most frequently target intellectual property, including new product plans, new product descriptions, research marketing plans, prospective customer lists, and similar information that is then sold to a competitor. The criminal may also sabotage a system to destroy databases or to conduct such terrorist activity as taking over a nation's power grid or air traffic control system. Most criminals, however, are in it for the money.

Computer vandals are motivated by revenge due to some real or imagined wrong. Vandals seek to destroy databases and wreak havoc, to shut down another's system or the entire Internet. Vandals may be employees who, when notified of being laid off or fired, will strike back against the employer by destroying the employer's databases. Vandals may also be outsiders who use the Internet to get even, such as an animal rights activist who targets companies dealing in fur coats and destroys their databases as a means of striking a blow for the cause.[8]

The tools of the vandal include viruses, Trojan horses, worms, and logic bombs. A **computer virus** is a type of malicious code that replicates itself and inserts copies or versions of itself in other programs. A virus may do something as simple as to let the user know that it exists or as malicious as to destroy the entire contents of the computer's memory. The 1999 Melissa virus was unleashed by a thirty-one-year-old New Jersey man and was designed to infect the e-mail of the first fifty e-mail addresses on the users' mailing lists. Because each infected computer could infect fifty additional computers, which in turn could infect another fifty computers, the virus proliferated rapidly and exponentially, overloading e-mail servers. The result was the shutdown of networks and significant costs to repair or cleanse computer systems. More than a million personal computers in North America were affected by Melissa—a virus that caused more than $80 million in damages.[9] Presently, well over 10,000 viruses are known worldwide.

Trojan horses are stand-alone programs that are disguised as other programs that innocent users pass to one another, usually in the form of an e-mail attachment. When the program is opened or executed, the malicious instructions are executed.

Worms are like viruses, but they do not replicate. Instead they make duplicates of themselves and steal system resources as they do so. Most worms are designed with intent to bring the user's system down.

Logic bombs are programs within programs that perform destructive acts based upon a trigger event. The trigger event might be a significant future date or an act such as the removal of a person's name from a payroll database, indicating that he or she has either been fired or laid off.[10]

COMPUTER FRAUD

The cybercriminal can forge business and government documents and create counterfeit ones of reasonable quality at relatively low cost. Documents such as checks, entertainment and transportation tickets, and stock certificates are relatively easy to produce with a computer and graphic software, scanners, color printers, and the appropriate paper stock. The U.S. government now redesigns its currency every seven to ten years to include security features that make it more difficult to counterfeit even with advanced computer technologies. Ticketless travel and electronic transfer of funds have reduced the need for paper documents and may lessen the threat of counterfeiting in the future.[11]

The Internet is a perfect forum for committing basic to complex frauds. Simple business frauds include offering items for sale and either supplying worthless goods or not sending the merchandise at all. For anyone making purchases over the Internet, the old adage "Buyer beware" is still sound advice. A more complex type of scheme is the **salami fraud,** which refers to the technique of taking small slices to deceptively acquire "the whole salami." For example, an enterprising programmer in a bank was asked to write a program that would refund excessive interest collections from credit cardholders. The program was written as requested with one important distinction. It reduced the refunds to randomly selected cardholders by twenty-five cents each and forwarded these amounts to the programmer's own account. Because the cardholders did not know exactly what they were supposed to receive as a refund, they were unable to detect the discrepancy. Fortunately, an alert bank auditor noticed the programmer's upscale lifestyle, and the programmer was successfully convicted of bank fraud.[12]

CHILD PORNOGRAPHY AND EXPLOITATION

The Internet, with its ability to transmit information around the world, is a mecca for persons distributing sexually explicit material. While pornography is not illegal in the United States, information and pictures depicting sex with children—child pornography—is prohibited by law. This material originates from Russia or Indonesia where it is not illegal and is then distributed in the United States. In one case, a thirty-seven-year-old man who ran the largest child pornography distribution company in the country was arrested and received a record 1,335-year prison term for trafficking in child pornography. Hundreds of the company's customers have also been arrested. To meet the standards for effective prosecution, federal agents sold and mailed child pornography videos, CDs, and floppy disks to the company's former customers. They then arrested the customers as they received the deliveries of the pornographic material. The names of another 30,000 alleged buyers of child pornography from the United States were offered to local police for investigation. The goal of these investigations was, according to then Attorney General John Ashcroft, "to help make the Internet a safe place for children to play and learn."[13] While all crimes committed by computer are a concern to law enforcement, perhaps the gravest concern is the use of a computer to harass and molest children. Computers and the Internet have made the predator's job easier. Historically, child predators found their victims in public places where children tend to gather—schoolyards, playgrounds, and shopping malls. Today, with so many children online, the Internet provides predators a new place—cyberspace—to target children for criminal acts.

Young children and teenagers are perfect targets for criminal acts because they are often trusting, naïve, curious, adventuresome, and eager for attention and affection. However, the most attractive factor to predators is that children and teenagers historically have not been viewed as credible witnesses. Today, the danger to children is even greater because the Internet provides predators anonymity. Whether the victimization occurs in person or over the Internet, the process is the same—the perpetrator uses information to target a child victim. For example, the predator may initiate an online friendship with a young person by sharing hobbies and interests. This may lead to the exchange of gifts and pictures. Just like the traditional predator who targets children in person, the online predator usually is willing to spend considerable time befriending and grooming a child. The predator wants to build the child's trust, which will allow the predator to get what he or she ultimately wants from the child.

Predators contact teenagers and children over the Internet and victimize them by enticing them through online contacts for the purpose of engaging them in sexual acts. These Internet contacts are also used for the production, manufacture, and distribution of child pornography and for exploiting children for the purposes of **sexual tourism**—travel with the intent to engage in sexual behavior for commercial gain or personal gratification.[14]

The investigation of the exploitation of children requires a proactive response to this type of victimization. Investigators, pretending to be children, go online and enter chat rooms that might be attractive to the predator. When approached, the investigator communicates with the predator as a child would, to determine the intent of the predator. Such contact may provide sufficient grounds to obtain a search warrant for the predator's computer or may lead to an arrest when the predator shows up at a predetermined location for the purpose of molesting the child.

CYBERCRIME INVESTIGATION AND PREVENTION

The foundation of dealing with computer crime is prevention. Antivirus programs that offer firewall software are available and useful in preventing unwanted intrusions into personal computers. These programs also track the Internet address of any person who launches an attack on the protected computer. This provides information useful in any subsequent criminal investigation. The computer forensic lab, using data-mining and tracking programs such as Silentrunner, which captures and analyzes all activity on a computer network, aids the investigation of computer crime. These programs are so powerful that they were at one time classified as government secrets. With this program, cybersleuths can pinpoint internal sources of misstated earnings, nab thieves of trade secrets, track down hackers, and uncover improper Internet use.

The FBI is well on its way to addressing many issues that challenge the new world of fighting computer crime. Most of the larger populated states now have full-time investigators dedicated to computer crime. Smaller jurisdictions should consider the creation of regional cybercrime investigation divisions.

Police academies should start offering training on the basics of assisting fully trained cybercrime investigation personnel in the proper methods of legally seizing and protecting computer criminal evidence. Every college and university that offers a curriculum in criminal justice should be offering training on the subject of computer crime investigation. In addition, all companies that are connected to a network should employ the services of a professional information system security officer as a cost of doing business in the cyberworld.[15]

HIT AND RUN

Investigators have difficulty avoiding personal involvement when attempting to solve a crime without motive and usually without witnesses. Standard police procedure calls for the issuance of a prompt alarm for the fleeing vehicle, an extensive crime scene search, and assignment of police investigators to the accident-and-crime scene around the time of occurrence, and on days following the accident, in a search for witnesses.

THE HIT-AND-RUN OPERATOR

Hit-and-run drivers have been grouped into three categories based upon possible psychological explanations for their motivation for flight:

1. The apprehensive, panic-driven, fearful driver
2. The projectionist—projects guilt
3. The sneak—inflicts minor property damage

The **apprehensive driver** has a greater sin to hide, either morally or criminally. This individual typically flees the scene for one or more of the following reasons: (1) driving while intoxicated, (2) operating without a license, (3) no insurance, (4) a companion in the car who is not the driver's mate or who is the mate of another, (5) stolen car, (6) stolen goods in the car, (7) leaving the scene of another accident, (8) fleeing a crime scene, (9) wanted for some crime, or (10) fear alone.

The **projectionist driver** tries the case—sitting as judge and jury, he or she finds the other driver at fault, refuses to be a party to the accident, and drives off as the offended person.

The **sneak operator** is one that crushes a fender and smashes grillwork as daily occupational activities and chalks up the action as the calculated risk shared by all vehicle owners who place their vehicles on the roadway.

Fortunately, hit-and-run operators do not have the attitudes of a professional criminal, nor are they skilled at concealing damage to a vehicle. They will usually be cooperative when found, and traces of vehicle damage can be easily located, even if recently repaired.

THE ALARM

The basic line of investigation in hit-and-run cases must be along the lines of opportunity: (1) What car was at the scene? (2) Who operated it? The ideal

(a)

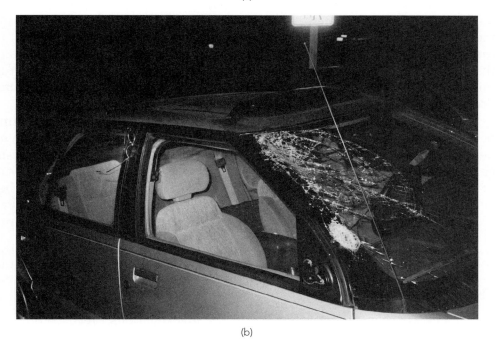

(b)

(a) This vehicle was involved in a hit and run of a pedestrian. (b) Note the victim's eyeglasses in the door frame of the suspect's vehicle.

time of apprehension is while the fugitive car is being operated by the hit-and-run driver. For this reason, time is most important in determining that the accident is a hit-and-run case and in getting a broadcast on the air.

When investigators find that the scene of an accident is a hit-and-run case, their first effort is to obtain from available witnesses a full description of the car involved. This should include all odd or unusual details. Even noises heard are sometimes useful clues. Descriptive items that may prove extremely valuable in locating the vehicle are (1) stickers on windows or windshield, (2) dented fenders, (3) fancy wheel covers, (4) broken radio aerials, (5) distinctive ornaments and fixtures, (6) broken window glass, (7) unusual colors and body styles, and (8) out-of-state license plates that are easily recognizable.

These data, together with a description of the occupants and the direction of the vehicle when last seen, should be immediately broadcast in a police radio alarm to all members of the department and to nearby police units. The alarm alerts police on patrol to look for abandoned vehicles or vehicles in transit with such damage and as described. Particular attention is usually directed along the possible escape routes of the fleeing vehicle.

Garages, parking lots, used car lots, and other places where a vehicle might be stored or taken for repairs should be promptly checked by police. Generally, if a car is not located within a reasonable time after the accident occurred, it may be assumed that the driver removed it from the streets and placed it in a private garage. A prearranged list of all public garages and other likely storage places will facilitate the assignment of police cars to conduct preliminary inquiries. Prearranged contacts with garages may result in immediate reporting of a damaged vehicle.

Officers at the accident scene should also check suspicious persons at the scene or inquisitive passersby. Sometimes hit-and-run drivers return to the scene, curious to find out how much evidence the police have discovered. In many cases the hit-and-run driver stops from habit, examines the injuries of the victim, stays a few minutes, and then flees. This habit should be kept in mind when questioning witnesses about persons who were at the scene but drove away.

Police officers should be alert for vehicles reported stolen after the time of the hit-and-run case and that fit the description of the fugitive car. When no description is available, all these cases of reported thefts should be investigated for possible involvement. It is a common technique of the hit-and-run driver, in attempting to explain vehicle damage and the presence of his or her vehicle at the scene, to flee and then park the vehicle in some out-of-the-way area and report it stolen so that they can explain any damage and the presence of the vehicle at the scene without implicating themselves.

THE SCENE SEARCH

Transfer evidence is important in hit-and-run investigations. Since the only investigative leads are along the line of opportunity, it is vital to search for evidence at the accident scene that will identify the vehicle and the driver involved. This should not be limited to prime identification that will lead to prompt recognition of either the vehicle or operator but should extend to any evidence that will connect the vehicle and its driver to the scene when the suspect vehicle is located or the fleeing operator is apprehended.

The search for physical evidence at the scene should be thorough. It should be planned so that every part of the area is carefully and methodically searched. A haphazard search procedure may frustrate the entire investigation by failing to discover evidence or by destroying or impairing the value of evidence. This is a most important step in the investigation. The scene must be protected and safeguarded, and then the search must be pointed toward broken headlight glass, door handles, hubcaps, paint marks or scrapings, soil and mud fallen from cars at impact, and any other debris. Objects carried in or on a hit-and-run vehicle are of value. Damage to fixed objects can also be studied for traces of paint and indication of damage to the vehicle.

Whenever the scene search reveals the nature of the damage to the car or the probable make or model of the car, this information should be added immediately to the alarm and broadcast to all units aiding in the search. Several police agencies use an artist or a special-effects photographer to prepare a graphic illustration of the wanted car on the basis of known information secured in the investigation and of probable damage, based on the damage sustained by vehicles involved in previous accidents of a similar nature.

Experienced hit-and-run investigators attempt to identify the original purpose of the hit-and-run driver. What brought the driver into the neighborhood of the accident scene? What brought him or her into this area at the time of the accident, on the day of the week on which the accident happened? This assumption of purposefulness is coupled with the habits of motorists who utilize the same routes to and from work or for leisure activity. This is the basis for the concept of returning to the accident scene on stakeout duty in a quest for witnesses. It is also an emerging concept for locating the vehicle involved in a hit-and-run case and for evidence that will connect the suspect with the scene or vice versa.

STAKEOUTS

Investigators should regularly return to the scene to look for new witnesses. The return should be at the same time of day and day of week as the accident. The neighborhood of the accident, route of travel, and other possible areas should be canvassed thoroughly for new witnesses. Perseverance is the rule, not the exception in locating witnesses.

TRANSFER EVIDENCE

Science has provided the police with one of their most effective weapons against hit-and-run cases. The scientific analysis of evidence found at an accident scene sometimes identifies the make and model of the wanted car. Comparison analysis of such evidence with that recovered from a suspect's automobile provides data placing the vehicle at the crime scene. Some of the most common types of evidence found in hit-and-run accident investigations are amenable to scientific analysis.

Since the advent of sealed-beam headlights, glass fragments found at accident scenes are not as productive of results as in former years. However, they are still excellent evidence for proving that a suspect car, when located, was at the accident scene. Broken automobile parts, paint, soil, hairs, fibers, bloodstains, and tire marks all lend themselves to the identification of the type and make of car in the first phase of searching for the vehicle, as well as to later comparison analysis when the suspect vehicle is located.

When a suspected vehicle is located, it should be impounded for an immediate search for evidence. All exterior parts of the vehicle should be carefully examined. Special attention should be given to all protruding parts where hairs or fibers might have been caught. All damaged parts should be noted and inspected for traces of blood or signs of contact with other objects. No foreign material should be discarded from consideration until its source is definitely determined. Evidence of recent damages, repairs, new paint, or wash jobs should be carefully noted. If damaged parts have been replaced, attempts should be made to obtain the original parts.

The undercarriage of the vehicle should receive special attention. The car should be placed over a mechanic's pit or up on a rack for a proper search. Spots that appear to have been brushed by an object and all protruding parts should be thoroughly examined for hairs, fibers, and blood spots.

The possibility of developing latent fingerprints to identify the driver of a vehicle must always be attempted. Frequently a suspect denies having driven the vehicle, and it may in fact have been driven by a thief. Fingerprints may tell the story.

All evidence should be properly preserved and compared with evidence found at the scene of the accident so that the investigating officer can prove that the suspect's vehicle was at the accident scene and was involved in the accident.

The vehicle is the key to the criminal in these cases. If transfer evidence will connect the vehicle with the accident scene, then police can look to its owner for honest answers in a fact-finding inquiry about the operator.

A common explanation by the owner of the vehicle is that his or her car may be involved, but he or she denies driving it at the time and claims it was loaned to a friend of recent acquaintance known only as "Joe." Don't believe it. In fact, do not believe it until "Joe" is identified, found, and confesses.

ACCOUNTABILITY

Apprehension of a hit-and-run driver is difficult because information can be secured only from victims and witnesses and from physical evidence found at the scene. Informers are of little use in such cases. No modus operandi is available to identify the criminal, and the suspect usually does not have a record of previous offenses and could be any member of the community.

Motive is not a potential line of inquiry in these cases insofar as a desire to kill or injure the victim. Motivation is only for flight from the scene and has no connection with the victim. Therefore, the line of inquiry as to who wanted to kill the deceased, which frequently leads to the criminal in homicide cases, is useless in hit-and-run cases.

Car dealers and motor vehicle license authorities can supply either the names and addresses of persons who recently purchased a vehicle similar to the wanted vehicle or a license number close to the license number of the wanted vehicle. Apprehension can be accomplished, but a great deal depends on chance.

Hit-and-run investigations should be conducted by accident investigators. When this work is assigned to detective units, it is only human for a detective working on criminal homicides, felonious assaults, kidnappings, and bank robberies to assign a role of lesser importance to hit-and-run cases. Yet in this field of traffic safety, the people of a community can be won over to the police side by the quick solution of these cases and prompt apprehension and trial of the offenders. Much of this work can be accomplished by accident investigators working in uniform, but permission should be granted to assigned investigators working out of uniform when necessary. Accident investigators are key personnel in getting these investigations started promptly. A prompt alarm and search will result in an apprehension before a car can be hidden and the damage repaired. It will also result in an emotional shock to the fleeing driver, which results in an offender's waiving the right to silence and legal counsel and making a prompt and full admission of fleeing the scene and the reasons for such flight.

POSSIBLE MURDER

Infrequently, a pedestrian, walking or jogging on a sidewalk or the side of a road, is struck by a fast-moving vehicle and is dead on arrival at the local hospital before police arrive. The case usually goes into the hit-and-run routine without producing results. The local homicide squad should be notified whenever the slightest evidence of murder is noted and asked to run a regular homicide check on who might profit from or want the victim dead. In the meantime, the hit-and-run investigator concentrates on finding the damaged car and witnesses.

CASE STUDY

Hit and Run

June 8

2045 Hours.   The city police dispatch center receives a 911 call of a pedestrian versus vehicle accident at 21st and Jay Streets. Patrol and medical units are dispatched to the scene.

2052 Hours.   The first police unit arrives on the scene and confirms that a pedestrian has been struck by a vehicle and that the victim is critically injured. According to witnesses, the vehicle involved has left the scene. The vehicle is described as a tan four-door sedan, last seen heading west on 21st Street. All available units are updated with this information and requested to search the area for the suspect vehicle.

2054 Hours.   An ambulance arrives on the scene and begins emergency medical treatment. The victim is transported to the nearest hospital, code 3: red lights and siren.

2105 Hours.   The highway patrol transfers a cellular 911 call to the city dispatch center. A young woman advises that she and her boyfriend are following a tan sedan that was just involved in an accident at 21st and Jay Streets in the city. The caller states that they were in light traffic when they observed the car in front of them run the light at the intersection and hit a pedestrian. The force of the impact caused the pedestrian to strike the windshield and be thrown over the roof of the vehicle and land in the street. As other drivers stopped to aid the victim, the couple decided to follow the suspect as he fled from the scene. The couple is now a few car lengths behind the suspect vehicle, headed east on the freeway toward the suburbs. The dispatcher asks the caller to stay on the line and to continue to follow the suspect at a discreet distance. The dispatcher obtains the suspect's license plate number from the caller and runs the number through the Department of Motor Vehicles (DMV) database.

2110 Hours.   Patrol units are advised of the suspect's location and possible destination. The DMV inquiry discloses that the suspect's vehicle is registered to a location in the eastern part of the county. As the suspect's residence is located in the jurisdiction of the sheriff's department, this department is advised.

2117 hours.   The couple following the suspect advises that the vehicle has stopped at a residence and that the suspect has parked the vehicle and gone inside. The address given by the couple matches the address supplied by DMV records.

2120 Hours.   Police and sheriff's units arrive at the suspect's residence and secure the area to prevent escape. Officers knock at the suspect's door, but no one responds to open the door.

2135 Hours.   The telephone number for the residence is obtained from the reverse directory and the dispatcher places a call to the suspect's residence. After a few minutes, a male answers the telephone and is advised to step outside to talk to the officers. When he opens the door and steps outside, he is taken into custody.

2215 Hours.   Crime scene technicians arrive at the suspect's residence and begin to photograph and process the vehicle for evidence. The victim's eyeglasses are recovered from the door frame of the vehicle.

2230 hours.   The officer at the hospital advises that the victim was just pronounced dead as a result of the injuries sustained in the accident. The suspect is subsequently booked at the county jail for vehicular homicide.

September 12

During a formal ceremony at City Hall, the young couple is presented with a citation from the chief of police commending their actions leading to the apprehension of this hit-and-run driver.

CHAPTER REVIEW

KEY TERMS

apprehensive driver   *362*
bookie   *353*
computer criminal   *359*
computer vandal   *359*
computer virus   *359*
cracker   *358*
cybercrime   *358*
cyberpunk   *358*
fix   *353*

hacker   *358*
john   *353*
line   *352*
logic bomb   *359*
madam   *353*
off the board   *353*
pimp   *353*
projectionist driver   *362*
salami fraud   *360*

sexual tourism   *361*
sneak operator   *362*
stroll   *353*
tong   *357*
Trojan horse   *359*
vice   *352*
worm   *359*

REVIEW QUESTIONS

1. Female undercover officers, or volunteer decoys, are used to arrest _____, who solicit females for prostitution.

2. The first characteristic that most distinguishes organized crime is _____ of _____.

3. A second major characteristic of syndicate operations is the _____ of weak and foolish public officials to secure immunity from arrest and successful prosecution.

4. A third major characteristic of syndicate operations is the extension of the _____ to the informer.

5. _____ are often antisocial misfits who are more comfortable online in front of a computer than with other people. They are usually intelligent, curious, and experts with computers. They rarely have a specific goal in mind beyond exploring another person's computer system.

6. _____ engage in fraud, sabotage, industrial sabotage, and theft. They are the mercenaries of cyberspace. These thieves most frequently target intellectual property.

7. _____ are programs within programs that perform destructive acts on the basis of a trigger event. The trigger event might be a significant future date or an act such as the removal of a person's name from the payroll database.

8. The type of hit-and-run driver involved in a hit and run because he or she has a greater sin to hide, either morally or criminally, such as drunk driving is known as the:
   a. Apprehensive driver
   b. Alarmist driver
   c. Projectionist driver
   d. Sneak operator

9. The type of hit-and-run driver involved in a hit and run because he or she has tried the case in his or her mind and has found the other driver at fault, refuses to be a party to the accident, and drives off is known as the:
   a. Apprehensive driver
   b. Alarmist driver
   c. Projectionist driver
   d. Sneak operator

10. The type of hit-and-run driver involved in a hit and run because he or she has justified the accident as the result of the calculated risk shared by all vehicle owners who place their vehicle on the roadway is known as the:
    a. Apprehensive driver
    b. Alarmist driver
    c. Projectionist driver
    d. Sneak operator

See Appendix D for the correct answers.

DISCUSSION QUESTIONS

1. Describe how a police agency can be criticized for actively enforcing vice laws in the community.
2. Explain how an agency can be criticized for not actively enforcing these very same laws?
3. Define organized crime.

4. What is an accomplice witness? Why do accomplice witnesses agree to cooperate with the police investigator? Do they require protection? Why?
5. Discuss how, as in the case study, the witnesses' use of a cell phone facilitated the suspect's identification and arrest.
6. Discuss how investigators can use other technology, such as security cameras, in solving hit-and-run cases.

RELATED WEB SITES

To get up-to-date information about organized crime, go to *www.ganglandnews.com.*

For the history of organized crime, including biographies, pictures, mugshots and more, go to *www.gangrule.com.*

For information regarding the U.S. federal government's response to cybercrime, visit the Web site of the Computer Crime and Intellectual Property section of the Department of Justice at *www.usdoj.gov/criminal/cybercrime.* This site provides information regarding investigative efforts, as well as employment opportunities.

chapter **eighteen**

Terrorism

CHAPTER OUTLINE

After reading this chapter you will be able to:

- Distinguish between domestic and international terrorism.
- List the various criminal acts committed by terrorists.
- Explain the historical development of domestic terrorists in the U.S. and identify the groups involved.
- Discuss the historical development of terrorism in the Middle East and the events that led to the formation of the groups involved.
- Appreciate the efforts involved in counterterrorism in the U.S. and the role of the agencies involved.

P rior to the attacks on the World Trade Center and the Pentagon on September 11, 2001, counterterrorism efforts in the United States were fragmented. After these attacks, Congress passed legislation, such as the Patriot Act, which removed the barriers preventing counterterrorist agencies from working together and sharing information. The Joint Terrorism Task Force concept was expanded, and now investigators from the state, federal, and local levels work together to respond to terrorist activity and prevent future attacks. The United States is a prime target for terrorists both from within its borders and from international terrorists groups.

DEFINING TERRORISM

Title 18, section 2331, of the United States Code defines **terrorism** as a "violent act or an act dangerous to human life in violation of the criminal laws of the United States or of any state to intimidate or coerce a government, the civilian population, or any segment thereof, in furtherance of political or social objective." More simply put, a terrorist is someone who commits criminal acts in furtherance of a political or social agenda.

The United States and other Western countries have an enormous capacity to conduct conventional warfare, and any direct confrontation on the battlefield would be fruitless. Therefore, dissident individuals and groups use unconventional means to strike symbolic blows designed to break the will of the stronger power and to advance the terrorist political agenda. Democracies, throughout history, have been the targets of terrorist attacks because democratic systems are expected to play by the rules and, therefore, cannot respond in comparable fashion to these attacks. Autocracies and totalitarian systems are able to respond more easily to terrorist attacks with terrorist acts of their own, which sometimes serves as effective deterrents, but democracies cannot respond in similar fashion.[1]

TERRORIST ACTS

The crimes a terrorist group chooses to commit may be based upon a political agenda or some other factor specific to that group. For instance, bombings are a common form of terrorist activity, yet some terrorist groups may prefer arson because the killing of human beings is inconsistent with the political agenda of those groups. The following are some of the more common crimes committed by terrorist groups:

1. *Bombings* are the most common terrorist tactic because a properly placed bomb can inflict massive numbers of casualties. For example, the 1995 bombing of the Murrah Federal Building in Oklahoma City killed 168 people and injured 500 others.
2. *Hijackings* of airliners, cruise ships, and other means of mass transportation have been committed primarily for their propaganda value. Such scenarios are played out in the media on a daily basis for the

duration of the event and bring the terrorists' names and objectives to the world's attention.

3. *Kidnapping* is committed for several reasons. As a maintenance function, the kidnapping of a wealthy subject may be a means of collecting ransom monies that terrorists then use to support their daily expenses and to finance future terrorist activity. Kidnapping is also useful as a propaganda tool, especially if the subject is a well-known individual or a member of the media.

4. *Physical assaults* such as **kneecapping** was a technique developed by the Irish Republican Army to cripple rather than kill. The process involves shooting an informant in the back of the knee and making that person a cripple for the rest of his or her life. A person in such a condition sends a strong visual message and thus becomes an example to others of the terrorists groups' power and the cost of informing on them.

5. *Arson,* unlike bombs, is designed to destroy property and not people. Arson has been a crime of choice for animal rights groups, such as those who set fire to and destroyed the animal research lab at the University of California at Davis.

6. *Vandalism* is a crime of choice for **ecoterrorists** who are dedicated to destroying the lumber industry due to its perceived negative impact on the environment. Damage to logging equipment is a prime objective. A favorite tactic known as **tree spiking** involves driving metal spikes into trees in logging areas for the purpose of damaging logging equipment.

7. *Assassinations* are usually carefully planned and executed. Victims are selected for both their symbolic and their publicity value.

8. *Robbery* is another crime committed for the maintenance of terrorists and their operations. Banks and armored cars are popular targets, and the money gained in the commission of these crimes is used to support terrorist groups' daily existence and future terrorist activities.

9. *Narcoterrorism* is another source of revenue for the terrorist. In the Middle East, **narcoterrorists** are involved in the production of opium, and in South America they are involved in the production of cocaine.

10. *Cyberterrorism* involves the hacking into automated control systems that run networks for electricity, water, gas, oil, communications, and more. Where such control systems are connected to the Internet, they are vulnerable. According to the FBI, terrorist groups have shown an interest in either developing hacking skills or hiring hackers to work for them.[2]

TERRORIST ATROCITIES

Terrorist atrocities, such as the events of September 11, 2001, serve several essential objectives for the terrorist. First and foremost, they can produce pure terror or paralyzing fear. A second major purpose is to attract attention and

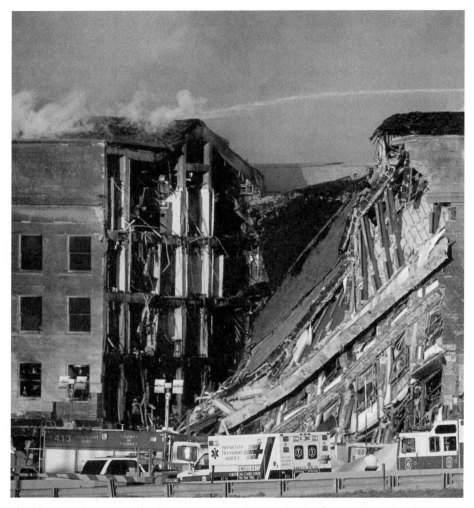

The damaged Pentagon building in Virginia surrounded by fire trucks and ambulances in the aftermath of the terrorist hijacking and airliner crash of September 11, 2001.

gain sympathy through publicity. The purpose of an atrocity is to attract widespread attention; thus, the more spectacular the act of terroristic violence, the more interest it arouses in the general population. Viewing the atrocity may lead one audience to supply recruits, another to supply material aid, and yet another to offer encouragement. In addition, the terrorist atrocity may increase the prestige of the terrorist group and strengthen its acceptability and influence among other terrorist groups. The boldness of the act of terrorism may also strengthen a terrorist group's claim that it is the only legitimate representative of "the people."

The third purpose of terrorist atrocities is to provoke the existing political establishment to commit counteratrocities. If the government is seen as employing the same tactics as the terrorist group, then potential sympathizers become allies and the strength of the terrorist group grows. The aim of the terrorist group is to enrage the establishment.[3]

DOMESTIC TERRORISM

According to Title 18, section 2331(5), of the United States Code, **domestic terrorism** refers to terrorist activities that occur primarily within the territorial jurisdiction of the United States. Domestic terrorists are active on the far left and the far right of the political spectrum in America.

The beginnings of the **Ku Klux Klan** can be traced back to 1865 in Pulaski, Tennessee, when a small group of Confederate veterans gathered together to form a social club. To show off their new club, the members disguised themselves in sheets and rode through the main street, which created quite a stir in the small town. The men adopted the sheets as official regalia and eventually added tall hats and masks. As the club grew, the men's actions began to have a chilling effect on the local blacks, an effect that was noted by the more violent members of the group.

Soon the hooded riders began intimidating night raids to black homes and advised blacks against exercising their newfound rights. As the Klan became more violent over time, its night rides included hangings, acid branding, tar and feathering, and other forms of terror. The numbers of Klan victims will never be known since many victims were too afraid to report their victimization. However, between 1889 and 1941 some 3,811 black persons were lynched by Klansmen for "crimes" and alleged "crimes" ranging from attempting to vote to being disrespectful to a white person. The image of a black male hanging from a tree by a rope became a symbol of the worst of the Klan violence.[4]

A second Klan movement emerged in 1915 and lasted until 1945. This new Klan, in addition to holding its prior beliefs of white Protestant

A typical Ku Klux Klan rally includes white robes and hats and a cross burning.

supremacy, added Catholics, Jews, and foreigners to its hate list. The Klan's membership was estimated to be between four and five million. The Klan controlled not only state and local politics but included at least two U.S. senators among its ranks. During World War II, the group's close association with the Nazi party became known and the Klan fell into disrepute.

The Klan reemerged a third time between 1960 and 1975 in response to the civil rights movement. In Birmingham, Alabama, more than a hundred bombs were detonated by Klan members in the early 1960s to intimidate blacks and civil rights workers. By 1966 the level of violence had overwhelmed local law enforcement, so the federal government stepped in and began to prosecute the top leadership of the Klan for the slaying of civil rights workers. Today Klan membership has dwindled, and many of its former and potential new members have been drawn to other groups committed to **white supremacy**.[5]

In 1985 William Pierce, a white supremacist headquarted in West Virginia, wrote a novel under the pseudonym of Andrew MacDonald. *The Turner Diaries*, as he named it, is a fictionalized account of an international white revolution and a how-to manual for terrorism. The book discusses the proper methods for making bombs and attacking targets. With is frequent diatribes against minorities and Jews, the book has become the philosophical standard for many antigovernment white supremacist groups. The lone wolf Timothy McVeigh, who was responsible for the Oklahoma City bombing of the Murrah Federal Building, had a well-worn copy of *The Turner Diaries* in his possession at the time of his arrest in 1995.[6]

In 1983 Robert Jay Mathews, inspired by *The Turner Diaries*, founded the Order, a violent white supremacist group. The Order's war against the "Zionist

Domestic terrorist Timothy McVeigh was convicted of bombing the Murrah Federal Building in Oklahoma City.

Occupation Government" included counterfeiting, bank robbery, armored car robberies, and murder. The Order was responsible for the 1984 murder of talk radio host Alan Berg, who regularly lambasted the **neo-Nazi** movement. Also in 1984 the group robbed an armored car in Ukiah, California, and made off with $3.6 million. Matthews was traced to Whidbey Island in Washington, where he died in an FBI-led siege. Mathews is considered a martyr and an inspiration to other hate groups.[7]

On the political left, two violent single-issue groups have surfaced that focus on one particular issue to the exclusion of all others. The **Animal Liberation Front (ALF)** and the **Earth Liberation Front (ELF)** have committed numerous acts of violence, including arson and vandalism. ALF members favor direct action to protest animal abuse, with the objective of saving as many animals as possible. ELF was founded in England by activists who split from the environmentalist group EarthFirst! because of its decision to abandon criminal activities. ALF and ELF have coordinated their activities and have made joint claims about taking responsibility for property damage and other acts of vandalism. Both groups have been nonviolent toward humans, but they have committed many incidents of property destruction. ALF/ELF actions have included the following:

- Destruction of a forest station in Oregon
- Destruction of the University of California at Davis livestock research laboratory
- Tree spiking, which involves pounding metal staves into trees in logging areas for the purpose of destroying logging equipment
- "Liberating" minks in Wisconsin
- Arson at the ski resort of Vail, Colorado

The FBI estimates that ELF alone has caused about $100 million in property damage since 1996. In one particularly destructive incident in August 2003, the group caused $50 million in damages to a condominium complex under construction in San Diego, California.[8]

INTERNATIONAL TERRORISM

Title 18, section 2331(1), of the United States Code defines **international terrorism** as occurring primarily outside the territorial jurisdiction of the United States or transcending national boundaries. The U.S. State Department has identified thirty-six groups as foreign terrorist organizations. The most dangerous of these is **Al Qaeda**, which means "the base" or "the base of Allah's support."

Al Qaeda was founded by Osama bin Laden in the early 1980s to support the effort in Afghanistan against the invasion by the former Soviet Union. These holy warriors, or **Mujahedeen**, were supported by the United States, and in 1989 the Soviets retreated. Bin Laden, born in 1957, is one of fifty-two siblings of a business tycoon who made billions of dollars in the construction business on the Arabian Peninsula. After the death of his father,

International terrorist Osama bin Laden is leader of the Al Qaeda network, which is responsible for the events of 9/11.

bin Laden allegedly inherited over $300 million. He studied engineering at a Saudi university where he was exposed to the writing and teachings of radical Muslim concepts.

In 1990 Iraq invaded Kuwait and the American-led coalition drove the invaders out in what was known as Operation Desert Storm. Radical Muslims, such as bin Laden, were appalled to find Muslims fighting Muslims under American leadership. In addition, Al Qaeda opposed the United States for its support of Israel and because of its perceived decadent society. Bin Laden declared war on the United States and began training his followers in terrorist tactics in training camps in Somalia and Afghanistan. Al Qaeda's presence has been confirmed in at least fifty-five countries and is believed responsible for the following terrorist attacks:[9]

1992 Bombed hotel in Yemen housing U.S. troops

1993 Bombed the World Trade Center in New York City

1993 Somalia firefight; 18 U.S. soldiers killed by Al Qaeda–trained extremists

1995 Bombed National Guard building in Riyadh, Saudi Arabia; 5 U.S. soldiers killed

1996 Bombed U.S. military housing known as Khobar Towers in Dharan, Saudi Arabia; 19 Americans killed

1998 Suicide bombings of U.S. embassies in Nairobi and Dar Es Salaam, Tanzania; more than 230 killed and 5,000 injured

1999 Planned "Millennium Bombing" attacks in Jordan and the Los
   Angeles airport; prevented by arrests

2000 Suicide bombing of the destroyer *U.S.S. Cole* in Aden, Yemen;
   17 sailors killed, 39 injured

2001 Suicide bombing of the World Trade Center and Pentagon;
   3,000 killed

2003 Multiple suicide bombing in Morocco; 32 killed at five locations

2003 Multiple suicide bombings in Saudi Arabia; 40 killed

When Israel invaded Lebanon in 1982, Iran responded by sending its Revolutionary Guards to Lebanon, which led to the creation of a new terrorist network called **Hizbollah**, or "the party of God." In the same year, French paratroopers and U.S. marines arrived in Beirut as part of a multinational peacekeeping force. Hizbollah viewed the peacekeeping force as an act of aggression, and on October 23, 1983, two suicide bombers driving vehicle bombs simultaneously struck the Marine barracks and the paratroopers' headquarters; 241 Marines and 58 paratroopers were killed. The remaining peacekeeping forces were withdrawn in early 1984.[10]

With the bombing of the marine barracks, Hizbollah introduced a new terrorist tactic, the suicide bomber that has plagued the Middle East since that time. Hizbollah kidnapped dozens of Western hostages from numerous countries for economic and political gain. Eighteen Americans were held hostage from 1983 until the release of the final hostage in 1991. During that time, three American hostages were killed. Hizbollah transcended Lebanon's borders in 1992 when it bombed the Israel embassy in Buenos Aires. It struck again two years later with the truck bombing of the Argentine–Jewish Mutual Association, which claimed the lives of nearly a hundred persons.[11]

Hizbollah continues to conduct military provocations by firing into Israel's territory and conducting cross-border raids. The kidnapping of three Israel soldiers in the summer of 2006 provoked a month-long war between Hizbollah and Israel.

One of the most volatile militant organizations in the Middle East is the Islamic Resistance Movement, better known as **Hamas**. Unlike Hizbollah, this group grew from the Palestinian liberation movement. Hamas's position is that the State of Israel should not exist. In its view the only acceptable solution to the Palestinian problem is to eliminate Israel and create a united Arab realm. According to Hamas, the State of Israel and anyone who supports it are abominations to Islam.

To understand Hamas, it is necessary to go back to the events right after World War I. Because of British promises, many Arabs felt that the entire Middle East would be united under one great Arabic banner, from North Africa to the Iranian border, known as **dar al-Islam**. When the European powers divided the area, taking control of some regions and placing their Arab allies in control of others, many Arabs were infuriated. One group, the Muslim Brotherhood, founded in 1925, rejected the new territorial lines and called for the unification of the entire Arab realm under the control of Islam.

The Muslim Brotherhood registered as a religious organization with the Israeli government in 1978 and attempted to convert followers into a more pristine version of Islam. In the 1980s as Yasser Arafat, the leader of the Palestinian Liberation Organization, moved toward moderation, the Muslim Brotherhood maintained its rigid views on the unification of the realm of Arabs and the necessity to rule through Islamic law. When the call for self-government began to dominate the Palestinian liberation movement, the Muslim Brotherhood rejected the idea because no nation should exist outside dar al-Islam. In 1987 the Muslim Brotherhood formed Hamas, an Arabic acronym for Harakat al-Muqawama al-Islamiyya, or "Islamic Resistance Movement."

Hamas states that it is at war with the Jewish people and the State of Israel. Its purpose is to kill Jews and drive the Zionist settlers and their allies from the area. The only acceptable outcome for Hamas is the united realm of Islam. Hamas is well financed, and its tentacles reach outside of the Middle East, including support bases in the United States. So far Hamas has been successful in disrupting the peace process and is engaged in a constant barrage of terrorist activities against the State of Israel, including suicide bombings and the shelling of Jewish settlements.[12]

WEAPONS OF MASS DESTRUCTION

The rationale for a terrorist to use weapons of mass destruction at the most basic level is simply the desire to kill as many people as possible. Chemical, biological, radiological, and nuclear weapons could give a terrorist group the ability to kill thousands, possibly even hundreds of thousands of people in a single strike.

Chemical agents include choking gases such as phosgene and chlorine, blood agents including hydrogen cyanide and cyanogen chloride, blister agents such as mustard gas, and nerve agents such as sarin. Due to the difficulty in obtaining these chemicals, terrorists would most likely reject most of them. However, sarin is relatively easy to make, and the Japanese terrorist group Aum Shinriko used this agent to attack the Tokyo subway system in 1995, killing 12 and injuring more than 5,000 others.

Biological agents are available to terrorists in a number of different ways, such as purchasing from one of the world's 1,500 germ banks, theft from a research laboratory, isolation and cultivation from natural sources, or through a rogue state or a state sponsor of terrorism. The principal obstacle in the use of biological agents is the development of sufficient quantities to cause mass casualties. In October 2001, a series of anthrax-laced letters were mailed to political and media targets, including two U.S. senators and news anchor Tom Brokaw. Although these letters did not reach their intended targets, five people who handled the letters died.

Radiological terrorism involves the dispersion of **radioactive agents** by conventional means, most commonly known as a "dirty bomb." The sources of material for such a device would include nuclear waste from fuel processing and radiological medical isotopes from hospitals or research laboratories. Such a weapon would have the ability to kill a large number of people, and the resulting panic would be devastating. In 2002 José Padilla, a follower of Osama bin Laden, was arrested in Chicago for allegedly planning a dirty-bomb attack.

Nuclear terrorism involves the detonation of a nuclear device in a major metropolitan city causing massive casualties. With the fall of the former Soviet Union, such materials were stolen from military bases and became available on the black market. Another possible source is a rogue nation with nuclear capabilities, such as North Korea. Due to the unthinkable destructive power of nuclear devices, this is the worst case scenario.[13]

COUNTERTERRORISM

The lack of a coordinated response to terrorism became evident in the analysis of the attack on the World Trade Center and the Pentagon on September 11, 2001. In response to these events, the FBI expanded the use of the Joint Terrorism Task Force concept to include a joint task force in each of its fifty-six field offices. These task forces include investigators from other federal, state, and local law enforcement agencies who bring a variety of skills to the task force environment. These field investigators have immediate access to the National Joint Terrorism Task Force located at FBI headquarters in Washington, D.C. The national task force includes members from the Central Intelligence Agency (CIA) and FBI, and well as agents and officers from the Naval Criminal Investigative Service, Transportation Security Agency, U.S. Coast Guard, U.S. Bureau of Prisons, and approximately fifty other significant contributors to the national counterterrorism mission.[14]

The purpose of these activities is to gather information, or intelligence, in order to have the ability to anticipate the behavior of terrorists and to thereby predict future terrorist incidents. The basis for these predictions is from two sources: signal and human intelligence.

With proper court authorization, **signal intelligence** is used to intercept financial data and to monitor communications such as land-line and cell phones and e-mail messages. Satellite imagery is also used, as are sophisticated computers that specialize in code breaking.

Due to the cellular organization of terrorist groups and their insular interactions, technology alone cannot provide a sufficient counterterrorism response. **Human intelligence** is a critical component, therefore, and the first step in this process is a cooperative venture with intelligence agencies and law enforcement investigators, which is the purpose of the Joint Terrorism concept. Another source of human intelligence includes the development of informants affiliated with terrorist organizations or their support groups. The use of undercover police officers is not only dangerous but usually not productive as the members of terrorist cells are made up of individuals who know each other very well.

The United States has a number of intelligence-gathering agencies. The director of national intelligence is responsible for coordinating the various components of the intelligence community, which include the following agencies:[15]

Central Intelligence Agency.   **The Central Intelligence Agency (CIA)** is responsible for collecting intelligence outside the borders of the United States. The agency uses covert human and technological assets to gather information on terrorist activity.

Federal Bureau of Investigation.   **The Federal Bureau of Investigation (FBI)** is within the U.S. Department of Justice and is charged with conducting domestic counterterrorism efforts. The agency engages in domestic intelligence collection efforts and has agents deployed to U.S. embassies around the world.

National Security Agency.   **The National Security Agency (NSA)** is the technological unit of the intelligence community. Its primary mission is to collect communications and signal intelligence and to conduct code-breaking activities.

Defense Intelligence Agency.   Each branch of the military collects intelligence, and the **Defense Intelligence Agency (DIA)** coordinates and analyzes this information.

ROLE OF POLICE OPERATIONS UNITS

Operations units of a police agency have responsibility for controlling the acts of terrorists once they are threatened or in progress. Patrol units are the first line of defense in these instances, with specialists available to them. Specialists in threat analysis will pass on the credibility and potential of the threat. Bomb detection and disposal specialists will direct the search for explosives and incendiary devices and effect their disposal if found. Hostage negotiators will establish communications with terrorists in hostage–kidnapping cases and conduct negotiations leading to termination of the event.

The commanding officer of the operational units also has the responsibility of the preliminary investigation:

Threats

1. Date and time of threat, how received, and who received it
2. Nature of act threatened, including target, time element, and weapon (e.g., fire, bomb)
3. Demands or grievances accompanying threat
4. Stated political or organizational affiliation of threat maker, including any claims of responsibility for prior terrorist threats or acts
5. Other data, such as background noises (telephone threat, speech characteristics, and apparent personal characteristics of threat maker

Events

1. Arrest any terrorist at scene; identify; collect data and prepare "alarm" for terrorists who have fled scene.
2. Assign personnel to interview victims and witnesses and to search scene for evidence likely to identify the terrorists and modus operandi.
3. Assign personnel to protect the scene until qualified personnel can assist in the search for physical evidence.
4. Assign a sworn officer or supervisor to collate all collected information and evidence, and to prepare the preliminary report.

ROLE OF THE CRIMINAL INVESTIGATOR

The role of a criminal investigator in relation to terrorist acts can be summed up as folows:

1. Identification of responsible parties—co-conspirators
2. Reinterview of victims and witnesses to get statements, check stories; follow-up on physical evidence and laboratory examinations
3. Identification of co-conspirators—individuals on the fringes of the crime or criminal conspiracy
4. Pursuit of unapprehended terrorists and co-conspirators
5. In kidnapping cases, immediate organization of pursuit in the attempt to locate victim and terrorists; immediate action seeking the identity of the terrorists and the hideout in which the captive is held; participating in rescue planning; and, if ransom is paid, probing for clues to the kidnappers during ransom negotiations and the ransom payment and on release of the person kidnapped
6. Apprehension of all persons wanted in connection with the terrorist act or conspiracy
7. Investigation of all arrestees to disclose associations, past history, and potential for cooperation: (a) to serve as an accomplice witness and (b) to provide information
8. Upgrading of preventive intelligence surveillance to secure more information on suspects
9. Case preparation highlighting the relevancy and probative value of various items of evidence in relation to prosecution for a specific crime or crimes

An investigation should be considered incomplete util evidence, direct or circumstantial, has been secured of an overt act that constitutes a "substantial step" in furtherance of the conspiracy (Figure 18–1). Forming or planning a conspiracy is not a true overt act, nor are acts done merely to cement the agreement.

A social network analysis is useful in investigating terrorism. This is a linking of known members of a group (or "cell") with suspected members or just a linking of suspects believed to be joined in a group. First, the individual suspects are linked to each other, then to the group, and then to incidents and their scenes.[16]

Another network analysis is how the terrorists secured reliable information about the targets of their attacks, particularly the targets to be killed or kidnapped. The link-up here relates to who was the source of information: members, sympathizers, collaborators, dissidents, and so on. The names of these individuals should be worked into the social network analysis for development of connections between known members of a group and sources of information.[17]

Investigators assigned to the activities of terrorists require all the standard skills of criminal investigators, plus a high level of integrity and an appreciation for the legal significance of collected evidence. One guarantees against illegal shortcuts that may ruin evidence; the other is a safeguard against building a case on evidence of little relevance or probative value.

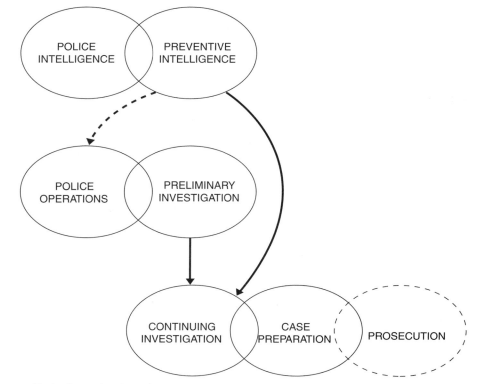

FIGURE 18–1   Investigation of terrorist activity.

PROBLEMS OF PROOF

Trials of terrorists in the United States have survived or perished on the issue of the legality or illegality of the means used by investigators to gather evidence. Electronic eavesdropping evidence has been attacked as an unreasonable and broad invasion of privacy; undercover agents have been described as partisan witnesses, unworthy of belief; and informants (and the rare accomplice witness) are perceived as persons of no credibility, intent on getting some benefit from the prosecution for their testimony. Unless the police–prosecutor team can overcome the damage wrought by these attacks, any jurors will downgrade the legal significance of the prosecution's evidence in these areas and conclude that a reasonable doubt of guilt exists.

CASE STUDY

Joint Terrorism Task Force

On February 23, 1997, a seventy-year-old Palestinian visited the observation deck of the Empire State Building in New York City. Shortly after arriving he opened fire with a handgun, killing one person and wounding seven others, before killing himself. A search of his clothing revealed a long rambling letter that expressed anti-U.S. and anti-Israel sentiments, along with a Florida identification card and a receipt for the weapon.

The FBI–New York City Police Department Joint Terrorism Task Force (JTTF) responded to the scene. The task force command center opened, and the various agencies that comprise the task force began working to ascertain the shooter's identity, his origin, and whether he had ties to any terrorist groups.

Within hours, the command center had answers. The FBI dispatched its legal attaché in Israel to the Gaza Strip to interview the subject's family.

The FBI and the local police in Florida interviewed several people who could help identify the shooter and track his movements while living in that state. It was determined that he had fulfilled the residency requirement and that he had legally purchased the murder weapon one month after arriving in this country.

The task force concluded that the shooter seemed mentally unstable. He had expressed hatred of Israel and the United States; however, he had no connection to any organized international terrorist group and had committed the attack alone. The speed at which these conclusions were reached is a testament to the effectiveness of the joint task force concept. According to investigators, had the JTTF not been in place, the investigation might have taken days or weeks, rather than hours, to complete.

Source: Robert A. Martin, "The Joint Terrorism Task Force: A Concept that Works," *FBI Law Enforcement Bulletin* 68, no. 3 (1999): 23–24.

CHAPTER REVIEW

KEY TERMS

Al Qaeda   *377*
Animal Liberation
   Front (ALF)   *377*
biological agent   *380*
Central Intelligence
   Agency (CIA)   *381*
chemical agent   *380*
dar al-Islam   *379*
Defense Intelligence
   Agency (DIA)   *382*
domestic
   terrorism   *375*

Earth Liberation
   Front (ELF)   *377*
ecoterrorist   *373*
Federal Bureau of
   Investigation (FBI)   *382*
Hamas   *379*
Hizbollah   *379*
human intelligence   *381*
international
   terrorism   *377*
kneecapping   *373*
Ku Klux Klan   *375*

Mujahedeen   *377*
narcoterrorist   *373*
National Security
   Agency (NSA)   *382*
neo-Nazi   *377*
nuclear terrorism   *381*
radiological agent   *380*
signal intelligence   *381*
terrorism   *372*
The Turner Diaries   *376*
tree spiking   *373*
white supremacy   *376*

REVIEW QUESTIONS

1. When Israel invaded Lebanon in 1982, Iran responded by sending its Revolutionary Guards into Lebanon, which led to the creation of a new terrorist network known as:
   a. Hamas
   b. Mujahedeen
   c. Al Qaeda
   d. Hizbollah

2. The group formed in Palestine to resist the moderate view of the acceptance of a separate Palestinian state is one of the most volatile militant

organizations in the Middle East and is known as:

a. Hamas
b. Mujahedeen
c. Al Qaeda
d. Hizbollah

3. The group founded in the early 1980s to support the Muslim effort in Afghanistan against the invasion by the former Soviet Union is known as:

a. Hamas
b. Mujahedeen
c. Al Qaeda
d. Hizbollah

4. The agency responsible for collecting intelligence inside the borders of the United States is known as the:

a. Central Intelligence Agency
b. Federal Bureau of Investigation
c. National Security Agency
d. Defense Intelligence Agency

5. The agency responsible for collecting intelligence outside the borders of the United States uses covert human and technological assets to gather information on terrorist activity and is known as the:

a. Central Intelligence Agency
b. Federal Bureau of Investigation
c. National Security Agency
d. Defense Intelligence Agency

6. The technological unit of the intelligence community whose primary mission is to collect communications and signal intelligence and conduct code-breaking activities is known as the:

a. Central Intelligence Agency
b. Federal Bureau of Investigation
c. National Security Agency
d. Defense Intelligence Agency

7. The group founded after the Civil War that used intimidating night raids to discourage newly freed blacks from voting is known as the:

a. Ku Klux Klan
b. Pierce Movement
c. Order
d. ALF/ELF

8. The group founded by Robert Mathews, who was inspired by the novel *The Turner Diaries*, has waged war against the U.S. government through counterfeiting, bank robberies, and murder and is known as the:

a. Ku Klux Klan
b. Pierce Movement
c. Order
d. ALF/ELF

9. The group concerned with a single issue that has committed numerous acts of arson and vandalism estimated in excess of $100 million since 1996 is known as the:

a. Ku Klux Klan
b. Pierce Movement
c. Order
d. ALF/ELF

10. The holy warriors supported by the United States for the purpose of repelling the invasion of Afghanistan by the Soviet Union in the early 1980s are known as the:

a. Hamas
b. Mujahedeen
c. Al Qaeda
d. Hizbollah

See Appendix D for the correct answers.

DISCUSSION QUESTIONS

1. Explain what a dirty bomb is and why terrorist groups would want to deploy such a weapon.
2. Define signal intelligence and explain how this information is gathered.

3. Define human intelligence and explain how this information is gathered.
4. What were the origins of the terrorist group Al Qaeda, and who is this group's founder?
5. Discuss the history of the Ku Klux Klan and the possibility of a reemergence of this group.
6. Explain the concept of the joint terrorism task force.

RELATED WEB SITES

For in-depth information on terrorism incidents and the groups responsible for them, visit the Web site of the Memorial Institute for the Prevention of Terrorism at *www.mipt.org*.

The Department of Homeland Security posts up-to-date information on the national threat level, press releases, current issues of national security, and employment opportunities on its Web page at *www.dhs.gov*.

You can go to the Central Intelligence Agency's Web page for information on its history, mission, values, and employment opportunities: *www.cia.gov*.

For information on foreign terrorist organizations and their activities, as well as a list of the most wanted terrorists, go to the United States Department of State Web site at *www.state.gov/s/ct*.

chapter **nineteen**

The Investigator as Witness and Ethical Awareness

CHAPTER OUTLINE

After reading this chapter you will be able to:

- Recognize the steps investigators take to prepare themselves for testifying in court.
- Identify the condition of stage fright that a witness may experience and how to deal with it.
- Discuss the role nonverbal communication plays in a witness's testimony.
- Describe how unethical conduct by law enforcement officers has impacted criminal investigations.
- Explain the remedies available to prevent future unethical conduct by law enforcement officers.

THE INVESTIGATOR AS WITNESS

At the conclusion of an investigation, an investigator does know the victim, the circumstances of the crime, the identity of the offender, and sometimes possesses data on the motive for the crime. He or she has collected facts, linked them together, and mentally shaped a pattern of the crime and a narrative of the event with form and order. However, the events and incidents of a crime are known to the investigator only indirectly, through the interviewing of witnesses and other techniques of investigation. No matter how much intelligence and honesty went into the many decisions common to any investigation, the sum total is a subjective impression in the mind of the investigator.

The investigator as a witness is confined to the same narrow band of personal knowledge as any other witness, and he or she is under the same requirement to establish a proper foundation to show personal knowledge prior to giving any oral evidence.

Criminal investigators have a basic obligation to court and community when testifying as a witness in a criminal case: to tell the truth as they have found it. They also have a basic obligation to themselves and their employing agency not to allow any item of their appearance or any act done within the courtroom to affect adversely their testimony on the witness stand. The legal significance of an investigator's testimony can be damaged by behavior not in harmony with his or her role as impartial fact finder and reporter. Men and women serving as trial jurors evaluate witnesses on what they say, how they say it, and their overt behavior while saying it.

ACTION PRIOR TO COURT APPEARANCE

Investigators should review the substance of their testimony before the trial of the defendant. Investigators can easily review areas of likely inquiry in direct examination by a friendly associate—the prosecutor. Unfortunately, investigators can never prepare fully for cross-examination, which is usually hostile questioning by the defense counsel. Major areas for this self-analysis are the following:

1. Is the possible testimony arrayed in a manner that allows the investigator to relate it simply and convincingly so that the triers of fact will both understand it and believe it?
2. Is the investigator willing to state that he or she does not know or cannot recall certain facts?
3. Is the investigator ready to acknowledge mistakes made in the investigation when questioned, and is he or she prepared to answer questions truthfully and directly, without hedging?
4. Is the investigator prepared to refute and rebut any allegation of "improving" the case against the defendant?
5. Will the investigator prepare for being a witness by refreshing his or her memory immediately prior to trial?

The legal significance of evidence demands a pretesting for credibility. Self-analysis is often difficult, but it is vital to the integrity of an investigator's testimony. The facts stated by the investigator as a witness will be tested in court against standard bases of credibility.

A short time prior to the date of court appearance, investigators should confer with the assigned prosecutor for a last-minute check. No doubt the prosecutor is well informed as to the expected testimony and possible areas of difficult cross-examination. A brief review just before a court appearance can be helpful to the investigator–witness. Ethical prosecutors will make certain that any conference with witnesses does not degenerate into a coaching session, and an investigator–witness should promptly admit to any such meetings under questioning, as they are normal case-preparation procedures.

On the date that an investigator is scheduled for a court appearance, he or she should allow a generous amount of time for the trip to the courthouse. This is a safeguard against unexpected traffic delays or other events that make the trip longer than anticipated. In court appearances, it is better to be very early than to rush in at the last minute.

On arrival at the courthouse and prior to opening of court, the investigator should sign in or check in as required by local regulations and make contact with the assigned prosecutor. If witnesses are excluded from the courtroom until they have testified and been excused, the investigator must wait outside the courtroom until a bailiff calls his or her name. If witnesses have not been excluded, the investigator should take a seat within the courtroom and await his or her call.

This is an excellent time to get rid of the **stage fright** not uncommon among witnesses about to testify. This is a nebulous fear, often based on no more than a reluctance to get up and talk in front of a group of people. With investigator–witnesses, it may be complicated by knowledge that the presiding judge is known to have a short-fuse temper or by the unpleasant memory of a previous experience with an aggressive cross-examiner.[1]

Stage fright is often cumulative. Initially, blood pressure and respiration rate of the witness increase, producing a feeling of being "charged up." This is accompanied by a noticeable dryness of the mouth and sometimes a shaking of the hands. This is unusual and uncomfortable, and the common reaction is greater anxiety.

Stage fright can be controlled. Planning ahead is the first step. Therefore, quickly review the substance of the case and possible questions. Second, mentally scan past experiences that can be termed "satisfactory" or better, and relax in the thought that such past experiences will be helpful in successfully concluding the forthcoming session as a witness. Finally, remember that anxiety at this time is nothing more than the witness's body preparing the person to do his or her best.[2]

GENERAL BEHAVIOR

Upon being called as a witness, the investigator walks promptly to the front of the courtroom. He or she stops in the "well" of the court, usually in front of the witness stand, to take the oath to tell the truth. This is an important stop on the way to the witness stand. A court officer proffers a Bible. The witness-to-be places his or her hand on it. The court officer then administers the oath (usually slowly and clearly), and the witness-to-be replies in the affirmative. The investigator's behavior during this portal ceremony should reflect a deep and sincere belief in the oath.

The first questioning of a witness that is not within the scope of any previous examination of the witness is the **direct examination** conducted by the party calling the witness (by subpoena). In the case of investigator–witnesses, this is most often the prosecutor. This questioner guides the witness to prevent deviation from relevant facts. This stage of the examination is followed by **cross-examination** by defense counsel. Cross-examiners are likely to be aggressive. In either stage of this examination, a witness is expected to be responsive to questions.

Cross-examiners often prefer to limit the responsiveness of a witness by phrasing questions calling for a yes-or-no answer. A "yes" means that the witness accepts the idea expressed in the question; a "no" indicates that the witness rejects the idea. If a cross-examiner does not use simple language in his or her query, then "yes" or "no" is not a simple response. Therefore, if a witness does not fully agree with the idea expressed in the question, he or she should give a negative response: "no." A "qualified yes" is often a responsive answer, but it is not usually allowed because the scope of the question may be extended when the witness explains the need to qualify the answer. As a general rule, the investigator–witness is not alone at this time. The prosecutor will usually speak out and ask the court to have the question withdrawn, reworded, or thrown out. Any witness who does not understand a question has the right to ask that the question be repeated, and it usually will be read by the court reporter. Sometimes, when this request is made, the questioner will withdraw the question and rephrase it.

How is it best to answer questions? Speak up! Speak clearly and loudly enough for everyone in the courtroom to hear all the testimony, and use simple language in making responses.

Simple language is plain talk. It helps people to understand the meaning of each answer. Beyond the limits of a yes-or-no answer, an investigator–witness should speak in complete sentences rather than sentence fragments. Normally, each sentence should express no more than one idea. Short sentences spread out ideas so that jurors, as well as others in the courtroom, get a breathing spell between them.[3]

Open-ended questions are often asked of investigator–witnesses during direct examination. These queries detail one segment of the investigation and ask the witness to respond in his or her own words. The key to a responsive answer, and one that will usually be understood by all listeners, is to use short sentences arranged in chronological order.

The time element in responding to questions is also important in any evaluation of a witness by in-court listeners. A short pause before responding is good behavior. It allows the prosecutor to interpose an objection to the question if he or she wishes. It also indicates a thoughtful reflection upon the substance of the question and the response.

Investigator–witnesses should avoid using underworld slang and police lingo. Jurors are unfamiliar with such language and will not understand it—and possibly will not understand a good portion of witnesses' responses in which this language is used. To many jurors a "hit" does not mean to kill, a "piece" does not indicate a pistol or revolver, and a "scam" does not describe a criminal conspiracy. Jurors also have little understanding of words common among police personnel—for instance, "pinch" (arrest), "frisk" (search), "DOA" (dead on arrival), and "FOA" (for other authority).

An investigator–witness must be courteous to questioners. It is an imperative rule, even with difficult defense attorneys. Questioners should be carefully addressed. Avoid the prefix "Mister," as it may be viewed as sarcasm. Be cautious of "Madam," as it not only means a lady but also is the title given to a woman in charge of a brothel. "Counselor" seems to be fairly safe as a general term for either the prosecutor or defense counsel, man or woman.

The apogee of discourtesy is to interrupt a questioner when he or she is phrasing a question. An interruption usually damages the ability of jurors to understand the question and any response made by the witness when the question is finally completed. Jurors, as well as others in the courtroom, view this conduct as argumentative. This evaluation can be harmful to the goals of the prosecution.

Another caution for any investigator–witness is not to argue with the defense counsel. Arguing destroys the image of the witness as an impartial fact finder and reporter. Jurors do not expect investigators to be "friendly with" the defendant or his or her counsel, but any argument during cross-examination can antagonize many jurors. It projects a hostility toward the defense beyond the expectations of these men and women. Remember: defendants are innocent until proven guilty.

A final caution is not to lie or misrecollect on the witness stand. Unfortunately, many investigator–witnesses are sensitive about one or more areas of the investigation in which they failed to perform up to standard or were overzealous in their performance. Rest assured that no circumstance of this area of the investigation will be left unexplored when a cross-examiner detects this sensitivity. It is also reasonably certain that any attempt to stonewall or cover-up can be disastrous to the credibility of the witness.

If any sensitive areas do exist, the best procedure is to discuss them with the assigned prosecutor prior to trial and then to obtain his or her guidance. These guidelines will probably be to admit to any substandard practice, inefficiency, or incompetence if questioning begins to exploit one or more of these areas. It is better to have the jurors think of a witness as a bungler (a common human condition) rather than a perjurer (an unacceptable human condition).

One survival technique for withstanding the most aggressive and belligerent cross-examination is to think and rethink constantly the fact that cross-examination of a witness is a constitutional right of all defendants—an absolute right.

NONVERBAL COMMUNICATION

Nonverbal communication is a process of a person transmitting unspoken cues that have potential meaning to one or more observers.[4] It includes anything someone does that another person finds meaningful. Nonverbal communication is body language, and body movement and eye behavior send signals to observers.

In the drama of witness and questioner as it is staged in U.S. courtrooms during criminal trials, the observers and listeners are jurors. These men and women are alert to what each witness is saying, and they are also alert to any body language signs that will help them to better understand the testimony of the witness and evaluate his or her credibility. Certainly many jurors mentally note what they do not hear to evaluate fully the net worth of what they do hear from a witness.

Communication without speech is transmitted through body movements and eye behavior. Facial expressions (smiles to frowns), head nods and shoulder shrugs, gestures (clenched fists to folded arms), leg crossing, and toe tapping are all body movements. The direction of eye movement, and the frequency and duration of eye contact, sum up common eye behavior.

A good portion of body language is involuntary and difficult or impossible to control. On the other hand, anyone can learn to mask some basic emotions.

Investigator–witnesses can easily learn the rudiments of masking nonverbal communication that indicates to observers that the witness is bored, impatient, anxious, surprised, angry, or fearful. Then a conscious effort to avoid these indicators while testifying should not interfere with the testimony of an investigator–witness.

As far as any body movement is concerned, most basic police academy lectures on being a witness have long emphasized "Don't fidget." Sit down. That's what witnesses are supposed to do on witness stands. Better yet, sit still.

Eye behavior is a nebulous area. "Do what comes naturally" is generally good advice. In making eye contact initially, the eyes should move casually to the presiding judge, the jury, prosecutor, defense counsel, defendant, and to the spectators. When asked a question, the eye contact is with the questioner. In answering, the eye contact moves from the questioner toward the jury, where the witness scans the jury box as he or she responds. If reading from notes or exhibits, the investigator–witness should look upward toward the jury box now and then and briefly make eye contact with one or two jurors. When extensive answers are called for by questions, the witness may pick out jurors who he or she believes to be more attentive than others and make eye contact without staring.

Clothing is also nonverbal communication, but investigator–witnesses are usually police officers, and most police departments have established rules for the appearance of their members in court. If a man or woman is working in uniform, these rules usually require court appearance in uniform. For members working as investigators in an out-of-uniform assignment, a dress code is usually specified—or stylized by custom—for appearance in so-called plainclothes. To identify the latter group as police officers, most departments require that badges or identification cards be pinned to the outer garment of the witness. Many badge cases are designed so that one-half of the case slips into the breast pocket of a coat and the other half hangs out and over the pocket, displaying the badge or ID card as if pinned to the coat.

To be identified as a police investigator by uniform or badge is not out of order. After being sworn in, a police witness must give his or her name, assignment, and the name of their employing agency. What may be considered a negative nonverbal communication is to stress this class membership by displaying a holstered revolver or pistol through an open jacket.

CONDUCT AFTER TESTIFYING

After testifying, the investigator–witness should make a graceful exit from the courtroom. Stopping to shake hands or chat with the prosecutor on the way out is definitely taboo. If the witness has not been excused by the court, he or she should wait in the hallway until the next recess prior to speaking to the prosecutor in low-key conversation. Also, this is the time for the witness to speak to the prosecutor about segments of his or her testimony about which the witness may be concerned.

Many prosecutors want the investigator–witness to be available for recall to the witness stand, and they will make whatever arrangements are necessary. While in or near the courtroom during this period, the investigator should not discuss his or her testimony with anyone except the prosecutor assigned to the case or a person designated by this official.

At this time, or shortly thereafter, the investigator should review in his or her own mind as much of the testimony given as possible. These are self-teaching sessions in which the investigator impartially examines his or her performance on the witness stand. In this fashion, every minute spent on the witness stand can be educational and serve as a means of improving future performance in court.

ETHICAL AWARENESS

Ethics is used as a euphemism for corruption and crime in U.S. police and law enforcement agencies. (A euphemism is the substitution of an inoffensive word or expression for one that might offend or suggest something unpleasant.) Law enforcement ethics includes two distinguishable topics: corruption and non-corrupt misconduct. The term **corruption**, as used in its traditional sense, involves an officer's misuse of police authority for personal gain; police **misconduct** may involve issues such as excessive use of force, violation of a suspect's constitutional rights, and a variety of other misdeeds.[5]

Dealing with these concerns can be called *ethical awareness*, as this term deals with some of the influences likely to cause criminal behavior and gets all the issues out on the table. **Ethical awareness**, even at average levels, warns a person that criminal behavior is "wrong," as well as unlawful, and warns that misconduct on the job is "wrong," substandard conduct. It also activates inner indications that it is not "right" for criminal investigators to use the wrong means to gain a desired result, the right means to achieve a wrong end, or to act out anything that is immoral or unprincipled.

CRIME AND OUTRAGEOUS CONDUCT

Corrupt conduct has a rich history in America's police establishment. Years ago, the locus of this corruption was vice and gambling. Madams, bookmakers, and other gambling-game operators paid police officers on vice squads for **protection** each month to avoid arrests. Today, the money tree includes narcotics and drug dealers and the thing of value is money—big money.

The money tree has shifted to narcotics law enforcement. Corrupt narcotics officers do not have a monthly "pad," similar to vice and gambling payments, for so-called protection. These agents depend on deals made at the time of the arrest or other threat to a drug dealer's business. It is a deal with the thing of value being money or drugs. Those deals, in fact, have the essential element of armed robbery![6]

IMPACT OF MISCONDUCT ON CRIMINAL INVESTIGATION

A major result of disclosures of misconduct is that the labor pool of men and women who want to become police officers will decrease and the most desirable candidates will not apply. Recruitment of working police officers will become more difficult as many applicants may now have records of prior misconduct.

Investigators have become aware of a change from the good old days when witnesses were not reluctant or unwilling to talk to investigating officers. They have identified this unfriendliness as a general mistrust of police, which indicates that simply blaming "a few bad apples" in a department cannot erase all of its recent transgressions. Investigators also are aware that the term **jury nullification** is becoming more common in the courthouses of America: the jury's not-guilty verdict is influenced by mistrust of police witnesses.

STANDARDS FOR CRIMINAL INVESTIGATORS

Investigators have obligations that derive from common membership in the community of investigators. A basic responsibility is to conform to prevailing practices and to be accountable when behavior is strange and unusual. In general, the behavior expected is that of a reasonable person exercising reasonable care, prudence, self-discipline, and judgment in his or her work. *Reasonable care*—in its legal definition—is care fairly and properly taken in response to the circumstances of a situation, such care as an ordinary prudent person would take in the same time frame, conditions, and act(s). *Self-discipline* and *judgment* mean jump-starting an inner moral sense in decisions on the moral quality of actions and discriminating between right and wrong.

Conforming to professional standards of conduct and having an appreciation of the ethical viewpoint of a reasonable person present a profile of an investigator who is conscientious, reliable, and responsible without regard for varying situations. It also describes a person who can justify, warrant, or excuse his or her conduct.

PREVENTION OF MISCONDUCT

Officers live and work in a constantly changing and dynamically social context in which they are exposed to a myriad of ethical conflicts. Those officers who are unprepared to meet these challenges are more likely to succumb to pressure from unethical peers and become compromised. The progression is predictable and for the most part preventable. If officers are going to survive ethical dilemmas, they need to be as mentally prepared as they would be for tactical encounters.

To be mentally prepared requires credible ethical instruction, proactive supervision, and continual ethical awareness. Ethical instruction begins at the academy and should continue throughout an officer's career. Ethical training taught in the academy should be reinforced by field training officers who have been selected as ethical role models and who have been provided with specific ethical awareness training. Ethical training should continue through ongoing professional training sessions and should be relevant, job-specific training on ethics rather than a knee-jerk reaction to some recent event.

Proactive supervision involves an acknowledgment of the existence of the **continuum of compromise** and the need to be ever vigilant for even the most minor unethical acts. Supervisors must be committed to acting quickly and must be held responsible for the unethical conduct of the officers under their command. Supervisors should strive to prevent small infractions of unethical conduct from becoming major problems. Proactive supervision also includes walking one's talk by setting the example of ethical professional conduct.[7]

CASE STUDY

The Special Crime Squad

Cast of Characters

Judge:	Anonymous
Defense Counsel:	Anonymous
Assistant District Attorney:	Anonymous
Defendant:	Bob (not otherwise identified)
Prosecution Witness:	Detective Sergeant Daniel Costello

SCENE: A courtroom. There is a high judicial bench, an adjacent witness stand and chair, and a table and two chairs in front of the bench and witness stand. As the scene opens, the judge is seated on the bench, the two chairs are occupied by the defendant and his counsel, the witness chair is empty, and the assistant district attorney is standing in front of it.

ASSISTANT DISTRICT ATTORNEY: I would like to call my first witness—Detective Sergeant Daniel Costello. (Sergeant Costello appears, is sworn in and sits down in witness chair.)

ASSISTANT DISTRICT ATTORNEY: What is your name and occupation?

DETECTIVE COSTELLO: Daniel Costello. I am a sergeant of detectives—all detectives are sergeants—and I work for the police force of this city.

ASSISTANT DISTRICT ATTORNEY: How long have you been in this occupation and rank?

DETECTIVE COSTELLO: Ten years in the police department, four years in the rank.

ASSISTANT DISTRICT ATTORNEY: About two years ago, I understand you were assigned to this new unit, the Organized Crime Suppression Squad, the OCSS, and that within a few days of working in your new job you visited a high official of your police force. Do you recall this event?

DETECTIVE COSTELLO: Yes, I do.

ASSISTANT DISTRICT ATTORNEY: When was it and who was involved?

DETECTIVE COSTELLO: It was just after St. Patrick's Day, March 18, of this year. It was about 10:00 in the morning, and the person involved was Captain Richard Jones of the Police Academy.

ASSISTANT DISTRICT ATTORNEY: Tell us in your own words what happened on this occasion.

DETECTIVE COSTELLO: I knew Captain Jones from the Academy—he was my instructor. He was a lieutenant, and I was a recruit. I told him I thought the OCSS, the whole group, was infiltrated or penetrated by the mob, the hoodlums, and drug pushers. He listened—I talked. His advice was to take it up with higher authorities in the department. He made a phone call arranging a meeting for me, and I thanked him and left the office.

ASSISTANT DISTRICT ATTORNEY: What happened next in direct relation to this talk?

DETECTIVE COSTELLO: I met a captain from the Internal Security Division that night, at a few minutes after 10:00, in the parking lot of the golf course—the city one.

ASSISTANT DISTRICT ATTORNEY: Please identify this man and tell us, again in your own words, what happened at this meeting.

DETECTIVE COSTELLO: His name is Captain John Behan. He works directly under the chief. He came over to my car, and I told him substantially what I had told Captain Jones. He told me that I had no specific evidence that he could use, but that if I was willing to work with him, I could get the evidence. Captain Behan gave me his home phone number and told me to call him. He said we would meet again where we were, in the golf course parking lot. That was for when I had something to tell him. We shook hands and split.

ASSISTANT DISTRICT ATTORNEY: Did you meet the captain again in this golf course parking lot? That is, Captain Behan?

DETECTIVE COSTELLO: Yes, I did. All told, I met with him about seven or eight times.

ASSISTANT DISTRICT ATTORNEY: At any of these meetings did Captain Behan spell out in any way what your job was in this new arrangement with him?

DETECTIVE COSTELLO: Yes, he did. Thoroughly. I was to work undercover, for him and the chief. I was to act as if nothing was out of order and to come up with some specific evidence of what I had said about dishonesty.

ASSISTANT DISTRICT ATTORNEY: In this new role, did you know the defendant?

DETECTIVE COSTELLO: Yes, he was one of my associates, another detective sergeant—a member of OCSS.

ASSISTANT DISTRICT ATTORNEY: During this time of your association with the defendant, did you at any time participate with the defendant in any event that led you to make a report about him to Captain Behan?

DETECTIVE COSTELLO: Yes, and it was on the Monday after I first met Captain Behan. That would be March 21 of this year.

ASSISTANT DISTRICT ATTORNEY: Tell us, in your own words, what happened at this time—on this occasion.

DETECTIVE COSTELLO: I met the defendant, Bob, in the Nitro Bar and Grill on Seventh and Main Streets. It was about 11:00 a.m. He had a hoodlum with him who I knew as Big Bart, Bart Nino, and he introduced us. Nino took some money from his pocket right away and handed some bills to me. I said, "What's that for?" Nino said, "Get yourself a hat." I said, "I don't wear a hat," and gave him back the money.

ASSISTANT DISTRICT ATTORNEY: Do you know the amount of money?

DETECTIVE COSTELLO: No, I don't. Several bills, folded up. No, I do not.

ASSISTANT DISTRICT ATTORNEY: What happened next?

DETECTIVE COSTELLO: Nino shrugged his shoulders and gave the money to Bob, the defendant. Then, Nino talked a little bit about nothing much, ball games and girls, and he left. I asked Bob, "What's he buying?" He said, "Not much." Then I said something like, "Why me?" He said, "Why not? You don't use money?" Then he told me that Nino wanted to get some records taken out of our squad files about his brother—his younger brother. Bob said the kid was trying to go legit, and our records were bugging him in getting a job. I heard him out, then left and went back to the office.

ASSISTANT DISTRICT ATTORNEY: Did you do anything in relation to this conversation?

DETECTIVE COSTELLO: Yes, I did. I went to our files. Everyone went out to lunch. I got young Nino's file folder out, looked at it, found he was wanted for suspicion of receiving stolen property and for suspicion of homicide in another case. I photocopied the file papers, and I put the photocopies copies in my desk drawer—which I locked—put the record file back in our filing cabinet, and then I went out to lunch myself.

ASSISTANT DISTRICT ATTORNEY: Now, at any future date, did you have anything to do with this record again?

DETECTIVE COSTELLO: Yes. It was the following Saturday—that's March 26, this year. I went into the office early, went to our files, and looked for young Nino's record. I took it out and examined it, and I found that the photo had been changed. Big Bart's photo was substituted for his brother's picture, and the wanted cards were missing.

ASSISTANT DISTRICT ATTORNEY: I show you a folder marked "Nino, Alberto," and I ask you, do you recognize it?

DETECTIVE COSTELLO: (Reading) Yes, it's the fixed-up, tampered-with folder.

ASSISTANT DISTRICT ATTORNEY: In relation to this photocopy of the original folder in your squad files about this young Nino—what happened to that?

DETECTIVE COSTELLO: I have that here (showing file folder) with me now.

ASSISTANT DISTRICT ATTORNEY: Your Honor, can I have both these files marked for identification? Thank you. Your witness (to defense counsel), counselor. (Defense counsel stands and begins cross-examination.)

DEFENSE COUNSEL: Are most of your fellow police officers honest?

DETECTIVE COSTELLO: Yes. Most of them are honest—and hard working.

DEFENSE COUNSEL: How many officers, in your knowledge, entered the police department for the purpose of becoming dishonest?

DETECTIVE COSTELLO: None, to my knowledge—not to my knowledge.

DEFENSE COUNSEL: I gather from your prompt answers that you know a great deal about your fellow police officers. Is that true?

DETECTIVE COSTELLO: Well—I guess I do. They're my coworkers. Why not?

DEFENSE COUNSEL: Now—tell the court if any conduct of yours has bothered or upset your fellow coworkers.

DETECTIVE COSTELLO: I don't—I don't understand the question.

DEFENSE COUNSEL: It's a simple question, but let me withdraw it, and phrase it in this fashion: To your knowledge has any of your conduct upset your fellow police officers?

DETECTIVE COSTELLO: Oh sure! That's a different thing. Sure, yes.

DEFENSE COUNSEL: Tell us of such an incident that you consider important.

DETECTIVE COSTELLO: Well—when I was transferred out of uniform, from patrol to the OCSS in plainclothes, I grew a beard (puts hands to face, indicating beard) and wore some clothes—well, the kind of clothes I only used to wear on my day off, kind of sharp, I suppose. The guys in the squad used to tell me, "What a disguise!"

DEFENSE COUNSEL: And that upset you, bothered you—emotionally disturbed you?

DETECTIVE COSTELLO: Well, I don't know all that. You asked the question. Say it bugged me a bit.

DEFENSE COUNSEL: Why? Why would this remark bother you—this "What a disguise!"?

DETECTIVE COSTELLO: It wasn't any makeup, really a disguise. It was just the clothes I liked. That's why it bothered me.

DEFENSE COUNSEL: Oh, I'm beginning to understand. Now—tell me this: In relation to the charges of dishonesty against my client, your fellow police officer, did you ever get any feedback from him about yourself as a person or as a police officer?

DETECTIVE COSTELLO: Yes, a few times, mostly about—or along the lines of—something like "Why don't you go along with the guys?" or "Why do you have to be different?"

DEFENSE COUNSEL: This was in relation to your manner of dress, your appearance?

DETECTIVE COSTELLO: No, it wasn't. It was in relation to the money he was making and that I didn't want to take—like from Nino.

DEFENSE COUNSEL: Your Honor, would you direct the witness just to answer the question?

JUDGE: No, I don't think I will. You asked the question, and it was open-ended. Let it stand along with its answer.

DEFENSE COUNSEL: Thank you, Your Honor.

DEFENSE COUNSEL: Did the defendant or any of your coworkers in this Organized Crime Squad ever actually do anything to indicate any dislike for you?

DETECTIVE COSTELLO: They—they sure did. All of them did. They stopped talking to me. Except when they had to, like a phone call for me, then it was a "Here, you—." Real brief. And they would stop talking to one another when I came in the room or walked up to them on the street.

DEFENSE COUNSEL: This animosity resulted from your dirty work—the role of informer or spying on your fellow workers?

DETECTIVE COSTELLO: No, counselor. At that time, no one knew of what you term "dirty work." All they knew was that I wouldn't do any business with the hoodlums—that I wanted to do my job just like I get paid for it.

DEFENSE COUNSEL: There is entrapment in your role, is there not?

ASSISTANT DISTRICT ATTORNEY: Your Honor, I object. The question—

JUDGE: (Interrupting) Sustained.

DEFENSE COUNSEL: (Resuming questioning) Since you place such a premium on doing what you get paid for, did you ever counsel or advise my client to do the same thing?

DETECTIVE COSTELLO: You sure you want to hear this?

DEFENSE COUNSEL: I asked the question.

DETECTIVE COSTELLO: Just before I left the Nitro Bar on the day we met Big Bart Nino, I said to Bob, the defendant, "My God, you're making good money as a police detective. You could never make this kind of money on the outside doing any other kind of work. You know you have a family, kids. Don't be stupid. Think about it." That was how it ended.

DEFENSE COUNSEL: Was there any response to these words of yours—any words said at all by my client?

DETECTIVE COSTELLO: No, not much. Something like "If I really did think about it, I'd blow my brains out."

Source: Paul B. Weston, *Criminal Justice and Law Enforcement: Cases* (Englewood Cliffs, NJ: Prentice Hall, 1972). Reprinted by permission of Prentice Hall.

CHAPTER REVIEW

KEY TERMS

continuum of
  compromise   *397*
corruption   *395*
cross-examination   *392*
direct examination   *392*

ethical awareness   *395*
ethics   *395*
jury nullification   *396*
misconduct   *395*

nonverbal
  communication   *393*
protection   *395*
stage fright   *391*

REVIEW QUESTIONS

1. The hostile questioning by the defense counsel in known as _____.

2. The first questioning of a witness that is conducted by the attorney calling the witness is known as _____.

3. A short _____ before responding to a question allows the prosecution to offer an objection to the question.

4. An officer's misuse of his or her police authority for personal gain is known as _____.

5. Police use of excessive force, or the violation of a suspect's constitutional rights, are both examples of police _____.

6. A jury's not-guilty verdict that is influenced by the mistrust of police witnesses is known as _____.

7. Ethical training should begin as part of the _____ curriculum.

8. Ethical training should be reinforced by _____ who have been selected as ethical role models.

9. Ethical training should continue throughout an officer's career with specific professional training sessions based on relevant _____ training.

10. The progression of a compromised officer is predictable and, therefore, _____ .

See Appendix D for the correct answers.

DISCUSSION QUESTIONS

1. Can stage fright be controlled? How?
2. Why are investigator–witnesses advised not to argue with a cross-examiner?
3. Define nonverbal communication.
4. What body movements indicate boredom, impatience, anxiety?
5. Do you believe eye contact between an investigator–witness and jurors in a criminal trial is important? Why?
6. Sum up the recommended behavior for investigator–witnesses following their appearance on the witness stand.
7. Do the facts of this case study justify a conclusion that police dishonesty is an inescapable part of the "system"?
8. In the case study, is the "thing of value" in this attempt to corrupt Detective Costello the money that would be given to him or the approval of his associates?
9. If you were a member of the jury in the case study, would you consider Detective Costello to be a credible witness and his testimony truthful?

RELATED WEB SITES

The U.S. Department of Justice (DOJ), Civil Rights Division, Special Litigation Section, seeks court orders to address systemic cases of police misconduct. To review the types of complaints addressed by this agency, consult the DOJ Web site at *www.usdoj.gov/crt/split/police.htm.*

The FBI's Civil Rights Division is responsible for investigating citizens' allegations of police misconduct, known as "color or law" violations. The FBI Web site can be accessed at *www.fbi.gov/hq/cid/civilrights/color.htm.*

Appendixes

Notes

Glossary

Selected Bibliography

Index

appendix A

Case Briefs

A. SEARCH AND SEIZURE

Fourth Amendment of the United States Constitution

Mapp v. Ohio, 367 U.S. 643 (1961)

Facts: Miss Dolly Mapp was convicted of the possession of lewd and lascivious books, pictures, and photographs. At her trial, evidence seized during a forcible search of her home without a warrant was admitted into evidence and was the primary evidence leading to her conviction.

Issue: Can evidence seized during an illegal search be admitted as evidence to convict a defendant?

Decision: No evidence seized illegally may be admitted in evidence in any case. It must be excluded as evidence in any state or federal court. The exclusionary sanction is to deter the police from unlawful acts and preserve the integrity of the court.

Katz v. United States, 389 U.S. 347 (1967)

Facts: Charles Katz was convicted in a U.S. district court of transmitting wagering information by telephone. At his trial, the prosecution was permitted to introduce evidence of Katz's portion of telephone conversations, despite defense counsel's objection. Eavesdropping was by agents of the Federal Bureau of Investigation, who had attached an electronic eavesdropping and recording device to the outside of the public telephone booth used by Katz.

Issue: Was the evidence obtained through a legal surveillance (electronic eavesdropping)?

Decision: It was reversible error to admit such evidence, in view of the lack of prior judicial authorization (search warrant).

Dalia v. United States, 441 U.S. 238 (1979)

Facts: Pursuant to Title III of the Omnibus Crime Control and Safe Streets Act of 1968, the federal district court found probable cause and authorized the government to intercept all oral conversations taking place in the suspect's business office. Even though the court order did not specifically authorize entry of the suspect's business office by government agents, FBI agents did secretly enter the business office at midnight and install an electronic bug.

Issue: Was the secret entry of the specified office a violation of the Fourth Amendment or the federal statute?

Decision: Secret entry to install an electronic device pursuant to a lawful search warrant is not a violation of the U.S. Constitution or the statute.

Terry v. Ohio, 392 U.S. 1 (1968)

Facts: A revolver was introduced in evidence at the trial of John W. Terry for carrying a concealed weapon unlawfully (after failure of a pretrial motion to suppress). A police officer had observed unusual conduct by Terry and two other men, and—concluding that they were contemplating a robbery—he stopped and frisked them, discovering the weapon carried by Terry and seizing it.

Issue: Is the police stop-and-frisk procedure constitutional?

Decision: The police stop-and-frisk procedure does not violate the Fourth Amendment rights of Terry (under the circumstances of the case), and the revolver seized from Terry was property admissible at his trial for carrying a concealed weapon unlawfully.

Chimel v. California, 395 U.S. 752 (1969)

Facts: Police officers armed with an arrest warrant but not a search warrant were admitted to Chimel's home by his wife in his absence. The officers awaited Chimel's arrival and then arrested him when he entered his home. Chimel refused consent to the officers' search of his home (to "look around"). Despite this refusal, officers searched the entire home on a claim that the lawful arrest justified the search. Chimel was convicted on burglary charges, items taken from his home during the police search having been admitted into evidence despite counsel's objection on constitutional grounds.

Issue: What is the scope of a search incidental to a lawful arrest?

Decision: Under the circumstances of this case, the scope of the police search was unreasonable under the Fourth and Fourteenth Amendments.

Gustafson v. Florida, 414 U.S. 260 (1973)

Facts: James F. Gustafson was convicted for unlawful possession of marijuana. The state introduced in evidence several marijuana cigarettes found in a box in Gustafson's coat pocket when a municipal police officer conducted a full body search of Gustafson after a lawful arrest for driving an automobile without having his driver's license in his possession.

Issue: Was the scope of this search connected with a lawful traffic arrest reasonable?

Decision: The scope of the search was reasonable under the Fourth and Fourteenth Amendments of the Constitution.

Rochin v. California, 342 U.S. 165 (1952)

Facts: Having "some information" that Rochin was selling narcotics, officers went to his home and found the defendant in bed. On the nightstand were some capsules, and when the officers asked what they were, Rochin put them in his mouth and swollowed them. He was taken to the hospital where his stomach was pumped against his will. Two capsules that contained morphine were recovered, and he was convicted for possession or narcotics.

Issue: Was the scope of this search—the pumping of his stomach—unreasonable?

Decision: The court found that this search was unreasonable as it runs counter to the decencies of civilized conduct and, as such, shocks the conscience of the court and society.

B. INTERROGATION

Payne v. Arkansas, 356 U.S. 560 (1958)

Facts: The suspect confessed to murder, was convicted by this and other evidence of murder in the first degree, and was sentenced to death. Undisputed evidence in this case showed that Payne, a mentally dull nineteen-year-old youth, (1) was arrested without a warrant; (2) was denied a hearing before a magistrate, at which he would have been advised of his right to remain silent and of his right to counsel, as required by Arkansas statutes; (3) was not advised of his right to remain silent or of his right to counsel; (4) was held incommunicado for three days, without counsel, advisor, or friend, during which time members of his family tried to see him but were turned away and he was refused permission to make even one telephone call; (5) was denied food for long periods; and finally, (6) was told by the chief of police "that there would be thirty or fourty people there in a few minutes that wanted to get him."

Issue: Did the acts and statements of the police deprive the suspect of due process of law?

Decision: The use in a state criminal trial of a defendant's confession obtained by coercion—whether physical or mental—is forbidden by the Fourteenth Amendment.

Lego v. Toomey, 404 U.S. 477 (1972)

Facts: The suspect was arrested and made a confession to the police. Evidence was conflicting on the issue of voluntariness (coercion) of the confession. The trial court admitted the confession into evidence.

Issue: What is the burden of proof necessary to admit a confession into evidence? Who determines the admissibility of the confession?

Decision: "By a preponderance of the evidence" is a constitutionally permissible burden of proof. Admissibility of evidence is a determination for the court, not the jury.

Miranda v. Arizona, 384 U.S. 436 (1966)

Facts: Ernesto A. Miranda was arrested by police for kidnapping and rape and taken to an interrogation room in a police building. In response to police questioning, Miranda signed a confession containing a typed paragraph stating that the confession was made voluntarily with full knowledge of his legal rights and with the understanding that any statement he made therein might be used against him. This confession was admitted in evidence at his trial on kidnapping and rape charges, and Miranda was convicted as charged.

Issue: Were Miranda's constitutional rights to counsel and against self-incrimination violated?

Decision: In the absence of intelligent waiver of the constitutional rights involved, confessions and other statements obtained by custodial police interrogation are inadmissible in evidence, where the suspect (as Miranda) was not informed of his right to counsel, or of his right to be silent, or of the possible use of his statements as evidence against him.

C. RIGHT TO AN ATTORNEY

Gideon v. Wainwright, 372 U.S. 335 (1963)

Facts: The defendant was charged and convicted of the felony of breaking and entering a poolroom with intent to commit a misdemeanor. The trial court denied defendant's request for an appointed attorney pursuant to Florida law, which allowed appointed attorneys for indigent defendants in capital cases only. The defendant proceeded to trial and was convicted without an attorney to represent him.

Issue: Does the Constitution require the appointment of an attorney for indigent defendants accused of crime?

Decision: The Sixth Amendment requires appointment of counsel unless waived for indigents accused of crime. The provision is obligatory on the states by the Fourteenth Amendment.

United States v. Wade, 388 U.S. 218 (1967)

Facts: Several weeks after Wade's indictment for robbery of a federally insured bank and for conspiracy, Wade was, without notice to his appointed counsel, placed in a lineup in which each person wore strips of tape on his face, as the robber allegedly had done and, on direction, repeated words like those the robber allegedly had used. Two bank employees identified Wade as the robber. At the trial, when asked if the robber was in the courtroom, they identified Wade. The prior lineup identifications were elicited on cross-examination. Urging that the conduct of the lineup violated his Fifth Amendment privilege against self-incrimination and his Sixth Amendment right to counsel, Wade filed a motion for judgment of acquittal or, alternatively, for a ruling to strike the courtroom identifications. The trial court denied the motions, and Wade was convicted.

Issue: Are courtroom identifications of an accused at trial to be excluded from evidence because the accused was exhibited to the witnesses before trial at a postindictment lineup conducted for identification purposes without notice to and in the absence of the accused's appointed counsel?

Decision: In-court identification by a witness to whom the accused was exhibited before trial in the absence of counsel must be excluded, unless it can be established that such evidence had an independent origin or that error in its admission was harmless beyond a reasonable doubt.

appendix B

Federal Controlled Substances Law*

TITLE 21, USC   *SECTION 812*

The five schedules of controlled substances and placement into any one of these schedules are as follows:

Schedule I

A. The drug has a high potential for abuse.
B. The drug has no currently accepted medical use in treatment in the United States.
C. There is a lack of accepted safety for use of the drug under medical supervision.

Schedule I Controlled Substances

Heroin
Lysergic acid diethylamide (LSD)
Marijuana
Mescaline
Peyote
Psilocybin

Schedule II

A. The drug has a high potential for abuse.
B. The drug has a currently accepted medical use in treatment in the United States or a currently accepted medical use with severe restrictions.
C. Abuse of the drug may lead to severe psychological or physical dependence.

---

*This section has been edited, and for a full understanding of the law in this area your attention is directed to Title 21 of the United States Code, sections 812–844.

Schedule II Controlled Substances

Cocaine
Opium
Fentanyl
Methadone
Injectable Methamphetamine

Schedule III

A. The drug has a potential for abuse less than the drugs in Schedules I and II.
B. The drug has a currently accepted medical use in treatment in the United States.
C. Abuse of the drug may lead to moderate or low physical dependence or high psychological dependence.

Schedule III Controlled Substances

Amphetamine
Methamphetamine
Barbituric acid
Phencyclidine
Codeine
Anabolic steroids

Schedule IV

A. The drug has a low potential for abuse relative to the drugs in Schedule III.
B. The drug has a currently accepted medical use in treatment in the United States.
C. Abuse of the drug may lead to limited physical dependence or psychological dependence relative to the drugs in Schedule III.

Schedule IV Controlled Substances

Barbital
Chloral hydrate

Schedule V

A. Any compound, mixture, or preparation containing limited quantities of narcotic drugs, such as the following:
Codeine
Dihydrocodeine
Ethylmorphine
Opium

TITLE 21, USC   *SECTION 841:   PROHIBITED ACTS*

It shall be unlawful for any person knowingly or intentionally to manufacture, distribute, or dispense, or possess 1 kilogram or more of heroin, 5 kilograms or more of cocaine, 100 grams or more of phencyclidine (PCP), 10 grams or more of lysergic acid diethylamide (LSD); 1,000 kilograms or more of marijuana, or 1,000 marijuana plants; 50 grams or more of methamphetamine. Such person shall be sentenced to a term of imprisonment that may not be less than 10 years or more than life, and if death or serious bodily injury results from the use of such substances shall be not less than 20 years or more than life, a fine not to exceed $4,000,000 if the defendant is an individual or $10,000,000 if the defendant is other than an individual.

After a prior conviction for a felony drug offense, such person shall be sentenced to a term of imprisonment that may not be less than 20 years and not more than life imprisonment, and if death or serious bodily injury results from the use of such substances shall be sentenced to life imprisonment, a fine not to exceed $8,000,000 if the defendant is an individual or $20,000,000 if the defendant is other than an individual, or both.

TITLE 21, USC   *SECTION 844:   PENALTIES FOR SIMPLE POSSESSION*

It shall be unlawful for any person knowingly or intentionally to possess a controlled substance unless such substance was obtained directly, or pursuant to a valid prescription or order, from a practitioner, while acting in the course of his or her professional practice. Any person who violates this subsection may be sentenced to a term of imprisonment of not more than 1 year and shall be fined a minimum of $1,000 or both. A person with a prior conviction shall be imprisoned for not less than 15 days but not more than 2 years and shall be fined a minimum of $2,500. After two prior convictions, the person shall be imprisoned for not less than 90 days but not more than 3 years and shall be fined a minimum of $5,000. Notwithstanding the preceding sentence, a person convicted under this section for the possession of a mixture or substance that contains cocaine base shall be imprisoned not less than 5 years and not more than 20 years and fined a minimum of $1,000.

appendix C

Identity Theft: What to Do if It Happens to You

This guide provides victims of identity theft with the major resources to contact for help. Unfortunately, at this time, victims themselves are burdened with resolving the problem. It is important to act quickly and assertively to minimize the damage.

In dealing with authorities and financial institutions, keep a log of all conversations, including dates, names, and phone numbers. Note time spent and any expenses incurred. Confirm conversations in writing. Send correspondence by certified mail (return receipt requested). Keep copies of all letters and documents.

WHAT TO DO

Once you discover you are a victim of identity theft, you should do the following:

1. *Credit Bureaus.* Immediately call the fraud units of the three credit-reporting companies: Experian (formerly TRW), Equifax, and Trans Union. Report the theft of your credit cards or numbers. Ask that your account be flagged. Also, add a victim's statement to your report, using up to 100 words. (Example: "My ID has been used to apply for credit fraudulently. Contact me to verify all applications.") Be sure to ask for how long the fraud alert will be posted on your account and how you can extend it if necessary. Be aware that these measures may not entirely stop new fraudulent accounts from being opened by the imposter. Ask the credit bureaus, in writing, to provide you with free copies every few months so you can monitor your credit reports.

Ask the credit bureaus for names and phone numbers of credit grantors with whom fraudulent accounts have been opened. Ask the credit bureaus to remove inquiries that have been generated as a result of the fraudulent access. You may also ask the credit bureaus to notify those who have received your credit report in the last six months to alert them to the disputed and erroneous information (2 years for employers).

2. *Creditors.*   Immediately contact by phone and in writing all creditors with whom your name has been used fraudulently. Get replacement cards with new account numbers for your own accounts that have been used fraudulently. Ask that old accounts be processed as "Account closed at consumer's request." (This is better than "Card lost or stolen," because when this statement is reported to credit bureaus it can be interpreted as blaming you for the loss.) Carefully monitor your mail and credit card bills for evidence of new fraudulent activity. Report it immediately to credit grantors.

   Creditors' requirements to verify fraud. You may be asked by banks and credit grantors to fill out and notarize fraud affidavits. This could become costly. The law does not require that a notarized affidavit be provided to creditors. A written statement and supporting documentation should be enough (unless the creditor offers to pay for the notary).

3. *Stolen Checks.*   If you have had checks stolen or bank accounts set up fraudulently, report it to the check verification companies. Put "Stop Payments" on any outstanding checks about which you are unsure. Cancel your checking and savings accounts and obtain new account numbers. Give the bank a secret password for your account (*not* your mother's maiden name).

4. *ATM Cards.*   If your ATM card has been stolen or compromised, get a new card, account number, and PIN. Do not use your old password. When creating a password, do not use common numbers such as the last four digits of your Social Security number or your birth date.

5. *Fraudulent Change of Address.*   Notify the local postal inspector if you suspect an identity thief has filed a change of your address with the post office or has used the mail to commit check or bank fraud. (Call the local postmaster to obtain the phone number.) Find out where the fraudulent credit cards were sent, and notify the local postmaster for that address to forward all mail in your name to your own address. You may also need to talk with the mail carrier.

6. *Social Security Number Misuse.*   Call the Social Security Administration (SSA) to report fraudulent use of your Social Security number. As a last resort, you might want to change your number. The SSA will only change it if you fit its fraud victim criteria. Also order a copy of your Earnings and Benefits Statement and check it for accuracy.

7. *Passports.*   If you have a passport, notify the passport office in writing to be on the lookout for anyone ordering a new passport fraudulently in your name.

8. *Phone Service.*   If your long-distance calling card has been stolen or you discover fraudulent charges on your bill, cancel the account and open a new one. Provide a password that must be used any time the account is changed.

9. *Driver's License Number Misuse.*   You may need to change your driver's license number if someone is using yours as identification on

bad checks. Call the Department of Motor Vehicles (DMV) to see if another license was issued in your name. Put a fraud alert on your license. Go to your local DMV to request a new number. Also, fill out the DMV's complaint form to begin the fraud investigation process. Send supporting documents with the complaint form to the nearest DMV investigation office.

10. ***Law Enforcement.***   Report the crime to the law enforcement agency within the jurisdiction for your case. Give the agency as much documented evidence as possible. Get a copy of your police report. Keep the phone number of your fraud investigator handy and give it to creditors and others who require verification of your case. Credit card companies and banks may require you to show the report to verify the crime. Some police departments have been known to refuse to write reports on such crimes. Be persistent!

11. ***False Civil and Criminal Judgments.***   Sometimes victims of identity theft are wrongfully accused of crimes committed by the imposter. If a civil judgment has been entered in your name for actions taken by your imposter, contact the court where the judgment was entered and report that you are a victim of identity theft. If you are wrongfully prosecuted for criminal charges, contact the Department of Justice in your state and the FBI. Ask how to clear your name.

12. ***Legal Help.***   You may want to consult an attorney to determine legal action to take against creditors or credit bureaus if they are not cooperative in removing fraudulent entries from your credit report or if negligence is a factor. Call the local bar association to find an attorney who specializes in consumer law and the Fair Credit Reporting Act.

13. ***Dealing with Emotional Stress.***   Psychological counseling may help you deal with the stress and anxiety commonly experienced by victims. Know that you are not alone.

Answers to Chapter Review Questions

CHAPTER 1

1. a 2. c 3. b 4. b 5. d 6. b 7. a 8. d 9. c 10. c

CHAPTER 2

1. a 2. b 3. a 4. c 5. d 6. b 7. c 8. b 9. d 10. a

CHAPTER 3

1. b 2. d 3. a 4. c 5. b 6. c 7. a 8. d 9. Open fields
10. Oath or affirmation

CHAPTER 4

1. a 2. b 3. Ruler 4. b 5. c 6. d 7. c 8. General/specific
9. Aerial 10. Do not

CHAPTER 5

1. a 2. b 3. c 4. d 5. d 6. Polymerase chain reaction
7. b 8. a 9. d 10. a

CHAPTER 6

1. a 2. c 3. Modus operandi 4. c 5. a 6. d 7. Dirty
business 8. b 9. a 10. c

CHAPTER 7

1. d 2. They make excellent witnesses 3. a 4. b 5. c
6. Intelligence 7. b 8. a 9. c 10. *United States v. Wade*

CHAPTER 8

1. b   2. a.   3. b   4. b   5. c   6. a   7. c   8. d   9. a
10. Examiner's

CHAPTER 9

1. a   2. c   3. Custody/interrogation   4. b   5. Emotional
6. Nonemotional   7. c   8. c   9. b   10. Private

CHAPTER 10

1. a   2. c   3. c   4. b   5. b   6. Chronological   7. c   8. d
9. Arrested   10. Pedigree

CHAPTER 11

1. Autopsy   2. a   3. b   4. d   5. c   6. d   7. a   8. c   9. b
10. c

CHAPTER 12

1. Rape trauma   2. a   3. b   4. d   5. c   6. a   7. e   8. c
9. b   10. d

CHAPTER 13

1. Home invasion   2. Spontaneous play groups   3. c
4. Unplanned   5. Single-teller 6. b   7. a   8. d   9. a   10. c

CHAPTER 14

1. Aggravated arson   2. Natural/accidental   3. Rational
4. Pyromaniac   5. Flashover   6. Wind/terrain   7. Trailers
8. Taggants   9. Hate   10. Irrational

CHAPTER 15

1. Passive   2. Disposal   3. b   4. a   5. c   6. b   7. a   8. c
9. d   10. Fences

CHAPTER 16

1. a   2. d   3. c   4. b   5. e   6. Date rape   7. Buy
8. Entrapment   9. Freebase   10. Crack cocaine

CHAPTER 17

1. Johns   2. Unity/action   3. Corruption   4. Death creed
5. Crackers   6. Computer criminals   7. Logic bombs   8. a
9. c   10. d

CHAPTER 18

1. d   2. a   3. c   4. b   5. a   6. c   7. a   8. c   9. d   10. b

CHAPTER 19

1. Cross-examination   2. Direct examination   3. Pause   4. Corruption
5. Misconduct   6. Jury nullification   7. Academy   8. Field training
officers   9. Job related   10 Preventable

Notes

CHAPTER 1: THE INITIAL INVESTIGATION

1. Hans G. A. Gross, *Criminal Investigation*, 5th ed., trans. John Adam and J. Collyer Adam, rev. R. L. Jackson (London: Sweet & Maxwell Ltd., 1962).

2. Richard Saferstein, *Criminalistics and Introduction to Forensic Science* (Upper Saddle River, NJ: Pearson Prentice Hall, 2004), 2–5.

3. U.S. Department of Justice, National Institute of Justice, Office of Justice Programs, *Crime Scene Investigation: A Guide for Law Enforcement* (Washington, DC: Government Printing Office, 2000), 11–14.

4. Evidence technicians are called *scenes-of-crime officers* in England. See H. J. Walls, *Forensic Science* (New York: Praeger Publishers, 1968), 4.

5. Vernon Geberth, "Physical Evidence in Sex-Related Death Investigation," *Law and Order* (July 2003): 106.

6. *Schmerber v. California*, 384 U.S. 757 (1966).

7. James P. Conway, *Evidential Documents* (Springfield, IL: Charles C Thomas, 1959), 73–83.

8. Claude W. Cook, *A Practical Guide to the Basics of Physical Evidence* (Springfield, IL: Charles C Thomas, 1984), 10–12.

9. *Gilbert v. California*, 388 U.S. 263 (1967); *United States v. Blount*, 315 F. Supp. 1321 (1970).

10. *United States v. Wade*, 388 U.S. 218 (1967). See also *United States v. Ash*, 413 U.S. 300 (1973), and *Kirby v. Illinois*, 406 U.S. 682 (1972).

11. *Miranda v. Arizona*, 384 U.S. 436 (1966).

12. Paul D. Bigbee, "Collecting and Handling Evidence Infected with Human Disease-Causing Organisms," *FBI Law Enforcement Technology* 18, (October 1991): 66–70.

13. U.S. Department of Justice, "Crime Scene Investigation," 30.

14. Bill Toohey, "Tips from the Trenches: Advice from a PIO," *The Police Chief* (April 2001): 43.

15. D. P. Blaricom, "The Media: Enemies or Allies?" *The Police Chief* (April 2001): 52.

CHAPTER 2: DIRECT AND CIRCUMSTANTIAL EVIDENCE

1. J. Stannard Baker, *Traffic Accident Investigator's Manual for Police*, 4th ed. (Evanston, IL: The Traffic Institute, Northwestern University, 1963).

2. Barbara Gelb, *On the Track of Murder: Behind the Scenes with a Homicide Commando Squad* (New York: William Morrow & Company, 1975), 26.

3. U.S. Department of Justice, Office of Justice Programs, National Institute of Justice "Eyewitness Evidence, a Guide for Law Enforcement," (Washington, DC: Government Printing Office, 1999), 15.

4. Larry Danaher, "The Investigative Paradigm," *Law and Order* (June 2003): 134.

5. Urgen Thornwald, *Century of the Detective*, trans. Richard Winston and Clara Winston (New York: Harcourt Brace Jovanovich, 1965), 434.

6. J. S. Hatcher, Frank J. Jury, and Joe Weller, *Firearms Identification and Evidence* (Harrisburg, PA: Stackpole Books, 1957), 286.

7. Nicole Lundrigan, "Gunshot Residue Technology," *Law and Order* (May 2004): 66.

8. Terrence McGinn, "The Forgotten Evidence," *Law and Order* (November 2002): 30.

9. Michael Deleo, "Bloodstain Pattern Analysis," *Law and Order* (November 2002): 43.

10. Richard Saferstein, *Criminalistics: An Introduction to Forensics Science*, 5th ed. (Englewood Cliffs, NJ: Prentice Hall, 1995), 424–32; See also J. B. Wallace, "In Defense of Traditional Technology in a High-Tech World," *Journal of Forensic Identification* 4, (July/August 1993): 378–85.

11. "Unsolved Case Fingerprint Matching," *FBI Law Enforcement Bulletin* (December 2000): 12–13.

12. Wilson R. Harrison, *Forgery Detection* (New York: Praeger, 1964), 209–12.

CHAPTER 3: RULES OF EVIDENCE

1. Stephen A. Saltzburg and Daniel J. Capra, *Basic Criminal Procedure,* 2nd ed. (St. Paul, MN: West Publishing, 1977), 77–135.

2. J. Scott Harr and Karen M. Hess, *Constitutional Law and the Criminal Justice System* (Belmont, CA: Thompson Wadsworth Publishing, 2005), 219–22.

3. Cliff Roberson, *Criminal Procedure Today: Issues and Cases,* 2nd ed. (Upper Saddle River, NJ: Prentice Hall, 2003), 148–50.

4. John N. Ferdico, *Criminal Procedure for the Criminal Justice Professional,* 7th ed. (Belmont, CA: West/ Wadsworth, 1999), 352–56.

5. Thomas D. Colbridge, "Search Incident to Arrest: Another Look," *FBI Law Enforcement Bulletin* 68, no. 5 (1999): 27–32.

6. Lisa A. Regina, "The Motor Vehicle Exception: When and Where to Search," *FBI Law Enforcement Bulletin* 68, no. 7 (1999): 26–30.

7. Ferdico, "Criminal Procedure for the Criminal Justice Professional," 385–90.

8. Roberson, "Criminal Procedure Today: Issues and Cases," 139.

9. Edward M. Hendrie, "Creating Exigent Circumstances," *FBI Law Enforcement Bulletin* 65, no. 9 (1996): 25.

CHAPTER 4: RECORDING THE CRIME SCENE

1. *Basic Police Photography,* 2nd ed. (Rochester, NY: Eastman Kodak, 1968), 16–22.

2. Paul B. Weston, *The Police Traffic Control Function,* 2nd ed. (Springfield, IL: Charles C Thomas, 1968), 196–99.

3. "The CAD Zone: Law Enforcement Drawing Software," *Police* (March 2004): 86.

4. Kenneth M. Wells and Paul B. Weston, *Criminal Procedure and Trial Practice* (Englewood Cliffs, NJ: Prentice Hall, 1977), 29–34.

5. Larry L. Miller, *Sansone's Police Photography,* 3rd ed. (Cincinnati, OH: Anderson Publishing, 1993), 111–113.

CHAPTER 5: LABORATORY AND TECHNICAL SERVICES

1. *Miller vs. Pate,* 386 U.S. 1 (1967).

2. Ibid.

3. James W. Osterberg, "What Problems Must Criminalistics Solve?" *Law Enforcement Science and Technology* (Chicago: Thompson, 1967), 297–303. The term *forensic science* is commonly used to describe criminalistics. See Richard Saferstein, *Criminalistics: An Introduction to Forensic Science,* 5th ed. (Englewood Cliffs, NJ: Prentice Hall, 1994).

4. Brian Parker and Joseph Peterson, "Physical Evidence Utilization in the Administration of Criminal Justice," in *Sourcebook in Criminalistics,* ed. Carroll R. Hormachea (Reston, VA: Reston, 1974), 50–58.

5. Holly Hammond and C. Thomas Caskey, U.S. Department of Justice, National Institute of Justice, *Automated DNA Typing: Method of the Future?* (Washington, DC: Government Printing Office), 1–2.

6. Victor Walter Weedn and John W. Hicks, U.S. Department of Justice, National Institute of Justice, *The Unrealized Potential of DNA Testing* (Washington, DC: Government Printing Office, 1998), 1–8.

7. Louise M. Robbins, *Footprints: Collection, Analysis, and Interpretation* (Springfield, IL: Charles C Thomas, 1985), 183–207.

8. Herbert L. Macdonell, U.S. Department of Justice, National Institute of Law Enforcement Assistance Administration, *Flight Characteristics of Stain Patterns of Human Blood,* Stock No. 2700-0079 (Washington, DC: Government Printing Office, 1971), 1–29.

9. Federal Bureau of Investigation, "Examination of Biological Fluids," *FBI Law Enforcement Bulletin* XLI (June 1972): 12–15, 30.

10. Ibid., 15, 30.

11. Richard L. Bru Belle and Robert W. Reed, *Forensic Examination of Ink and Paper* (Springfield, IL: Charles C Thomas, 1984), 6–8.

12. H. J. Walls, *Forensic Science* (New York: Praeger, 1968), 60–61.

13. Ibid., 49–55.

14. Donald E. Bryan, et al., "High-Flux Neutron Activation Analysis as an Investigative Tool in the Field of Criminalistics," in *Law Enforcement Science and Technology* (Chicago: Thompson, 1967), 371–77.

15. U.S. Department of Justice, National Institute of Law Enforcement and Criminal Justice, Law Enforcement Assistance Administration, *Trace Metal Detection Technique in Law Enforcement* (Washington, DC: Government Printing Office, 1970), 1–16.

16. Richard S. Treptow, *Handbook of Methods for the Restoration of Obliterated Serial Numbers* (Cleveland, OH: Lewis Research Center, prepared for the National Aeronautics and Space Administration, 1978), 73–82.

17. Ronald E. Blacklock, "The Laser: A Tool for Questioned Document Examination," *The Journal of Police Science and Administration* XV, (July 1987): 125–26.

18. R. W. Becker, F. R. Clarke, F. Poza, and J. R. Young, U.S. Department of Justice, Law Enforcement Assistance Administration, *A Semiautomatic Speaker Recognition System* (Washington, DC: Government Printing Office, 1973), 1–26.

19. Parker Hitt, *Manual for the Solution of Military Ciphers* (Fort Leavenworth, KS: Press of the Army Service Schools, 1966), vii; David Kahn, *The Code-Breakers* (New York: Macmillan, 1966), passim.

20. Dan Tyler Moore and Martha Waller, *Cloak and Cipher* (Indianapolis, IN: Bobbs-Merrill, 1962), 17–19, 98–112.

CHAPTER 6: BASIC INVESTIGATIVE LEADS AND INFORMATION

1. M. A. P. Willmer, "Criminal Investigation from the Small Town to the Large Urban Conurbation," *British Journal of Criminology* VIII, (July 1968): 259–74.

2. James W. Osterberg, "The Investigative Process," in *Law Enforcement Science and Technology* (Chicago: Thompson, 1967), 591.

3. Truman Capote, *In Cold Blood* (New York: Random House, 1965), 159–64.

4. Joan Petersilia, *Processing Latent Fingerprints: What Are the Payoffs?* (Santa Monica, CA: The Rand Corporation, 1977), 13–14.

5. John E. Eck, *Solving Crimes: The Investigation of Burglary and Robbery* (Washington, DC: U.S. Department of Justice, Police Executive Research Forum and the National Institute of Justice, 1983), 269–70.

6. Stephanie L. Hitt, "NCIC 2000," *FBI Law Enforcement Bulletin* (July 2000): 12–15.

7. Jennifer Budden, "Linking Crime Through Ballistic Evidence," *Law and Order* (November 2002): 51–54.

8. Alan Scholle, "Sex Offender Registration Community Notification Laws," *FBI Law Enforcement Bulletin* (July 2000): 17–19.

9. Juliet Eilperin, "Congress Approves 'Amber Alert' System," *Washington Post*, April 11, 2003, A2.

10. Christopher Swope, "The Digital Mugshot," *Governing* (August 1998): 54.

11. James Q. Wilson, *The Investigators: Managing FBI and Narcotics Agents* (New York: Basic Books, 1978), 62.

12. Ira Rosen, "Wheeler, Dealer, Squealer," *60 Minutes* transcript, March 6, 1988, 5–9.

13. Irvin B. Nathan, "ABSCAM: A Fair and Effective Method for Fighting Public Corruption," in *ABSCAM Ethics: Moral Issues and Deception in Law Enforcement*, eds. Gerald M. Caplan and The Police Foundation (Cambridge, MA: Ballinger, 1983), 1–16.

14. Thomas Whiteside, *An Agent in Place: The Wennestrom Affair* (New York: Viking, 1966), 150.

15. Carole De Vault (with William Johnson), *The Informer: Confessions of an Ex-Terrorist* (Toronto, Canada: Fleet Books, 1982), 115–44.

16. James M. Poland, *Understanding Terrorism: Groups, Strategies, and Responses* (Englewood Cliffs, NJ: Prentice Hall, 1988), 196.

17. Mike McAlary, *Buddy Boys: When Good Cops Turn Bad* (New York: Putnam, 1987), 25–37.

18. Richard Hammer, *The CBS Murders* (New York: William Morrow, 1987), 215–20.

CHAPTER 7: MAJOR INVESTIGATIVE TECHNIQUES

1. Jeffrey Selingo, "Protecting the Cellphone User's Right to Hide," *New York Times*, February 5, 2004, E5.

2. Richard G. Schott, "Warrantless Interception of Communications: When, Where, and Why It Can Be Done," *FBI Law Enforcement Bulletin* (January 2003): 25–31.

3. National Commission for the Review of Federal and State Laws Relating to Wire-Tapping and Electronic Surveillance (NWC), *Electronic Surveillance* (Washington, DC: U.S. Government Printing Office, 1976), 151–52.

4. Thomas D. Colbridge, "Electronic Surveillance, a Matter of Necessity," *FBI Law Enforcement Bulletin* (February 2000): 25–31.

5. E. Drexel Godfrey, Jr., and Don R. Harris, *Basic Elements of Intelligence: A Manual of Theory, Structure and Procedure for Use by Law Enforcement Agencies Against Organized Crime* (Washington, DC: U.S. Department of Justice, Law Enforcement Assistance Administration, 1971), 11–35.

6. Don R. Harris, *Criminal Investigation Information Center: A Manual Describing the Organization and Analysis of Criminal Information* (Washington, DC: U.S. Department of Justice, 1979), 1–8.

CHAPTER 8: INTERVIEWING AND THE DETECTION OF DECEPTION

1. Paul Szczesny, "Suspect Interviews: Asking for the Necessary Information," *Law and Order* (June 2002): 126.

2. Larry Danaher, "The Investigative Paradigm," *Law and Order* (June 2003): 133–34.

3. Fred Inbau, John Reid, Joseph Buckley, and Brian Jayne, *Criminal Interrogation and Confessions*, 4th ed. (Gaithersburg, MD: Aspen Publications, 2001), 51.

4. Edgar Miner, "The Importance of Listening in the Interview and Interrogation Process," *FBI Law Enforcement Bulletin* (June 1984): 12–16.

5. Paul Ekman, *Telling Lies: Clues to Deceit in the Marketplace, Politics, and Marriage* (New York: Norton, 1985), 287.

6. Joe Navarro, "A Four-Domain Model for Detecting Deception," *FBI Law Enforcement Bulletin* (June 2003): 19–24.

7. *California Evidence Code,* sec. 795 (1984).

8. Margo Bennett and John Hess, "Cognitive Interviewing," *FBI Law Enforcement Bulletin* (March 1991): 8–12.

CHAPTER 9: INTERROGATION OF SUSPECTS

1. *Miranda v. Arizona,* 384 U.S. 436 (1966).

2. *Brown v. State of Mississippi,* 297 U.S. 278 (1936).

3. *Ward v. State of Texas,* 316 U.S. 547 (1942).

4. *Fikes v. Alabama,* 352 U.S. 191 (1957).

5. *Ashcraft v. State of Tennessee,* 322 U.S. 143 (1944).

6. *Haley v. Ohio,* 332 U.S. 596 (1948).

7. *Davis v. North Carolina,* 384 U.S. 737 (1966).

8. *Mincey v. Arizona,* 437 U.S. 385 (1978).

9. *Townsend v. Sain,* 372 U.S. 293 (1963).

10. *Escobedo v. Illinois,* 378 U.S. 478 (1964).

11. *Beckwith v. United States,* 245 U.S. 341 (1976).

12. *Rhode Island v. Innis,* 446 U.S. 291 (1980).

13. *Miranda v. Arizona,* 384 U.S. 436 (1966).

14. Fred Inbau, John Reid, Joseph Buckley, and Brian Jayne, *Criminal Interrogation and Confessions,* 4th ed. (Gaithersburg, MD: Aspen Publications, 2001), 51–58.

15. Ibid., 209–11.

16. David Tousignant, "Why Suspects Confess," *FBI Law Enforcement Bulletin* (March 1991): 14–18.

17. U.S. Department of Justice, National Institute of Justice, Office of Justice Programs, *Videotaping Interrogations and Confessions,* (Washington, DC: Government Printing Office, 1993), 4.

CHAPTER 10: THE ARREST OF THE ACCUSED PERSON

1. These contacts are invaluable when a speedy response to queries is necessary, despite the reciprocity inherent in these calls. Some networks include graduates of the FBI Academy, former members of the FBI and the New York City Police Department, and alumni of college/university criminal justice degree programs.

2. Herbert Edelhertz, Ezra Stotland, Marilyn Walsh, and Milton Weinberg, *The Investigation of White-Collar Crime: A Manual for Law Enforcement Agencies* (Washington, DC: U.S. Department of Justice, Law Enforcement Assistance Administration, 1977), 267–75 (Appendix B, Sample Guide to Sources of Information). For in-depth coverage of the sources on information, see Harry J. Murphy, *Where's What: Sources of Information for Federal Investigators* (Washington, DC: The Brookings Institution, 1975).

3. *Agnello v. United States,* 296 U.S. 20 (1925).

4. *Rochin v. California,* 342 U.S. 165 (1952).

5. Hans G. A. Gross, *Criminal Investigation,* trans. John Adam and J. Collyer Adam (Madras, India: Higginbotham, 1906), 34–35.

6. Wayne R. Lafave, *Arrest: The Decision to Take a Suspect into Custody* (Boston: Little, Brown, 1965), S-6, 320–24.

7. Institute of Defense Analyses, *Task Force Report: The Courts—A Report to the President's Commission on Law Enforcement and Administration of Justice* (Washington, DC: U.S. Government Printing Office, 1967), 5–7.

8. International Association of Chiefs of Police, Case No. S. Criminal Investigation (Washington, D.C. International Association of Chiefs of Police, Inc., 1966), 18.

CHAPTER 11: PHYSICAL ASSAULTS

1. Thomas A. Gonzalez, et al., *Legal Medicine: Pathology and Toxicology* (New York: Appleton-Century Crofts, 1954).

2. William F. Kessler and Paul B. Weston, *The Detection of Murder* (New York: Arco Publishing, 1961), 44–47.

3. Lowell J. Levine, "Forensic Odontology Today: A New Forensic Science," *FBI Law Enforcement Bulletin* XLI, no. 8 (August 1972): 6–9, 26–28.

4. T. D. Stewart, "What the Bones Tell Today," *FBI Law Enforcement Bulletin* XLI, no. 2 (February 1972): 16–20, 30–31.

5. Kessler and Weston, *The Detection of Murder,* 1–9.

6. Larry Miller, et al., *Human Evidence in Criminal Justice* (Cincinnati, OH: Anderson Publishing, 1983), 115–46.

7. Edward A. Dieckmann, Sr., *Practical Homicide Investigation* (Springfield, IL: Charles C Thomas, 1901), 23–25.

8. Barry A. J. Fisher, *Techniques of Crime Scene Investigation* (New York: CRC Press, 2000), 445–50.

9. Donald John Geise, *The Carol Thompson Murder Case* (NewYork: Scope Reports, 1969), 5–20, 38–50.

10. Vernon J. Geberth, *Practical Homicide Investigation: Tactics, Procedures, and Forensic Techniques* (New York: CRC Press, 1996), 849.

11. Eric W. Hickey, *Serial Murderers and Their Victims* (Pacific Grove, CA: Brooks/Cole Publishing, 1991), 5.

12. Ronald M. Holmes and Stephen T. Holmes, *Mass Murder in the United States* (Upper Saddle River, NJ: Prentice Hall, 2001), 3.

13. Geberth, *Practical Homicide Investigation*, 348.

14. Ronald M. Holmes and Stephen T. Holmes, *Profiling Violent Crimes*, 2nd ed. (Thousand Oaks, CA: Sage Publications, 1996), 63–67.

15. Geberth, *Practical Homicide Investigation*, 419–21.

16. James B. Howleit, Kenneth A. Hanflang, and Robert K. Ressler, "The Violent Criminal Apprehension Program—VICAP: A Progress Report," *FBI Law Enforcement Bulletin* LV, no. 12 (December 1986): 14–22.

17. R. M. Holmes, "Stalking in America: Types and Methods of Criminal Stalkers," *Contemporary Criminal Justice* 8, no. 4 (December 1993): 318–26.

18. Joseph Goldstein, Anna Freud, and Albert J. Solnit, *Before the Best Interests of the Child* (New York: The Free Press—Macmillan Publishing Company, 1979), 72–77.

19. California Department of Justice, *Child Abuse Prevention Handbook* (Sacramento, CA: California Department of Justice, 1982), 7–9.

20. U.S. Department of Justice, Office of Justice Programs, Office of Juvenile Justice and Delinquency Prevention, *Burn Injuries in Child Abuse: Portable Guides to Investigating Child Abuse* (Washington, DC: U.S. Department of Justice, Office of Justice Programs, Office of Juvenile Justice and Delinquency Prevention, 1997), 1–8.

21. U.S. Department of Justice, Office of Justice Programs, Office of Juvenile Justice and Delinquency Prevention, *Battered Child Syndrome: Investigating Physical Abuse and Homicide* (Washington, DC: U.S. Department of Justice, Office of Justice Programs, Office of Juvenile Justice and Delinquency Prevention, 1996), 1–11.

CHAPTER 12: SEXUAL ASSAULTS

1. Paul B. Weston and Kenneth M. Wells, *Criminal Law* (Santa Monica, CA: Goodyear Publishing, 1978), 253–62.

2. Susan Estrich, *Real Rape* (Cambridge, MA: Harvard University Press, 1987), 7–26.

3. Joseph A. Zeccardi and Diana Dickerman, "Medical Exam in the Live Sexual Assault Victim," in *Practical Aspects of Rape Investigation—A Multidisciplinary Approach*, eds. Robert R. Hazelwood and Ann Wolbert Burgess (New York: Elsevier Science Publishing, 1987), 315–25.

4. Lisa Brodyaga, et al., *Rape and Its Victims: A Report for Citizens, Health Facilities, and Criminal Justice Agencies* (Washington, DC: U.S. Department of Justice, Law Enforcement Assistance Administration, 1975), 37–42.

5. Jerry D. Moody and Vicki Ellen Hayes, "Responsible Reporting: The Initial Step," in *Rape and Sexual Assault: Management and Intervention*, ed. Carmen Germaine Warner (Rockville, MD: Aspen Systems Corp., 1980), 27–45.

6. Robert R. Hazelwood, "The Behavior-Oriented Interview of Rape Victims: The Key to Profiling," *FBI Law Enforcement Bulletin* LII, no. 9 (September 1983): 8–15.

7. Ronald H. Holmes and Stephen T. Holmes, *Profiling Violent Crimes: An Investigative Tool*, 3rd ed. (Thousand Oaks, CA: Sage Publications, 2002), 145–52.

8. A. Nicholas Groth, *Men Who Rape: The Psychology of the Offender* (New York: Plenum Press, 1979) 12–59.

9. Richard Braen, "Examination of the Accused: The Heterosexual and Homosexual Rapists," *Rape and Sexual Assault: Management and Intervention*, ed. Carmen Germaine Warner (Rockville, MD: Aspen Systems Corp., 1980), 85–91.

10. C. R. Van Zandt and S. E. Ether, "Real Silence of the Lambs," *Police Chief* 61, no. 4 (April 1994): 45–52.

11. R. D. Blackledge, "Collection and Identification Guidelines for Traces from Latex Condoms in Sexual Abuse Cases," *Crime Laboratory Digest* 21, no. 4 (October 1994): 57–61.

12. Robert J. Barry, "Incest: The Last Taboo," *FBI Law Enforcement Bulletin* LIII, no. 1 (January 1984): 2–9.

13. Marvin R. Janssen, "Incest: Exploitive Child Abuse," *The Police Chief* LI, no. 2 (February 1984): 46–47.

14. Holmes and Holmes, *Profiling Violent Crimes*, 161–71.

15. Vincent DeFrancis, *Protecting the Child Victim of Sex Crimes Committed by Adults* (Denver, CO: The American Humane Association, 1969), 1–2.

16. T. M. Dees, "Cyberchip Chickenhawks: A Mix of Kids, Computers, and Pedophiles," *Law Enforcement Technology* 21, no. 10 (October 1994): 52–55.

17. Nancy Walker Perry and Lawrence S. Wrightman, *The Child Witness: Legal Issues and Dilemmas* (Newbury Park, CA: Sage Publications, 1991), 2–10.

CHAPTER 13: ROBBERY

1. Kenneth M. Wells and Paul B. Weston, *Criminal Law* (Santa Monica, CA: Goodyear, 1978), 200–11.

2. *People v. Timmons*, 482 F.2d 648 (1971).

3. Ernest Volkman and John Cummings, *The Heist: How a Gang Stole $8,000,000 at Kennedy Airport and Lived to Regret It* (New York: Franklin Watts, 1986), 1–27.

4. Henry Williamson, *Hustler* (New York: Doubleday, 1965), 117.

5. John Bartlow Martin, *My Life in Crime: The Autobiography of a Professional Criminal* (New York: Harper & Brothers, 1952), 68.

6. Gerald D. Wolcott, "A Typology of Armed Robbers" (Master's thesis, Sacramento State College, 1968), 30.

7. Williamson, *Hustler,* 188–206.

8. U.S. Department of Justice, Law Enforcement Assistance Administration, *Selection and Application Guide to Fixed Surveillance Cameras* (Washington, DC: U.S. Department of Justice, Law Enforcement Assistance Administration, 1974), 1–5; *United States v. McNair,* 439 F. Supp. 103 (1977).

9. U.S. Department of Justice, Law Enforcement Assistance Administration, *Curbing the Repeat Offender: A Strategy for Prosecutors* (Washington, DC: U.S. Department of Justice, Law Enforcement Assistance Administration, 1977), 16–17.

CHAPTER 14: ARSON, BOMBINGS, AND HATE CRIMES

1. William Blackstone, *Commentaries on the Laws of England* (Oxford, England: Clarendon Press, 1765–1769), bk. 4, chap. 16.

2. Kenneth M. Wells and Paul B. Weston, *Criminal Law* (Santa Monica, CA: Goodyear, 1978), 221–28.

3. *Kehoe v. Commonwealth,* 149 Ky. 400 (1912).

4. Brendan P. Battle and Paul B. Weston, *Arson: Detection and Investigation* (New York: Arco, 1978), 30–42.

5. "Fire Marshalls on Duty: The Intelligence Unit in Fire Investigation," *The Fire Journal* LXIV (September 1970): 92–93.

6. Noland D. C. Lewis and Helen Yarnell, *Pathological Firesetting: Pyromania* (New York: Nervous and Mental Disease Monographs, 1951), 86–134.

7. W. Hurley and T. M. Monahan, "Arson: The Criminal and the Crime," *British Journal of Criminology* IX (1969): 4–21.

8. Paul Kirk, *Fire Investigation* (New York: Wiley, 1969), 71–81.

9. Edwin E. Smith, "An Experimental Determination of Combustibility," *Fire Technology* VII, no. 2 (May 1971): 109–19.

10. T. E. Waterman, "Room Flashover: Criteria and Synthesis," *Fire Technology* IV, no. 1 (February 1968): 25–31.

11. T. E. Waterman and W. J. Christian, "Characteristics of Full-Scale Fires in Various Occupancies," *Fire Technology* VII, no. 3 (August 1971): 205–17; and "Fire Behavior of Interior Finish Materials," *Fire Technology* VI, no. 3 (August 1970): 165–78.

12. Kirk, *Fire Investigation,* 82–88.

13. C. M. Countryman, M. A. Fosberg, R. C. Rothernel, and M. J. Schroeder, "Fire Weather and Fire Behavior in the 1966 Loop Fire," *Fire Technology* IV, no. 2 (May 1968): 126–41.

14. Bruce V. Etting and Mark F. Adams, "Spontaneous Combustion of Linseed Oil and Sawdust," *Fire Technology* VII, no. 3 (August 1971): 225–36.

15. Battle and Weston, *Arson,* 17–29.

16. Richard D. Fitch and Edward A. Porter, *Accidental or Incendiary* (Springfield, IL: Charles C Thomas, 1968), 3–26; and John J. O'Connor, *Practical Fire and Arson Investigation* (New York: Elsevier, 1987), 81–105.

17. John F. Boudreau, Quon Y. Kwan, William E. Faragher, and Genevieve C. Denault, *Arson and Arson Investigation: A Survey and Assessment* (Washington, DC: U.S. Department of Justice, Law Enforcement Assistance Administration, 1977), 77–89.

18. L. V. Waters and L. A. Palmer, "Multiple Analysis of Fire Debris Samples Using Passive Headspace Concentration," *Journal of Forensic Sciences* 18, no. 1 (January 1993): 165–83.

19. Jack Levin and Jack McDevitt, *Hate Crimes: The Rising Tide of Bigotry and Bloodshed* (New York: Plenum, 1993), 1–5.

20. James D. Tabor and Eugene V. Gallager, *Why Waco? Cults and the Battle for Religious Freedom in America* (Los Angeles: University of California Press, 1995), 147–48.

CHAPTER 15: PROPERTY CRIMES

1. *State v. Wiley,* 173 Maryland 119 (1937).

2. California Penal Code, sec. 459.

3. Ibid., sec. 461.

4. Ibid., sec. 459.

5. George Rengert and John Wasilchick, *Surburban Burglary: A Time and a Place for Everything* (Springfield, IL: Charles C Thomas, 1985), 53–75.

6. Maurice J. Fitzgerald, *Handbook of Criminal Investigation* (New York: Arco, 1960), 131.

7. Harry A. Scarr, et al. *Patterns of Burglary* (Washington, DC: U.S. Department of Justice, Law Enforcement Assistance Administration, National Institute of Law Enforcement and Criminal Justice, 1972), 4–5.

8. U.S. Department of Justice, *Criminal Victimization in the United States: 1992* (Washington, DC: U.S. Department of Justice, 1994), 154–55.

9. M. A. Wilmer, "Criminal Investigation from the Small Town to the Large Urban Conurbation," *British Journal of Criminology* VIII, No. 3 (July 1968): 259–74.

10. Darrel J. Stefensmeier, *The Fence: In the Shadow of Two Worlds* (Totowa, NJ: Rowman & Littlefield, 1986), 13–35, 157–86.

11. U.S. Department of Justice, Law Enforcement Assistance Administration, *Strategies for Combating the Criminal Receiver of Stolen Goods: An Antifencing Manual for Law Enforcement Agencies* (Washington, DC: U.S. Department of Justice, Law Enforcement Assistance Administration, 1976), 89–97. Also see Ron Shaffer and Kevin Kloss (with Alfred R. Lewis), *Surprise! Surprise! How the Lawmen Conned the Thieves* (New York: Viking Press, 1977).

12. G. Jack Bolongna and Robert J. Lindquist, *Fraud Auditing and Forensic Accounting: New Tools and Techniques* (New York: Wiley, 1987), 27–42.

13. Mary Carey and George Sherman, *A Compendium of Bunk: Or, How to Spot a Con Artist—A Handbook for Fraud Investigators, Bankers, and Other Custodians of the Public Trust* (Springfield, IL: Charles C Thomas, 1976), 9–20.

14. Ibid., 28–38.

15. David W. Maurer, *The American Confidence Man* (Springfield, IL: Charles C Thomas, 1974), 30–47.

16. See Herbert Edelhertz, Ezra Stotland, Marilyn Walsh, and Milton Weinberg, *The Investigation of White-Collar Crime: A Manual for Law Enforcement Agencies* (Washington, DC: U.S. Department of Justice, Law Enforcement Assistance Administration, 1977).

17. Brendan P. Battle and Paul B. Weston, *Arson: Detection and Investigation* (New York: Arco, 1979), 108.

18. Edelhertz, et al., *The Investigation of White Collar Crime*, 200; and Lee J. Seidler, Fredrick Andrews, and Marc J. Epstein, *The Equity Funding Papers: The Anatomy of a Fraud* (New York: Wiley, 1977), 3–19.

19. Tsutomu Shimomura, *Takedown* (New York: Hyperion/New York Times, 1996), 313–14.

CHAPTER 16: DANGEROUS DRUGS

1. *People v. Martinez,* 256 P.2d 1028 (Dist. Ct. App. 1953).

2. *Robinson v. California,* 370 U.S. 660 (1962).

3. *People v. Monteverde,* 46 Cal. Rptr. 2-7 (1965).

4. *People v. Muñoz,* 18 Cal. Rptr. 82 (1962).

5. Paul B. Weston, "The Illicit Traffic in Drugs," *Narcotics, U.S.A.* (New York: Greenberg, 1952), 127–40.

6. Phillip C. McGuire, "Jamaican Posses: A Call for Cooperation Among Law Enforcement Agencies," *The Police Chief* LV, no. 1 (January 1988): 20–27.

7. William D. Hyatt, "Investigation of Major Drug Distribution Cartels," in *Critical Issues in Criminal Investigation,* 2nd ed., ed. Michael J. Palmiotto (Cincinnati, OH: Anderson, 1988), 113–39.

8. Scott H. Decker and Barrik Van Winkle, "Sling Dope: The Role of Gang Members in Drug Sales," *Justice Quarterly* 11, no. 4 (December 1994): 583–604.

9. *Draper v. United States,* 358 U.S. 307 (1959).

10. *Aguilar v. Texas,* 378 U.S. 108 (1964); *Spinelli v. United States,* 393 U.S. 410 (1969); *United States v. Garrett,* 565 F. 2nd 1065 (1977).

11. *United States v. Johnson,* 561 F. 2nd 832 (1977).

12. Peter K. Manning, *The Narcs' Game: Organizational and Informational Limits on Drug Law Enforcement* (Cambridge, MA: The MIT Press, 1980), 161.

13. Mark Harrison Moore, *Buy and Bust* (Lexington, MA: D. C. Heath, 1977), 135.

14. James Mills, *The Underground Empire: Where Crime and Government Embrace* (New York: Doubleday, 1986), 72–113, 283–394, 520–618.

CHAPTER 17: SPECIAL INVESTIGATIONS

1. Frederick W. Egen, *Plainclothesman: A Handbook of Vice and Gambling Investigation* (New York: Arco, 1968), 3–104.

2. Donald R. Cressey, *Theft of the Nation* (New York: Harper & Row, 1969), 248–89.

3. Drexel Godfrey, Jr., and Don R. Harris, *Basic Elements of Intelligence: A Manual of Theory, Structure and Procedures for Use by Law Enforcement Agencies Against Organized Crime* (Washington, DC: U. S. Department of Justice, Technical Assistance Division, Law Enforcement Assistance Administration, 1971), 11–35.

4. James Burro, *Mob Rule: Inside the Canadian Mafia* (Toronto: Macmillan, 1985), 256–58.

5. Francis M. Roache, "Organized Crime in Boston's Chinatown," *The Police Chief* 45, no. 1 (January 1988): 48–51.

6. Gannett News Service, "Computer Security Lacking, Experts Warn," *Sacrameto Bee,* March 23, 2001, A6.

7. Stephen Frothingham, "Jailed Hacker Builds Firm," *Sacramento Bee,* September 4, 2001, D1.

8. Peter Stephenson, *Investigating Computer Related Crime* (Boca Raton: CRC Press, 2000) 31–38.

9. U.S. Department of Justice, United States Attorney for the District of New Jersey, "Creator of 'Melissa' Computer Virus Pleads Guilty to State and Federal Charges," United States Attorney for the District of New Jersey, U.S. Department of Justice, press release, December 9, 1999, 1–3.

10. Stephenson, *Investigating Computer Related Crime,* 81–88.

11. Donn B. Parker, *Fighting Computer Crime* (New York: Wiley, 1998), 98.
12. Ibid., 126.
13. Lenny Savino, "Web Child Porn: A Test for Police," *Sacramento Bee*, August 15, 2001, A7.
14. U.S. Department of Justice, Office of Juvenile Programs, "Internet Crimes Against Children," *OVC Bulletin* (2001): 2–5.
15. Jim E. Reames, "Computer Crimes, Hacking and Cybernetic Warfare," *The Journal of California Law Enforcement*, vol. 34, no. 1 (2000) 22–25.

CHAPTER 18: TERRORISM

1. Cindy C. Combs, *Terrorism in the Twenty-First Century*, 3rd ed. (Upper Saddle River, NJ: Prentice Hall, 2003), 9.
2. Robert Lenzner and Nathan Vardi, "The Next Threat," *Forbes*, September 20, 2004, http://www.forbes.com/forbes/2004/0920/070.html.
3. James M. Poland, *Understanding Terrorism, Groups, Strategies and Responses*, 2nd ed. (Upper Saddle River, NJ: Prentice Hall, 2005), 17.
4. Clifford E. Simonsen and Jeremy R. Spinlove, *Terrorism Today: The Past, The Players, The Future* (Upper Saddle River, NJ: Prentice Hall, 2000), 39–43.
5. Poland, *Understanding Terrorism, Groups, Strategies and Responses*, 29–31.
6. Jonathan R. White, *Terrorism: An Introduction*, 4th ed. (Belmont, CA: Thompson, 2003), 229–30.
7. Gus Martin, *Understanding Terrorism*, 2nd ed. (Thousand Oaks, CA: Sage, 2006), 459–60.
8. Ibid, 447.
9. Poland, *Understanding Terrorism, Groups, Strategies and Responses*, 102–107.
10. Martin, *Understanding Terrorism*, 385.
11. Poland, *Understanding Terrorism, Groups, Strategies and Responses*, 93–95.
12. White, *Terrorism*, 159–61.
13. Yonah Alexander and Milton Hoenig, *Super Terrorism: Biological, Chemical, and Nuclear* (Ardsley, NY: Transnational Publishers, 2001), 12–17.
14. James Casey, "Managing Joint Terrorism Task Force Resources," *FBI Law Enforcement Bulletin* 76, no. 11 (2004): 1–6.
15. Martin, *Understanding Terrorism*, 495–97.
16. Christopher A. Hertig, "The Investigation of Terrorist Activity," in *Critical Issues in Criminal Investigation*, ed. Michael J. Palmiotto (Cincinnati, OH: Anderson, 1988), 235–45.
17. Walter Laqueur, *The Age of Terrorism* (Boston: Little, Brown, 1987), 109–11.

CHAPTER 19: THE INVESTIGATOR AS WITNESS AND ETHICAL AWARENESS

1. John J. Burke, "Testifying in Court," *FBI Law Enforcement Bulletin*, XLIV, no. 9 (September 1975): 8–13.
2. John F. Wilson and Carroll C. Arnold, *Dimensions of Public Communication* (Boston: Allyn and Bacon, 1976), 34–36.
3. Rudolf Flesch, *The Art of Plain Talk* (New York: Harper & Brothers, 1946), 31–56.
4. Loretta A. Malandro and Larry Barker, *Nonverbal Communication* (Reading, MA: Addison-Wesley, 1983), 4–28.
5. William Geller, ed., *Local Government Police Management* (Washington, DC: The International City Management Association, 1991), 239.
6. James Lardner and Thomas Reppetto, *NYPD: A City and Its Police* (New York: Henry Holt, 2000), 276–77.
7. Kevin Gilmartin and John Harris, "The Continuum of Compromise," *The Police Chief* (January 1998): 25–28.

Glossary

Active information. Establishes a group of suspects.

Aka, a.k.a., A.K.A., AKA. Also known as, alias, nickname, street name.

Algor mortis. The cooling of a body after death.

Anger rapist. Someone who commits the crime of rape as a means of expressing and discharging feelings of pent-up anger and rage.

Ante mortem. Before death.

Autonomic nervous system. Governs respiration, heartbeat, and perspiration.

Backup man. Shooter for a robbery gang. Mixes with bystanders as robbery is in progress; acts only when police or armed guards appear and threaten overt robbers.

Badger game extortion. Male and female crime partners operate a three-act scam: (1) victim (sucker) is placed in compromising position; (2) offender discovers, claims to be husband or lover of female, screams and threatens, demands money; (3) goes to bank with victim to get cash.

Ballistics. The identification of firearms, bullets, cartridges, and shotgun shells.

Benefit. Basic investigative lead regarding who might gain by committing the crime in question.

"Better him than me." Crime partner agrees to testify for prosecution in return for a reduced charge or reduced sentence.

Blind date bombings. Acts of violence against random victims.

Bugging. Secret wiring of suspect's home, office, or car with electronic eavesdropping device—bug.

Bumper beeper. Electronic tracking device hidden on underside of suspect vehicle; monitored by receiver in police surveillance car; allows pursuit without fear of discovery.

Canvass. Systematic inquiry for witnesses in view, shopping, and neighborhood areas.

Carjacking. Vehicle taken from driver by force or fear; handgun most popular weapon; if handbag left in car, contents may be "bonus" loot.

Chain of possession. A written document that can account for an item of evidence from the time it came into an agency's possession to the time it is presented in court.

Chicken hawk. Pedophile, child molester; commonly an older man seeking out young boys as sexual partners.

Chromatography. A laboratory method of separating compounds to identify the components.

Circumstantial evidence. Evidence from which an inference may be drawn.

Community threat groups. Organizations engaging in hate crimes and their advocacy (i.e., Klu Klux Klan, skinheads, Aryan Nation).

Con (confidence) game. Fraud, rip-off, or scam based on promise of high profit in a "sure thing."

Conspiracy. Two or more persons combine to commit or to cause a violation of the criminal law.

Contaminated fingerprints. Prints that are observable with the naked eye, such as bloody fingerprints.

Corpus delicti. Body of a crime; essential elements.

Corruption. The misuse of police authority for personal gain.

Crack. A smokeable form of cocaine.

Crank. See Meth.

Crime laboratory. A facility equipped for the scientific examination of evidentiary material submitted by police evidence gatherers, staffed by qualified forensic scientists or criminalists; has the capacity to provide reports explaining what was discovered in the lab, by whom, relevancy to the issue of guilt or innocence, and whether examiner is qualified as an expert witness in court in the scientific area of the examination.

Criminalistics. Individualization of physical evidence in a crime lab, also referred to as forensic science.

Cryptography. Ciphers and codes (cloak and dagger) used to protect the security of underworld communications; decoding.

Cult. An organization, group, or sect (not a gang) bound together by a charismatic leader and his or her spin on one or more segments of the Bible or areas of religious worship; often accused of child abuse, unorthodox lifestyles, misuse of funds, and undue influence in recruiting members and mind-bending techniques to retain them.

Date rape. Prior relationship between rapist and victim.

Direct evidence. Witness testimony as it relates to what they saw or heard.

DNA (deoxyribonucleic acid). Identification by genetic code analysis in crime labs of blood samples and samples of other body fluids. Accuracy, reliability, and validity established by in-court testimony of DNA experts in a growing number of cases.

Drive-by shooting. One or more cars filled with members of a street gang who have large-caliber, fast-firing assault rifles and handguns with large-capacity magazines drive by a house suspected of containing one or more members of a rival gang and open fire. This barrage of bullets threatens all occupants in the target, as well as nearby yards, houses, and people. It is nondiscriminating, threatening young and old, boy and girl, involved and uninvolved.

Drugs, narcotics. See Appendix B.

Entrapment. A crime or wrongful act that was induced by the investigator and otherwise would not have occurred.

Ethical awareness. An alertness to behavior that is wrong, immoral, unprincipled, substandard, and criminal.

Exhumation. A court order for the removal of a body of a deceased person from its burial place for a medicolegal examination.

Fence. Professional receiver of stolen property.

Field contact report. A report of a suspicious occurrence not amounting to a crime.

Firebug. See Pyromania.

Flipped. Confronted with evidence of his or her guilt, suspect agrees to become accomplice witness in return for reduced charge or lesser sentence.

Forensic science. See Criminalistics.

Hackers. Intruders who enter into another's computer system without authorization.

Hate crime. Vandalism and violent crime motivated by apparent hate of victim's religion, race, ethnic heritage, or sexual orientation; may be linked to offender's membership in community threat group.

Home invasion (robbery). A vicious and violent robbery of a family in its home. Pistol whipping and threats to kill force victims into disclosing hiding places of cash, jewelry, and other valuables.

Jury nullification. Jury verdict apparently influenced by mistrust of police witnesses or testimony.

Knowledge. Basic investigative lead regarding the identification of the person who had the knowledge, skill, or capacity to commit the crime in question.

Known standard of evidence. Evidence collected from a known source.

Latent fingerprints. Must be developed or dusted as cannot be seen with the naked eye.

Linkage. Relationship formed between persons engaged in criminal activity.

Lividity. Irreversible postmortem process in which blood settles to the lowest part of the body.

Malice. An offender's inexcusable, unjustified, unmitigated, person-endangering state of mind.

Mass murder. The homicide of four or more victims during a single event at one location.

Match (matching). Most favorable term in a crime lab report of a comparison analysis of evidence submitted by police investigators.

Meth (methamphetamine). An illegal drug. A stimulant, popular because of "hit," low price, and availability. Usually made in clandestine labs or at home (kitchen lab) from legal substances. Also known as crank, speed.

Misconduct. Involves issues such as excessive use of force, violation of a suspect's constitutional rights, and a variety of other misdeeds.

Modus operandi. Involves the choice of a particular crime to commit and the selection of a method of committing it.

Munchausen syndrome by proxy. A psychological disorder in which a parent or caretaker suffering from Munchausen syndrome attempts to bring medical attention to themselves by injuring or inducing illness in their children.

Mushroom factor. Diligent investigation of child molester likely to lead to exposure of a network of these offenders.

Neighborhood canvass. A method of contacting people in the area of a crime scene to locate potential witnesses.

Neutron activation analysis. A laboratory technique used to determine the presence of gunshot residue on a subject's hands. The test can detect the presence of antimony and barium, common gunshot residues.

Omission. A failure to act when such action is required by law.

Opportunity. A basic investigative lead that places the suspect at the scene of a crime at or about the time of its occurrence.

Passive information. Data are useful when a group of suspects is developed in a crime investigation.

Pedophilia. A sexual perversion in which children are the preferred sexual object.

Physical evidence. Liquid to solid material amenable to scientific analysis by forensic science technicians in a crime lab.

Plastic fingerprint. Prints left in soft material such as tar or tacky paint.

Ponzi scheme. A con in which the swindler uses money invested by new victims to pay high interest on the investments of earlier victims whose money the swindler has appropriated to his or her own use.

Postmortem. After death.

Pot (marijuana). Most popular illegal drug in the United States, and usually the most available and inexpensive.

Power rapist. Uses sex as a means of compensating for underlying feelings of inadequacy and serves to express issues of mastery, strength, authority, and control over another person.

Prima facie. On the face of, at first view, uncontradicted.

Pyromania. Obsessional impulse to set fires; a *pyro* is a fire bug, a pyromaniac.

Ransom. Money or other consideration paid or demanded for the release of the victim.

Reasonable care. Care fairly and properly taken in response to the circumstances of a situation; such care as an ordinarily prudent person would take in the same time frame, conditions, and act(s).

Rigor mortis. Body appearance after death—stiffening; factor in determining time of death in criminal homicides.

Sadistic rapist. Finds the intentional maltreatment of the victim intensely gratifying and takes pleasure in victim's torment, anguish, distress, helplessness, and suffering.

Scam. See Con games.

Search warrant. Judicial authorization to enter a specified place for the purpose of gathering evidence or arresting a suspect.

Serial murder. Two or more separate murders when an individual, acting alone or with another, commits multiple homicides over a period of time with time breaks between each murder event.

Shaken baby syndrome. Injuries caused by a violent sustained shaking action in which the infant's head is violently whipped forward and backward, hitting the chest and shoulders; occurs primarily in children eighteen months of age or younger because their necks lack muscle control and their heads are heavier than the rest of their bodies.

Signature. The so-called trademark that is part of the modus operandi of a crime and distinguishes it as the work of a specific criminal or group of criminals who have committed previous crimes in which the same identifying circumstances occurred.

Stakeout (Plant). Fixed visual surveillance.

Stalking. Aggressive and threatening pursuit of a victim selected because of celebrity status, past relationship, or some irrational motive; initial harassing letters and telephone calls escalate to threats and demands and then to serious injury or even fatal attack.

Stash. Hiding place of a drug seller's inventory of drugs; generally, hiding place of cash, weapons, stolen property.

Sting. Police-operated "fencing" operation to trap thieves as they sell their stolen property to undercover police; thieves are videotaped and identified for future arrest at completion of operation; also modified and used to trap graft-taking public officials and others.

Sudden infant death syndrome (SIDS). Is not a positive finding but rather is a diagnosis made without other medical explanation for the abrupt death of an apparently healthy infant.

Surveillance. The observation of people and places by investigators to develop investigative leads.

Taggants. Coded microparticles added to explosives during manufacture; these particles survive detonation, can be recovered at the bombing scene, and can be decoded by the crime laboratory to indicate where and when the explosives were made.

Target blue. The ambush slaying of police officers by terrorist groups—killed not because of who they are but because of what they represent; the attention getter is the willingness of the terrorist group to kill the armed representatives of law and order.

Trailers. Used by arsonists to spread fires from a point of ignition to other parts of a room or building; the trailer may be nothing more than a rope or ropelike string or toilet paper, newspaper, or rags soaked in a fire accelerant.

Ultrasonic cavitation. A method "of restoring obliterated serial numbers on firearms and other metal objects.

"Working off a beef." The process of an arrestee making a deal with the arresting officers and prosecutor for exchanging information and cooperation in an investigation in return for leniency in drafting the indictment or at the time of sentencing.

X-ray crystallography. A laboratory process used for the identification of any crystalline solid or compound from which a crystalline solid derivative can be made.

Selected Bibliography

ABRAHAMS, PETER. *The Fan.* New York: McGraw-Hill, 1990.

ADLER, MORTIMORE J. *Desires: Right and Wrong—The Ethics of Enough.* New York: Macmillan, 1991.

ALLEN, BUD, and DIANA BOSTA. *Games Criminals Play—How You Can Profit by Knowing Them.* Sacramento, CA: Rae John Publishers, 1981.

BATTLE, BRENDON P., and PAUL B. WESTON. *Arson Detection and Investigation.* New York: Arco Publishing, 1979.

BING, LEON. *Do or Die.* New York: Harper Perennial (HarperCollins), 1993.

BIONDI, RAY, and WALT HECOX. *All His Fathers Sins.* New York: Pocket Books, 1988.

BOLOGNA, JACK G., and ROBERT J. LINDQUIST. *Fraud Auditing and Forensic Accounting—New Tools and Techniques.* New York: Wiley, 1987.

BUBRO, JAMES. *Mob Rule—Inside the Canadian Mafia.* Toronto: Macmillan, 1985.

CAREY, MARY, and GEORGE SHERMAN. *Compendium of Bunk, or How to Spot a Con Artist: A Handbook for Fraud Investigators, Bankers and Other Custodians of the Public Trust.* Springfield, IL: Charles C Thomas, 1976.

CLARKE, MICHAEL. *Business Crime: Its Nature and Control.* New York: St. Martin's, 1990.

CONWAY, JAMES P. *Evidential Documents.* Springfield, IL: Charles C Thomas, 1959.

COOK, CLAUDE W. *A Practical Guide to the Basics of Physical Evidence.* Springfield, IL: Charles C Thomas, 1984.

COUNT, E. W. *Cop Talk—True Detective Stories from the NYPD.* New York: Pocket Books, 1994.

CUOMO, GEORGE. *A Couple of Cops—On the Street, in the Crime Lab.* New York: Random House, 1995.

DALY, ROBERT. *Prince of the City—The True Story of a Cop Who Knew Too Much.* Boston: Houghton Mifflin, 1978.

DELATTRE, EDWIN J. *Character and Cops: Ethics in Policing.* Washington, DC: American Enterprise Institute for Public Policy Research, 1989.

DILNOT, GEORGE. *Great Detectives and Their Methods.* Boston: Houghton Mifflin, 1928.

ECK, JOHN E. *Solving Crime—The Investigation of Burglary and Robbery.* Washington, DC: U.S. Department of Justice, National Institute of Justice, 1983.

ESTRICK, SUSAN. *Real Rape.* Cambridge, MA: Harvard University Press, 1987.

FARR, ROBERT. *The Electronic Criminals.* New York: McGraw-Hill, 1975.

FISHER, BARRY. *Techniques of Crime Scene Investigation.* New York: CRC Press, 2000.

GARBARINO, JAMES, EDNA GUTTMAN, and JANIS WILSON-SEELEY. *The Psychologically Battered Child—Strategies for Identification, Assessment, and Intervention.* San Francisco: Jossey-Bass, 1986.

GEBERTH, VERNON J. *Practical Homicide Investigation, Tactics, Procedures, and Forensic Techniques.* New York: CRC Press, 1996.

GODDARD, DONALD. *Undercover—The Secret Lives of a Federal Agent.* New York: New York Times Books, 1988.

GRAYSMITH, ROBERT. *The Sleeping Lady—The Trailside Murders Above the Golden Gate Bridge.* New York: Onyx (Penguin Books), 1990.

GREEN, GARY S. *Occupational Crime.* Chicago: Nelson-Hall, 1990.

GROSS, HANS G. A. *Criminal Investigation,* 5th ed. Translated by John Adam and J. Collyer Adam, Revised by R. L. Jackson. Sweet & Maxwell Ltd., 1962.

GROTH, NICHOLAS A. *Men Who Rape: The Psychology of the Offender.* New York: Plenum Press, 1979.

HAMMER, RICHARD. *The CBS Murders.* New York: William Morrow, 1987.

HAZELWOOD, ROBERT R., and ANN WOLBERT BURGESS. *Practical Aspects of Rape Investigation—A Multidisciplinary Approach.* New York: Elsevier Science, 1987.

HIBBARD, WHITNEY S., and RAYMOND W. WORRING. *Forensic Hypnosis in Criminal Investigations.* Springfield, IL: Charles C Thomas, 1987.

HICKEY, ERIC W. *Serial Murderers and Their Victims.* Pacific Grove, CA: Brooks/Cole, 1991.

HOLMES, RONALD M., and STEPHEN T. HOLMES. *Profiling Violent Crimes,* 2nd ed. Thousand Oaks, CA: Sage, 1996.

KESSLER, WILLIAM F., and PAUL B. WESTON. *The Detection of Murder.* New York: Arco, 1961.

KIRK, PAUL. *Fire Investigation.* New York: Wiley, 1969.

LAQUEUR, WALTER. *The Age of Terrorism.* Boston: Little, Brown, 1987.

LARSEN, RICHARD W. *Bundy—The Deliberate Stranger.* Englewood Cliffs, NJ: Prentice Hall, 1980.

LARSON, ERIK. *Lethal Passage.* New York: Viking, 1995.

LEVIN, JACK, and JACK MCDEVITT. *Hate Crimes—The Rising Tide of Bigotry and Bloodshed.* New York: Plenum Press, 1993.

LEVINE, MICHAEL. *Deep Cover—The Inside Story of How DEA Infighting, Incompetence, and Subterfuge Lost Us the Biggest Battle of the Drug War.* New York: Delacorte, 1990.

LOFTUS, ELIZABETH, and KATHERINE KETCHAM. *Witness for the Defense—The Accused, the Eyewitness, and the Expert Who Puts Memory on Trial.* New York: St. Martin's, 1991.

MAAS, PETER. *Serpico.* New York: Viking, 1973.

MANNING, PETER K. *The Narcs' Game—Organizational and Informational Limits on Drug Law Enforcement.* Cambridge, MA: MIT Press, 1980.

MAURER, DAVID W. *Language of the Underworld.* Lexington: The University Press of Kentucky, 1981.

——————. *The American Confidence Man.* Springfield, IL: Charles C Thomas, 1974.

MCALARY, MIKE. *Buddy Boys—When Good Cops Turn Bad.* New York: Putnam, 1987.

MCCARTHY, BILL, and MIKE MALLOWE. *Vice Cop—My Twenty-Year Battle with New York's Dark Side.* New York: William Morrow, 1991.

MCDONALD, PETER. *Tire Imprint Evidence.* New York: Elsevier, 1989.

MCGINNISS, JOE. *Cruel Doubts.* New York: Pocket Star Books (Simon & Schuster), 1991.

MILLER, LARRY. *Human Evidence in Criminal Justice.* Cincinnati, OH: Anderson, 1983.

MILLS, JAMES. *The Underground Empire—Where Crime and Government Embrace.* New York: Doubleday, 1986.

MOORE, MARK HARRISON. *Buy and Bust.* Lexington, MA: D. C. Heath, 1977.

MURPHY, HARRY J. *Where's What: Sources of Information for Federal Investigators.* Washington, DC: Brookings Institution, 1975.

NEFF, JAMES. *Mobbed Up—Jackie Presser's High-Wire Life in the Teamsters, the Mafia, and the FBI.* New York: Dell, 1989.

O'BRIEN, DARCY. *Two of a Kind—The Hillside Stranglers.* New York: New American Library, 1985.

O'CONNOR, JOHN J. *Practical Fire and Arson Investigation.* New York: Elsevier-Ndu, 1987.

PALMIOTTO, MICHAEL J., ed. *Critical Issues in Criminal Investigation.* Cincinnati, OH: Anderson, 1988.

PARKER, DONN B. *Fighting Computer Crime.* New York: Wiley, 1998.

PERRY, NANCY, and LAWRENCE WRIGHTSMAN. *The Child Witness: Legal Issues and Dilemmas.* Newbury Park, CA: Sage, 1991.

POLAND, JAMES M. *Understanding Terrorism—Groups, Strategies, and Responses.* Englewood Cliffs, NJ: Prentice Hall, 1988.

POLLOCK-BYRNE, JOCELYN. *Ethics in Crime and Justice—Dilemmas and Decisions.* Pacific Grove, CA: Brooks/Cole, 1988.

RENGERT, GEORGE, and JOHN WASILCHICK. *Suburban Burglary—A Time and Place for Everything.* Springfield, IL: Charles C Thomas, 1985.

ROBBINS, LOUISE M. *Footprints—Collection, Analysis, and Interpretation.* Springfield, IL: Charles C Thomas, 1985.

SAFERSTEIN, RICHARD. *Criminalistics: An Introduction to Forensic Science, 5th ed.* Englewood Cliffs, NJ: Prentice Hall, 1975.

SCHMALLEGER, FRANK. *Ethics in Criminal Justice.* Bristol, IN: Wyndham Hall, 1990.

SHIMOMURA, TSUTOMU. *Takedown.* New York: Hyperion, 1996.

SIMON, DAVID. *Homicide—A Year on the Killing Streets.* Boston: Houghton Mifflin, 1991.

SLOAN, STEPHEN. *Simulating Terrorism.* Norman: University of Oklahoma Press, 1981.

STEFFENSMEIER, DARREL J. *The Fence—In the Shadow of Two Worlds.* Totowa, NJ: Rowman & Littlefield, 1986.

STEPHENSON, PETER. *Investigating Computer Related Crime.* Boca Raton: CRC Press, 2000.

TABOR, HAMES D., and EUGENE V GALLAGHER. *Why Waco? Cults and the Battle for Religious Freedom in America.* Los Angeles: University of California Press, 1995.

THORNWALD, JURGEN. *Century of the Detective.* Translated by Richard Winston and Clara Winston. New York: Harcourt Brace Jovanovich, 1965.

TOSI, OSCAR. *Voice Identification: Theory and Practice.* Baltimore: University Park Press, 1979.

VOLKMAN, ERNEST, and JOHN CUMMINGS. *The Heist—How a Gang Stole $8,000,000 at Kennedy Airport and Lived to Regret It.* New York: Franklin Watts, 1986.

WAKEFIELD, HOLLIDA, and RALPH UNDERWAGER. *Accusations of Child Sexual Abuse.* Springfield, IL: Charles C Thomas, 1988.

WALLS, H. J. *Forensic Science, 2nd ed.* New York: Praeger, 1974.

WAMBAUGH, JOSEPH. *The Blooding.* New York: Perigord Press (Bantam Books), 1989.

WARNER, CARMEN GERMAINE, ed., *Rape and Sexual Assault: Management and Intervention.* Rockville, MD: Aspen Systems, 1980.

WELLS, KENNETH M., and PAUL B. WESTON. *Criminal Procedure and Trial Practice.* Englewood Cliffs, NJ: Prentice Hall, 1977.

WESTON, PAUL B., and KENNETH M. WELLS. *Criminal Law.* Santa Monica, CA: Goodyear Publishing, 1978.

WESTON, PAUL B., KENNETH M. WELLS, and MARLENE HERTOGHE. *Criminal Evidence for Police, 4th ed.* Upper Saddle River, NJ: Prentice Hall, 1995.

WHITED, CHARLES. *The Decoy Man—The Extraordinary Adventures of an Undercover Cop.* Chicago: Playboy Press, 1973.

WILSON, JAMES Q. *The Moral Sense.* New York: Free Press, 1993.

Index